W9-BDD-112

Personality and Psychotherapy is a book of
ideas, of hypotheses which provide a basis for
research. It begins with a definition of
neurosis, from which an analysis of the basic
principles of learning evolves. After a
treatment of normal behavior in solving
emotional problems, it considers neurosis as
a learned set of responses. The role of therapy
as another kind of learning is followed by
analysis of conflict in the neurotic patient,
some special aspects of therapy, and their
application in normal life. Few studies in this
rapidly expanding field display the originality
which has assured the usefulness of this
book for over a decade.

Both authors are Professors in the Department
of Psychology, and on the faculty of the
Institute of Human Relations, Yale University.

McGRAW-HILL PAPERBACKS
PSYCHOLOGY

DAVID G. SCHROT

PERSONALITY and
PSYCHOTHERAPY

An Analysis in Terms of
Learning, Thinking, and Culture

Personality
and Psychotherapy

An Analysis in Terms of
Learning, Thinking, and Culture

John Dollard
Neal E. Miller

McGraw-Hill Book Company, Inc.
New York   Toronto   London

PERSONALITY AND PSYCHOTHERAPY

121314151617 MUMU 76

ISBN 07-017371-0

To

Freud and Pavlov
and
Their Students

PREFACE

Before the Second World War we began teaching some of the main ideas in this book in classes and discussing them with colleagues. At that time our goal was to write a book on psychotherapy, formulating in behavior theory and culture concepts what is done by the therapist and patient. We found, however, that in order to discuss therapy intelligently, we had to work out a theory of the neurosis, and from there we were driven back to a consideration of the normal use of the higher mental processes in the solution of emotional problems. Thus our project grew from one book to three. A completely systematic coverage of this wide area was too large to be manageable, and additonal data were needed at many points. Therefore we decided to cut the work down to a progress report on those ideas that were clearest to us at the time, without fretting about the many obvious gaps and unsolved problems. The emphasis on normal personality and adjustment mechanisms emerged inevitably as the work proceeded.

This book is addressed to students, teachers, and researchers in the fields of personality, adjustment, abnormal psychology, and psychotherapy. Personality theory is indivisible. Normal and abnormal aspects, routine functioning, and therapeutic reconstruction all derive from a common set of principles. A knowledge of these principles should be brought early to college students in psychology and other relevant disciplines. Graduate students and research scientists may be expected to help us modify and extend the theory. We offer the book also to that circle of intelligent adults who keep up with the new things in the science of human personality, and we hope that they will find here some clarification and stimulation.

Most of the ideas in this book are hypotheses, the basis for research, not proven principles. Furthermore, it has not been possible to formulate these hypotheses in as rigorous, systematic, and quantitative a form as will eventually be desirable.

The need for new research in the therapeutic situation itself is especially evident. Sound recorded interviews preserve larger portions of the effective stimuli of the interview than do written transcripts or the therapist's notes. Reliable scales for measuring aspects of the therapeutic situation must be developed and validated by other scales which measure the results of therapy in subsequent life. Especially, we need to watch for ways of subjecting critical variables to experiment and other forms of empirical test. Sociologists can help us greatly by further clarifying the social conditions which affect therapeutic results. We feel a great need for a science of child rearing based on observations in the home where the fundamental social learning occurs. Such a science will supply the rationale for the prevention of much neurotic behavior.

We have concentrated our analysis on the one type of therapeutic practice with which we are familiar—namely, the Freudian. Even here, we have attempted to analyze only those features of theory and practice that we understand best. The principles, if sound, and with appropriate extensions, should be found applicable to all forms of therapy. The sympathetic reader who is familiar with Rogerian therapy will make many applications to it. The problems presented by group therapy, the psychodrama, and various institutional systems of reassurance should all be analyzed to see how well they can be embraced by one comprehensive set of principles of this sort.

Our analysis is based on the way neuroses and psychotherapy appear in our own culture. This constitutes a restriction of unknown severity and may have prevented us from exploring many significant possibilities. It seems almost inevitable that cross-cultural investigations would put our principles to a severe test and force considerable modifications and extensions.

This book by itself is not meant to teach anyone to be a therapist. Many invaluable bits of therapeutic wisdom that have been omitted did not seem crucially related to the main theoretical principles. Students who are learning to practice therapy must have firsthand experience with therapeutic material. As will be seen, it is impossible to teach therapy at the highest level without giving the students an opportunity to discover and repair their own repressions. As a systematic attempt to deal with the relevant variables, however, it is hoped that this book may help to make the teaching of therapy easier.

The growth of systematic thought takes time. We are therefore greatly indebted to Yale University and its Institute of Human Relations for funding our work for so long. To the Institute itself we are obliged for bringing together the various streams of ideas that we believe are essential to the understanding of human social behavior. The names of Freud, Pavlov, Thorndike, Hull, Sumner, Murdock, Kluckhohn, and Warner symbolize this new integration. We are grateful to all these sources of crucial ideas and to our colleagues at the Institute who helped us to correlate them. Dr. Mark A. May, the Institute's director, graciously allowed us to borrow and adapt for this book the introductory material on learning contained in several chapters of our "Social Learning and Imitation"—thus aiding us to make this work more complete and teachable.

We are especially grateful to Alice M. White, who, in every sense of the word, aided in the preparation of the book; to Robert F. Grose, who acted as research assistant; and to Hilda B. Young, who helped us in preparing the manuscript for publication.

Work and pain can be shared rather evenly, but the assessment of the source of creative ideas becomes more difficult as one becomes more deeply involved in collaborative work. The result in this case is that there is no senior author of the book.

Acknowledgment is made to the following publishers from whose publications quotations are reproduced: Appleton-Century-Crofts, The Blakiston Company, Hogarth Press and Institute of Psycho-Analysis, Oxford University Press, The Ronald Press Company, John Wiley & Sons, Inc., and Yale University Press. Acknowledgment for permission to quote is also extended to the editors of the *Journal of Abnormal and Social Psychology* and the *Yale Journal of Biology and Medicine*.

JOHN DOLLARD
NEAL E. MILLER

New Haven, Conn.
September, 1950

CONTENTS

PART I
ORIENTATION

CHAPTER I

MAIN POINTS

This book is an attempt to aid in the creation of a psychological base for a general science of human behavior. Three great traditions, heretofore followed separately, are brought together. One of these is psychoanalysis, initiated by the genius of Freud and carried on by his many able students in the art of psychotherapy. Another stems from the work of Pavlov, Thorndike, Hull, and a host of other experimentalists. They have applied the exactness of natural-science method to the study of the principles of learning. Finally, modern social science is crucial because it describes the social conditions under which human beings learn. The ultimate goal is to combine the vitality of psychoanalysis, the rigor of the natural-science laboratory, and the facts of culture. We believe that a psychology of this kind should occupy a fundamental position in the social sciences and humanities—making it unnecessary for each of them to invent its own special assumptions about human nature and personality.

Psychotherapy, the Window to Higher Mental Life

If psychotherapy were used only as a way of curing neurotic persons, it would have a real but limited interest to students of human personality. The psychotherapeutic situation, however, provides a kind of window to mental life. Advanced research students in psychology are taught the rudiments of the therapist's art so that they may sit at this window. Learning something of the work of the therapist is a small price to pay for what the researcher sees.

The elementary student similarly can profit by the reports on human personality which can be made only by the psychotherapist. As the therapist sees it, there is no artificial separation between intelligence, emotion, childhood, social influences, and behavior deviations. He must understand the patient's childhood, see him

3

struggling in the grip of his social system, watch his intelligence contending with emotion, and identify behavior deviations. The mental-emotional life of man is seen the way it feels—as a single system.

If normal people could be got to accept the conditions of psychotherapy, it would be possible to learn from them almost everything which has been discovered by studying neurotic persons. It has proved difficult to get normal people to spend the money, take the time, and accept the conditions of the psychotherapeutic situation. There is a tendency for everyone to wear a mask, to put his best foot forward, and to be on guard against exposure, criticism, or exploitation. But we need not doubt, as novelists are forever telling us, that there is much that even friends do not suspect behind the composed mask.

The difficulty lies in the field of motivation. Normal people have low motivation to talk frankly and extensively about their most significant problems. Only neurotic misery seems to provide the strong drive required. Further, high motivation is needed to get people to talk long enough to cover the wonderfully intricate details of the human personality in action. Likewise, the investigator must have enough time to listen so that he can absorb the patient's account. Outside of psychotherapy, how many subjects have been studied for an hour a day for five days a week for from one to three years? With the motivation of therapy, some thousands of analytic patients have been studied this thoroughly.

In many situations where human behavior must be studied with normal people, the motives are slight and the situation is trivial. Just the opposite is the case with psychotherapy. Not only is motivation strong, but the life situation is vital. The alternatives are years of misery or years of relative peace and success. Such urgent circumstances tend to bring every resource of the patient and the therapist into play, with the result that the patient exhibits himself more fully than he will ever do again to any one person. The patient must report and the therapist must deal with the most vexing and vital problems of adjustment. The attention of the therapist is forced on the drives that motivate human behavior. He sees the wonderful higher mental processes of reasoning and thought in their natural context. He can observe how rational thought and action are crippled by conflict and repression. Only if the therapist has a practical working knowledge of human nature—of the kind we all aspire to—can he conduct therapy successfully.

The notion of "abnormal" behavior misleads many people. They think it to be the study of persons entirely different from the rest of mankind. Practically all specialists agree now that such is not the case. The very same variables which are operating in an extreme degree in mentally ill people are present in people who are not ill. Neurotic people should therefore be seen rather as a population in which the study of higher mental life is especially convenient than as a group of people different in kind from others. Important variables which are hard to see in mild degrees become very clear when presented in extreme degrees. Once the significant variables and their effects are identified in abnormal persons it becomes easier to know what to look for and where to look among the normal population. Such inferences from neurotics need, of course, to be checked in every way possible in order to evaluate the importance of selective factors among neurotic patients.

Of particular interest are the changes that occur in a neurotic person during and after psychotherapy. After therapy he is indistinguishable from the mine run of people; he too has low motivation for further psychotherapy. But in his case therapists have the invaluable information of how he came to transfer from the neurotic to the normal group. The study of psychotherapy, in distinction from the isolated study of abnormal behavior, is a description of the process by which *normality is created*. If some persons acquire a normal personality in childhood and others from the work of psychotherapy, there must be fundamental similarities between the two processes.

Working for a half century under the favorable conditions of psychotherapy, Freud and his brilliant students have collected much significant information about human behavior and personality. They have advanced the most fruitful hypotheses which exist in this field. Freud insisted upon the lawfulness of mental life, even in the most bizarre bits of human behavior. He emphasized the importance of motivation and conflict, the role of the family in early childhood, and discovered the significance of unconscious mental life. This is the reason why we emphasize the importance of experience with psychotherapy for experimentalists. The hypotheses of Freud are a rich source of significant research problems.

Observations made in the situation of psychotherapy are a kind of natural history. They have the advantage of locating significant problems in a realistic setting; by necessity they also have the disadvantage of lacking rigorous control. Clinical observations likewise are difficult to condense and transmit to others. Clinical observations are often not convincing enough to other persons and too convincing to the person who makes them.

Testing Freudian principles may seem to some therapists to be proving the obvious, but sometimes when one starts out to prove the obvious (*e.g.*, heavy stones fall faster than light ones) it turns out to be false. We shall not be able to present many new experiments or other rigorously controlled, empirical observations in the present book. We hope that this attempt at systematization, in terms of principles derived from the laboratory, will help ingenious investigators to find ways to put propositions to experimental and other forms of empirical test. Whatever be the difficulties of data and concept, an attention to Freudian hypotheses can help the experimenter spend his time on important problems and build toward that general systematic account of human personality which is expected of psychologists.

Advantages of Scientific Theory

This book is an attempt at integration of the data on mental and emotional life via scientific principles. As is well known, a scientific theory has great advantages over an aggregation of empirical facts. A theory is more powerful the more generally applicable its principles are. As Einstein has emphasized, the goal is to account for the most facts with the fewest principles.

Integrating facts around principles makes them easier to remember. In this connection we are reminded of the superiority of logical over rote memory. Facts which are easier to remember are likewise easier to teach.

Similarly, scientific principles are easier to adapt to new situations (the superior *transfer* of logical over rote learning). A purely empirical generalization ("This happened frequently in the past; therefore it is likely to happen again") can only be applied when a similar situation repeats itself; but one can use principles to make predictions about what will occur in new situations. If one understands the principles, one knows better whether a new application will be relevant or not. Understanding the principles should make it easier for the student to adapt his techniques to the infinitely variable and complex problems of therapy.

In the same connection, correct principles can be used as a basis for creating innovations. Every adult can call the roll of deadly diseases which have been made harmless during his lifetime. These advances in the therapy of physical disease have been made possible as a result of fundamental theoretical advances in bacteriology, physiology, chemistry, and relevant natural sciences. Innovations have been made that were not hit upon previously by hundreds of generations of purely empirical trial and error (Bush, 1945; Conant, 1947).[1]

There is a further advantage to scientific principles—the fact that they allow one to make predictions about new situations gives a powerful method of testing them in a greater variety of situations. Thus, after principles of psychotherapy have been systematized in general terms, one can predict what should happen under rigidly controlled experimental conditions and use this prediction as a powerful method of testing and refining the principles. We hope that deductions of effect in therapeutic situations will suggest innovations in therapeutic technique. New ways of meeting the inevitable dilemmas of therapy are much needed. Likewise, deductions of effect in experimental situations which are easier to control and measure may provide a method of testing and refining the principles of psychotherapy.

Similarly, the clinic is constantly suggesting new problems for laboratory study, such as the list of learned social drives discussed later in this book. If a systematic theory of psychotherapy can be created, the clinic and laboratory should interact to a much greater degree and in a much more potent way than heretofore.

If neurotic behavior is learned, it should be unlearned by some combination of the same principles by which it was taught. We believe this to be the case. Psychotherapy establishes a set of

[1] Names and dates in parentheses refer to items listed in the bibliography at the end of the book.

conditions by which neurotic habits may be unlearned and non-neurotic habits learned. Therefore, we view the therapist as a kind of teacher and the patient as a learner. In the same way and by the same principles that bad tennis habits can be corrected by a good coach, so bad mental and emotional habits can be corrected by a psychotherapist. There is this difference, however. Whereas only a few people want to play tennis, all the world wants a clear, free, efficient mind.

We believe that giving the solid, systematic basis of learning theory to the data of psychotherapy is a matter of importance. Application of these laws and the investigation of the new conditions of learning which psychotherapy involves should provide us with a rational foundation for practice in psychotherapy analogous to that provided by the science of bacteriology to treatment of contagious diseases. As a learning theorist sees it, the existence of neuroses is an automatic criticism of our culture of child rearing. Misery-producing, neurotic habits which the therapist must painfully unteach have been as painfully taught in the confused situation of childhood. A system of child training built on the laws of learning might have the same powerful effect on the neurotic misery of our time as Pasteur's work had on infectious diseases.

The Problem of Teaching Scientific Theory

As larger areas of psychology move nearer to the status of a natural science, a new dilemma is presented to the teacher. He may have to make sure, as in the natural sciences, that the first units of the theory are heavily overlearned. He may have to resist the temptation to give the students large amounts of material, hoping that they will get something out of the mere quantity. Good theory is the best form of simplification, and good teaching consists of hammering home the basic elements of such theory.

Basic Assumption That Neurosis and Psychotherapy Obey Laws of Learning

If a neurosis is functional (*i.e.*, a product of experience rather than of organic damage or instinct), it must be learned. If it is learned, it must be learned according to already known, experimentally verified laws of learning or according to new, and as yet undiscovered, laws of learning. In the former case, such laws, meticulously studied by investigators such as Pavlov, Thorndike, Hull, and their students, should make a material contribution to the understanding of the phenomenon. If new laws are involved, the attempt to study neuroses from the learning standpoint should help to reveal the gaps in our present knowledge and to suggest new principles which could be fruitfully submitted to investigation in the laboratory. It seems likely that not only laws we know but also those we do not know are involved. However, the laws that we *do* know seem sufficient to carry us a long way toward a systematic analysis of psychotherapy.[2]

Main Consequences of This Approach

We have attempted to give a systematic analysis of neurosis and psychotherapy in terms of the psychological principles and social conditions of learning. In order to give the reader a better perspective on this attempt, we shall swiftly list some of its main consequences.

1. The principle of reinforcement has been substituted for Freud's pleasure principle. The concept of "pleasure" has proved a difficult and slippery notion in the history of psychology. The same is true of the idea that the behavior that occurs is "adaptive," because it is awkward to have to explain maladaptive behavior on the basis of a principle of adaptiveness. The principle of reinforcement is more exact and rigorous than either the pleasure principle or the adaptiveness principle. Since the effect of immediate reinforcement is greater than that of reinforcement after a delay, the investigator is forced to examine the exact temporal relationships between responses, stimuli, and reinforcement. He is thus provided with a better basis for predicting whether or not adaptive behavior will be learned. Where reinforcement is delayed, some account must be given of the means by which the temporal gap is bridged.

2. The relatively neglected and catchall concept of Ego strength

[2] Early, brilliant work on the unification of the great traditions of Freud and Pavlov has been done by French (1933) and Sears (1936).

has been elaborated in two directions: first is the beginning of a careful account of higher mental processes; second is the description of the culturally valuable, learned drives and skills. The importance of the foregoing factors in human behavior can hardly be overemphasized. The functioning of higher mental processes and learned drives is not limited to neuroses or psychotherapy. It is an essential part of the science of human personality.

3. A naturalistic account is given of the immensely important mechanism of repression. Repression is explained as the inhibition of the cue-producing responses which mediate thinking and reasoning. Just what is lost by repression and gained by therapy is much clearer in the light of this account.

4. Transference is seen as a special case of a wider concept, generalization. This explanation draws attention to the fact that many humdrum habits which facilitate therapy are transferred along with those that obstruct it. The analysis shows also why such intense emotional responses should be directed toward the therapist in the transference situation.

5. The dynamics of conflict behavior are systematically deduced from more basic principles. Thus, a fundamental fact of neurosis—that of conflict—is tied in with general learning theory. A clear understanding of the nature of conflict serves to provide a more rational framework for therapeutic practice.

6. We have been obliged to put great stress on the fact that the patient gets well in real life. Only part of the work essential to therapy is done in the therapeutic situation. Reinforcement theory supplies logical reasons why this should be expected.

7. The somewhat vague concept of "reality" is elaborated in terms of the physical and social conditions of learning, especially the conditions provided by the social structure of a society. In order to predict behavior we must know these conditions as well as the psychological principles involved. Psychology supplies the principles while sociology and social anthropology supply the systematic treatment of the crucial social conditions.

8. The concepts of repression and suppression are supplemented by the parallel ones of inhibition and restraint. The idea that it is important to suppress and restrain tendencies to unconventional thoughts and acts is not a novelty with us, but our

type of analysis has forced us to reaffirm and expand it.   In a study of this kind, it is necessary to discuss matters that are not ordinarily the subject of polite conversation.   But those who have used a misinterpretation of psychoanalysis to justify their own undisciplined behavior will find scant comfort in this book.

CHAPTER II

WHAT IS A NEUROSIS?

Most people, even scientists, are vague about neurosis. Neither the neurotic victim nor those who know him seem able to state precisely what is involved. The victim feels a mysterious malady. The witness observes inexplicable behavior. The neurotic is mysterious because he is *capable* of acting and yet he is *unable* to act and enjoy. Though physically capable of attaining sex rewards, he is anesthetic; though capable of aggression, he is meek; though capable of affection, he is cold and unresponsive. As seen by the outside witness, the neurotic does not make use of the obvious opportunities for satisfaction which life offers him.

To Be Explained: Misery, Stupidity, Symptoms

The therapist confronts a person who is miserable, stupid (in some ways), and who has symptoms. These are the three major factors to be accounted for. Why is he miserable, in what curious way is he stupid, and whence arise the symptoms? The waiting room of every psychiatric clinic is crowded with patients showing these common signs.

Neurotic Misery Is Real

Neurotic misery is real—not imaginary. Observers, not understanding the neurotic conflict, often belittle the suffering of neurotics and confuse neurosis with malingering. Neurotic habits are forced upon an individual by peculiar conditions of life and are not cheap attempts to escape duty and responsibility. In most cases the misery is attested by many specific complaints. These complaints or symptoms differ with each category of neurosis but sleeplessness, restlessness, irritability, sexual inhibitions, distaste for life, lack

12

of clear personal goals, phobias, headaches, and irrational fears are among the more common ones.

At times the depth of the misery of the neurotic is concealed by his symptoms. Only when they are withdrawn does his true anguish appear. Occasionally the misery will be private, not easily visible to outside observers because friends and relatives are ringed around the neurotic person and prevent observation of his pain. In still other cases, the neurotic person is miserable but apathetic. He has lost even the hope that complaining and attracting attention will be helpful. However this may be, *if the neurotic takes the usual risks of life* he is miserable. He suffers if he attempts to love, marry, and be a parent. He fails if he tries to work responsibly and independently. His social relations tend to be invaded by peculiar demands and conditions. Neurotic misery is thus often masked by the protective conditions of life (as in childhood) and appears only when the individual has to "go it on his own."

Conflict produces misery. Suffering so intense as that shown by neurotics must have powerful causes, and it does. The neurotic is miserable because he is in conflict. As a usual thing two or more strong drives are operating in him and producing incompatible responses. Strongly driven to approach and as strongly to flee, he is not able to act to reduce either of the conflicting drives. These drives therefore remain dammed up, active, and nagging.

Where such a drive conflict is conscious there is no problem in convincing anyone why it should produce misery. If we picture a very hungry man confronting food which he knows to be poisoned, we can understand that he is driven on the one hand by hunger and on the other by fear. He oscillates at some distance from the tempting food, fearing to grasp but unable to leave. Everyone understands immediately the turmoil produced by such a conflict of hunger and fear.

Many people remember from their adolescence the tension of a strong sex conflict. Primary sex responses heightened by imaginative elaboration are met by intense fear. Though usually not allowed to talk about such matters, children sometimes can, and the misery they reveal is one of the most serious prices exacted of adolescents in our culture. That this conflict is acquired and not innate was shown by Margaret Mead in her brilliant book, "Coming of Age in Samoa" (1928). It is also agonizingly depicted in a novel by Vardis Fisher (1932).

Our third example of conscious conflict shows anger pitted against fear. In the early part of the war, an officer, newly commissioned from civilian life and without the habits of the professional soldier, was sent to an Army post. There he met a superior officer who decided to make an example of some minor mistake. The ranking officer lectured and berated the subordinate, refusing to let him speak and explain his behavior. He made him stand at attention against the wall for half an hour while this lecture was going on. The new-made officer quaked in fearful conflict. He detected the sadistic satisfaction which his superior got in dressing him down. He had never so much wanted to kill anyone. On the other hand, the junior officer felt the strong pressure of his own conscience to be a competent soldier and some real fear about what the consequence of assault might be. We met him shortly after this episode, and he still shook with rage when he described the experience. There was no doubt in his mind but that bearing strong, conflicting drives is one of the most severe causes of misery.

Repression Causes Stupidity

In each of the above cases, however, the individual could eventually solve his conflict. The hungry man could find nourishing food; the sex-tortured adolescent could eventually marry; the new officer could and did avoid his punishing superior.

With the neurotic this is not the case. He is not able to solve his conflict even with the passage of time. Though obviously intelligent in some ways, he is stupid in-so-far as his neurotic conflict is concerned. This stupidity is not an over-all affair, however. It is really a stupid area in the mind of a person who is quite intelligent in other respects. For some reason he cannot use his head on his neurotic conflicts.

Though the neurotic is sure he is miserable and is vocal about his symptoms, he is vague about what it is within him that could produce such painful effects. The fact that the neurotic cannot describe his own conflicts has been the source of great confusion in dealing with him either in terms of scientific theory or in terms of clinical practice. Nor can the therapist immediately spot these areas of stupidity. Only after extensive study of the patient's life can the areas of repression be clearly identified. Then the surprising fact emerges that the competing drives which afflict the neurotic person are not labeled. He has no language to describe the conflicting forces within him.

Without language and adequate labeling the higher mental processes cannot function. When these processes are knocked out by repression, the person cannot guide himself by mental means to a resolution of his conflict. Since the neurotic cannot help himself, he must have the help of others if he is to be helped at all—though millions today live out their lives in strong neurotic pain and never get help. The neurotic, therefore, is, or appears to be, stupid because he is unable to use his mind in dealing with certain of his problems. He feels that someone should help him, but he does not know how to ask for help since he does not know what his problem is. He may feel aggrieved that he is suffering, but he cannot explain his case.

Symptoms Slightly Reduce Conflict

Although in many ways superficial, the symptoms of the neurotic are the most obvious aspects of his problems. These are what the patient is familiar with and feels he should be rid of. The phobias, inhibitions, avoidances, compulsions, rationalizations, and psychosomatic symptoms of the neurotic are experienced as a nuisance by him and by all who have to deal with him. The symptoms cannot be integrated into the texture of sensible social relations. The patient, however, believes that the symptoms *are* his disorder. It is these he wishes to be rid of and, not knowing that a serious conflict underlies them, he would like to confine the therapeutic discussion to getting rid of the symptoms.

The symptoms do not solve the basic conflict in which the neurotic person is plunged, but they mitigate it. They are responses which tend to reduce the conflict, and in part they succeed. When a successful symptom occurs it is reinforced because it reduces neurotic misery. The symptom is thus learned as a habit. One very common function of symptoms is to keep the neurotic person away from those stimuli which would activate and intensify his neurotic conflict. Thus, the combat pilot with a harrowing military disaster behind him may "walk away" from the sight of any airplane. As he walks toward the plane his anxiety goes up; as he walks away it goes down. "Walking away" is thus reinforced. It is this phobic walking away which constitutes his symptom. If the whole situation is not understood, such behavior seems bizarre to the casual witness.

Conflict, Repression, and Symptoms Closely Related

In the foregoing discussion we have "taken apart" the most conspicious factors which define the neurosis and have separately discussed conflict, stupidity, and misery. We hope that the discussion has clarified the problem even at the expense of slightly distorting the actual relationships. In every human case of neurosis the three basic factors are closely and dynamically interrelated. The conflict could not be unconscious and insoluble were it not for the repressive factors involved. The symptoms could not exist did they not somewhat relieve the pressure of conflict. The mental paralysis of repression has been created by the very same forces which originally imposed the emotional conflict on the neurotic person.

THE CASE OF MRS. A [1]

We are presenting the facts about Mrs. A for two reasons: (1) as background material on a case from which we will draw many concrete examples throughout the book; (2) as a set of facts from which we can illustrate the relationships between misery and conflict, stupidity and repression, symptoms and reinforcement. The reader will understand, of course, that the sole function of this case material is to give a clear exposition of principles by means of concrete illustrations; it is *not* presented as evidence or proof.

[1] We are allowed to present and analyze the material on Mrs. A through the kindness of a New York colleague, a man so remarkable as to provide this laboriously gathered material and yet be willing to remain anonymous to aid in the complete disguise of the case.

The facts. Mrs. A was an unusually pretty twenty-three-year-old married woman. Her husband worked in the offices of an insurance company. When she came to the therapist she was exceedingly upset. She had a number of fears. One of the strongest of these was that her heart would stop beating if she did not concentrate on counting the beats.

The therapist, who saw Mrs. A twice a week over a three-month period, took careful notes. The life-history data that we present were pieced together from the patient's statements during a total of 26 hours. The scope of the material is necessarily limited by the brevity of the treatment. The treatment had to end when a change in the husband's work forced her to move to another city.

Her first neurotic symptoms had appeared five months before she came to the psychiatrist. While she was shopping in a New York store, she felt faint and became afraid that something would happen to her and "no one would know where I was." She telephoned her husband's office and asked him to come and get her. Thereafter she was afraid to go out alone. Shortly after this time, she talked with an aunt who had a neurotic fear of heart trouble. After a conversation with this aunt, Mrs. A's fears changed from a fear of fainting to a concern about her heart.

Mrs. A was an orphan, born of unknown parents in a city in the upper South. She spent the first few months of life in an orphanage, then was placed in a foster home, where she lived, except for a year when she was doing war work in Washington, until her marriage at the age of twenty.

The foster parents belonged to the working class, had three children of their own, two girls and a boy, all of them older than the patient. The foster mother, who dominated the family, was cruel, strict, and miserly toward all the children. She had a coarse and vulgar demeanor, swore continually, and punished the foster child for the least offense. Mrs. A recalls: "She whipped me all the time—whether I'd done anything or not."

The foster mother had imposed a very repressive sex training on the patient, making her feel that sex was dirty and wrong. Moreover, the foster mother never let the patient think independently. She discouraged the patient's striving for an education, taking her out of school at sixteen when the family could have afforded to let her go on.

Despite the repressive sex training she received, Mrs. A had developed strong sexual appetites. In early childhood she had overheard parental intercourse, had masturbated, and had witnessed animal copulation. When she was ten or twelve, her foster brother seduced her. During the years before her marriage a dozen men tried to seduce her and most of them succeeded.

Nevertheless, sex was to her a dirty, loathesome thing that was painful for her to discuss or think about. She found sexual relations with her husband disgusting and was morbidly shy in her relations with him.

The patient had met her husband-to-be while she was working as a typist in Washington during the war. He was an Army officer and a college graduate. Her beauty enabled the patient to make a marriage that improved her social position; her husband's family were middle-class people. At the time of treatment Mrs. A had not yet learned all the habits of middle-class life. She was still somewhat awkward about entertaining or being entertained and made glaring errors in grammar and pronunciation. She was dominated, socially subordinated, and partly rejected by her husband's family.

When they were first married, Mr. and Mrs. A lived with his parents in a small town north of New York City and commuted to the city for work. Mrs. A had an office job there. Later, they were able to get an apartment in New York, but they stayed with the in-laws every week end. Although she described her mother-in-law in glowing terms at the beginning of the treatment, Mrs. A later came to express considerable hostility toward her.

When she came to the psychiatrist, Mrs. A was in great distress. She had to pay continual attention to her heart lest it stop beating. She lived under a burden of vague anxiety and had a number of specific phobias that prevented her from enjoying many of the normal pleasures of her life, such as going to the movies. She felt helpless to cope with her problems. Her constant complaints had tired out and alienated her friends. Her husband was fed up with her troubles and had threatened to divorce her. She could not get along with her foster mother and her mother-in-law had rejected her. She had no one left to talk to. She was hurt, baffled, and terrified by the thought that she might be going crazy.

Analysis in Terms of Conflict, Repression, Reinforcement

We have described Mrs. A as of the moment when she came to treatment. The analysis of the case, however, presents the facts as they were afterward ordered and clarified by study.

Misery. Mrs. A's misery was obvious to her family, her therapist, and herself. She suffered from a strong, vague, unremitting fear. She was tantalized by a mysterious temptation. The phobic limitations on her life prevented her from having much ordinary fun, as by shopping or going to the movies. Her husband and mother-in-law criticized her painfully. She feared that her husband would carry out his threat and divorce her. She feared that her heart would stop. She feared to be left all alone, sick and rejected. Her friends and relatives pitied her at first, then became put out with her when her condition persisted despite well-meant advice. Her misery, though baffling, was recognized as entirely real.

Conflict. Mrs. A suffered from two conflicts which produced her misery. The first might be described as a sex-fear conflict. Thanks to childhood circumstances she had developed strong sex appetites. At the same time strong anxieties were created in her and attached to the cues produced by sex excitement. However, she saw no connection between these remembered circumstances and the miserable life she was leading. The connective thoughts had been knocked out and the conflict was thus unconscious. The presence of the sexual appetites showed up in a kind of driven behavior in which she seemed to court seduction. Her fear was exhibited in her revulsion from sexual acts and thoughts and in her inability to take responsibility for a reasonable sexual expressiveness with her husband. The conflict was greatly intensified after her marriage because of her wish to be a dutiful wife. Guilt about the prospect of adultery was added to fear about sex motives.

Mrs. A was involved in a second, though less severe, conflict between aggression and fear. She was a gentle person who had been very badly treated by her mother-in-law. Resentful tendencies arose in her but they were quickly inhibited by fear. She attempted to escape the anger-fear conflict by exceptionally submissive behavior, putting up meekly with slights and subordination and protesting her fondness for the mother-in-law. She was tormented by it nevertheless, especially by feelings of worthlessness and helplessness. She felt much better, late in therapy, when she was able to state her resentment and begin to put it into effect in a measured way. (After all, she had the husband and his love, and if the mother-in-law wanted to see her son and prospective grandchildren she would have to take a decent attitude toward Mrs. A.)

Stupidity. Mrs. A's mind was certainly of little use to her in solving her problem. She tried the usual medical help with no result. She took a trip, as advised, and got no help. Her symptoms waxed and waned in unpredictable ways. She knew that she was helpless. At the time she came for therapy she had no plans for dealing with her problem and no hope of solving it. In addition to being unable to deal with her basic problems, Mrs. A did many things that were quite unintelligent and maladaptive. For example, in spite of the fact that she wanted very much to make a success of her marriage and was consciously trying to live a proper married life, she frequently exposed herself to danger of seduction. She went out on drinking parties with single girls. She hitchhiked rides with truck drivers. She was completely unaware of the motivation for this behavior and often unable to foresee its consequences until it was too late. While her behavior seems stupid in the light of a knowledge of the actual state of affairs, there were many ways in which Mrs. A did not seem at all stupid—for example, when debating with the therapist to protect herself against fear-producing thoughts. She then gave hopeful evidence of what she could do with her mind when she had available all the necessary units to think with.

Repression. Mrs. A gave abundant evidence of the laming effects of repression. At the outset she thought she had no sex feelings or appetites. She described behavior obviously motivated by fear but could not label the fear itself. The closest she came was to express the idea that she was going insane. Further, Mrs. A thought she had an organic disease and clung desperately to this idea, inviting any kind of treatment so long as it did not force her to think about matters which would produce fear. Such mental gaps and distortions are a characteristic result of repression. They are what produce the stupidity.

Symptoms. Mrs. A's chief symptoms were the spreading phobia which drove her out of theaters and stores and the compulsive counting of breaths and heartbeats. These symptoms almost incapacitated her. She had lost her freedom to think and to move.

Reinforcement of symptoms. An analysis of the phobia revealed the following events. When on the streets alone, her fear of sex temptation was increased. Someone might speak to her, wink at her, make an approach to her. Such an approach would increase her sex desire and make her more vulnerable to seduction. Increased sex desire, however, touched off both anxiety and guilt, and this intensified her conflict when she was on the street. When she "escaped home," the temptation stimuli were lessened, along with a reduction of the fear which they elicited. Going home and, later, avoiding the temptation situation by anticipation were reinforced. Naturally, the basic sex-anxiety conflict was not resolved by the defensive measure of the symptom. The conflict persisted but was not so keen.

The counting of heartbeats can be analytically taken apart in a similar way. When sexy thoughts came to mind or other sex stimuli tended to occur, these stimuli elicited anxiety. It is clear that these stimuli were occurring frequently because Mrs. A was responding with anxiety much of the time. Since counting is a highly preoccupying kind of response, no other thoughts could enter her mind during this time. While counting, the sexy thoughts which excited fear dropped out. Mrs. A "felt better" immediately when she started counting, and the counting habit was reinforced by the drop in anxiety. Occasionally, Mrs. A would forget to count and then her intense anxiety would recur. In this case, as in that of the phobia, the counting symptom does not resolve the basic conflict—it only avoids exacerbating it.

Thus Mrs. A's case illustrates the analysis of neurotic mechanisms made in the earlier part of the chapter. Conflict produced high drives experienced as misery; repression interfered with higher mental processes and so with the intelligent solution of the conflict; the symptoms were learned responses which were reinforced by producing some reduction in the strength of drive. We will discuss later how higher mental life can be restored and how actions which *will* resolve the poisonous conflict can be made to occur.

PART II
BASIC PRINCIPLES OF LEARNING

CHAPTER III

FOUR FUNDAMENTALS OF LEARNING [1]

Human behavior is learned; precisely that behavior which is widely felt to characterize man as a rational being, or as a member of a particular nation or social class, is learned rather than innate. We also learn fears, guilt, and other socially acquired motivations, as well as symptoms and rationalizations—factors which are characteristic of normal personality but show up more clearly in extreme form as neurosis. Successful psychotherapy provides new conditions under which neurosis is unlearned and other more adaptive habits are learned.

Certain simple basic principles of learning are needed for a clear understanding of the kinds of behavior involved in normal personality, neurosis, and psychotherapy. Other principles would be useful in explaining some of the details of the behavior, and probably all of the known facts about learning are relevant in some way or another. In the interest of a sharp focus on the fundamentals, however, only the most essential principles will be included in this discussion, which is not considered to be a complete survey of the facts and theories of learning. [2]

The field of human learning covers phenomena which range all the way from the simple, almost reflex, learning of a child to avoid a hot radiator, to the complex processes of insight by which a scientist constructs a theory. Throughout the whole range, however, the same fundamental factors seem to be exceedingly important. [3] These factors are: *drive, response, cue,* and *reinforce-*

[1] The material in this chapter has been adapted from our "Social Learning and Imitation" (Miller and Dollard, 1941).

[2] For more complete summaries see Hull (1943), Spence (1950), Hilgard and Marquis (1940), Skinner (1938), McGeoch (1942), and Hilgard (1948) and his references.

[3] From the point of view of constructing a parsimonious and rigorous theory most likely to stimulate significant research on fundamental problems of learn-

ment. They are frequently referred to with other roughly equivalent words—drive as motivation, cue as stimulus, response as act or thought, and reinforcement as reward.

In order to give a bird's-eye view of the manner in which these factors are interrelated, a concrete example of learning will be analyzed first; then each of the factors will be discussed separately.

A Simple Experiment

The fundamental principles of learning can be illustrated by a simple experiment which can easily be repeated by anyone who desires firsthand experience with the operation of the factors involved in learning.[4] The subject is a girl six years old. It is known that she is hungry and wants candy. While she is out of the room, a small flat piece of her favorite candy is hidden under the bottom edge of the center book on the lower shelf of a bookcase about four feet long. The books in the center of this row are all dark in color and about the same size. The other shelves contain a radio, some magazines, and a few more books.

The little girl is brought into the room; she is told there is a candy hidden under one of the books in the bookcase and asked if she wants to try to find it. After she answers, "Yes," she is directed to put each book back after looking under it and is told that if she finds the candy, she can keep the candy and eat it.

---

ing, we believe that it is best to assume that these factors are *essential.* For the logic of this book, however, all that is necessary is to make the less controversial assumption that they are *important.*

Almost everyone agrees that these factors are important; the disagreement is about whether any learning at all can occur in the complete absence of one or more of them. For example, it is known that more learning occurs when drive and reinforcement are present (MacCorquodale and Meehl, 1948), but it is not agreed that no learning at all occurs in the complete absence of drive and reinforcement. This is probably due to the fact that, while the presence of a strong drive and reinforcement is relatively easy to establish, it is much harder to be certain that all drives and reinforcements are completely absent. If anything important is at stake, it is safest to assume that all of these factors are essential to learning.

[4] See also a sound film, *Motivation and Reward in Learning,* by N. E. Miller and G. Hart, obtainable from the Psychological Cinema Register, Pennsylvania State College, State College, Pa.

Immediately after receiving these instructions, the little girl eagerly starts to work. First, she looks under the few books on the top shelf. Then she turns around. After a brief pause, she starts taking out the books on the lower shelf, one by one. When she has removed eight of these books without finding the candy, she temporarily leaves the books and starts looking under the magazines on the top shelf. Then she returns to look again on the top shelf under several of the books that she has already picked up. After this, she turns toward the experimenter and asks, "Where is the candy?" He does not answer.

After a pause, she pulls out a few more books on the bottom shelf, stops, sits down, and looks at the books for about half a minute, turns away from the bookcase, looks under a book on a nearby table, then returns and pulls out more books.

Under the thirty-seventh book which she examines, she finds the piece of candy. Uttering an exclamation of delight, she picks it up and eats it. On this trial, it has taken her 210 seconds to find the candy.

She is sent out of the room, candy is hidden under the same book, and she is called back again for another trial. This time she goes directly to the lower shelf of books, taking out each book methodically. She does not stop to sit down, turn away, or ask the experimenter questions. Under the twelfth book she finds the candy. She has finished in 86 seconds.

On the third trial, she goes almost directly to the right place, finding the candy under the second book picked up. She has taken only 11 seconds.

On the following trial, the girl does not do so well. Either the previous spectacular success has been due partly to chance, or some uncontrolled factor has intervened.[5] This time the girl begins at the far end of the shelf and examines 15 books before finding the candy. She has required 86 seconds.

Thereafter, her scores improve progressively until, on the ninth trial, she picks up the correct book immediately and secures

[5] For example, the little girl might say to herself as a result of previous experience with hiding games, "He'll probably change the place now that I know it."

the candy in three seconds. On the tenth trial, she again goes directly to the correct book and gets the candy in two seconds.

Her behavior has changed markedly. Instead of requiring 210 seconds and stopping, asking questions, turning away, looking

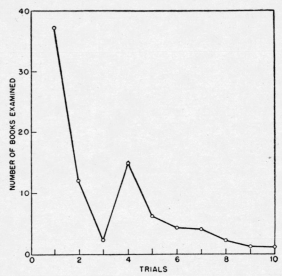

FIG. 1. The elimination of errors. On the first trial the child looks under 36 wrong books and makes other incorrect responses not indicated on the graph before finding candy under the thirty-seventh book examined; errors are gradually eliminated until on the ninth and tenth trials the child makes only the one response of going directly to the correct book. (*Adapted from Miller and Dollard*, 1941.)

under magazines, searching in other parts of the room, picking up wrong books, and making other useless responses, she now goes directly to the right book and gets the candy in two seconds. She has learned. The dramatic manner in which her behavior has changed is illustrated in Fig. 1.

Factors Involved in Learning

The first factor involved in learning is drive. Before beginning, the experimenters had to be sure that the little girl wanted candy. Had she not been motivated, the experiment would certainly have been doomed to failure.

Drive impels the subject to act or respond. Response is the second factor involved in learning. Had the act of picking up a book not been in the girl's repertory of responses, it would have been impossible to teach her to find the candy.

Responses are elicited by cues. In this case, the drive for candy, the directions given to the girl, and the whole setting of the room are parts of the general pattern of cues. Possible specific cues to the response of picking up a given book are the color, size, and markings of the book, and the position of that book in relation to the rest of the bookcase. Were there nothing distinctive about the correct book to serve as a cue, it would be impossible for the girl to learn to solve this problem.

Since the girl's first natural response to the situation, looking under the top book on the upper shelf, does not bring her the candy, she is not rewarded, *i.e.,* this response is not reinforced. Since reinforcement is essential to the maintenance of a habit, the unsuccessful response tends to be weakened and not to reappear. This gives other responses a chance to occur. The girl tries successively a number of different responses, asking questions, turning away, sitting down, and picking up other books. This is what is often wrongly called random behavior.

Finally, one of the responses is followed by seeing, seizing, and eating the candy. This is the reward or, to describe it more technically, *reinforcement.* On subsequent trials a response that has been followed by reward will be more likely to recur. This increase in the probability of recurrence of a rewarded response may be expressed in shorthand fashion by saying that the reward has strengthened the connection between the cues and the rewarded response. Without some sort of reward, the girl would never learn to go regularly to the correct book. The rewarding effect of the candy depends upon the presence of the drive and tends to produce a reduction in strength of this drive. After eating a large amount of candy, the girl would be satiated and stop looking for it.

The relationship among the fundamental factors may be grasped in a brief summary. The drive impels responses, which are usually also determined by cues from other stimuli not strong enough to act as drives but more specifically distinctive than the drive. If the first response is not rewarded by an event reducing the drive, this response tends to drop out and others to appear. The extinction of successive nonrewarded responses produces so-called random behavior. If some one response is followed by reward, the connection between the cue and this response is strengthened, so that the next time that the same drive and other cues are present, this response is more likely to occur. This strengthening of the cue-response connection is the essence of learning. The functions of each of the four factors will become clearer as they are described separately in more detail.

Drive

Strong stimuli which impel action are drives. Any stimulus can become a drive if it is made strong enough. The stronger the stimulus, the more drive function it possesses. The faint murmur of distant music has but little primary drive function; the infernal blare of the neighbor's radio has considerably more.

While any stimulus may become strong enough to act as a drive, certain special classes of stimuli seem to be the primary basis for the greater proportion of motivation. These might be called the *primary* or *innate* drives. One of these is pain. Pain can reach stabbing heights of greater strength than probably any other single drive. The parching sensation of thirst, the pangs of extreme hunger, and the sore weight of fatigue are other examples of powerful innate drives. The bitter sting of cold and the insistent goading of sex are further examples.[6]

[6] Where subjective terms are used, they were adopted in order to express the main point in briefer phrases more meaningful to many readers and were not meant to have any refined technical or philosophical significance. Thus the specialist will understand that hunger can be defined objectively in terms of the effects of food deprivation. In further examples, it will be understood that hearing a sound of a given pitch means being stimulated by sound waves of a given frequency; feeling oneself run means stimulating certain proprioceptors in the course of the responses involved in running; and trying a response means that the response is elicited.

It is perfectly clear that intense stimuli of external origin (like the direct glare of the sun which motivates the man driving west in the late afternoon to pull down the sunshade) can function as drives. As nearly as we can see, drives of internal origin, such as those resulting from deprivation of food or water, seem to have the same functional properties, even though it is possible that the excitation is produced centrally either by direct chemical action on the synapses, by lowering of thresholds (producing an effect like

The strength of the primary drives varies with the conditions of deprivation. For example, if you hold your breath for more than 60 seconds, you experience a tremendous drive to breathe. But this drive is important to only a few people like asthmatics because it is rare for anyone to have his breathing interrupted.

To people living in a society protected by a technology as efficient as ours, it is difficult to realize the full height to which these primary drives can mount. One of the basic aims of any social organization is to protect its members from the unpleasant force of severe motivation by providing satiation for drives before they mount to agonizing heights. Thus it is only when the social organization breaks down under extreme conditions of war, famine, and revolution that the full strength of the primary drives is realized by the social scientist in his usually secure social circumstances.

The importance of the innate drives is further obscured by social inhibitions. In those cases in which our society allows a primary drive, for example, the sex drive before marriage, to rise to considerable heights, a certain amount of negative sanction or social opprobrium generally attaches to frank statements about the drive and to vivid descriptions of its intensity. In some cases, the effects of this taboo upon speech spread even to thoughts, so that consciousness of the drive tends to be weakened and, in extreme cases, obliterated.[7]

The conditions of society tend, besides obscuring the role of certain primary or innate drives, to emphasize certain *secondary* or *learned* drives. These learned drives are acquired on the basis of the primary drives, represent elaborations of them, and

---

increasing the intensity of stimulation), or by learned connections that cause many neurons to fire in some area that has afferent connections to the cortex. But we do not care to press this view in the present book. All that needs to be assumed here is (1) that intense enough stimuli serve as drives (but not that all drives are strong stimuli), (2) that the reduction in painfully strong stimuli (or of other states of drive) acts as a reinforcement, and (3) that the presence of a drive increases the tendency for a habit to be performed.

While many needs produce drives, not all of them do. Thus the need to escape carbon monoxide does not produce any drive. Patients with pernicious anemia may need to eat raw liver in order to keep alive but have no appetite for it.

[7] The mechanism for this will be discussed in Chap. XII.

serve as a façade behind which the functions of the underlying innate drives are hidden. These learned drives are exceedingly important in human behavior; Chap. V will be devoted to them.

In the experiment with the little girl, part of the drive may have been the primary one of hunger but it is exceedingly probable that sheer hunger was not as important as various learned drives such as an appetite for candy aroused by the statement that there was candy to be found, the desire to please the experimenter, the desire to succeed, and possibly annoyance at delay in finding the candy.

Any teacher who has tried to teach unmotivated students is aware of the relationship between drive and learning. Completely self-satisfied people are poor learners. Colonial governments have sometimes found it necessary to tax satisfied natives in order to create a need for money. Spurred by the prospect of interference with the satisfaction of their more primary drives, the natives would then learn the new work and continue to perform it for money.

Cue

The drive impels a person to respond. Cues determine when he will respond, where he will respond, and which response he will make.[8] Simple examples of stimuli which function primarily as cues are the five o'clock whistle determining when the tired worker will stop, the restaurant sign determining where the hungry man will go, and the traffic light determining whether the driver will step on the brake or on the accelerator.

The relationship between the drive and cue functions of stimuli must be considered in more detail. Stimuli may vary in two respects: in strength and in kind. Thus sounds may differ in loudness and in pitch. Weak sounds have little innate drive value; the naïve child is not stirred to action by the onset of a cricket's chirp nor rewarded by its cessation. But weak sounds may be distinctive and have cue value; the individual can be trained to make one response to a weak sound of high pitch and a different response to a weak sound of low pitch. The more the two sounds differ in pitch,

[8] This way of describing cues was suggested to the authors in conversation by Dr. John W. M. Whiting

the easier it is to connect different responses to them; they are more *distinctive* as cues.

As sounds become louder, they increase in drive value. A noise of medium intensity may have a dynamogenic effect, causing the individual to be slightly more active and less likely to fall asleep. As sounds become extremely loud, they possess definite innate drive value and can arouse even the naïve infant to action. Furthermore, escape from an exceedingly loud noise acts as a reward. But loud sounds may vary in pitch and hence can serve as cues as well as drives. The individual can be trained to make one response to one loud sound and a different response to another.

As we have said, a strong stimulus of external origin, like an extremely loud sound or bright light, can have drive value, and hence motivate a person to do something; at the same time it can be distinctive, and hence serve as a cue to elicit a specific response. Apparently the same thing is true of "stimuli" produced by internal states such as hunger; in addition to their impelling or drive function, they may have a selective or cue function. Thus a person can learn to make one response (opening the pantry) when hungry, and a different response (turning on the faucet) when thirsty. Similarly people learn to respond with one word "hungry" when deprived of food and another word "thirsty" when deprived of water, just as they learn to respond to light of one wave length by saying "red" and light of another wave length by saying "green."

Finally, different strengths of stimulation may themselves be distinctive and hence serve as cues. Thus a person can learn to make one response to a weak knocking sound in the engine of his car and a different response to a louder knocking sound. People also learn to give different verbal responses, "weak sound" and "loud sound," to different intensities of auditory stimulation. Exactly the same thing seems to be true of "stimuli" produced by internal states, such as hunger. People learn to respond with one phrase, "slightly hungry," after a short period of food deprivation and another phrase, "very hungry," after a longer period of food deprivation.[9]

[9] Similarly Jenkins and Hanratty (1949) have shown that different intensities of hunger have cue value for the rat by training rats to turn right in a T maze after a short period of food deprivation and to turn left after a longer period of food deprivation. The functional similarities between the

To summarize, stimuli may vary quantitatively and qualitatively; any stimulus may be thought of having a certain drive value, depending on its strength, and a certain cue value, depending on its distinctiveness.

Differences and patterns as cues. Usually a change in an external source of stimulation is a more distinctive cue than the absolute value of that source. Thus if one is reading in a room illuminated by a floor lamp with a six-way switch, it is much easier to report when someone turns the lamp to a higher level of illumination than to say offhand at which of the six levels the light has been constantly burning. Relatively few people are able to learn to name the exact note that they hear played on a piano, but almost anyone can learn to report whether two notes hit in rapid succession are the same or different, and to report the direction of the difference, whether the second note is a little higher or lower than the first. Changes, differences, the direction of differences, and the size of differences all can serve as cues.[10]

Finally, the occurrence of a specific response can be made to depend not upon any single stimulus alone but upon a specific combination of stimuli. A hurried driver speeding down the highway may respond differently to the combination of a sign indicating a reduced speed limit and a police car seen in the rear vision mirror than he would to either the sign without the police car or the car without the sign. This is called *patterning* (Pavlov, 1927; and Hull, 1943). Man has a marvelous capacity to learn to respond to intricate and subtle relationships and patterns.

Importance of cues. The importance of cues in the learning process becomes apparent from an examination of cases in which learning fails through the absence of cues. The experiment already described

---

effects of these internal states, such as hunger and thirst, and those of external sources of stimulation, such as illumination and sound, are our justification for tentatively expanding the concept of stimulus to include both of them.

[10] In their analysis of copying, Miller and Dollard (1941) have shown that this type of cue seems to follow exactly the same laws (*e.g.*, stimulus generalization) as any other and thus can be used in a stimulus-response analysis. We maintain that any specifiable attribute of the environment, which the gestalt psychologists or other students of perception discover as a consistent basis for discriminations, can be used in the stimulus, or cue position of a stimulus-response formula.

of hiding candy under a certain book was repeated on a four-year-old child. When the candy was hidden under a distinctive red book in the middle of a row of black books, he learned to respond perfectly by the third trial. When the candy was hidden under a dark book in the middle of a long row of books of similar color, he learned during the first few trials to select books in that general region but thereafter failed to show improvement during the next ten trials. If the cues are too obscure, as in this case, it is impossible to learn to make the correct response with precision.

Noticing a cue can in itself be a response which may be learned. This is called learning to pay attention.

Response

Drive impels the individual to respond to certain cues. Before any given response to a specific cue can be rewarded and learned, this response must occur. A good part of the trick of animal training, clinical therapy, and schoolteaching is to arrange the situation so that the learner will somehow make the first correct response. A bashful boy at his first dance cannot begin to learn either that girls will not bite him or how to make the correct dance step until he begins responding by trying to dance.

The role of response in human learning is sometimes rather difficult to observe. Because of the fact that the individual already has a good deal of social learning behind him, verbal and other non-overt anticipatory responses may play an important part in controlling his behavior. But cases of verbal behavior are no exception to the rule. A person cannot learn a new way of speaking or thinking until he has first tried a new statement or thought. Much of the difficulty in teaching arises in finding a situation which will produce thoughts that can be rewarded.[11]

[11] A response does not need to be a movement of a given absolute magnitude; it can be a change in a given direction. Learning to attach relative responses to relative cues (*e.g.,* tensing the vocal cords to the cue of hearing that one is singing lower than the model or changing the motion of the hand from left to right to the cue of seeing that one's hand is to the left of the object one is trying to reach) can result in an extremely flexible type of behavior. See the analysis of copying in Miller and Dollard (1941) and of goal-directed learned drives in Miller (1950) and in Chap. V.

Hierarchies of responses. The ease with which a response can be learned in a certain situation depends upon the probability that the cues present can be made to elicit that response. It is a case of "to everyone that hath shall be given." If the response occurs relatively frequently, it is easy to reward that response and still further increase its frequency of occurrence. If the response occurs only rarely, it is difficult to find an occasion when it occurs and can be rewarded. Thus, the initial tendency for a stimulus situation to evoke a response is an important factor in learning.

In order to describe this factor, one may arrange the responses in the order of their probability of occurrence and call this the *initial hierarchy* of responses. The most likely response to occur is called the dominant response in the initial hierarchy; the response least likely to occur is called the weakest response. The same situation may be described in another way. It may be said that there is a strong connection between the stimulus and the dominant response and a weak connection between the stimulus and the weakest response. The word "connection" is used to refer to a causal sequence, the details of which are practically unknown, rather than to specific neural strands.

Learning changes the order of the responses in the hierarchy. The rewarded response, though it may have been initially weak, now occupies the dominant position. The new hierarchy produced by learning may be called the *resultant hierarchy*. At the beginning of the experiment with the books, the response of selecting the correct book happened to be a late response in the initial hierarchy, coming after 36 responses of looking under other books and after other responses such as asking questions. At the end of the experiment, this response had become the first or dominant response in the resultant hierarchy.

Usually the order of responses in an initial hierarchy is the result of previous learning in similar situations. In those cases in which the order of the response is primarily determined not by learning, but by hereditary factors, the initial hierarchy may be called an *innate hierarchy*. In the human infant, crying occupies a higher position in the innate hierarchy than does saying the word "No." Therefore it is much easier for an infant to learn to respond to the sight of a spoonful of medicine by crying than by saying "No."

How novelty is produced. Once having learned, the person responds in a new way. But if the correct response must always occur before it can be rewarded, what novelty is added by learning? The new feature is that the particular response rewarded now occurs regularly to a specific cue, whereas previously its occurrence at just that time and place may have been exceedingly infrequent. The connection between cue and response is the new product of learning. Often a number of different response units are connected to cues so that they all occur together, either simultaneously or successively. Thus a new pattern of responses is produced; the responses are old, but the combination is new. Once this new combination occurs frequently, variations in it may be points of departure for still further learning.

Eliciting the first correct response. There are a number of different ways in which the response to be connected to a given cue as a new habit may first be elicited. The least efficient of these is the mechanism of trial and error. The drive elicits responses, one after another. As those high in the initial hierarchy are nonrewarded and extinguished, various weaker responses appear. These are new in the sense that they would not have been likely to occur before the stronger competing responses were extinguished. If one of these happens to be the desired response, it can be rewarded and the habit established. It should be noted that, even in trial and error, the responses are far from random; they are determined by the initial hierarchy which may vary from situation to situation. Thus it is much more exact to refer to the behavior as *variable* than random.

After a person has learned to attach appropriate responses to specific words as cues, language can be of enormous assistance in eliciting the correct response early in the sequence. The problem confronting the little girl was vastly simplified by eliminating many irrelevant responses through the simple expedient of telling her that the candy was under a book in the bookcase.

Similarly, after a person has learned to attach appropriate responses to the cue of seeing another person perform an act, imitation can help the person to limit his range of trial and error. Provided he has learned the particular units essential to successful copying (Miller and Dollard, 1941), watching a demonstration of the correct response may enable the student to perform perfectly on the first trial. But if not all the units and the techniques of combining them have been learned, the first trial may be halting and involve errors.

One important function of culture, as Ford (1937; 1939) has pointed out, is that it represents a storehouse of solutions to recurrent problems. Various means of instruction (Whiting, 1941) are employed by the older members of society to get the younger members to perform just those responses which are most likely to be rewarded.

In psychological literature, insight and conditioning are often thought to be at the opposite poles, yet both are mechanisms which can cause the individual to perform the correct response on the first trial. As an example of conditioning, a child may thrust his hand against a hot radiator, be burned, and learn to withdraw it at the sight of the radiator. The question here is: How does the child come eventually to withdraw his hand from the radiator before he is burned? Obviously it is the primary or unconditioned stimulus of the burn which causes the child immediately to respond with withdrawal—the dominant response in his innate hierarchy of responses to this situation. This withdrawal is rewarded by escape from pain. Consequently, the first trial is a successful one; there are no errors. But at the same time that the child is withdrawing from pain, he is also withdrawing from the sight of the radiator and is rewarded for doing this. A tendency is thus established for visual cues to elicit withdrawal before his hand touches the radiator. The important fact about conditioning, or associative learning, is that the correct response is dominant in the hierarchy of responses to the unconditioned stimulus. Therefore, that stimulus causes the subject to make the correct response on the first trial.

In cases involving insight or reasoning, a more complicated and less understood mechanism may achieve the same result. In a new situation, the function of reasoning or insight seems to be to produce a response which might otherwise not be made. If this response is rewarded, it will be learned as the response to that situation. If the insight is not rewarded, it will be abandoned. As teachers, we use all the insight at our command, facilitating our reasoning by the use of verbal and even mathematical symbols, in attempting to prepare demonstrations for our classes. If these demonstrations are successful, they are repeated year after year; if not, they tend to be abandoned.

Insight, the conditioning technique, imitation, and verbal instruction are different ways of producing responses likely to be rewarded. Once produced, the responses are all subject to the same laws of trial-and-error learning, to rejection or selection on the basis of the effects of reinforcement or nonreinforcement.

If a response which would be rewarded does not occur, it is not learned. Radically new inventions are rare because the occurrence of the correct combination of responses is improbable. No one in the pre-Columbian New World ever used a wheel in transportation, even though the Mayas built huge pyramids and the Incas had paved roads. In all the rest of the world, the wheel seems to have been invented only once. The history of human society is teeming with the unborn spirits of useful responses which for centuries did not occur, were therefore not rewarded, and did not become cultural habits.

Reinforcement

Repetition does not always strengthen the tendency for a response to occur. When the little girl picked up the wrong book on the top shelf and did not find candy, her tendency to repeat this response was weakened. Such weakening of a response is called experimental extinction; it will be discussed in the next chapter.

When the little girl picked up the correct book and found the candy, her tendency to repeat this response was strengthened. Any specified event, such as finding candy when you want it, that strengthens the tendency for a response to be repeated is called reinforcement.

At first glance it might be thought that this definition is completely circular, but that is not the case. Once it has been discovered that a given event, such as giving candy to a hungry child, can be used as a reinforcement to strengthen a given stimulus-response connection (*e.g.*, the connection between the cue of the sight of the book and the response of reaching for it), it is assumed that this same event can be used as a reinforcement to strengthen any other stimulus-response connection.[12] This assumption could be wrong and if so would be capable of disproof. Therefore, although the definition is circular with respect to the defining response, it is non-circular with respect to all other responses.

Reduction in painfully strong stimulation. When the glare of the sun is bright enough to have a high drive value, any reduction in the strength of this drive stimulus will have the effect of reinforcing any immediately preceding response. Thus a person will tend to learn any response (such as squinting, pulling down a sunshade, or putting on dark glasses) that acts to reduce the painful glare. Similarly when stimulation from a painful headache is intense, any act that produces a prompt reduction in this stimulation—turning off the radio, lying down, rubbing the back of the neck, or taking aspirin—will be reinforced and learned. In animal experiments, escape from the stimulation of an electric shock is frequently used as a strong reinforcement. As we shall subsequently show, a sudden reduction in the strength of fear also acts as a reinforcement.

Observations of the foregoing type may be generalized into the principle that the prompt reduction in the strength of a strong drive stimulus acts as a reinforcement. This principle is essential to the logic of subsequent sections of the book.[13] It is so well supported by evidence that it will scarcely be doubted as an empirical fact.

Drive and reinforcement. Where the drive is a strong stimulus from an external source that is easy to measure independently (like an intense light or an electric current), the following relationships between drive and reinforcement are clear: (1) a prompt reduction in the strength of the drive acts as a reinforcement; (2) reinforcement is impossible in the absence of drive because the strength of stimulation cannot be reduced when it is already at zero; and (3) the drive must inevitably be lower after the reinforcement so that unless something is done to increase it, it will eventually be reduced to zero, at which point further reinforcement is impossible. This fact makes the process self-limiting and so provides a mechanism

[12] A similar definition was given in Miller and Dollard (1941, pp. 29–30). Meehl (1950) has clearly stated in elegant detail the logic of this type of definition.

[13] It is not essential for the logic of the present book, however, to assume that all reinforcement is produced in that way.

for causing the individual to stop one type of behavior and turn to another.

In the case of drives with an internal source, the same general pattern can be observed, but it is harder to be sure of the details because we have no independent measure of the strength of stimulation. Thus food only acts as a strong reinforcement (*i.e.*, reward) if the animal is hungry; the administration of sufficient food will eliminate the drive of hunger and produce satiation. Similarly, water acts as a reinforcement for the thirsty animal and tends to remove the thirst.[14] When responses to the sex drive result in an orgasm, the same general pattern of drive reduction appears quite clearly. Sexual responses short of orgasm are also reinforcing, even in animals that presumably are inexperienced sexually (Sheffield, Wulff, and Backer, 1950). It seems, at least superficially, that they involve increases rather than decreases in stimulation, although in the absence of an independent measure, it is difficult to determine this with certainty (Miller, 1950). Even those activities, sexual and otherwise, that appear to be reinforcing because they produce an increase in pleasure rather than a decrease in drive seem to vary with drive and to become temporarily satiated after sufficient repetition. The failure of the subject to continue repeating them forever must be explained in some way.

So far we have been emphasizing primary, or innate, reinforcement. Many of the most important reinforcements in adult human behavior are social rewards that are learned. Thus paper money and coins do not serve as the powerful reinforcements for small children that they do for adults who have "learned the value of money." An elaborate variety of learned rewards is extremely important in human behavior; they will be discussed separately in Chap. V.

The effects of these learned rewards also seem to be related to drive (they are only reinforcing if the person wants them), but since

[14] When an animal is fed relatively small pellets of food or sips of water, it is possible that the chief reinforcing effect is produced by the removal of the annoyance or restlessness produced by being hungry without food in a situation in which a habit of eating has been established (McCulloch, 1939; Guthrie, 1939) and/or that a good part of the reinforcement comes from a learned reward (Miller, 1950). Even in the absence of enough hunger to make the animal eat, the sight of food apparently has some learned reward value (Myers, 1949).

we do not yet have independent measures of the drives involved, it is difficult to be certain that all of these learned rewards are completely without effect in the absence of drive or that each of them produces a reduction in the strength of some drive.

Although we believe that a consistent, parsimonious drive-reduction theory of reinforcement (Miller and Dollard, 1941) is possible and has the advantage of being more likely to stimulate penetrating research on fundamental problems of learning, such a view is not essential to the main line of argument in the present book. All we need to assume here is that a sudden reduction in a strong drive acts as a reinforcement; we do not need to make the more controversial assumption that all reinforcement is produced in that way.[15]

Direct vs. indirect effects of reinforcement. In order to give a clear introduction, we have greatly simplified the exposition of the experiment with the little girl. While she was looking for the candy, she was almost certainly thinking words and sentences about the candy and perhaps also having visual images of it. The reward of

[15] All that is needed for the present purpose is a reinforcement theory in the broadest sense of those words. One could maintain, like Guthrie (1935), that drive is chiefly important in eliciting strong responses and that the effect of reinforcement is to protect learning by contiguity from being unlearned; like Nuttin (1947) that reinforcement produces an automatic integration of the response into a tension system; or like Skinner (1938) and Mowrer (1947) that there are two kinds of reinforcement: drive reduction for somatic, and contiguity for autonomic responses. It would even be possible to assume, as Tolman (1949) and Hilgard (1948) have done, that there are a considerable number of different kinds of learning. The basic logic of this book would not be affected materially by any of these different views, provided the following two assumptions are retained: (1) that a sudden reduction in the strength of a strong drive has the automatic effect of making contiguous acts more prepotent, and (2) that verbal and other cue-producing responses play an important role in the higher mental processes. The reason we do not need to go into more detail in this book is that, as far as is known, all habits seem to obey exactly the same laws, *e.g.*, the gradient of reinforcement, generalization, extinction, spontaneous recovery, etc. There seems to be no difference in this respect between habits reinforced by a clear-cut reduction in the strength of an external drive such as electric shock and those reinforced by feeding hungry animals, by sexual rewards, or by the sweet taste of saccharin. This seems to apply to habits that involve instrumental responses under the control of the somatic nervous system as well as to those that involve emotional or glandular responses under the control of the autonomic nervous system.

finding the candy not only reinforced the response of reaching for a certain book, it also elicited and reinforced thoughts about the location of the candy. Then as a result of previous training, these words, sentences, and images about the location of the candy helped to elicit the correct reaching responses. In fact, in this example of learning the major role may have been played by such thoughts (technically called cue-producing responses) intervening between the external cues and the overt instrumental responses of reaching for the books. Higher mental processes of this kind are exceedingly important in human behavior; four chapters will be devoted to them in Part III of this book.

Although many of the effects of reinforcement may be mediated by intervening thoughts, others seem to be direct and independent of thought or insight. For example, in the course of trying to find out what was wrong with a radio set, one of the authors was probing into it with the nearest available tool, which happened to be a long darning needle. As he inadvertently touched the wrong wire, he received an extremely powerful electric shock which jerked his whole arm and body back and left him feeling shaken. The intense stimulus from the electric shock was a strong drive and its termination as his hand jerked back was a powerful reinforcement. After receiving this shock, he unplugged the radio and shorted out the condensers. After doing this, he was completely convinced that it was impossible to get another shock. Nevertheless, as he resumed probing in the same location, he felt a certain uneasiness and observed his hand involuntarily jerking back. He had no thought of further shock, but the one strong reinforcement had produced a strong automatic effect.

An experiment by Greenspoon on the reinforcement of a response (1950) provides another clear example of direct, automatic, or, in other words, unconscious learning. He had his subjects sit facing away from him so that they could not see him. He asked them to say all the words they could think of, pronouncing them individually without using any sentences or phrases, and he recorded their responses on a tape recorder. The response he was reinforcing was that of saying plural nouns; he did this by saying "Mmm-hmm" immediately after the subject said a plural noun. In this case the response was a highly generalized part of language habits and the reinforcing value of the stimulus "Mmm-hmm" must have been acquired as a part of social learning.

Greenspoon found that during the "training" period the experimental group, to whom he said "Mmm-hmm" after each plural noun, greatly increased the percentage of plural nouns spoken, while the control group, to whom nothing was said after plural nouns, showed no such increase. Furthermore this happened with subjects who on subsequent questioning showed that they had no idea what the purpose of the "Mmm-hmm" was and were completely unaware of the fact that they were increasing their percentage of plural nouns. This clearly demonstrates that the effects of a reinforcement can be entirely unconscious and automatic. Somewhat similar experiments have been performed by Thorndike (1932) and Thorndike and Rock (1934). A great deal of human learning seems to be of this direct, unconscious kind. Apparently many attitudes, prejudices, emotions, motor skills, and mannerisms are acquired in this way.

The assumption that reinforcement has a direct, unconscious effect is essential to the logic of this book. We fail to see how any theory that bases *all* learning on the cognitive, intelligent selection of responses can adequately explain unconscious, unintelligent behavior.

Importance of reinforcement. As has already been pointed out, learning does not occur under all conditions. Cases in which learning fails to occur because of the absence of reinforcement, or, as it is commonly called, reward, serve to emphasize the great practical importance of this fact. For example, a certain boy never learned much about playing a piano because his mother failed to understand the importance of praise and escape from anxiety as necessary rewards in this situation. She sat at his side during practice. As soon as he finally hit the right note, she would say, "Now, can't you get the fingering correct?" As soon as he got the fingering correct, she would say, "Now, can't you play a little faster?" As soon as he played a little faster, she would say, "But the expression is very poor." Thus no response except that of walking away from the piano at the end of the session was followed by a complete escape from the anxiety-provoking criticism. The boy was never allowed to bask in the relaxing sense of achievement and reduced anxiety that comes with praise or the cessation of criticism. Under these conditions, the one response which was significantly rewarded, to wit, walking away from the piano, became more and more dominant in the situation. The boy failed to learn and, as soon as he was able, escaped practicing altogether.

Part of the seeming mental inferiority of lower-class children at school may be traced to lack of reward. In the first place, the teachers are not so likely to pay attention to them, praise them, and confer little signs of status, such as special tasks, as they are to reward middle-class children in these ways. In the second place, these children have never experienced or seen at close hand in the lives of relatives those advantages of better jobs which are the rewards for educational merit, and they consequently see less promise of attaining such positions. The teacher is less likely to reward them, and their own training has invested the types of event which the teacher controls with less learned reward value.[16]

As long as an individual is being rewarded for what he is doing, he will learn these particular responses more thoroughly, but he may not learn anything new by trial and error.[17] This is partly because the further strengthening of the dominant responses makes the occurrence of any new responses less likely, and partly because its rewards, if ample, will keep the drive at a low level. Thus, in order to get the individual to try a new response which it is desired that he learn, it is often necessary to place him in a situation where his old responses will not be rewarded. Such a situation may be called a *learning dilemma*. The importance of a problem, or dilemma, in producing learning and thinking has been emphasized by John Dewey (1910).

In the absence of a dilemma, no new learning of either the trial-and-error or the thoughtful problem-solving type occurs. For example, a mother was worried because her child seemed to be retarded in learning to talk. Brief questioning revealed that she was adept at understanding the child's every want as expressed by its gestures. Having other successful means of responding, the child was not in a dilemma. He learned only his old habits of using gestures more thoroughly, and consequently he did not perform that

---

[16] For a more detailed description of these conditions, see Davis and Dollard (1940), Chap. XIII.

[17] His behavior may change through other mechanisms, however, such as that of the *anticipatory response*. This will be described later.

type of random vocal behavior which would lead to speech. By gradually pretending to become more stupid at understanding gestures, the mother put the child in a dilemma and probably facilitated the learning of speech. At least, under these modified conditions, this child rapidly learned to talk.

The absence of a dilemma is one of the reasons why it is often difficult to teach successful people new things. Old, heavily rewarded habits must be interrupted before new learning can occur. When the accustomed rewards are withdrawn by unusual circumstances such as revolution, new responses may occur and, if rewarded, may be learned; Russian counts *can* learn to drive taxicabs and countesses to become cooks.

Examples of seemingly incidental learning may appear to contradict the assertion that drive and reward are important conditions of learning. It seems possible, however, that such examples are merely instances of faulty analysis of obscure conditions of learned drive and reward. An individual whose life history is rather well known to the authors shows almost no incidental learning during many trips from New Haven to New York in the cars of various friends. That he is not mentally deficient is demonstrated by the fact that he shows a good deal of incidental learning when walking through strange forests. He has never been punished for failing to note directions while driving with intelligent friends. But, for failing to note directions carefully enough in the woods, he has on earlier occasions suffered the fatigue of plowing through dense underbrush and crossing steep gullies, has been scratched by thorns, stung by hornets, and gone hungry. Finding the blazes of a trail has been followed by a reduction in the strength of a number of innate drives. As a result of these primary experiences, he now finds that he is slightly anxious whenever disoriented in the woods and that the response of rehearsing landmarks produces a rewarding reduction in this anxiety. Thus, what might be superficially taken to be an exception actually illustrates the importance of motivation and reward in human learning.[18]

---

[18] Electrical recording of the responses of afferent nerves indicates that the sudden onset of a new stimulus produces at first a strong burst of impulses from the sense organ which rapidly diminishes in strength till a plateau of stimulation is reached (Adrian, 1928, pp. 67, 116). This diminution is

Summary

Four factors are exceedingly important in learning. These are: drive, cue, response, and reinforcement. The drive impels responses which are usually channelized by cues from other stimuli not strong enough to act as drives but more specifically distinctive than the drive. If the first response is not rewarded, this creates a dilemma in which the extinction of successive nonreinforced responses leads to so-called random behavior. If some one response is followed by reinforcement, the connection between the stimulus pattern and this response is strengthened, so that the next time the same drive and other cues are present this response is more likely to occur. Since reinforcements presumably produce their effect by reducing the strength of the drive stimulus, events cannot be rewarding in the absence of an appropriate drive. After the drive has been satiated by sufficient reward, the tendency to make the rewarded response is weakened so that other responses occur until the drive reappears.

---

called adaptation. According to the principles which have been outlined, such a reduction in strength of stimulation should, if marked enough (as might be the case following the sudden onset of a relatively strong stimulus), act to reinforce any responses associated with it. Careful experiments may reveal that such a mechanism, or the downward part of rapid fluctuations in the strength of stimulation, accounts for certain cases of learning which might superficially appear to be exceptions to a rigorous drive-reduction theory of reinforcement.

In other instances the explanation may be far simpler. For example, a great deal of confusion has occurred in interpreting the "fixated" behavior of Maier's (1949) rats by failing to note that they are rewarded on every trial (irrespective of whether they jump to the correct window or not) by escaping from the punishing air blast. This reward maintains the response that the experimenter has defined as incorrect. Then the function of guidance is to elicit a different response which will be more strongly rewarded.

For a more detailed analysis, showing that the factor of partial reinforcement is involved in Maier's "fixations" and that no qualitatively new type of process needs to be postulated, see Wilcoxon (1951).

CHAPTER IV

SIGNIFICANT DETAILS OF THE LEARNING PROCESS [1]

Principles governing significant aspects of the learning process have been formulated as a result of many careful experimental studies. The most important of these principles will be described briefly. For ease in reference, each principle will first be defined and then illustrated before its function is discussed. Since adequate summaries are available elsewhere,[2] no attempt will be made to describe the evidence supporting each of these principles.

Extinction

Reinforcement is essential to the learning of a habit; it is also essential to the maintenance of a habit. When a learned response is repeated without reinforcement, the strength of the tendency to perform that response undergoes a progressive decrease. This decrement is called *experimental extinction,* or, more simply, extinction.

When the little girl, looking for candy, picked up a book and did not find any candy under it, her tendency to pick up the same book again was reduced. In this case, previous training had already established a general habit of not looking in the same place twice in this kind of a situation. One performance of a nonrewarded response, therefore, usually eliminated it for the rest of that trial. In the absence of previous training, the process of extinction is often much slower. A fisherman who has been rewarded by catching many fish in a certain creek may come back to that creek repeatedly, but if these visits are never again rewarded by securing fish (as a subgoal with learned reward value), his visits will gradually become less frequent and less enthusiastic.

The process of extinction should not be confused with forgetting.

[1] The material in this chapter has been adapted from parts of our "Social Learning and Imitation" (Miller and Dollard, 1941).

[2] See Hull (1934a; 1943), Hilgard and Marquis (1940) and their references.

48

Forgetting occurs during an interval in which a response is not practiced. Extinction occurs when a response is practiced without reinforcement.

If nonreinforced performances did not weaken the tendency to repeat a habit, maladaptive habits would persist indefinitely. The apparent function of extinction is to eliminate responses which do not lead to reinforcement, so that other responses can occur. Thus, when the little girl did not find candy under the first book, she ceased looking under that book and went on to pick up other books. Nonreinforced responses occur when the innate hierarchy is not adapted to the conditions of the specific environment, when the conditions in the environment change so that a previously reinforced response no longer is adequate, or when a response has previously been reinforced by chance. The effects of extinction tend to correct the results of these conditions.

Rate of extinction. The process of extinction is usually not immediate but extends over a number of trials. The number of trials required for the complete extinction of a response varies with certain conditions.

Stronger habits are more resistant to extinction than weaker habits. Other things equal, any factor which will produce a stronger habit will increase its resistance to extinction. One such factor is a greater number of rewarded training trials. Thus a storekeeper is more likely to give up trying to sell a new line of goods if he fails to make sales to a series of customers near the beginning of his experience with these goods than he is if he has the same streak of bad luck after having made many successful sales. Two additional factors producing a stronger habit and hence a greater resistance to extinction are: a stronger drive during training and a greater amount of reward per trial during training.

The resistance to extinction is also influenced by the conditions of extinction. Fewer trials are required to cause the subject to abandon a given response when the drive during extinction is weaker, when there is more effort involved in the responses being extinguished, when the interval between extinction trials is shorter, and when the alternative responses competing with the extinguished response are stronger.

Finally, the rapidity with which a response is abandoned can be influenced by habits established during previous experiences with nonreward in similar situations. For the child in the experiment with the books, not finding candy under an object was a cue which, during the child's previous life history, had always been associated with nonreward for the response of looking again under the same object during the same trial. Under different circumstances, a fisherman who happens to cast many times in the same pool and then is rewarded by catching a fish on a cast, which follows the cue of a previously unsuccessful cast, can learn to try many casts in the same pool.[3]

Learned drives and rewards seem to be as subject to extinction as is any other form of habit. A little girl acquired a great desire to see a certain guest during a period when he happened to bring the girl presents on his visits to the family. After a number of visits on which the guest did not bring her presents, her desire to see him waned. Similarly, the delicious aroma of foods can lose its ability to whet the appetite of professional cooks; and promises, if not fulfilled some of the time, can lose their learned reward value.

Although the process of extinction may be slowed down by certain factors, all habits that have to date been carefully investigated in the laboratory have been found to be subject to extinction. Thus, there is reason to believe that seeming exceptions to extinction, such as the examples of so-called functional autonomy cited by G. W. Allport (1937, pp. 190–212), are either cases in which the habit has become so strong that evidence of extinction is hard to notice during the number of nonrewarded repetitions observed, or cases in which the habit is actually being supported periodically by unrecognized conditions of drive and reward. It seems inadvisable to depend on the eternal persistence without reward of crucial responses from one's employer or one's wife.

In conclusion, mere repetition does not strengthen a habit. Instead, nonrewarded repetitions progressively weaken the strength of the tendency to perform a habit. Usually the tendency to perform a habit does not disappear immediately. The number of trials required for extinction depends on the strength of the habit, on the

---

[3] This procedure is called partial reinforcement. For a more detailed stimulus-response explanation of why it increases resistance to extinction, see V. Sheffield (1949).

particular conditions of extinction, and on past experience with non-rewarded trials.

Spontaneous Recovery

The effects of extinction tend to disappear with the passage of time. After a series of unsuccessful expeditions, a fisherman may have abandoned the idea of making any further trips to a particular stream. As time goes on, his tendency to try that stream again gradually recovers from the effects of extinction, so that next month or next year he may take another chance. This tendency for an extinguished habit to reappear after an interval of time during which no nonrewarded trials occur is called *spontaneous recovery*.

The fact of recovery demonstrates that extinction does not destroy the old habit but merely inhibits it. With the passage of time, the strength of the inhibiting factors produced during extinction is weakened more rapidly than the strength of the original tendency to perform the habit. In this manner, a net gain is produced in the strength of the tendency to perform the habit.

Many carefully controlled experiments have demonstrated that a certain amount of spontaneous recovery is a regular characteristic of extinguished habits. After enough repeated extinctions, however, the habit may become so completely inhibited that it shows little tendency to reappear. Habits that have been disrupted by punishment are much less subject to recovery than habits that have been disrupted by extinction.

The function of extinction is to force the subject to perform new responses. If any of these responses are rewarded, they will be strengthened to the point where their competition may permanently eliminate the old habit. If none of these new responses is rewarded, however, their extinction plus the recovery of the old response will induce the subject to perform the old response again. Recovery is adaptive in those situations in which the absence of reward is only temporary.

Generalization

The effects of learning in one situation transfer to other situations; the less similar the situation, the less transfer occurs. Stated more exactly, reinforcement for making a specific response to a given pattern of cues strengthens not only the tendency for that pattern of cues to elicit that response but also the tendency for other similar patterns of cues to elicit the same response.   The innate tendency for transfer to occur is called innate stimulus generalization.[4]   The less similar the cue or pattern of cues, the less the generalization. This variation in the transfer is referred to as a *gradient of generalization*.

No two situations are ever completely the same.   In the experiment with the little girl, for example, the books were put back into the bookcase in slightly different patterns of unevenness on different trials, and the girl approached the bookcase from different angles. In many other types of learning situations, the variability of the correct cues is considerably greater than in this experiment.   Therefore, if the response were completely specific to the pattern of cues associated with its reward, learning would be impossible because the specific pattern of cues would never repeat itself in exact detail. If the cues eliciting the response were completely generalized, on the other hand, the correct response would also be impossible to learn; the girl could never learn to select a specific book because she would have an equally strong tendency to pick up each of the other books.   This dilemma is partially resolved by an innate gradient of generalization, so that there is a stronger tendency to respond to cues in proportion to their similarity to those present in preceding situations in which the response was rewarded.   As a solution to this dilemma, the gradient of generalization is supplemented by the process of discrimination and by the mechanism of learned or secondary generalization.

Examples of generalization are common in everyday experience. A child bitten by one dog is afraid of other animals and more afraid of other dogs than of cats and horses.   As will be shown, the patient likewise generalizes many responses to the therapist.

The phenomena of generalization have been studied in detail by Pavlov (1927), Bekhterev (1932), and a host of other subsequent experimenters.   Generalization can occur either on the basis of the qualitative similarity of the cues involved or on the basis of identical elements in the two situations.   Perhaps ultimately these are reducible to the same thing.

[4] Learned, or secondary, generalization is discussed in Chap. VI.

The gradient of generalization refers to the qualitative differences or cue aspect of stimuli. The *distinctiveness* of a cue is measured by its dissimilarity from other cues in the same situation, so that little generalization occurs from one cue to other cues in the situation. Thus the distinctiveness of a cue varies with the other cues that are present. A red book in a row of black books is a more distinctive cue than is the same volume in a row of other red books, because less generalization occurs from red to black than from one shade of red to another.

Once a response has been reinforced in one situation, the function of generalization is to increase the probability that the response will occur in other similar situations. For example, after the response of stopping at a tourist cabin near one town has been rewarded by an exceptionally good, quiet, cheap night's rest, generalization will increase the probability that the individual will try stopping at similar tourist cabins near other towns. If a generalized response is rewarded in the new, but similar, situations, the tendency to perform that response in these situations will be further strengthened.

Effect of drive. As Brown (1942) has shown, the strength of generalized responses increases with the strength of drive. One way of expressing this fact is to say that an increase in the strength of drive raises the height of the entire gradient of generalization. From this principle it would be expected that stimuli that are too dissimilar to the original one to elicit a generalized response should become able to do so when the strength of drive is increased. An experiment by Beach (1942) confirms this deduction. He found that an injection of male hormone (which we presume strengthened sexual motivation) increased the variety of stimulus objects that could elicit sexual behavior from the male rat.

Discrimination

If a generalized response is not rewarded, the tendency to perform that response is weakened. By the reward of the response to one pattern of cues and the nonreward or punishment of the response to a somewhat different pattern of cues, a discrimination may gradually be established. The process of discrimination tends to correct maladaptive generalizations. It increases the specificity of the cue-response connection.

By being rewarded for stopping at tourist cabins in the West and nonrewarded for stopping at tourist cabins in the East, a person may gradually learn to discriminate between the two situations on the basis of the geographical cue. But the process of learning to discriminate is complicated by the fact that the effects of extinction also generalize. Thus, after being nonrewarded for stopping at a series of tourist cabins in the East, our heroes of the highway may be reluctant to stop at tourist cabins in the West.

The less different the cues in the two situations, the more generalization will be expected to occur, and hence the more difficult it will be to learn discrimination. If the cues are too similar, so much of the effects of reward may generalize from the rewarded cue to the nonrewarded one, and so much of the effects of extinction may generalize from the nonrewarded cue to the rewarded one, that it will be impossible to learn a discrimination.

Gradient in the Effects of Reinforcement

Delayed reinforcements are less effective than immediate ones. In other words, if a number of different responses are made to a cue and the last of these responses is followed by reward, the connection to the last response will be strengthened the most and the connection to each of the preceding responses will be strengthened by a progressively smaller amount. Similarly, in a series of responses to a series of cues—as when a hungry boy takes off his hat in the hall, dashes through the dining room into the kitchen, opens the icebox, and takes a bite to eat—the connections more remote from the reward are strengthened less than those closer to the reward. In this series, the connection between the sight of the hall closet and the response of hanging up the hat will be strengthened less than the connection between the sight of the icebox door and the response of opening it.

In the experiment performed with the little girl, it was necessary for her to make the response of approaching the bookcase as well as the response of selecting a specific book. If the effects of reward were completely specific to the final response performed (picking up the correct book), she would not learn to approach the bookcase and hence would not find the candy. On the other hand, if the effects of reward were completely general, the response of taking out the wrong book would be strengthened just as much as would the response of taking out the correct book, and learning would be impossible. This dilemma is resolved by the *gradient of reinforcement*.[5] The connection between the cue of the sight of the bookcase at a distance and the response of going toward the bookcase is sufficiently strengthened by each reward to cause the little girl to run toward the bookcase faster and more eagerly on successive trials. But the response of picking out the correct book is strengthened more by the reward than are the earlier responses of picking out the wrong books. Thus the response of selecting the correct book eventually crowds out the responses of picking out the preceding wrong books, and the sequence of behavior is shortened. Since it is physically impossible for the girl to take a book from the bookcase before she arrives there, the responses of taking out a book do not crowd out those of running to the bookcase.

The gradient of reinforcement accounts for an increase in tendency to respond, the nearer the goal is approached. Because cue-response connections near the reward are strengthened more than connections remote from the reward, a hungry man on his way to dinner has a tendency to quicken his pace in rounding the last corner on the way home.

The gradient of reinforcement also explains why, after both a longer and a shorter route to the goal have been tried, the shorter route tends to be preferred. A thirsty child learns to secure water from drinking fountains in the park. Approach to a fountain seen nearby is usually followed more immediately by the rewarding goal response of drinking than is approach to a fountain seen at a distance. During a series of trials in which both fountains are approached, the connection between the cue of seeing the near fountain and the response of approaching that fountain is the more firmly established. The response with the stronger connections crowds out the weaker connection; approaching the near fountain becomes dominant in the hierarchy. Similarly, a child will learn

[5] The gradient of reinforcement is what Hull originally called the goal gradient (1932; 1934b). See Spence (1947) for a paper suggesting that the gradient of reinforcement may be deduced from two more fundamental principles: stimulus generalization and secondary (*i.e.*, learned) reinforcement.

to approach that one of two equally distant fountains where fewer people are waiting in line for a drink.

With human subjects who have had the proper social training, symbolic stimuli that have a learned reward value are often used to bridge the gap between the performance of an act and the occurrence of an innate reward. Money or even the thought of making money can be immediately associated with the performance of a task; after an interval, the money can be immediately associated with some primary reward, such as eating. In this way, the decrement which would be expected on the basis of the gradient of reward is markedly lessened. As would be expected, younger children who have had less training in responding to symbolic stimuli are less affected by such a procedure and hence more influenced by immediacy of reward. Similarly, lower-class individuals who have not been taught to save—that is, have had less opportunity of having the presence of a bank balance immediately associated with primary rewards—are more influenced by immediacy of reward. But even in the cases in which well-established habits of responding to symbolic stimuli help to bridge the gap between the response to a cue and the reward of that response, the gradient of reinforcement is not completely masked; more immediate rewards are regularly more effective than more remote ones.

In summary, the effects of reinforcement are not limited to the particular cue-response sequence which is immediately associated with reward but they also strengthen other cue-response connections less immediately associated with reward. This spread of the effects of reinforcement has the function of strengthening the connections to responses comprising the first steps of the sequence leading to reward. It can be greatly facilitated if certain stimuli involved in the sequence acquire a subgoal, or learned rewarding value, by repeated association with the primary reward. Nevertheless, the effects of reward taper off in a gradient so that the connections immediately associated with the reward are strengthened more than remoter connections. This gradient of reinforcement has the function of tending to force the subject to choose the shortest of alternative paths to a goal and to eliminate unnecessary responses from a sequence.

Anticipatory Response

From the principle of the gradient of reinforcement and from that of generalization, an additional principle can be deduced: that responses near the point of reinforcement tend, wherever physically possible, to occur before their original time in the response series, that is, to become anticipatory. When the little girl was looking for candy, the response of selecting the correct book moved forward in the series and crowded out the originally prior response of selecting the wrong book. Since the same cue, the bookcase within reach, elicited both responses, it was not necessary for generalization to occur. But the cues from the bookcase were fairly similar at different distances—when it was just beyond reach and when the girl was removing one of the books. Thus the response of reaching generalized from the near to the farther cues; the girl tended to start reaching before she actually arrived at the bookcase.

This tendency for responses to occur before their original point in the reinforced series is an exceedingly important aspect of behavior.[6] Under many circumstances, it is responsible for the crowding out of useless acts in the response sequence; under other circumstances, it produces anticipatory errors. As will be noted in following chapters, anticipatory responses may produce stimuli playing an important role in learned motivation and in reasoning and foresight. At present, the simpler dynamics of anticipatory response will be illustrated.

A child touches a hot radiator. The pain elicits an avoidance response, and the escape from pain reinforces this response. Since the sight and the muscular "feel" of the hand approaching the radiator are similar in certain respects to the sight and the muscular "feel" of the hand touching the radiator, the strongly reinforced response of withdrawal will be expected to generalize from the latter situation to the former. After one or more trials, the child will reach out his hand toward the radiator and then withdraw it before touching the radiator. The withdrawal response will become anticipatory; it will occur before that of actually

[6] The functional significance of anticipatory responses has been pointed out by Hull (1929; 1930; 1931).

touching the radiator. This is obviously adaptive, since it enables the child to avoid getting burned.

A person at a restaurant orders a delicious steak, sees it, and then eats it. The taste and eating of the steak elicits and reinforces salivation. On subsequent occasions, the sight of the steak or even its ordering may elicit salivation before the food has actually entered the mouth.

A person sees a green persimmon, picks it up, and bites into it. The astringent taste evokes the response of puckering the lips and spitting out the fruit. This response is reinforced by a decrease in the extreme bitterness of the taste. Upon subsequent occasions, puckering of the lips and incipient spitting responses are likely to have moved forward in the sequence so that they now occur to the cue of seeing a green persimmon instead of to the cue of tasting it.

Anticipatory tendency is involuntary. In the foregoing examples, the anticipatory aspects of the learned responses was adaptive. The tendency for responses to move forward in a sequence, however, does not depend upon the subject's insight into the adaptive value of the mechanism. That the principle of anticipation functions in a more primitive way than this is indicated most clearly by examples in which it functions in a maladaptive manner.

A rifleman pulls the trigger of his gun and then hears a loud report which elicits blinking of the eyes and a startle response by the whole body. The end of the loud stimulus is closely associated with these responses and has a reinforcing effect.[7] On subsequent occasions, the cues involved in pressing the trigger tend to elicit the blinking and the startle. These anticipatory responses are likely to occur before the gun is actually fired and to cause the bullet to swerve from its mark. This tendency is maladaptive,

---

[7] This reinforcing effect of the termination of the sound is clearer in cases where sounds of this loudness persist longer. Then the individual may try a number of different responses and be more likely to repeat on subsequent occasions those which were more closely associated with the escape from the sound than those which were less closely associated with the escape. The basic logic of our exposition in the present book would not be changed if it should be found that it is the onset of the strong stimulus or its ability to elicit an unconditioned response that is the source of the reinforcement in examples of this kind.

but, as all marksmen know, is so strong that it can be inhibited only with difficulty. In this example, it should be noticed that the cues that touch off the anticipatory response are proprioceptive ones that the rifleman receives as a part of the act of tensing his muscles to pull the trigger. Thus, the maladaptive startle can be eliminated readily if the rifleman squeezes the trigger so gradually that no specific cues precede the explosion in a regularly predictable manner. That such a practice has been found desirable is a tribute to the strength and the involuntariness of the tendency for responses to become anticipatory.

Shortening behavior sequence. A small boy comes home at night hungry from play. He cleans his shoes on the doormat, comes in, passes the door of the dining room, where he can see food on the table, hangs his hat carefully on the hook, goes upstairs, straightens his tie, brushes his hair, washes his face and hands, comes downstairs to the dining room, sits down, waits for grace to be said, and then asks, "May I have some meat and potatoes, please?" Eating the food is the reinforcing goal response to this long series of activities. On subsequent occasions, there will be a strong tendency for responses in this sequence to become anticipatory. He will tend to open the door without stopping to clean off his shoes, and to turn directly into the dining room without stopping to hang up his hat or to go through the remainder of the sequence. These acts will be likely to crowd out other preceding responses in the series because the connections to these acts have been strengthened relatively more by being nearer to the point of reward. If he secures food, the anticipatory responses will be still more strongly rewarded and will be more likely to occur on subsequent occasions. The response sequence will be short-circuited. In this way, the principle of anticipation often leads to the adaptive elimination of useless acts from a response sequence.

Discrimination of anticipatory responses. If the response of turning directly into the dining room without stopping to remove the hat and clean up is not followed by food, however, it will tend to be extinguished as a response to cues at this inappropriate point in the series. A discrimination may eventually be established. Similarly, the acts of washing, brushing the hair, waiting quietly during grace, and saying "please" will tend to be abbreviated and crowded out by competition with anticipatory responses unless the latter are either punished or continuously extinguished. Those short cuts which are physically and socially possible will be strengthened by more immediate rewards; others will be punished or extinguished. Thus behavior tends gradually to approximate the shortest, most efficient possible sequence.

Like all other discriminations, the type which results in the elimination of a nonrewarded anticipatory response from a sequence becomes easier as the cues to be discriminated become more distinctive. According to the principle of generalization, anticipatory responses are more likely to occur the more similar the cues in the different parts of the sequence. For instance, the boy is most likely to make an anticipatory entry when passing the dining-room door if his hands happen to be relatively clean and his hair well brushed. If the cues are too similar, anticipatory errors will regularly be expected to intrude.

Anticipatory responses in communication. Anticipatory responses may play an important role in communication between people by providing significant stimuli to other persons. An infant not yet old enough to talk was accustomed to being lifted up into its mother's arms. Because often followed by innate rewards, being in the mother's arms had achieved learned reward value. As a part of the response of being picked up, the infant learned to stand up on his toes, spread his arms, arch his back in a characteristic way. Subsequently, when the child was motivated to be picked up, this response moved forward in a series; the infant performed in an anticipatory manner the part of the subgoal response that was physically possible under the circumstances. He stood on his toes, spread his arms, and threw his head and shoulders back. He could not, however, bend his knees, which would have been a part of the total response, because this would have conflicted with the activity of standing. Since his parents rewarded this gesture by picking him up, he used it more and more often.

All the stages in the evolution of a gesture have been observed in pairs of albino rats. The hungry animals are placed in a cage in which there is a single small dish of powdered food. The first rat discovers the food and commences to eat. The second rat comes over, notices the food, braces himself, and violently bats the first rat out of the way. To the strong stimulus of receiving the blow, the first rat withdraws and is rewarded for this withdrawal by escaping from the blow. After a number of such episodes, the response of withdrawing becomes anticipatory so that it occurs at the sight of the second animal's starting his blow. As this procedure is repeated, the second rat's response of returning to his food becomes more and more anticipatory so that the sweep of his paws in batting at the first animal is progressively shortened. Eventually the whole process is reduced to a mere gesture. The second rat raises his paw, the first retreats from the food, and the second goes directly to the food without attempting to strike a full blow. The tendency for the responses of both rats to become anticipatory has caused a gesture to be substituted for a fight.

A similar type of communication by means of involuntary anticipatory responses occurs when an athlete unwittingly "telegraphs" his punches or points his play. The clever opponent learns to observe such gestures and to respond appropriately. The role of anticipatory responses as a means of communication is enormously elaborated by the conditions of social life.

One of the reasons why verbal responses and thoughts are so likely to become anticipatory is that they can occur without interference from other activities such as standing or using the hands.

CHAPTER V

LEARNED DRIVE AND LEARNED REINFORCEMENT [1]

The helpless, naked, human infant is born with primary drives such as hunger, thirst, and reactions to pain and cold. He does not have, however, many of the motives that distinguish the adult as a member of a particular tribe, nation, social class, occupation, or profession. Many extremely important drives, such as the desire for money, the ambition to become an artist or a scholar, and particular fears and guilts are learned during socialization. [2]

At present only a modest beginning has been made in the experimental study of learned drives and rewards. The work has a long way to go before it bridges completely the gap between the fundamental biological drives and the wonderfully complex web of socially learned motives that determine adult human behavior. The facts that have been learned, however, are extremely important for an understanding of normal and abnormal personality and of psychotherapy.

As Allport (1937) points out, the ability for drives to be acquired

[1] For the experimental evidence supporting many of the conclusions given in this chapter, and the original, more detailed discussion of theory, see Miller (1950). Minor portions of this chapter are adapted from Miller and Dollard (1941).

[2] It is entirely possible that the infant acquires a number of significant new drives (*e.g.*, an increase in sexual motivation) as a physiological result of the process of maturation. But the extreme variability from society to society (Ford, 1949) and even among the social classes in our own society (Davis, 1948; and Warner *et al.*, 1949) is conclusive proof that many of the most important human motivations must be learned. It seems highly probable that other, more universal drives are also learned as the product of more universal conditions of human learning, such as the family. The presence of conditions favorable for the learning of such drives along with evidence that they can be modified by learning places the burden of proof on those who would claim that they are entirely the product of maturation.

is an exceedingly important factor in the development of the distinguishing characteristics of personality. No two people are exactly alike because each has learned different combinations of motives and values under the different conditions of life to which he has been exposed. Freudian theory contains many assumptions about how drives are changed by experience and how these changes affect the personality. Finally, an important part of what has often been called Ego strength, or strength of character, is the ability of socially learned drives to compete with primary ones.

FEAR AS A LEARNED DRIVE AND FEAR REDUCTION AS A REINFORCEMENT

Fear will be discussed first and in the most detail because it has been studied most thoroughly, provides the clearest examples of basic concepts, and is so important as a learned drive. When the source of fear is vague or obscured by repression, it is often called *anxiety*.

Rationale of experiments on animals. The basic facts and concepts can best be introduced by the discussion of a simple experiment on albino rats. In using the results from an experiment of this kind we are working on the hypothesis that people have all the learning capacities of rats so that any general phenomena of learning found in rats will also be found in people, although, of course, people may display additional phenomena not found in rats. Even though the facts must be verified at the human level, it is often easier to notice the operation of principles after they have been studied and isolated in simpler situations so that one knows exactly what to look for. Furthermore, in those cases in which it is impossible to use as rigorous experimental controls at the human level, our faith in what evidence can be gathered at that level will be increased if it is in line with the results of more carefully controlled experiments on other mammals.

Experiments Verifying Basic Principles

In an experiment on albino rats, Miller (1948a) used the apparatus illustrated in Fig. 2. It consisted of two compartments, one black and one white, separated by a little door. Before beginning the experiment proper, he tested the animals in this apparatus and showed that they had no fear of either compartment. Then he gave the animals electric shocks in the white compartment and

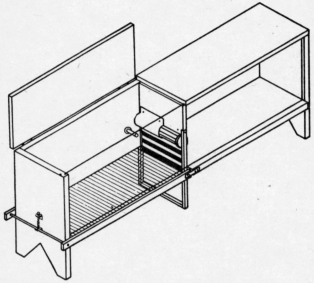

Fig. 2. Apparatus for studying fear as a learned drive. The left compartment is painted white, the right one, black. In order to train the animals to fear the white compartment, a mild shock is administered through the floor of this compartment, which is a grid. During this training the experimenter, by pressing a button, causes the door between the compartments to drop open in front of the animal. In order to see whether the animal can learn a *new* habit when he is motivated by fear alone (without the primary drive of shock) the experimenter leaves the door closed and adjusts the apparatus so that the door drops when the animal performs the correct response, which is turning the wheel or pressing the bar as the case may be. An electric clock is automatically started when the animal is placed in the white compartment and stopped when the animal performs the correct response. (*From Miller,* 1948a.)

trained them to escape these shocks by running through the door (which was open) into the black compartment.

On later trials the electric shock was turned off so that the primary drive of pain was absent, but the animals still continued to run rapidly through the open door. When the door was closed so that they were confined in the white compartment, the rats showed obvious symptoms of fear such as urination, defecation, tenseness, and crouching.   This fear must have been learned since it had not been present before the training with the electric shock.

Next, a test was made to see whether the fear would serve to motivate, and the escape from fear to reinforce, the learning of a new habit.[3]   The animals were placed in the white compartment *without shock*, the door was closed but could be released by rotating a little wheel above it.   Under these circumstances the fear motivated a variety of responses in the compartment: the animals stood up in front of the door, placed their paws on it, sniffed around the edges, bit the bars of the grid they were standing on, ran back and forth and gave other signs of agitation.   In the course of this behavior they eventually touched and moved the wheel above the door.   This caused the door to drop so they could run out of the fear-provoking white compartment.   If this reduction in fear was a reinforcement, we would expect it to strengthen the response of turning the wheel.   As Fig. 3 shows, this is exactly what happened; the animals learned to move the wheel much faster during the series of test trials.

If escaping from the fear-producing white compartment was the reinforcement, we would expect the response to change when the reinforcement was changed.   In order to test this, the conditions were changed so that turning the wheel would not open the door, but pressing a bar would.   When wheel turning was no longer reinforced by escape from the fear-producing white compartment, this response was gradually extinguished, and variable, trial-and-error behavior reappeared.   Figure 4 shows the disappearance of the response of turning the wheel during the trials in which it was not reinforced.   At the same time, as Fig. 5 shows, the new response, bar pressing, that allowed the animal to escape from the fear-producing white compartment, was learned.

In the foregoing experiment the fear was elicited by the cues in a specific place, the white compartment, and reduced by the

[3] Mowrer (1939) was the first to state clearly the hypothesis that fear can serve as a drive and fear reduction as a reinforcement.   Without working out the details, he suggested that this hypothesis should be applicable to the learning of neurotic behavior, superstitions, etc.

removal of those cues when the animal escaped from that place. But it does not make any difference how the fear is elicited or reduced. For example, in another experiment a monkey was trained to fear a buzzer by pairing it with electric shock (Miller, 1950). Throughout this experiment the monkey remained in the

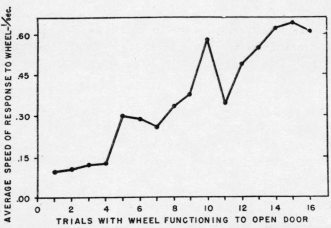

FIG. 3. Learning the first new habit, turning the wheel, in order to escape from the fear-provoking cues in the white compartment. With mild pain produced by an electric shock as a primary drive, the animals have previously learned to fear the white compartment (see Fig. 2) and to run out of it through an open door into the black compartment. Then they are given trials without any electric shock. During these trials they are presumably motivated by fear. The door is closed but can be opened by turning a little wheel. Under these conditions the animals learn to turn the wheel. The curve indicates their progressive increase in speed on successive trials. (*From Miller*, 1948a.)

same place, which was a special cage. It was found that any response that was followed by cessation of the fear-provoking buzzer would be strongly reinforced. For example, the monkey was taught to respond to the buzzer by immediately pulling a handle that turned it off.

The type of behavior that we have been describing is shown by people as well as by animals. A child who has not previously feared dogs learns to fear them after having been bitten, and this fear can motivate him to learn and perform a variety of new responses such as closing gates, climbing over fences, and avoiding certain streets.   The clinical data to be discussed later will be full of many other examples.

Behavior puzzling when conditions of learning are unknown.   In the preceding experiments the behavior is easy to understand because the white compartment and the buzzer are conspicuous

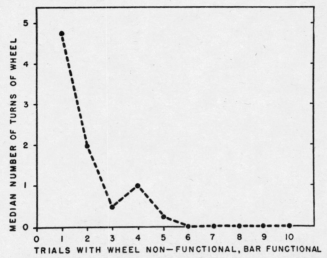

Fig. 4.   Unlearning the habit of turning the wheel when it fails to reduce the learned drive of fear.   Conditions are changed so that turning the wheel no longer causes the door to drop open allowing the animal to escape from the fear-provoking cues in the white compartment.   The animal can escape, however, by pressing a bar.   The curve shows the progressive decrease in the amount of wheel turning during trials when it is no longer rewarded by a reduction in the strength of fear.   (*From Miller,* 1948*a.*)

external cues and the observer knows that they have been associated with pain produced by electric shocks.   If the cues were more obscure or produced by internal thoughts or drives and the observer entered after the training with electric shock was completed, the behavior might be quite puzzling.   In many examples of abnormal behavior it is only after time-consuming study that the therapist learns that certain cues are eliciting fear, exactly what these cues are, and why they are eliciting the fear.

To summarize, we say that fear is *learned* because it can be attached to previously neutral cues, such as those in the white compartment; we say that it is a *drive* because it can motivate, and its reduction can reinforce, the learning and performance of new responses, such as turning the wheel or pressing the bar. Therefore, we call the fear of a previously neutral cue a *learned drive*.

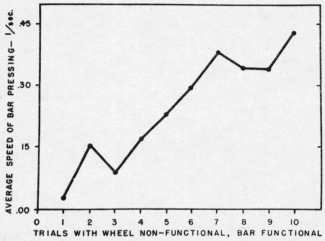

FIG. 5. Learning a second new habit, bar pressing, with the learned drive of fear as a motivation. During further trials without shock, conditions are changed so that only pressing the bar will cause the door to drop open and allow the animals to escape from the fear-provoking cues in the white compartment. The curve shows the increase in speed in the performance of the second new habit, pressing the bar. (*From Miller,* 1948a.)

Functional Definitions of Stimulus and Response

Overt responses can be observed easily and have been fairly well studied. Many of their functional properties are known; they can be learned, generalized to new stimuli, extinguished, inhibited by conflicting responses, facilitated by summation, and so forth. Fear is more difficult to observe, but we are advancing the tentative hypothesis that it has all the functional properties of a response. We have already shown that it has one of these—it can be learned; we shall show that it has others.

Similarly, external sources of stimulation are easy to control so the properties of exteroceptive stimuli are relatively well known: they can vary in distinctiveness and serve as cues; they can vary in strength, and, if strong enough, act as drives. On the basis of the fact that fear has one of the properties of a strong external stimulus (namely, drive) we shall tentatively assume that it has the other property.

In short, we are assuming (1) that fear obeys the same laws as do external responses; and (2) that it has the same drive and cue properties as strong external stimuli. These hypotheses are purely functional; they say nothing about the anatomical location, central or peripheral, of the inferred process. According to them, fear could be a central state that obeys the same laws as an external response and has the same drive and cue properties as a strong external stimulus.

As a short way of expressing the first hypothesis, fear will be called a response; to express the second one, it will be called stimulus-producing. This is a somewhat unorthodox expansion of the use of these two words. Throughout this book we shall use these expanded, purely functional definitions (Miller and Dollard, 1941, p. 59). We shall call anything a stimulus that seems to have the functional properties of a stimulus and anything a response that seems to have the functional properties of a response. Whenever we find that anything has one of the characteristics of a stimulus or a response, we shall look for the other characteristics.

Innate Factors in Fear

The neurological and physiological basis of fear is, of course, innate. Furthermore, the fear of the painful electric shock was presumably not learned, but was rather an innate response to that stimulus. Finally, there is some evidence suggesting that fear, like other responses, may occupy different positions in the innate hierarchy of responses to different cues so that it is easier to learn to be afraid of some situations than of others. Therefore, in referring to the fear drive *per se*, it is more exact to describe it as *learnable* than learned. The fear of a previously neutral cue, however, may be described accurately as a learned drive.

With human subjects it is exceedingly difficult to separate innate from learned factors. We need not be surprised, however, if it is eventually found that there are individual differences in fear, as in other responses. Such differences could come from a number of sources. For example, there could be individual differences in the capacity of the mechanism producing fear so that people would differ in the strength of their maximum fear responses just as they differ in strength of grip. The strength of the innate connections between pain and fear could also differ so that fear would be more readily elicited in some people than it would be in others.

Reinforcement of Fear

It is well known that animals or people can be made to fear a neutral stimulus by pairing it with some other stimulus that already elicits strong fear. In this case the stimulus, such as pain, that already elicits the fear is called the reinforcing stimulus, but the exact nature of the reinforcement is still controversial. According to a strict drive-reduction theory, the reinforcement would have to be a reduction in the strength of pain occurring immediately after its sudden onset or as a part of throbbing changes in intensity. According to other hypotheses, contiguity is all that is necessary; pain reinforces the fear by eliciting it in the presense of the neutral stimulus. This controversy (Miller, 1950) is important for the basic theory of learning, but for our present purposes we do not need to go into it. We can be satisfied with the empirical fact that pain and other stimuli that innately elicit strong fear serve as a primary reinforcement for it,[4] and that stimuli eliciting fear as a learned response have the properties of secondary, or learned, reinforcement.

Although it is not certain that emotional responses, such as fear, are reinforced by drive reduction, it is known that they obey the same laws (gradient of reinforcement, generalization, extinction, spontaneous recovery, etc.) as do those instrumental habits that clearly are reinforced by drive reduction. Because the same general laws seem to apply to both situations, we need not take a definite stand in this book on the question of whether or not drive reduction is the sole mechanism of reinforcement.

[4] We assume that pain has an innate capacity to elicit fear but not that this is the only stimulus that has this capacity. For a further discussion of this complex problem, see Miller (1950).

Strength of Fear

Fear is an important drive because it can be learned so readily and can become so strong. Its great strength is shown by experiments on conflict. Brown (1948) found that albino rats motivated by 46-hour hunger pulled with a force of 50 grams when they were stopped near food they had learned to approach. Other rats pulled with a force of 200 grams when stopped near the place where they had received electric shock. Since this test was without shock, they presumably were motivated by fear. Furthermore, animals first trained to approach food and then shocked there remained far away showing that the habits motivated by fear were prepotent over those motivated by hunger (Miller, 1944). This experimental evidence is supported by many clinical observations (e.g., Freud, 1936) which indicate that fear (or, as it is often called, anxiety) plays a leading role in the production of the conflicts leading to neurotic behavior.

So far as is known, the strength of fear seems to vary with the same factors that are known to affect the strength of overt responses. The strength of fear varies with the strength of the primary drive involved in its reinforcement and with the number of reinforced trials, although in some situations it seems to reach great strength in one or two trials. The gradient of reinforcement applies: stimuli more immediately associated with the reinforcement acquire stronger fear. Fear generalizes to new stimuli and, following the principle of the gradient of generalization, is stronger the more similar those stimuli are to the originally reinforced ones.[5] The fears elicited by different cues summate to produce more intense fear.

Extinction of Fear

Like other habits, learned fears seem to be subject to experimental extinction so that they become weaker during a series of trials without primary reinforcements. Many fears, however, are extremely resistant to extinction. Figure 6 presents extinction curves for animals performing the response of pressing a bar to

[5] The different ways that fear can transfer to new situations will be discussed in more detail in Chap. XI.

escape from a white compartment they have learned to fear. It can be seen that if only the first 200 nonreinforced trials (distributed over 10 days) of the first rat were observed, one might falsely con-

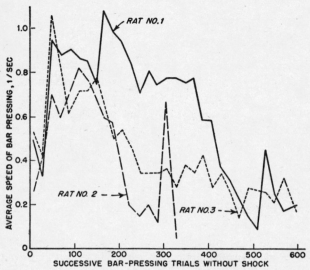

FIG. 6. The resistance to extinction of a habit based on fear. Albino rats were first trained to escape shock in the white compartment of a learned-drive apparatus (illustrated in Fig. 2) by running through a door which opened in front of them. During this training they received 20 trials with shocks interspersed among a larger number of nonshock trials. Then, during trials without shock, they learned and performed a new habit, bar pressing, to open the door that allowed them to escape. Each point on each curve represents the average of 20 trials given to an animal on one day. It can be seen that all animals performed vigorously for more than 100 trials. If only the first 100 trials were observed, the false conclusion might be drawn that the fear motivating this habit was not subject to extinction. (*From Miller,* 1950.)

clude that the fear motivating this habit was not subject to any extinction; in fact, during these trials the fear remained strong enough to motivate continued improvement in the habit of pressing the bar. As trials are continued, however, it is obvious that the fear motivating this habit is being extinguished.

Fear is so resistant to extinction that it is sometimes difficult to determine whether the curve of extinction will eventually reach zero or flatten off at some constant level above zero. Sometimes it is even difficult to be certain that any extinction at all is taking place.

The resistance of fear to extinction seems to be affected by the same factors that apply to other responses. The difficulty of extinguishing fear is increased by anything that makes it stronger: reinforcement by a more painful stimulus, more reinforced trials, more immediate reinforcement, or greater similarity to the originally reinforced stimulus. Furthermore, the procedure of so-called partial reinforcement greatly increases the resistance of fear to extinction. In other words, a painful experience occurring after a number of extinction trials is far more effective in specifically training the subject to remain afraid than the same painful experience would have been as a part of the original learning. This is particularly important in the avoidance of dangerous objects where the person gets hurt only after his fear has extinguished to the point where he begins to be careless.

Although there is no direct experimental evidence on the point, we have every theoretical reason to expect fears to be more resistant to extinction when they are attached to a greater number of variable cues (that are sometimes present and sometimes absent) in complex stimulus situations.

It is quite likely that the preceding list does not exhaust the factors that may be involved in determining the resistance of fears to extinction. For example, clinical evidence suggests that fears are much more resistant to extinction when the subject is unable to remember the traumatic situation in which they were learned. Possible reasons for this effect will be discussed in Chap. XIX.

If an interval of time without further trials is allowed to elapse after a fear has been extinguished, it shows spontaneous recovery just as other responses do. This suggests that the extinction has inhibited rather than eliminated the habit responsible for the fear. The phenomena of spontaneous recovery leads us to expect that massed nonreinforced trials will be more effective in producing an immediate extinction of fear, but that the results of distributed ones will be more permanent.

Responses Inhibiting Fear

Like any other response, fear apparently can be inhibited by responses that are incompatible with it. Apparently eating and the emotional responses that accompany it are at least partially incompatible with fear. If fear is relatively strong with respect to hunger, the eating is inhibited; if hunger is relatively strong with respect to fear, the eating tends to inhibit the fear. Thus Jones (1924) eliminated a child's fear of a rabbit by first showing the rabbit at a distance while the child was eating and then gradually bringing it nearer until the child ate with one hand and petted the rabbit with the other. The rabbit had to be kept at a distance at first so that the responses involved in eating would inhibit the fear instead of the fear inhibiting the eating.

Watson and Rayner (1920) observed that it was much harder to elicit fear from the child, Albert, when he was sucking his thumb. If thumb sucking should have some tendency to elicit responses incompatible with fear (either innately or by generalization from eating) it can be seen that the reduction in fear produced in this way would be a powerful reinforcement for the habit of sucking the thumb when anxious. Unfortunately we do not yet have any definitive list of the responses incompatible with fear and of their degrees of incompatibility.[6]

Other ways of eliminating fear will be discussed in Chap. XII under the topic of the ways responses producing a drive can be prevented; they will also come up in the chapters on psychotherapy where the importance of establishing a discrimination will be emphasized.

FEAR AS A CUE

If our hypothesis that drives are strong stimuli is correct, we would expect fear to have the other properties of a stimulus and thus be able to function as a cue. That seems to be true. People can be taught to make a specific verbal response, saying the word "afraid," in situations that arouse fear. Once this word is learned as a response to the cue of fear, it will transfer to any new situa-

---

[6] For a discussion of different types of incompatibility see Miller (1944, p. 456).

tion that elicits the response producing this cue. This kind of a transfer, mediated by a response-produced cue, is called secondary, or *learned generalization*. Furthermore, people can learn to respond to different degrees of fear with different verbal responses just as they can learn to attach different labels to weak and loud sounds. The same thing applies to overt responses; people who have learned to respond in different ways (by meek muteness, or by verbose bluster) to social situations that frighten them will tend to transfer these different patterns of response to any new social situation that arouses fear. The function of fear as a cue to mediate the transfer of responses to new situations has even been demonstrated in an experiment on albino rats (May, 1948).

After the individual has learned to escape from many different painful and fear-evoking situations by stopping and withdrawing, a sudden increase in fear may become a cue for stopping and reversing whatever response is in progress. Then any cues eliciting fear will be expected to tend to elicit stopping and retreating even though the subject has not had a chance to stop and retreat in the original painful situation responsible for connecting the fear to those cues.

How Punishment Works

Although a reinforcement makes a response more likely to occur and a punishment usually makes it less likely to occur, the two are not simple opposites. It is the *end* of the punishment (*i.e.*, reduction in pain or fear) that strengthens whatever response is associated with it. When this response is incompatible with the one leading to punishment, it tends to eliminate that response. Thus if withdrawal from a hot object coincides with some reduction in the pain, withdrawal is reinforced and tends to prevent the subject from reaching.

But punishment also functions in another way: it attaches fear to the cues involved in performing the punished response. If the person is caught in the act and punished immediately, the connection is simple and direct. If the punishment is long delayed, the process involves more steps and hence is less certain. Fear must be attached to the cues produced by the thought of performing the punished act. For this process to be effective the person has to be made to think about that act while he is being punished for it.

After effective punishment, the person tends to feel afraid whenever he thinks about or starts to perform the punished act. This fear tends to motivate stopping, at least in experienced people, and since the stopping or withdrawing eliminates the cues eliciting the fear, it is reinforced by a reduction in the strength of that fear. Thus a child who has been punished for a forbidden act tends to be frightened when he starts to do it and less frightened when he stops. If he stops, the reduction in fear reinforces stopping.

If the conditions are not arranged correctly so that the foregoing processes can occur, punishment will be expected to be ineffective. In fact, experiments have shown that, when the conditions are arranged so that the reduction in fear reinforces the response leading to punishment, punishment may increase the tendency for the punished act to occur (Gwinn, 1949, and Miller, 1950).

Common Effects of Fear

Mahl (1949) has shown that some of the effects of chronic fear are an increase in stomach acidity and an increase in the rate and irregularity of the heartbeat. Presumably these are innate physiological reactions that do not have to be learned or reinforced as responses to fear.

Two of the overt behavioral effects of fear present a striking contrast. One is the tendency to remain motionless and mute, which reaches its extreme form in the death-feigning of certain animals and sometimes produces results suggestive of the waxy flexibility of catatonics. The other is the pattern of startle, withdrawal, running, and screaming. Both these incompatible patterns seem to be high in the innate hierarchy of responses to fear, and behavior may shift rapidly from one to the other, as when a frightened animal first freezes, then suddenly scurries to shelter and remains motionless there. Although there seems to be a strong innate tendency to respond with these patterns, it is obvious that they can be modified by learning.

Studies of normal men under severe conditions of combat show responses to fear that are either innate or frequently learned (Dollard, 1943; Wickert, 1947, p. 128; Hastings et al., 1944). It is interesting to note how many of the common neurotic and psychotic symptoms are included among the responses normally produced by strong fear in combat or by the conflict between loyalty and fear.   In fact, Grinker and Spiegel (1945*b*, p. 4) report that the symptoms of severe combat anxiety often resemble those of schizophrenia so closely that there is danger of making a wrong diagnosis.

Some of the most frequent reactions to fear in combat are a pounding heart and rapid pulse, a strong feeling of muscular tension, trembling, exaggerated startle, dryness of the throat and mouth, a sinking feeling in the stomach, perspiration, a frequent need to urinate, irritability and aggression, an overpowering urge to cry, run, or hide, feelings of unreality, confusion, feeling faint, nausea, and sometimes stuttering, mutism, and amnesia.   Common chronic effects of fear between missions in combat aircraft are unwillingness to go on any more missions, fatigue, depression and a slowing down of movements and thoughts, restlessness, aggression, loss of appetite, trembling, tendency to be easily startled, insomnia, nightmares, interference with speech, the use of meaningless gestures, and the maintaining of peculiar postures.

In order to get a balanced picture, one must remember that fear, like any other drive, can motivate the learning and performance of socially useful responses such as driving carefully or having a medical examination.   Even in aerial combat, between 35 and 40 per cent of the men reported that they performed their duties better when they were very much afraid, and 50 per cent reported that mild fear had a beneficial effect (Wickert, 1947, p. 131).

SUMMARY OF FUNCTIONS OF FEAR

Fear is important because it can be learned so quickly and become so strong.   Some of its chief effects are:

1. When the fear is learned as a response to a new situation, it brings with it a number of reactions that are either parts of the innate pattern of fear or high in the innate hierarchy of responses to it.

2. When fear is learned as a response to a new situation, it serves as a cue to elicit responses that have previously been learned in other frightening situations.

3. When fear is learned as a response to a new situation, it serves as a drive to motivate trial-and-error behavior. A reduction in the strength of the fear reinforces the learning of any new response that accompanies it. This learning will be influenced by the preceding two factors through their roles in determining which responses are likely to occur.

4. When the responses reducing other drives are punished, fear will be learned and will tend to motivate responses that prevent the reduction of those drives. As we shall show, the conflict between responses motivated by fear and those motivated by other drives, such as aggression and sex, can cause these drives to mount, create misery, and motivate symptoms.

LEARNED REINFORCEMENT

Definitions of learned drive and learned reinforcement. When, as the result of learning, previously neutral cues gain the capacity to play the same functional role in the learning and performance of new responses as do primary drives, such as hunger and thirst, these cues are said to have *learned-drive value.*

When, as the result of learning, previously neutral cues gain the capacity to play the same functional role in the learning and performance of new responses as other reinforcements, such as food for the hungry animal or water for the thirsty one, they are described as *learned reinforcements.* They may also be called learned rewards or secondary reinforcements.

Money is a common example of a learned reinforcement. To infants or to people who have not been subject to the influence of Western society, bits of paper with printing on them by the United States Treasury are relatively neutral cues. With most adults in our society who have "learned the value of money," these same bits of paper may be used to reinforce the learning of new habits and to maintain the performance of old ones. Thus money functions as a learned reinforcement.

Experiments on token reward. Experiments by Wolfe (1936) and Cowles (1937) show how poker chips can acquire learned reinforcement value for chimpanzees. In order to give reinforcement value to the poker chips, Wolfe first trained hungry chimpanzees to insert them into a vending machine which delivered a grape for each token inserted. After sufficient training of this kind, he found that the chimpanzees could be taught to work for the chips by pulling a handle against a weight.

Cowles found that after the poker chips had been associated with primary reinforcement, they could be used to reinforce the learning of a variety of new habits. In one experiment he confronted the animal with two boxes. If they opened the one on the left they found a token; if they opened the one on the right they found nothing. Under these conditions they quickly learned to open the box on the left in spite of the fact that they were not allowed to exchange the tokens for food until after the end of the day's session. In other experiments the possible innate reward value of the token was controlled by giving the animal a token that had been associated with food if he performed the correct response and a different token that had been associated with the nondelivery of food if he performed the incorrect response. The learning of the correct response under these circumstances showed that the reinforcement value of the token depended upon its previous association with the primary reinforcement of eating food when hungry.

Learned rewards follow same laws as other habits. Other experiments on subjects ranging from chickens to children have shown that a variety of sounds and visual stimuli (and hence presumably any cue) can be made to function as a learned reinforcement by repeated, immediate association with primary reinforcement. In the experiments that have been done to date, the acquisition of learned reinforcement seems to follow exactly the same laws as the learning of any other habit. The learned reinforcement effect of the stimulus is strengthened by trials with primary reinforcement and extinguished by repeated nonreinforced trials.[7] According to

---

[7] In adult human subjects many learned reinforcements seem to be exceedingly resistant to extinction, but some are readily extinguished. For example, in a completely uncontrolled inflation, the learned reinforcement value of money extinguishes. Presumably the resistance of learned reinforcement to extinction varies with the same conditions that affect the resistance of learned drives to extinction and presents the same problems in complex human situations involving interlocking hierarchies of learned drives and reinforcement.

the principle of the gradient of reinforcement, immediate associations between a cue and primary reinforcement are more effective in establishing learned reinforcement than are delayed ones. Learned reinforcement generalizes to other similar cues, but, with repeated primary reinforcement of one cue and nonreinforcement of another somewhat different one, a discrimination can be established. Learned reinforcements are more effective in the presence of a drive, and even the presence of an irrelevant drive (*i.e.*, hunger for a learned reinforcement based on giving water to a thirsty animal) can increase their effectiveness somewhat. As with the performance of other responses, it is difficult to be certain whether or not their effectiveness is reduced all the way to zero in the absence of any drive.[8]

Reduce effects of delay. One of the important functions of learned reinforcement is to extend the effects of the gradient of reinforcement over longer intervals of delay between the performance of a response and its reinforcement by a primary reward.[9] Thus in Cowles' (1937) experiment the primary reward of food did not come until the end of the day's session. Learning was possible in spite of this delay because the chimpanzees received the poker chips as a learned reinforcement immediately after the selection of the correct box. Then later the learned-reinforcement value of the poker chips was maintained by immediate association with the primary reinforcement of food.

It is obvious that money functions in a similar fashion in our society. But this effect of learned reinforcement is not limited to one stimulus, such as money: after a child has learned to respond to promises, promises may be used in a similar way, provided the learned reinforcement value of the promises is maintained by regular enough associations with primary reinforcement. After sufficient training, words that the child says to himself may function in the same way. As will be seen, this is a part of the mechanism

[8] According to a strict drive-reduction theory, their effectiveness would, of course, have to be zero in the absence of any drive to be reduced.

[9] In fact, Spence (1947) has made a good case for the hypothesis that all the effects of delayed reinforcement are mediated in this way. If his hypothesis is correct, the gradient of reinforcement emerges as a deduction from two more fundamental principles: stimulus generalization and learned reinforcement.

of "hope" and plays an important role in the response to remote goals.

Relationship between Learned Drive and Learned Reinforcement

In an experiment that we have already mentioned, albino rats were given an electric shock in the white compartment. In the learning process, they established not only a new drive (fear of the white compartment) but also a new reinforcement (escape from the white compartment). In this case it is clear that escape from the white compartment served as a reinforcement because it reduced the drive. Any cue that acquires the ability to stop the fear responses, and hence reduce the strong fear stimulus, will be expected to serve as a reinforcement for the frightened individual.

Conversely, when a child is being taught the value of money, not only is the money established as a learned reinforcement but also the need for money becomes a new drive. Similarly, after Wolfe (1936) had trained the chimpanzees to exchange poker chips for grapes, the sight of a poker chip out of reach in the work apparatus served as an *incentive* to motivate him to pull it in, and getting the poker chip served as a reinforcement for the response of pulling it in. The fact that the chimpanzees would refuse to work if they were given a free supply of poker chips suggests that getting the poker chips served to reduce their learned drive for them.

To a hungry infant, the sudden appearance of the mother with the bottle would be expected to function as a learned reinforcement; it also seems to soothe the infant and temporarily reduce crying and other signs of high drive. But if the bottle is not given to the child, its being near but not near enough eventually elicits responses that indicate increased drive. It is conceivable that in some cases in which the appearance of a rewarding object seems to produce an immediate increase in excitement, the foregoing sequence may occur so rapidly that an initial, temporary decrease in drive is not noted. On the other hand, it is entirely possible that the relationships we have been describing are not universal. For the purposes of this book it is enough to know that both learned drives and learned reinforcements can be established.[10]

---

[10] According to a strict drive-reduction theory, the same cue could not serve as a learned drive (increasing stimulation) and a learned reinforcement

ADDITIONAL SOURCES OF LEARNED MOTIVATION

Anger. Anger is another of the learnable drives. Evidence from newborn children and from the behavior of decorticate animals seems to indicate that an already patterned response of anger and potential aggression exists as one of the learnable responses in the innate hierarchy. One part of this reaction consists of very vigorous external responses, such as the pattern of threshing, striking, and clawing exhibited in a severe temper tantrum. Another part of this pattern consists of various internal responses which prepare the body physiologically for vigorous action and also produce strong internal stimulation exciting the body to vigorous action. Physiological studies (Bard, 1934; Cannon, 1929) indicate that a considerable number of the peripheral stimulus-producing responses involved in anger are similar to those in fear. It is thought (though the evidence is not completely conclusive) that the differences between anger and fear are the result of differences in the central, or thalamic, responses supposedly involved. Whatever their ultimate locus, the responses producing the drive of anger seem to be subject to the laws of learning.

Since anger appears to be a learnable drive, the pattern of anger and aggression is subject to modification at several points. These are represented diagrammatically in Fig. 7. The first of them is the connection between various cues and the responses producing the anger; the individual learns in which situations to become angry. The second is the connection between these same cues and the overt responses of aggression; the individual learns which responses of aggression to make in various situations. The innate pattern of threshing and striking already referred to seems to determine the likelihood of occurrence of certain responses in initial trial-and-error situations. With further learning, various responses can be eliminated from the innate pattern (including even

(decreasing stimulation) simultaneously, but it could serve as first one and then the other in slightly different contexts or at slightly different times. Other theories of reinforcement have not been applied rigorously to this problem, but it is conceivable that they would allow the same object to function in these two different ways simultaneously.

the internal responses producing the anger), or other responses, such as swearing, can be inserted into the pattern. The third of these points, subject to modification, is the connection between the response-produced stimulus of anger and the overt responses of aggression. Through learning, anger becomes connected to those responses which are most rewarded in the same way that external stimuli ordinarily become connected to rewarded responses. Actually, the final aggression usually is a response to a pattern involving

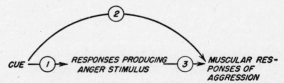

FIG. 7. Different points at which the pattern of anger and aggression is subject to modification by learning. (1) The responses producing the anger stimulus can be connected to different cues; (2) different muscular responses of aggression can be connected to different cues; (3) different muscular responses of aggression can be connected to the anger stimulus.

cues from the external situation and from the internal drive stimulus of anger.

Reinforcement is the selective agent in the learning which produces the adult habits of aggression. It seems probable that a more detailed analysis of social conditions will indicate that there are two sets of circumstances in which the responses involved in the anger pattern are likely to be rewarded. In one, habits motivated by a drive and leading to a reward are blocked by the intervention of another individual. Under these circumstances, responses of aggression are likely to cause the other individual to get out of the way and thus allow the reward to be secured.[11] Another

[11] Whiting has adopted this hypothesis, testing it in his analysis of data on the socialization of the Kwoma (1941). He finds that an additional important condition for the reward of responses of aggression among children is that the opponent be younger than the aggressor. He also finds that, as would be expected under these circumstances, children are likely to respond to interference by younger children with aggression and by older children with avoidance or fear. Similar behavior has been observed in goats (Scott, 1948).

condition is that in which a motivated response usually leading to reward is prevented by some sort of a physical obstacle, such as a sticking door. Both of these conditions will be recognized as the type of situation usually referred to as a frustration. It can readily be seen that aggression will not be likely to be rewarded unless some habit capable of achieving the reward is already present and unless a drive to be reduced is also present.

According to this analysis, whether or not aggression will be high in the hierarchy of responses to frustration or any other pattern of cues will depend upon whether past conditions have been such as to reinforce aggression as a response to the cues in question or ones similar to them.[12]

A reduction in anger can serve as a reinforcement in the same way as can a reduction in fear or any other learned drive. Thus any situation capable of eliciting a relaxation of the responses producing the anger stimuli acquires a reinforcing capacity. It seems probable that individuals learn to relax after completing a successful act of aggression because relaxation before completing successful aggression is not rewarded whereas relaxation afterward is. Thus the performance of certain acts of aggression (as indicated by the cues of seeing and feeling oneself perform these acts) may acquire a rewarding capacity to reduce the strength of the anger stimulus. Furthermore, acts of aggression may acquire learned reward value by association with the more primary rewards secured by the aggression.

Nausea and disgust. Various conditions such as middle-ear stimulation, drugs, or bad food can produce nausea. The response of reverse peristalsis seems to be one of the sources of this strong stimulus. Whatever its source, the response of nausea can be

---

[12] In a previous book, "Frustration and Aggression" (Dollard *et al.*, 1939), no stand was taken on the issue of whether the frustration-aggression relationship was innate or acquired. The hypothesis put forward here (and in Miller and Dollard, 1941) is that the position aggression will occupy in the initial hierarchy of responses to any situation is largely a product of learning. It is a refinement of the original frustration-aggression hypothesis. See also Miller (1941). In emphasizing learning we do not wish to deny the role of innate factors. Thus different strains of animals are known to vary in their savageness, and aggression seems to be influenced by factors such as male hormone (Collias, 1944; Hall, 1941; and Richter, 1949).

readily attached to new cues so that, for example, it tends to be elicited by the sight of the food that has made one sick. The stimulus produced by nausea is distinctive enough to serve as a definite cue, so that a person can learn to respond to it with a specific verbal label or with a specific instrumental response such as going out for a breath of fresh air. It also can be strong enough to have drive value and motivate a person to learn to avoid the cues eliciting it. Similarly, a reduction in the intensity of strong nausea serves as a reinforcement. On this basis a person may learn a variety of responses such as avoiding certain situations or taking appropriate pills. Nausea appears to be an important component of disgust.

Sexual excitement. General observations on man and also on animals (Beach, 1947) show that sexual excitement can readily be learned as a response to previously neutral cues and result in a considerable increase in drive. Similarly, such observations indicate that previously neutral cues can acquire learned-reinforcement value by association with sexual reinforcements.[13] The fact that components of sexual drive and reinforcement can be learned as readily as responses to new cues appears to be a basis for perversion and fetishism. That the components can be learned is also illustrated by the extreme variability of cultural standards of sexual desirableness from society to society and even during different historical periods in our own society.

Appetites and oral drives. It is well know that the primary drive of hunger can be modified by learning so that it becomes a desire for a particular kind of food prepared in a particular way. Thus the infant has to learn to like solid foods and many adults

[13] As has already been pointed out, the separation between drive as an increase in stimulation and reinforcement as a decrease, demanded by a strict drive-reduction theory of reinforcement, is more difficult to make in the case of sex. This may be either because the two frequently occur in rapid alternation or possibly because sexual reinforcements are a genuine exception to the drive-reduction hypotheses. It should be noted, however, that the sexual subgoals that are reinforcing in spite of an apparent increase in excitation tend to lose their reinforcing value and to be avoided rather than sought if they consistently fail to be associated with eventual drive reduction, either directly or through the mediation of phantasies associated with masturbation and nocturnal emission.

can remember learning to like beer, oysters, olives, or snails. After a person has learned to like a particular kind of food, the cues of seeing or smelling it when only slightly hungry may materially increase the appetite. This effect has not been studied in detail, but casual observation suggests that the learning to like a food varies with the strength of the primary drive of hunger, so that one learns to like a new food faster if one is introduced to it on a camping trip when one is extremely hungry. Similarly, the ability of cues to elicit the appetite seems to vary with the amount of hunger at the time of elicitation, so that it is easier to whet one's appetite before a Thanksgiving dinner than afterward.

On the basis of Levy's (1934) experiments on dogs, it has sometimes been assumed that the infant has an innate drive to perform a certain amount of sucking. More recent observations (Sears, Davis *et al.*, 1948, and Sears and Wise, 1949) raise serious question as to the presence of such an innate drive in the human infant. Infants who were cup-fed from birth, and hence did not get a chance to perform a large amount of sucking during eating, did not perform more nonnutritive sucking than suckled infants—though such would be demanded by the hypothesis that there is an innate drive for a certain amount of this activity. If anything, they showed less thumb sucking and other nonnutritive oral activity. Furthermore, with children who had been nursed for various periods of time before weaning to the cup, those who were weaned very early showed less signs of frustration than those who were weaned later. This seems to indicate that the specific desire for nursing at the breast or bottle is at least in part learned as a result of the primary reinforcement of getting food when hungry.

Some General Considerations

Let us return for a moment to the first experiment described in this chapter. After the rats had learned to fear the white compartment, any response that removed these cues was reinforced. Thus a certain directedness was given to their behavior, namely, away from the white compartment. Since the black compartment was the only possible place of escape, this became a goal, and any response that would allow them to get there (running through the open door, rotating the wheel, or pressing the bar) was learned.

Let us consider a slightly more complex example. A child who has experienced severe pain and other forms of discomfort when away from the mother and who has had the close presence of the mother associated with relief will be expected to learn to feel anxious when separated from the mother and safer when closer to her. Thus motivated he will learn to approach the mother by turning to the left to the cue of seeing her to the left, to the right to the cue of seeing her to the right, and going forward to the cue of seeing her straight ahead. After he has learned these relative responses (turning to the left or right or going forward) to the cues of relative differences in position, his behavior will be oriented toward her as a goal. In short, he will respond to the cues of distance from the mother with the drive of fear and the cues of the relative direction with appropriate approach responses. In the same way, he may learn much more complicated habits of approach, such as going around or under obstacles and even taking busses and streetcars to get home. The fact that the mother is the one stimulus object that will reduce his fear will cause his behavior to be oriented toward her as a goal.

Many learned drives seem to be goal-oriented in exactly this same way. The cue that elicits them is a difference between the immediate stimulus situation and a goal.[14] With the sophisticated subject, the cue may be a discrepancy between a verbal statement of the goal and the current stimulus situation. Thus the discrepancy between a verbally defined desirable bank balance and the statement rendered by the bank may motivate a man to a variety of attempts to increase income and reduce expenses. It is obvious that the rigorous analysis of such behavior may involve complex problems in the fields of perception and language.

Differences between Innate and Learned Drives

In our analysis of fear we have said that the physiological basis of the fear mechanism is innate and that fear may be an innate

[14] Miller and Dollard (1941) have analyzed copying in these terms, making a stimulus-response deduction of the type of behavior ordinarily called approximation and correction.

response to certain cues such as pain. Fear is learnable in that it can be acquired as a response to previously neutral cues; the response to those cues is a learned drive. We have seen that even with primary drives, such as hunger and sex, learning can play an important role in determining the situation under which the drive will be intensified and in defining the goal object that will be most sought after and satisfying. We know that certain drives, such as fear, can be learned very easily and that other drives, such as pain, are difficult to attach to new cues by learning, although hallucinations of pain suggest that even this drive may conceivably be learned under suitable conditions. To date we have no definitive list of the "learnableness" of different drives.

We would expect innate drives to vary with the physiological state of the organism. By contrast we would expect learned drives to vary with the principles and conditions of learning.

In the first place, learned drives should be weakened by nonreinforcement; innate drives should not. Thus the ambitious young worker who never gets rewarded for his extra effort should gradually tend to lose his ambition. But an adolescent who is prevented from any direct expression of sex should not lose the innate components of his sex drive, although the *learned* components might be lower than those of someone else who had precocious sexual experience.

Similarly, learned drives should be strengthened by reinforcement. When an ambitious instructor has his hard work rewarded by a promotion to an assistant professorship and then experiences a considerable number of greater rewards associated with his increased prestige and salary, we might expect his ambition to increase. Having been rewarded for striving to move up in the academic hierarchy, it is not surprising that he should continue so to strive; having been rewarded with one promotion it is not surprising that the prospects of a second promotion should become an increased incentive and elicit stronger motivation. In this case, of course, most of the rewards resulting from the promotion are learned rewards and their effect on the ambition is mediated by thoughts and other cue-producing responses of the kind that will be described in the next chapter.

The fact that different conditions of learning may attach learned drives or reinforcements to different cues leads us to expect great variability in them. The variety of stimulus situations that potentially can elicit learned drives and the variety that can serve as their goals and elicit learned reinforcement is practically infinite.

Different learnable drives may be attached to the same cue. Thus both fear and anger may be aroused in the same situation. To make the problem still more complicated, slightly different proportions of two or more learned drives may be attached to different cues. For instance, one situation may make a person very angry and slightly afraid while another may make him slightly angry and very afraid. Furthermore, different individuals may learn to respond to the same pattern of cues with different mixtures of stimulus-producing responses. One individual may be angry, disgusted, and afraid while another is only afraid. One person's desire for money may be motivated chiefly by fear, another by his wish to support his acquired taste as a gourmet, and yet another by his wish to have leisure for artistic or scientific pursuits. In this way learned drives would be expected to blend with each other in a baffling series of combinations, varying with the complex social conditions under which they were learned.

In the same way the rewards which reduce, or are the goals of, learned drives, will be expected to vary from situation to situation, from individual to individual, and from culture to culture. Thus a child may learn to reduce his fear about having broken a dish by crying and seeming penitent when his parents are present and by picking up and hiding the broken pieces when no one has seen the accident. In different societies, different symbols of status are evolved by associating the conventional stimuli of the culture with the reduction of primary drives.

Certain learned drives such as fear and nausea are named with some reference to the physiological responses producing them; others such as vanity, avarice, and the desire to be with people seem to be named for the situations arousing them or the goals satisfying them. In these latter cases the internal components may differ from person to person. One person's avarice may be motivated by fear, and another's by lust.

In the light of this analysis one can see why it is impossible to make any complete list of unitary and independent learned drives and reinforcements.

Fear as a possible component of many socially learned drives.
We may speculate that many socially learned drives, such as guilt, suspicion, shame, pride, the need for social conformity, and the desires for money, power, or status are composed to a considerable extent of fear. According to this speculation, the fear might be blended with different mixtures of other motives, such as disgust. But the main distinctiveness of these motives would lie in the social training that causes specific culturally defined categories of external cues or internal cue-producing responses to arouse the fear or to serve as goals because they reduce it. In this connection it is interesting to note that we speak of the fear of loss of love, the fear of criticism, the fear of losing status, the fear of failure, and the fear of poverty.

Age-grading and Social Mobility: Responses to Relative Cues

In the example of the ambitious instructor who was promoted, part of the pattern of cues was the label "assistant professorship," which might be considered an absolute cue because it represents an absolute position in the culturally defined academic hierarchy. Another part of the pattern of cues, however, was the relative cue of a position higher than his present one in the hierarchy. This is called relative because it is relative to whatever position he occupies; it is described by the label "a promotion." Once the instructor got his assistant professorship, a different absolute cue, "associate professorship," loomed ahead in the same relative position in the status hierarchy. Therefore his reward for the promotion to one position, assistant professor, motivated him to strive for a promotion to a different one, associate professor.

People respond to the relative cue of a culturally defined higher status by making the relative response of "striving to move up." We would expect this response to be strongly established as a result of a great deal of training under the social conditions of age-grading. Thus the small child is first motivated to try to put on his shoes before his mother laces them for him. If he does not try to do this, he is made to feel somewhat anxious by being called a baby; if he succeeds, he is rewarded by praise. But after he has learned to put on his shoes easily, he can no longer escape anxiety and secure praise by continuing to perform this same act; now he is a big enough boy to try lacing his shoes. And so it goes, until he is eventually expected to be able to earn the money to buy shoes for his own children.

The conditions of age-grading establish a strong learned drive in most children to become like their elders—to grow up. At each stage of growing up they achieve new rewards, but the goal is always a relative one that recedes ahead of them. As a result of this kind of social demand, which in our society tends to extend on into adulthood, many individuals learn to feel uneasy whenever they are standing still, not making progress or getting somewhere. This drive can only be reduced by responses that result in something that can be defined as "showing an improvement." It may be speculated that the training that all children receive as a part of age-grading is one of the sources of the motivation for social and professional mobility.[15]

A Sample of Other Socially Learned Drives and Rewards

We have shown that the socially learned drives will only be expected to be as constant, unitary, and independent as the conditions of learning that produce them. In this section we want to say a few words about some of the drives that seem to be produced by relatively constant and important conditions of learning in our society. We shall concentrate on motives that are important in personality and therapy and shall not pretend to give a comprehensive coverage of this exceedingly important subject. Other learned drives that are important in the higher mental processes will be mentioned in Chap. IX.

In the first year of its life the human infant has the cues from its mother associated with the primary reward of feeding on more than 2,000 occasions. Meanwhile the mother and other people are ministering to many other needs. In general there is a correlation between the absence of people and the prolongation of suffering from hunger, cold, pain, and other drives; the appearance of a person is

---

[15] It is the relative nature of the cues and responses and the culturally defined structure of the situation which solves the dilemma posed by Allport (1946). He correctly observes that the (absolute) response that is reinforced is often not the one that is repeated, e.g., a student rewarded by getting an "A" in a course, does not tend to repeat the same course but rather to enroll for a more advanced one in the same department.

associated with a reinforcing reduction in the drive. Therefore the proper conditions are present for the infant to learn to attach strong reinforcement value to a variety of cues from the nearness of the mother and other adults.

Under ordinary circumstances sheep are known to be extremely gregarious. But bottle-fed sheep (Scott, 1945) do not exhibit this trait; they graze apart from the rest of the herd and show more of a tendency to follow the people who have fed them than to follow other sheep. This indicates that learning plays an important role in the development of the strong drive of gregariousness in sheep. Since favorable conditions are present for the learning of gregariousness in the human infant, it seems probable that human gregariousness is also learned.

In the light of the fact that the required social conditions for learning exist in the family, it seems reasonable to advance the hypothesis that the related human motives of sociability, dependence, need to receive and show affection, and desire for approval from others are learned. For example, approval tends to be associated with escape from punishment and with a large number of rewards, while disapproval tends to be associated with nonreward and punishment. Thus it is not hard to see why people display considerable anxiety at even slight indications of social disapproval or dislike and are rewarded by various signs of approval. In fact, a generalization from other stimuli indicating approval was probably the basis for the unconscious reinforcing effect of "Mmm-hmm" in Greenspoon's (1950) experiment.

Similarly, it seems likely that a large number of punishments for being different establish fear of nonconformity and that escape from punishment and rewards for conformity establish the desire to keep within the culturally defined range of permissible variation. As was pointed out in more detail in a previous book (Miller and Dollard, 1941), after the cues of difference arouse anxiety and the cues of sameness reduce it the individual may be motivated to perform verbally guided, conscious copying or may learn to copy another's behavior by unconscious trial and error.

In general there is more reward for copying people with prestige. This establishes a tendency to imitate such people. Where the copying of certain classes of people is consistently nonrewarded or punished, a tendency to try to be different from them may also be learned. Copying the other person's feelings or responding with the appropriate signs of emotion is called empathy or sympathy.

Pride can be a strong motive in many cases. It seems to be related to the desire to escape disapproval and get approval, but sentences of self-disapproval or self-approval play an important role in it. The details of how pride is learned are not known, but the variability from person to person and culture to culture in what will wound pride and what will restore it shows that it must be a product of learning. In our society people learn independence, the desire to be able to do things for themselves, along with pride.

In the course of socialization children learn to try not to be cowards. They learn motivation to resist fears that are labeled unreasonable. When authorities say that doing something is safe, the average person feels some compulsion to try it, even though he is afraid. Calling a small boy "a sissy" or "a pantywaist" can arouse a strong learned drive.

Other important social motivations are fairness and honesty. Labeling an act as "unfair" or "dishonest" elicits a considerable motivation to avoid it. As would be expected with a learned drive, careful studies (Hartshorne and May, 1928) show that honesty is far from uniform or unitary. The same individual can be honest in some situations and dishonest in others. That the motivational factors are important, in addition to the intellectual ones, is shown by the fact that delinquents may have as good a knowledge of what is right and wrong as have nondelinquents; the difference seems to be that they are not as strongly motivated to do the honest thing in certain socially important situations.

Cultural Differences in Learned Drives

As has been pointed out, we would expect learned drives and reinforcements to vary with different conditions of learning. That seems to be the case. There are tremendous differences from society to society and even among the social classes in our own society. In some cultures husbands feel no jealousy when certain other men make love to their wives, and, still more incredibly, a number of women seem to be able to share the same husband amicably. In certain cultures the son feels it his filial duty to kill his parents as soon as they have outlived their economic usefulness, and the parents seem to want to be killed. Among some people, blackened teeth filed to a sharp point or greatly distended ears are considered to be the ultimate feminine allure. Many other such differences have been summarized by Ford (1949).

Even within our own society there are important differences (Davis, 1948; and Warner *et al.*, 1949). Being a good fighter is highly valued in the lower class and controlling one's temper in the middle class. The types of houses, furniture, clothing that are valued, and the attitude toward saving, religion, and family vary in the different social classes. As has been suggested, one of the important reasons why lower-class children are likely to do poorly in school is the fact that they have not learned to be interested in the types of tasks included in the curriculum and that their parents have not taught them to want to please the teacher and to be rewarded by good grades. The middle-class teacher does not have the same values that they do, nor does she understand how to motivate them. Finally, as Kinsey (1948) has shown, the degree of disapproval of various sexual practices is quite different among different social class groups.

A person usually chooses as intimate associates others whose interests, tastes, and morals are relatively similar to his own because they come from the same general social background. Therefore almost everyone greatly underestimates the variability within our own society. Therapists, social workers, psychologists, and other students of personality should be aware of this whenever they are dealing with people from a social background different from their own. An amount of aggression or sexual promiscuity that would suggest neurotic motivation if it occurred in a middle-class individual may be quite normal in a lower-class clique. A fear of expressing physical aggression that would be quite maladaptive in the lower class may be quite adaptive in the middle class. Much of human motivation is a product of learning and varies with the specific conditions of learning.

PART III

THE NORMAL USE OF THE MIND IN SOLVING EMOTIONAL PROBLEMS

CHAPTER VI

INTRODUCTION TO HIGHER MENTAL PROCESSES: EFFECT ON TRANSFER AND DISCRIMINATION

One of the important normal functions of the higher mental processes is the solution of emotional problems. Analyzing this function will help the nonspecialist to dissipate the aura of spookiness surrounding psychotherapy and to understand it in terms of his own experience. It will show what resources have been tried and have failed before the person is driven to get help from the therapist, what is lost when neurosis interferes, and what is regained through proper therapy. It will clarify some of the extremely important functions that psychoanalysts subsume under the category of Ego strength.

Theories and experiments on the higher mental processes have dealt almost exclusively with the solution of problems in the physical environment (Wertheimer, 1945; Ryan, 1948; and Miller and Dollard, 1941, Chap. V). They have largely neglected the process of solving social and emotional problems. The same emphasis pervades the school curriculum. It stresses arithmetic, physical science, and other ways of solving problems in the physical environment but does not give any comparable training in the techniques for handling emotional problems.

The chapters in this part of the book will concentrate mainly, but not exclusively, on the solution of emotional problems. Since so little is known scientifically about the magnificent higher mental processes of man, the treatment cannot be more than a humble beginning to an immensely significant subject. We will probably make the error of overemphasizing the importance of those factors that we understand. Most of the material in this chapter must be taken as hypotheses and illustrations. It cannot be rigorous, comprehensive, and detailed. Having made these general qualifications, we shall not continue to repeat encumbering conditional clauses.

A great deal more research is needed in this area. One of the advantages of the psychotherapeutic situation is that it affords a unique opportunity to observe the mental life of a patient who is struggling with the solution of vital problems. This naturalistic observation should help the student with sound theoretical and experimental training to discover ways of increasing our knowledge of the higher mental processes.

Two "Levels" of Learned Behavior

A great deal of human behavior is made up of simple automatic habits. We respond directly to the cues in our environment and to our internal drives without taking time to think first. For example, a driver sees a child run in front of a car and quickly and automatically presses the brake. Even a passenger is likely to perform the useless response of pressing the floorboards. This shows that the response is direct and automatic rather than the product of thought.

In a second type of behavior people do not respond immediately and automatically to cues and drives. The final overt response follows a series of internal responses, commonly called a train of thought. For example, a driver may see a steep hill, remember that his brakes are poor, and then decide to shift gears.

Many acts are a complex blend of both types of behavior. Man has a much greater capacity for the second, or thoughtful, type called the "higher mental processes." These chapters are primarily concerned with this second, or "higher," type of adjustment.

Cue-producing Responses

In order to talk about the higher mental processes we need to make the distinction between instrumental and cue-producing responses (Hull, 1930). An instrumental act is one whose main function is to produce an immediate change in the relationship to the external environment. Opening a door, lifting a box, jumping back on the curb are examples of instrumental acts. A cue-producing response is one whose main function is to produce a cue that is part of the stimulus pattern leading to another response. Counting is a cue-producing response. The chief function of counting the money one receives as change is to produce the cue that will lead to the proper instrumental response of putting it in one's pocket, giving some back, or asking for more.

When the counting is done out loud, it is perfectly obvious that it is a response and that it produces a cue to which other responses can be attached. When the counting is done silently, it seems to function in exactly the same way. Since we are interested in the functional laws of the responses rather than in their anatomical location, we shall call both counting aloud and counting silently cue-producing responses.[1]

Other examples of cue-producing responses are: writing down numbers in the course of long division, drawing diagrams in the course of designing apparatus, thinking in a silent train of words and sentences, and having images of diagrams, scenes, smells, etc.

It will be noted that certain cue-producing responses can be used in two different ways: (1) they can be used as cues to another person, often in place of an instrumental response, as when one asks for a drink of water instead of getting it oneself, or (2) they can supply cues to the person who makes them, as in the example of counting change. It is primarily with the second function that we are concerned, but we shall see that it is greatly influenced by the first. It is because of its social origin that language and its derivatives, such as mathematics, are the most highly developed form of human

---

[1] This is a somewhat unorthodox extension of the common usage of the words "response" and "cue." The usefulness of this functional definition depends on the validity of two hypotheses: (1) that the laws governing the learning and performance of the internal processes involved in thought are the same as those governing external responses, such as speaking aloud; and (2) that differential responses can be attached to these internal processes, generalize to and from them, etc., in exactly the same way as they can to external cues. Though these hypotheses are far from being definitely established, such evidence as we do have seems to favor them. For example, the internal "response" of thinking of numbers seems to be dependent on the same kind of social learning as the overt response of saying them out loud. Its performance seems to depend on motivation in the same way and it seems to be interfered with in the same way by competing responses; *e.g.*, it is difficult to think of two different numbers simultaneously. Similarly, a response conditioned to the cue of saying a number out loud will generalize to the "cue" of thinking the number, and thinking of different numbers and letters can be a "cue" for a differential conditioned response in apparently exactly the same way as different external cues can, as will be shown in Fig. 12.

cue-producing response. Most human thinking is done in words and sentences.

As has already been pointed out, a person can learn to respond to specific combinations of stimuli or relationships among them and to make different responses to the same cues in different contexts. This is called patterning. A person's responses to the words that he hears someone else speak obviously involve patterning. Thus a parent will respond quite differently to the following two reports containing the same words in different sequences: "Jim hit Mary" and "Mary hit Jim." This is an exceedingly simple example. Although scarcely a beginning has been made toward the study of language from the point of view of learning theory, it is obvious that man's great innate capacity and rigorous social training have produced marvelously intricate and subtle patterning in his responses to spoken language.

Our hypothesis is that all the laws that have been discovered for learned responses to external cues also apply to internal response-produced cues. Therefore we would expect just as much complex patterning in a person's responses to the words in sentences that he says or thinks to himself as we observe in those that he hears other people say.

Role of Cue-producing Responses in Higher Mental Processes

Having made the distinction between instrumental and cue-producing responses, we can improve our description of the distinction between the "lower" and "higher" types of adjustment. In the former, the instrumental response is made directly to the pattern of external cues and internal drives; in the latter, one or more cue-producing responses intervenes.

Our basic assumption is that language and other cue-producing responses play a central role in the higher mental processes. This should be contrasted with the approach of some philosophers who seem to believe that language is a mere means of communicating thoughts which somehow "exist" independently of speech rather than an essential part of most thinking and reasoning. According to our theory, teaching a student the specialized "language" of tensor analysis may enable him to solve problems that for centuries baffled the best minds of the ancients.

It should be noted, however, that by emphasizing the hypothesis that verbal and other cue-producing responses play an essential role in the higher mental processes, *we are not denying the fact that the organism must possess certain capacities, the exact nature of which is still unknown, before such responses can operate in this way.* A parrot can learn to imitate words but not to become a great thinker.

The rest of this part of the book will deal with some of the main functions of cue-producing responses in the solution of problems. The emphasis will be on emotional problems but instrumental ones will also be included.[2]

Influence of Labeling on Transfer and Discrimination

Attaching the same cue-producing response to two distinctive stimulus objects gives them a certain *learned equivalence* increasing the extent to which instrumental and emotional responses will generalize from one to the other (Birge, 1941; Foley and Cofer, 1943; Miller, 1935). This may be illustrated from our previous example of counting change. Five dimes and a fifty-cent piece present cues that are innately quite different. Since they both elicit the same label (*i.e.*, verbal cue-producing response), "fifty cents," they have a certain amount of learned equivalence for adults in our culture. To give another example, once a child has learned to be slightly afraid of objects that are labeled "sharp" and to handle them carefully, these responses can be generalized to a new object by the simple expedient of labeling it "sharp." The child thus may often be taught to fear the new object and be cautious without first being cut by it. Similarly, the label of "Doctor" tends to mediate the transfer of confidence and respect to anyone to whom it is attached.[3]

Conversely, attaching distinctive cue-producing responses to similar stimulus objects tends to increase their distinctiveness. To use

[2] This analysis of the higher mental processes may be supplemented by the one in Chap. V of Miller and Dollard (1941), which emphasizes their use in the solution of instrumental problems.

[3] The cues involved in verbally mediated generalization apparently can be quite complex, including factors such as spelling, context, and the other words and images aroused by the original one. As would be expected from the way our language functions, there is more generalization from one synonym to another than from one homonym to another (Foley and Cofer, 1943).

the example of counting change again, an array of nineteen nickels is sufficiently similar to an array of twenty nickels so that few people would be able to make the discrimination by merely looking. When the nickels are counted, however, they lead to the distinctive cue-producing responses "nineteen" and "twenty," so that the discrimination is easy.

By facilitating a discrimination, cue-producing responses can have an important effect on emotional responses. A girl whose older brother had died of a ruptured appendix suffered acute fear when she learned that her other brother had a ruptured appendix. In this case the drive of strong fear was her emotional problem; it motivated trial-and-error behavior. The girl tried unsuccessfully to concentrate on cleaning the house and then on reading. She also tried thinking. Eventually she thought: "My first brother died before they had sulfa drugs and penicillin; now that they have these new drugs it is different." This labeling of before and after the availability of the new drugs made the two situations more distinctive and cut down on the generalization of fear from the case of the one brother to the other. At the same time the thoughts about the drugs mediated the generalization of fear-reducing responses from other situations in which drugs and medical science had been effective. Both of these effects reduced the fear. The reduction in fear reinforced the thoughts about the drugs so that they recurred whenever the fear was revived. In this example, the labeling that facilitated the discrimination between the cases of the two brothers was the solution to an emotional problem.

To cite another example, a faculty member was anxious, disappointed, and annoyed at not being invited to a large party given by a close friend. These painful emotions motivated problem-solving behavior. Turning it over in his mind, he suddenly noticed that all of the guests were members of his friend's department, which was different from his own. As soon as he labeled it "a departmental party," his fear that he had offended his friend or had been ungenerously neglected, and his ensuing disappointment and aggression, were eliminated; he no longer had an emotional problem.

Other words and sentences can be labeled as well as objects in the external environment. Labeling a statement "a lie" tends to mediate the generalization of emotions that have been learned in response to other lies.   Likewise, pointing out a contradiction in his logic may have considerable emotional effect on a scientist.

Similar results can be secured by nonverbal cue-producing responses such as images and perceptual responses, or by focusing the attention on the parts of complex stimulus objects that are similar or different.   Sometimes the focusing of attention is done by the overt response of turning the eyes in a particular direction; at other times it seems to be accomplished by internal "responses" that are not as well understood (Lawrence, 1950a and b).

Part of the effectiveness of the verbal labels probably comes from the nonverbal cue-producing responses which are attached to them in the course of extensive social learning.   As the result of this learning, words and sentences become able to direct attention toward relevant differences, to influence perception, and to elicit images and other nonverbal cue-producing responses.

Language Contains Culturally Important Generalizations and Discriminations

The verbal responses of labeling are especially important because language contains those discriminations and equivalences that have been found useful by generations of trial and error in a given society (Miller, 1948b).   Common examples are "boy" vs. "girl," "big boy" vs. "little boy," "friend" vs. "enemy," "married" vs. "single," and "my wife" vs. "other woman."

In our society, where discriminating different stages in the ripeness of cocoanuts is not important, we have only two phrases, "green" cocoanuts and "ripe" cocoanuts.   Among the Cook Islanders (Hiroa, 1932) in Polynesia, in whose economy cocoanuts play a paramount role as source of food, drink, and fiber, there are 12 distinctive words and phrases, each describing a different stage in the maturity of this nut.   Learning to use these words to describe correctly the state of the cocoanut is of great assistance in subsequent behavior where correct discrimination or generalization is important.   The kinship terminology used in a society likewise reflects the special behavior patterns required in relations to kinsmen. In a society where a man is expected to treat his mother's brother differently from his father's brother, he does not call them both "uncle" but uses a special designation for his mother's brother (Murdock, 1949, pp. 138, 152).

Scientific terminology is often chosen to bring out similarities between superficially dissimilar phenomena and facilitate discrimination among the superficially similar. This is one of the reasons why logical learning transfers to new situations so much more adaptively than rote learning. Logical learning is in terms of words and sentences and scientific principles, the general applicability of which has already been discovered and conserved as a part of the culture.

SUMMARY OF THREE "LEVELS" OF GENERALIZATION AND DISCRIMINATION

By way of summary and refinement, three "levels" of generalization and discrimination may be distinguished:

1. *Those based solely on innate similarities and differences.* After the subject learns a response to one cue, this response will tend to generalize to other similar cues, with more generalization occurring to cues that are more similar. This is called a *gradient of innate stimulus generalization.* For example, a child who is burned by one object will tend to fear other similar objects, showing more fear of objects that are more similar.

If the response to the original cue is repeatedly reinforced and that to the dissimilar cue is repeatedly nonreinforced, the response to the former will tend to be strengthened while that to the latter will be weakened until a *discrimination* is established. With further experience of being burned by one object but not by others, the child's fear will tend to become restricted to the hot object. Because of generalization, the difficulty in establishing a discrimination will be a function of the similarity of the cues, and if the cues are too similar, it will be impossible to establish a discrimination.

2. *Those in which innate similarities or differences are enhanced by appropriate labels or other cue-producing responses.* Attaching the same label to different cues increases the amount of generalization. Attaching different labels to similar cues decreases the amount of generalization and thus makes subsequent discriminations easier to learn. For example, if a child has already learned to apply the words "hot" and "cold" to the right objects but has had no experi-

ence with being burned, he will be more likely to generalize the fear caused by his first serious burn to other objects labeled "hot," and it will be somewhat easier for him to learn to discriminate these from ones labeled "cold."

3. *Those in which labels or other cue-producing responses mediate the transfer of already learned responses.* If the correct instrumental or emotional responses have already been learned to the appropriate labels, these responses can be immediately transferred to a new cue by learning to label it correctly. For example, if the child has already learned to respond appropriately to objects labeled "hot" and "cold" it is possible to transfer this discrimination to the new objects by teaching him to label one "hot" and the other "cold."

It can be seen that the first "level" differs from the other two in that no labeling or other cue-producing response is involved. In the second, the label is already learned but the appropriate response to the label still has to be learned. In the third, the appropriate response to the label has already been learned and is thus available for immediate transfer as soon as new objects are given the correct labels.

Actually the three "levels" blend into one another, as when a child tends to fear a new object because it has been labeled "hot" but is overcome by curiosity, touches it, and is burned, so that fear is reinforced as a response to the label and also as a direct response to the new object. Furthermore, if the label elicits strong enough responses, it may serve as a learned reinforcement. Then the responses that it elicits may become conditioned to the new stimulus object, so that by repeated labeling (without any primary reinforcement such as a burn) the new object becomes able to elicit the responses directly without the need for the continued intervention of the label.

CHAPTER VII

THE ROLE OF WORDS AND SENTENCES IN
AROUSING DRIVES, MEDIATING REWARDS,
AND PRODUCING FORESIGHT

In the course of showing how labels can influence generalization and discrimination we have already used examples in which labels arouse drives. This point is so important, however, that it deserves separate emphasis. The doctor's announcement of a diagnosis of cancer can arouse strong fear. A letter may make one homesick or a pep talk, ambitious. Similarly, the words and sentences that a person thinks to himself can have a strong motivating effect. For a student, the thought of an important examination may arouse a fear that drives him to work hard instead of going to the movies. Thinking about an insult can make one angry. Sometimes thoughts are so motivating that in order to go to sleep it is necessary to suppress them by performing an incompatible response, such as counting sheep.

Since words have no innate tendency to arouse drives, it is apparent that only drives that are learnable (that is, by our definition, response-produced) can be attached to words. After the drive-producing response has been attached to the word as a cue, the response of saying the word will elicit the drive. Since the learned drive is elicited via the word, it is called a *mediated learned drive*. For a more detailed discussion, see Miller (1950).

Verbal responses mediate rewards. Spoken words and thoughts can also lower painful drives and give reassurance or reward. Tremendous relief from a nagging fear can be produced when the doctor says, "I've made the test and it's definitely not tuberculosis." The anxious·child is reassured by being told, "Mama's coming soon." He may then reassure himself by repeating this either out loud or silently. To give a more complex example, a person may take a discouragingly large task with a remote reward, such as writing a book, and break it up into small units by verbally defining a series of subgoals. Then he may reward himself by noting the completion of each step, excluding for the moment all thoughts about the many incompleted steps ahead.[1]

Foresight. Verbal and other cue-producing responses play an important role in helping man to respond to what is likely to happen in the future.[2] Many of the examples that have already been given involve this feature. The disturbing thought that he may not be able to provide for his children's education may help to motivate a father to buy insurance and to keep working hard in the shop or office. In this way, words and thoughts help to sustain motivation over a period of time. Without them people would be less foresightful and consistent and more at the mercy of the stimuli present here and now. Their behavior would be deflected whenever these stimuli changed.

Great Economy of Verbal Learning Once Necessary Units Have Been Acquired

The absence of necessary units (*i.e.,* motivational and instrumental responses attached to verbal cues) can impose a severe limitation on social control, including psychotherapy, and on the use of the higher mental processes. For example, one cannot use words to motivate, reassure, reward, or guide very small children; one cannot reason with them. Similarly, they cannot use words in this way for themselves. Thus they lack foresight and the ability to sustain hope or tolerate delay and tend to live in the present only.

---

[1] Theoretically drives can be reduced by words in two different ways: (1) the cue of the verbal response can elicit a response that is incompatible with the one producing the drive—for example, the part of the drive that is produced by muscular tension can be reduced by the command to relax; (2) in the case of mediated learned drives, the response to the cue of the word can be incompatible with the mediating response eliciting the drive—for example, the words "the train leaves on standard time" can eliminate the thoughts of being late that are, in turn, arousing fear.

[2] Miller (1935) has shown that introducing a distinctive cue-producing response into a simple experimental situation in which animals had been unable to show foresightful behavior enabled them to show an elementary kind of foresight.

Older children who have not received the proper training show similar defects. Lower-class children, for instance, are not readily motivated to do better school work by threats of poor grades (Davis, 1948). It is hard, likewise, to reassure a suspicious adult. Conversely, it is much easier to give technical directions to an expert than to a novice because the expert has more essential response units that can be elicited by words and sentences.

Once the necessary units have been acquired, verbal learning can be extremely economical. Calling a person "an enemy" is a relatively simple response that can be learned quickly. But if the necessary subunits have been learned, the word "enemy" can elicit the performance of a complicated variety of habits, including the emotional responses of hate and fear and the intricate instrumental responses involved in caution, avoidance, defense, and offense. Through patterning (Hull, 1943), the responses to the same verbal cue may be different when it occurs in the context of different environmental cues. Thus one set of responses may be elicited at a formal social event, and another in a competitive situation. The responses may vary with the presence of the individual's friends, of the enemy's friends, and with the particular advantages and disadvantages that the enemy has at the moment. To learn all of these responses separately for each new enemy would be exceedingly laborious; to learn the *one* verbal response that mediates them in different contexts is much easier. Later, of course, the responses mediated by the label can be refined by further learning dependent on characteristics specific to this particular enemy.

Changing one verbal response from "friend" to "enemy" is an economical way of changing a large number of complex instrumental and emotional responses. Similarly, labeling an object as "expensive and fragile," a wire as "high voltage," an idea as "the Chief's," or an act as "dishonest," may immediately elicit motivations that originally were slowly learned (Miller, 1950).

Because of this tremendous economy, a great deal of human learning is in terms of verbal responses, often called hypotheses. Thus a tennis player up against a new opponent is making a variety of responses both instrumental and verbal. One of these may be the thought, "I believe he has a weak backhand." If this response is present and reinforced by success when the opponent returns poorly a forcing shot to his backhand, it may influence a great variety of other responses occurring during the remainder of the game.

It can be seen that the quick learning of a single verbal response of this kind will be expected to produce a sudden change in many other responses. This will contrast dramatically with the gradual changes that occur without any such verbal response. The sudden generalized change mediated by the verbal hypothesis (or other cue-producing response) is often called *insight;* the slow piecemeal accumulation of specific changes in the absence of any such verbal response is usually called *trial and error*.

The two are not mutually exclusive. Because placements on a certain opponent's backhand are more often reinforced with success, a player may drift into a greater proportion of them without realizing it. Then, he may suddenly have the thought that mediates the more drastic change. On the other hand, he may begin by giving himself verbal directions to play this opponent's backhand, and after sufficient practice the postural and other responses involved in following this strategy may become directly connected to the sight of this opponent so that the verbal cues are no longer necessary.

Superiority of logical over rote learning. Learning that involves words, sentences, and thoughts is often described as *logical learning*. Learning that involves more direct associations between cues and responses is often described as *rote learning*. In the light of the foregoing discussion it can be seen why logical learning is often so superior to rote learning and why it is important to teach children by logical instead of rote methods. The advantages of teaching words, sentences, and other cue-producing responses will become still clearer as we discuss their function in reasoning.

CHAPTER VIII

REASONING AND PLANNING

The function of reasoning is to shorten the process of overt trial and error by producing successful sequences of responses on the first trial. Frequently reasoning produces new sequences that would not be likely to occur at all in the course of mere trial and error.

Reasoning often involves trial and error in which safe, effortless cue-producing responses, usually verbal, substitute for the more dangerous and effortful overt instrumental ones. In everyday language, this is called canvassing the various alternatives. The subject responds with various sequences of sentences or images. Those that result in cues that elicit responses of frustration, anxiety, or stopping are abandoned. Those that lead to verbal statements or images of the desired goal are reinforced by the learned reward value of such cues and thus tend to lead to overt action.

Although this aspect of reasoning involves trial and error, the cue-producing responses are not random; they are a function of internal drives, external cues, and the way the subject has stated the problem to himself.

Reasoning Involves More Than Symbolic Trial and Error

If reasoning were nothing more than the substitution of verbal for instrumental trial and error, it would be somewhat quicker and a great deal less effortful and dangerous but could not accomplish anything essentially different. Fortunately this is not the case. There is one enormously important difference between a sequence of instrumental responses and one of cue-producing responses. Because of the structure of the environment, a series of instrumental responses can occur in one sequence only, the one leading from the problem situation to the goal. If the individual could achieve the goal without the intervening steps, he would have no problem. A series of cue-producing responses is not limited in this way. It is

110

possible for certain cue-producing responses that have been associated with the goal to move forward in the sequence and provide cues that have a selective effect on subsequent responses. Hull (1935) calls these *anticipatory goal responses* and presents a rigorous deduction of how they could make the adaptive combination of habits more likely to occur in a novel situation. A similar but more radical possibility is for the chain of cue-producing responses to begin at the goal and unreel backward step by step till the correct response in the problem situation is reached. According to stimulus-response theory, it is these two possibilities that give cue-producing responses their great superiority over instrumental trial and error in the solution of problems. When they are operating, the process can truly be called reasoning or creative thinking.

A Simple Example of Reasoning

The way reasoning works may be illustrated by a simple example. In the heavy traffic leaving a football game, a driver was caught in a long line of cars all waiting to make a left turn on a four-lane highway. The situation is shown in Fig. 8. Most of the cars leaving the game were all waiting to make the same left turn. There was just enough traffic coming from the other direction to make the left turn difficult so the line was advancing quite slowly. Once the cars negotiated the difficult left turn, they could drive ahead rapidly on the other highway.

As the long line of cars crept slowly ahead, the man became increasingly impatient. He wished he could pull out of the line into the almost empty lane on the right and drive ahead. But this thought led to the one of being stopped by the other drivers when he tried to turn left in front of the long line so this solution was immediately rejected. The driver continued, however, to think of the road he would like to get onto. He noticed that the few cars coming in the opposite direction had no difficulty in making their right turns onto this road and driving rapidly on down it. He said to himself, "If I were only going the other way, it would be so easy." This led to the question, "How could I be going the other way?" From here on he was dealing with a problem that he had a great deal of practice in solving. He immediately thought of pulling out into the outside lane, driving up the highway, finding a place to

turn around, coming back the other way, and making the right
turn onto the other highway. While thinking of this, he felt a tri-

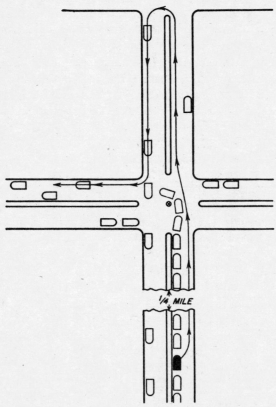

FIG. 8. An example of reasoning. The driver in the black car is blocked from
making a left turn by the traffic jam in the left lane. In the distance he sees
the cars in the much lighter traffic coming from the opposite direction making
the right turn easily on to the road he wants to take. He thinks, "If I were only
going the other way." This stimulates him to think of how he could be going
the other way. He pulls out into the right lane, passes the cars ahead, turns
around, comes back the other way, and makes a right turn on to the highway.
(The small circle at the center intersection indicates a traffic light.)

umphant sense of relief from the frustration of waiting in line and
immediately proceeded to carry his ideas through to successful action.

The first part of this example illustrates the operation of symbolic trial and error. The train of thoughts started with the immediate situation (pulling out of line) and progressed toward the goal in the same sequence that would be required in a series of instrumental responses. This sequence of thoughts, however, was much less effortful and embarrassing than actually driving up and getting stopped when trying to turn in front of the other drivers. Furthermore, these thoughts did not lose this driver his place in line. In the second part of the example, the sequence of cue-producing responses started at the goal in what might almost be called wishful thinking ("If I were only going the other way it would be so easy") and worked backward without any trial and error. It resulted in a new and adaptive sequence of instrumental responses that probably never would have occurred by mere trial and error.

In this example the crucial cue-producing responses were verbal. Words and sentences play an exceedingly important role in human reasoning, but reasoning can also involve nonverbal cue-producing responses such as visual images.

Importance of the Way the Problem Is Defined

Since reasoning is guided by anticipatory goal responses and often works backward from the goal, it can be seen that the way the goal is described, or in other words the way the problem is posed, will be important. A problem is often very hard if stated one way and easy if stated in another. For example, *how* to build a house with an all southern exposure is a difficult question, but *where* to build one is easy—at the North Pole.

The way the problem is stated is also of importance in problems involving emotional responses. A pilot who had just been assigned to a new type of airplane was having a great deal of trouble landing it properly. He asked himself, "What am I doing wrong with this airplane?" He thought of and tried a number of different changes in his technique but did not seem to be able to find any way to solve this particular problem. Finally he noticed that he was tense and wondered: "Am I scared?" Then he remembered that he had heard that this plane had bad stalling characteristics. He redefined his problem as "how to get over being afraid of stalls on landing." As soon as he did this, he knew the solution. He went up to a safe altitude and practiced stalls until he had a relaxed feeling of complete confidence. Having overcome the distracting fear that was producing conflicts and muscular tension, he was able to come down and make the delicate discriminations and smooth motor responses required for a good landing.

Planning

Planning is similar to reasoning except that the emphasis is much more on future and less on immediately present problems. The thinking is done in advance while there is more time for it and for preparatory action. Therefore, planning often prevents the occurrence of situations that would produce emotional problems.

The following case illustrates a complex mixture of reasoning and planning in the solution of an emotional problem. A supervisory vacancy occurred in a large business organization. A contemporary of an employee was promoted and made his supervisor. This resulted in considerable friction. The employee tended to blame the supervisor for various incidents, to disagree with his ideas, and to quarrel with him. He went around feeling angry, depressed, and quite unhappy. He asked himself the question, "What can I do about the supervisor's stupid and unreasonable behavior?" He canvassed various alternatives, such as going over the supervisor's head and complaining but abandoned these because he knew from observing other cases that none of them would work.

Finally, he asked himself, "Am I being unreasonable?" This caused him to admit to himself how much he had hoped for this promotion and how disappointed he was when his rival got it. Then he told himself that the rival had had a right to compete too and had played fair in competing. He told himself that there were other opportunities, that his turn might come next, and that he would only spoil his chances for this turn if he continued to fight with his supervisor. It also occurred to him that the supervisor might be somewhat insecure at first in the new role and hence especially reactive to signs of jealous competition from his former rival.

With these thoughts in mind, he set out to make a plan. He canvassed the kinds of situations in which his jealous rivalry would be most likely to show itself and planned to avoid these when possible and to be on guard when it was impossible to avoid the situation completely. He decided to withhold all criticisms and suggestions until things had settled down and to recognize and appreciate any good changes that the new supervisor made. The employee was especially careful to avoid any appearance of by-passing the supervisor in any way. As soon as he put this plan into action, he got on much better and felt better. Occasionally, however, he had to rehearse his thoughts and put himself back on guard.

Although we are in no position to make a rigorous analysis of the detailed dynamics of this example, it is clear that the sentences that the employee thought to himself helped to reduce the generalization of aggression, to restrain rash acts that might have been disastrous, and to elicit a planned course of action that was more likely to succeed.

Summary of Conditions for Successful Reasoning and Planning

From the foregoing analysis, one can see that a number of different conditions have to be met before reasoning and planning can produce adaptive behavior in a given dilemma. First, the direct instrumental responses to the internal drives and external cues must be inhibited in order to give the cue-producing responses time to occur; the subject must stop and think before rushing precipitately into action. Then, the proper thoughts must occur. These can fail to occur either because they are not in the individual's repertory of learned responses or because they are inhibited by competing thoughts. If the cue-producing responses that have been learned do not parallel objects and events in the environment, the solution or plan will be unrealistic. Finally, it is necessary for the thoughts to be carried over into action. In other words, the instrumental responses elicited indirectly via the cue-producing sequence must be stronger than the direct responses to internal drives and external cues. As we shall see, the likelihood of these conditions being met is enormously increased by specific kinds of training that the child receives in the process of socialization.

CHAPTER IX

SOCIAL TRAINING IN THE USE OF HIGHER
MENTAL PROCESSES

Man's wonderful capacity for using his higher mental processes is greatly facilitated by social training. The problem solutions painfully acquired during centuries of trial and error, and by the highest order of creative reasoning by rare geniuses, are preserved and accumulate as a part of the culture. Thus each new generation builds on the discoveries of the past. This applies not only to material culture but also to the use of language and other techniques of thinking. People receive an enormous amount of social training in putting words and sentences together in ways that lead to the adaptive solution of problems. This social training also establishes learned drives, such as the motivation to be logical, which play an important role in effective thinking.

How sentences copied from others can help. Sentences copied from others can function in the same way in reasoning and planning as those that the individual produces by himself. Thus a child who was frequently teased by a bully on the playground came to his father for help and was told: "He's trying to get your goat; the thing to do is ignore him." The next time the child was confronted with the bully he repeated this to himself, acted accordingly, and eventually succeeded in getting the bully to stop teasing him.

Everyone has a great deal of experience in getting help from others. In fact the use of verbal responses in reasoning seems to begin by copying the sentences of others. While the child is young, others do most of the reasoning and planning for him and he learns to respond to what they say.

We have been emphasizing the private function of verbal responses as cues in reasoning and planning. The verbal responses, however, were learned originally not as private but as social cues. The details of this learning are not thoroughly understood. Since

116

it is the foundation of all social communication, including psychotherapy, and has a profound influence on the use of language as thought, we shall have to consider it as best we can.

Listening and rehearsal. The child is first taught to respond to words as commands and to use them as requests. He learns to stop when someone says "No, no!" and to ask for a toy that is out of reach. At the same time he slowly is learning to repeat words that he hears. This imitative verbal behavior (Miller and Dollard, 1941) plays a central role in the process of learning to talk. Children receive a tremendous amount of training in repeating words that they hear.

This learning to repeat words also seems to play an important role in learning to obey commands and follow out directions. Often the young child is required to repeat, either in exact or paraphrased form, what he has just been told. Frequently young children can be heard rehearsing such things aloud to themselves.

In adults overt verbal imitation and rehearsal is less frequent but some similar process still seems to be necessary. This is called listening, or paying attention to what is being said. It seems to have functional characteristics similar to those of the overt response of rehearsal. It is dependent upon similar types of learning, as witnessed by the difficulty of paying attention to and remembering the sounds of a strange language. It can be inhibited by other responses. Thus it is impossible to listen to two different conversations simultaneously, although it may be possible to get something by shifting rapidly back and forth from one to the other. As with overt responses, the performance of listening seems to vary with the motivation to listen.

Acting on suggestions. While learning to listen and obey, the child learns to discriminate between cues from his own verbal responses and those from others or his rehearsal of what others have said. Suggestions from others often are not related to his own drives and hence are unrewarded, as when the mother says, "Johnny, go to bed," when he is not tired. Children are given a good deal of formal and informal training in not being too gullible. Thus they learn to respond to suggestions from others with a certain amount of restraint and are said to acquire "a mind of their own." [1]

---

[1] It may be speculated that hypnotism is one way of removing this restraint.

It is as if the child had learned to think first: "That's what he says, but do I want to do it?" Then the suggestion may be rejected, tentatively accepted, or enthusiastically accepted.

Prestige vs. suspicion. We would expect the tendency to listen to and follow suggestions to be subject to strengthening by reward and extinction by nonreward. Furthermore, punishment for acting on a suggestion should establish fear of acting on the suggestion. Such a fear is often called "suspicion." It motivates rejecting suggestions; and the reduction in the strength of this fear when the suggestion is rejected reinforces the response of rejection. It is obvious that if suspicion is strong and generalized enough it can seriously interfere with getting help from others.

If following one person's suggestion is consistently rewarded and following another person's is consistently punished, a discrimination can be formed so that one will trust certain people but not others. Similarly, one can learn to trust a person for some things but not for others.[2] Such discriminations determine whose advice will be sought and the extent to which it will be followed; they are the basis for prestige.

Training to stop and think. If a person makes an immediate, direct, instrumental response to a given problem situation, there may not be sufficient time for the proper cue-producing responses to occur. The first step in any but the simplest types of reasoning is to stop and think. Children are given a great deal of social training in doing this. They are specifically told to stop and think, are criticized when their actions are ill-considered and hasty, and rewarded when they have shown evidence of rational thought.

The tendency for people to use cue-producing responses in a dilemma is strengthened by training of this kind. It can also be weakened by inadvertent punishment and failures. In some people, so much fear has been attached to the cue-producing responses involved in mathematics that they never try this mode of problem solution. Often, if such people can be encouraged to try learning mathematics again, they become able to solve problems which have previously been impossible for them.

[2] For experiments showing how the tendency to copy can be increased by reward and decreased by nonreward, how this generalizes, etc., see Miller and Dollard (1941); for experimental work on the learning of suggestion, see Hull (1933), and Jenness (1944).

Sometimes people fail to show the intelligence of which they are capable because they are afraid of the cue-producing responses involved in a particular kind of problem. Other times people fail to show intelligence because they have not been trained to stop and think or because they cannot tolerate the anxiety aroused by a period of indecision during which action is postponed and thought occurs.

Making a correct report of the environment. While learning to talk the child receives training in matching words, sentences, and descriptive paragraphs with important features of the environment. He is trained not to call the sky "green" or the grass "blue." He is corrected for mistakes, and eventually learns to have anxiety about responding differently from other people. He is also taught to distinguish between the make-believe and the real—in other words, between the situations in which sentences that do not run parallel to sequences in the environment will be tolerated and those in which they will not. He is taught to discriminate between his own private dreams, images, and phantasies, and the perceptions that can be verified by cross-checking with other senses and that agree with the reports of other people. Finally, he is trained to be self-critical, to avoid agreeable but false ideas.

We believe that this training serves to provide motivation against hallucinations and delusions. The strength of this motivation is shown by the anxiety that a normal person will show if through some unexpected illusion he seems to be seeing things that others do not see.

The training in matching words to important features of the environment applies to the social as well as the physical environment. The child is trained to give an accurate account of social events and to make his statements about the probable social consequences of acts match the cultural pattern. He is also trained to be fair and not to blame others when it is his own fault, although blaming others is sometimes inadvertently rewarded. This training, imperfect as it often is, tends to operate against showing behavior of the types called displacement, projection, and rationalization.

Orderly narration; being understood. Along with training in putting words together in ways that match features of the environment, there are also years of training in orderly, intelligible narration. Whenever the child is not understood he is likely to fail to get what he wants; he also may be criticized for not talking sense. In this way, not being understood comes to elicit frustration and anxiety and being understood tends to become somewhat of a goal in itself. Even as adults, people react to small signs that they are not understood.

Being logical; eliminating contradictions. Along with the training in certain minimum standards of orderly narration, there is great stress on detecting and eliminating obvious logical contradictions and absurdities. These are punished, especially in arguments or alibis. There is a good deal of social training in the culture's practical everyday rules of logic. The child may discover for himself that illogical plans do not work and that contradictory ones lead to conflict and wasted efforts. After he is in trouble, someone else is likely to come along and label the plan or course of action "illogical." As a result of all this training, the cues produced by the response of labeling something as "a contradiction" or "illogical" tend to make most people feel quite uncomfortable; they have a learned drive to make their explanations and plans seem logical. In the same way, they learn to try to make their plans seem practical.

Being oriented; having an explanation. Somewhat similarly, but on a more primitive level, there is a good deal of training in being oriented in time and place and in the social group. Thus training results in a motivation to notice and label salient features of where one is and what is going on around one. Adults feel uncomfortable when they are unable to do this in strange surroundings and the child may get terror-stricken when lost.

In addition to the social training that results in the need to be oriented, there is also training that results in a learned drive, or need, to have an explanation. Children are frequently called on by parents and teachers to give an explanation of their behavior or of factors in the environment. They are rewarded if they can give a correct explanation and punished or ridiculed if they cannot.

Besides the direct social training, there is a good deal of indirect training. When things are occurring that one does not understand, one is less likely to succeed and more likely to have bad things happen. Thus, the absence of an explanation would be expected to arouse a certain amount of frustration and anxiety. This anxiety is commonly called "fear of the unknown." Furthermore, when things are not succeeding, the child frequently has the situation explained, rehearses the explanation, modifies his behavior, and then succeeds. When things seem emotionally bad, discouraging, or frightening, the parent frequently gives a reassuring explanation which is rehearsed and rewarded so that such explanations acquire learned reward value. All these factors tend to produce a need for an explanation, which, as we have already seen, must meet cultural standards of logic and reasonableness. Similarly, the intellectual curiosity which is such an important component of the motivation of a scientist is at least in part a product of social learning.

Responding to verbal cues with appropriate action and emotion. Along with all of this training in labeling the environment correctly and putting words and sentences together in reasonable and intelligible sequences, there is also training in responding to the verbal cues with the appropriate instrumental and emotional responses. Promises are to be kept, plans are to be carried over into the realm of action and not to remain as daydreams. Words are to be matched with deeds. One must not say "the man is innocent" and then punish him.

There is a great deal of social training in attaching many appropriate instrumental responses to verbal cues. Similarly there is training in appropriate emotional responses. One must not respond to solemn or sad words by laughing or to gay ones by crying. One should not show "unreasonable" fear in situations that authorities have labeled as "safe." This emotional training is much less perfect than the training in appropriate action and is probably a by-product of the latter. This is because emotional responses are not so readily subject to social observation and thus can only be rewarded or punished when they produce observable overt results. For precisely this reason many people learn to disguise their emotions.

As a result of this kind of training and of rewards for social conformity and punishments for nonconformity, there is a desire to make one's behavior appropriate to the social situation. Labeling a response as "inappropriate" usually arouses considerable motivation to change it.[3]

"Sense of reality" and "Ego strength."   A large part of the social training in using words and sentences to mediate adaptive behavior occurs more or less informally as a part of the everyday life of the child and young adult.   Further training in special techniques of thinking such as arithmetic, calculus, tensor analysis, and science are given in the school.   The effectiveness of this training and the importance of our cultural heritage of concepts and techniques for problem solving is illustrated by the fact that thousands of modern students can solve problems, such as the prediction of the flight of a projectile, that were insoluble to the greatest of minds before the time of Galileo.[4]

When training in the techniques and learned drives involved in clear thinking is defective, the individual is often described as having a weak Ego or a poor sense of reality.   As will be seen, such deficits can be limiting factors in psychotherapy.   This is one of the reasons why special techniques must be used with small children who have not had time to acquire the types of social training that we have been describing.

Private vs. social cue-producing responses.   We have emphasized the tremendous amount of social training that people receive in the use of verbal responses.   They receive this training because speaking and its derivatives, such as writing, are the responses most used in the elaborate social communication that is a necessary feature of human society.   Language is the human example *par excellence* of a cue-producing response.   Responses such as making gestures and drawing diagrams are also used in social communica-

---

[3] The training in social conformity that results in the fear of being different (Chap. V) can also interfere with creative thinking, even in science.   By its very nature, every truly original idea must be somewhat different from the previous conventional ones.   Some otherwise highly intelligent people seem to be so afraid of original ideas that they cannot express them either to others or to themselves, and therefore cannot be creative.   To be scientifically creative one must have enough social training in conformity to be disciplined and critical and yet have enough courage to be original.   Apparently, this can be learned only under especially favorable, but as yet imperfectly defined, conditions.

[4] We are grateful to Professor F. S. C. Northrop for suggesting this example.

tion and so are subject to social learning. The usefulness of these responses in social communication and the ease of giving social training in their use is obviously due to the fact that speaking, drawing diagrams, etc., provide cues that are easily observable by others.

By contrast, visual, tactile, olfactory, and kinesthetic images cannot be observed by others. Since such cue-producing responses are private, the lessons learned from ages of trial and error cannot readily be passed on from generation to generation and accumulated as a rich cultural heritage.

In the case of such cue-producing responses, there is no special training in the rules of logic, in avoiding contradiction, or in orderly, intelligible narration. These private cue-producing responses are less useful in culturally sophisticated types of problem solution. Because they cannot be directly observed and punished when taboo, they would also be expected to be less subject to social inhibition. Perhaps this is one of the reasons why dreams, in which visual imagery is predominant, are (as Freud discovered) less inhibited than waking verbal thought and also are often illogical and unintelligible by the ordinary standards of narration.

SUMMARY

The various "levels" of adjustment may now be recapitulated.

At the lower level are direct responses to cues. These may be innate reflexes (like a blink to a cinder in the eye), responses that are originally learned as direct responses (like the blink to a sudden motion toward the eye), or ones that were originally learned as responses to verbal instructions and later so strongly associated with the external cues that they are out of verbal control (like pressing on the floorboards when a child runs in front of a car in which one is a passenger).

On a higher level are responses mediated by one or more intervening cue-producing responses. Because these responses are not limited by the mechanical and social possibilities of the immediate environment, they can become anticipatory or work backward from the goal step by step. This enables them to mediate adaptive, new combinations of responses that would be unlikely to occur otherwise. Thought is obviously highly creative and vastly superior to instrumental trial and error.

Attaching the same label (or other cue-producing response) to two distinctive stimulus objects increases the generalization of emotional and instrumental responses from one to the other. Attaching different labels (or other distinctive cue-producing responses) to two similar stimulus situations increases the discrimination between the two. If the proper habits have been learned, words can arouse strong learned drives or give powerful reward and reassurance. In this way, verbal responses play an especially important role in mediating the foresightful response to remote rewards or punishments.

Cue-producing responses, such as imagery, that are not socially observable are not subject to direct, intensive social training. The use of these private cue-producing responses thus tends to be relatively unsophisticated. On the other hand, the public cue-producing responses, like words and sentences, that are used in social communication receive an enormous amount of social training. The accumulated cultural heritage of generations of trial and error is represented in the categories, common-sense rules of logic, standards of reasonableness, and sequences of orderly narration of language. This greatly increases the usefulness of verbal responses and their derivatives, such as mathematics, in the solution of social, emotional, and instrumental problems.

In our society, there seems to be much more emphasis on formal training in special techniques for solving problems in the physical environment than on ones for solving emotional problems.

Only a modest and uncertain start has been made toward understanding the marvelous intricacies of language and the higher mental processes. In this extremely important area there is a great need for more detailed observations of patients in therapy and of the socialization of children in the home, for a more rigorous theoretical formulation and a more penetrating experimental analysis.

As we increase our scientific knowledge in this area, we may be able to improve our social training in the use of the higher mental processes.

PART IV
HOW NEUROSIS IS LEARNED

CHAPTER X

SOCIAL CONDITIONS FOR THE LEARNING OF UNCONSCIOUS CONFLICTS

An intense emotional conflict is the necessary basis for neurotic behavior. The conflict must further be unconscious. As a usual thing, such conflicts are created only in childhood. How can it be that neurotic conflicts are engendered when there is no deliberate plan to do so? Society must force children to grow up, but it does not idealize neurosis and makes no formal provision in its system of training for the production of neurotic children. Indeed we deplore the neurotic and recognize him as a burden to himself and to others. How then does it happen? Our answer is that neurotic conflicts are taught by parents and learned by children. We will examine the circumstance under which this strange result occurs.

Discovery of childhood. A first answer to the puzzle is that until recently the relationship between childhood conditions of learning and adult neurotic behavior has not been understood. Freud (1924, Vol. I, pp. 145–154) first called attention to this possibility. He avowed that society could and did create serious emotional conflicts in some of its children and that these conflicts were the basis of later neurotic behavior. He noted that a serious conflict in the young child (infantile neurosis) usually precedes later neurotic behavior in the adult (Freud, 1936, pp. 90–91).

Patterns of child training confused. Culture, according to Freud, is not a logical structure designed with experimental nicety. Rather, it is a loose historical system with many strains and conflicts. Some of the elements of current child-training procedures are undoubtedly thousands of years old. They represent a long history of conflict and confusion, of survivals from older times and unassimilated increments of the present. For example, modern society attempts to make children meek and obedient in the family but strong and competitive outside. Sometimes training in docility is so strong that the child is never able to hold its own later in the world outside the family. In other cases, rebellious traits are strongly developed and barely restrained within family life but are later freely generalized to the adult milieu. The problem of getting meekness exactly where it is wanted and strength displayed where it is appropriate is not an easy one, and it is not surprising that children frequently fail to make the correct discriminations.

A strain toward consistency in the culture patterns of child rearing there may indeed be, but these patterns are as yet far from a coherent structure. Not only are the advised methods of child training confused and changing in a "fadistic" manner, but the characters of the parents who apply these rules are variously corrupted and ineffectual. Occasionally the parents themselves may be infantile, selfish, lazy, obsessed, or timid. In one way and another, they compete with their children, overtrain them, underlove them, or fail to make the vigorous demands required to force children up the inclined plane of culture. Out of confused instructions to parents, combined with the character faults of parents themselves, arise the situations in which children are put in severe conflict.

The problem of the socialization of children has been solved only in a very rough and ready way. The laws of learning required to understand it are still but partly known. Hence it is difficult to arrange the conditions of learning correctly, and even if one granted the existence of a science of child rearing, it would still be necessary to get the correct rules into the habit systems of whole generations of parents.

Inherent difficulty of the problem. Granted that the human infant is the organism most amenable to social training, there is still the problem of converting this organism into a complex socialized being (Dollard, 1935). Many skills must be developed; innumerable complex restraints have to be imposed and internalized; difficult discriminations must be learned. In some cases, responses which have a considerable innate likelihood of occurrence must be reversed and habits opposed to the natural ones acquired. Even if scientists knew the rules, could arrange the conditions, and could indoctrinate the parents, they would face the problem of what kind of children to produce. Since the conditions of material and social life are constantly changing under the impact of science (Ogburn, 1922), it is difficult to envision exactly the kind of child who will be best adapted to the world of 1975 (Dollard, 1949).

Idealization of childhood.   The idealization of childhood in the "myth of the happy child" has prevented candid discussion of the strains of family life and the frequent misery and conflict of children.   Each turbulent family has supposed that the inward life of other families was more serene, and each conflicted individual accepted the myth of the happy child—but for someone else. Thanks much to Freud's work we all now seem ready to tell the truth at the same time and admit that growing up in a family is a strenuous affair.

Weakness of conventional child research.   Most of the conventional research on childhood does not deal with these important matters, nor is it carried on in the home where emotional conflicts are first learned.   The early researchers on childhood grasped at the measuring instruments at hand and measured whatever could be measured with these instruments.   Emotional conflict could not be easily measured.   Hence though the physical maturation of the child is quite well understood, its emotional growth has been studied hardly at all.   The instruments for this purpose have yet to be fashioned.   Furthermore, the study of the child in the convenient clinic has tended to obscure the effect of the home and parents on the child's learning.   The result is that there is little formal knowledge about some of those aspects of child development which are most important.

A hypothesis on early learning must be risked.   Confessing this inadequacy in our scientific data, we must yet make the best picture we can of the sources of emotional conflict in child life.   On the basis of behavior theory we know that the learning of childhood is likely to be important.   On the basis of common sense, we know that many significant changes in behavior are forced upon the child during the first five or six years of life.   On the basis of clinical studies and histories we get some firsthand (though retrospective) accounts of these conflict areas.

We have this consolation: If some such reconstruction as that attempted here is *not* made, adult life, as all know it, is unintelligible. We prefer to run the risk of being found wrong on many points, while yet giving a coherent and reasonable account of social and emotional development, to being utterly right on a few points while leaving out many important variables because they are not yet carefully described. Leaving out the critical variables leads to a nonsensical account—which can never be a merit of science.

Helplessness exposes children to conflict. Because of their physical, mental, and emotional helplessness, children are particularly vulnerable to harsh or confusing patterns of training. They have few skills at evading the effects of unfavorable circumstances. On the physical side, the child has progressed greatly by the age of 18 months (Gesell, 1940, pp. 77–78); yet he is still much smaller and weaker and can be hauled around, picked up, or spanked by adult giants. The gap between child and adult is even greater in the mental and emotional spheres. Children cannot understand the world and cannot control their emotional reactions. Therefore young children can be subject to more extreme conditions than adults endure, except perhaps when adults are exposed to combat situations in time of war. In combat and in infancy the extremes of hunger, fear, helplessness, confusion, and timeless strain are reproduced. Only in childhood and in combat are the individual's own capacities to control his life so meager and ineffectual.

It is not surprising, then, that acute emotional conflicts occur in childhood. The infant has not learned to wait, not knowing the world's inescapable routines; to hope, and thus to assure itself that the good moment will return and that the evil occasion will pass; to reason and plan, and thus to escape present disorder by constructing the future in a controlled way. Rather, the child is urgently, hopelessly, planlessly impelled, living by moments in eternal pain and then suddenly finding itself bathed in endless bliss. The young child is necessarily disoriented, confused, deluded, and hallucinated—in short, has just those symptoms that we recognize as a psychosis in the adult. Infancy, indeed, may be viewed as a period of transitory psychosis. Savage drives within the infant impel to action. These drives are unmodified by hope or concept of time. The higher mental processes (the Ego) cannot do their benign work of comforting, directing effort, and binding the world into a planful sequence. What is gone may never return. The present pain may never fade. These are the tumultuous circumstances in which severe unconscious mental conflicts can be created. Only when the child has been taught to speak and think at a rather high level can the impact of the raw, drastic character of these circumstances be reduced.

Greatest indulgence when child most helpless. Ideally, of course, young children should not be called upon to face severe conflicts until they have the mental means for doing so. They should have the greatest support from the parents during earliest weeks,[1] months, and years. Strong drives should be kept at low level through constant attentiveness by those who care for the child. Tasks should be imposed, but in a graded series. The most important objective of training in this period is teaching the child to speak and think, for only with the aid of his language can he learn to wait, hope, reason, and plan.

But parents are far from resolved to keep the strongest drives at a low level of urgency or from knowing how to impose the burdens of civilized life in a reasonable way. The young child is often taught too fast. He is treated as a mental adult when he cannot understand the instructions which he is given. Adult powers to control emotions are assumed. Incompatible demands are made and impossible tasks set. He is expected to produce discriminations which he has not been taught. He is sometimes expected to learn a habit perfectly in one trial. Heavy sanctions are applied for mistakes and failures.

Single drives can produce misery. Not all the painful circumstances of life are produced by *conflicts* although some of the worst are. Disturbance tends to be greatest when two drives are pitted one against the other and the individual must bear the pain of both. However, any *one* drive can be raised to traumatic heights and the bearing of it at such heights can be a source of important consequences. In the nursing period the child can learn some good or bad habits and develop some benign or ominous expectations of the world depending on how its feeding is handled.

---

[1] We should mention here the pioneering work of Dr. Edith B. Jackson (Jackson *et al.*, 1948) in developing the "rooming-in plan" in which mothers have their newborn infants near them in the hospital so that they may feed and care for the infants as need be.

FOUR CRITICAL TRAINING SITUATIONS

The culture, of course, takes a position—a traditional position—on the various needs of the child. It has a design for the feeding situation, for cleanliness training, for sex training, for the treatment of anger responses in the child; and as the society imposes its will through the acts of the parents, the child reacts in its blind emotional way. Each one of the above-mentioned training situations can produce long-lasting effects on the character and habits of the individual and each is worth a brief discussion. We are by no means sure that these four are all of the dilemmas which can produce acute emotional conflicts, but we do know that each one of them has, in known cases, done so.

1. *The Feeding Situation: Conflicts and Attitudes*

Much important learning takes place in reference to the hunger drive and the strong responses it excites. During the nursing period the child cannot "comfort" itself. It cannot, so to say, tell itself "It won't be long now," or "Only twenty minutes 'til feeding time." The hunger of the child is an urgent, incessant, and timeless pressure which, obviously, produces the most intense activation. If the child is fed when hungry, it can learn that the one simple thing it can do to get results (*i.e.*, cry) can make a difference in what happens. Learning to cry as a signal for food is one small unit in its control of the world. Such a trait could be the basis of a later tendency to be "up and doing" when in trouble, of a belief that there is always a way out of a painful situation.

Apathy and apprehensiveness. If the child is not fed when it is crying, but is instead left to "cry itself out," it can, similarly, learn that there is nothing it can do at that time to change the painful circumstances. Such training may also lay the basis for the habit of apathy and not "trying something else" when in trouble. In a second case, when drive is allowed to mount, the child can also learn that being a little bit hungry is followed by being very painfully hungry. When the child is then fed, only its most violent responses are reinforced. In this case the child can learn to fear being very hungry when it is only slightly hungry and to make the frightened response appropriate to severe hunger when only mild hunger exists.

It is thus learning to "overreact," to be apprehensive of evil even when the circumstances of life seem calm. This learning occurs through the behavior mechanism of anticipation.

Sociability and "love." On the other hand, probably the feeding experience can be the occasion for the child to learn to like to be with others; that is, it can establish the basis of sociability. When the hungry infant is fed, some of the wonderful relaxation responses which it experiences can be conditioned to the stimuli of those persons who are caring for the child. Thereafter the mere appearance of the mother can produce a momentary feeling of well-being. The child will learn to stop crying at the sound of her footstep, the rustle of her dress, or the sound of the tap water which is warming its bottle. These experiences have an intense emotional quality which is often attached thereafter to the word "mother" as the source of all beneficence.

Likewise, if the child is properly held, cared for, and played with, the blessed relaxing quality of these experiences also will attach to those who care for it. Since the mother or caretaker stands at the very head of the parade of persons who become "society" for the child, it is quite important that she evoke such benign and positive responses in the child.

Lack of social feeling. The reverse of all this can also take place if the child is stuffed when it is not hungry. If its food rewards are in various ways cut down and spoiled, it may not care much whether "the others" are there or not. It may tend to be "low in social feeling." If the child is actually punished for crying when it is hungry, as by being slapped, a true hunger-anxiety conflict will be created. Though this may be rare, it does undoubtedly happen, especially when the child is overactive as a result of gastric upset and so is able to provoke anger in the ill-disciplined parent.

One origin of fear of being alone. The child can learn another dangerous habit in this period. It can learn to fear being alone. Teaching a child to fear being alone is easy to do and is often done inadvertently. Let the child get very hungry when it is alone, let it cry and not be heard or attended to, but let the quantity of stimulation in its body from hunger and from crying continue to rise. When the child is finally fed, these very strong terminal responses are reinforced and can be attached to all the stimuli which were present during the period of its intense hunger. These responses can produce stimuli of drivelike strength. Similarly responses which produce strong drives can be attached to the darkness, to the immobility of objects, to quietness, to absence of parental stimuli. Once the child has inadvertently learned to "fear" darkness and quietness and immobility, it will also learn to escape from the darkness into the light, from the quietness into noise, and from immobility into the presence of others.

This escape may be perceived by the parents as an additional nuisance when they are expecting their hours of relaxation; the child insists on being with them even though "there is nothing wrong with it." They may then take punitive measures, forcing the child back into the dark or the quiet and creating a true conflict between fear of darkness and the newly learned fear of the irate parent. This must indeed be a very common conflict, since fear of quietness and darkness are not innate in children and yet are frequently seen.

If this fear persists into adult life, it can be an element in the character of a person who is compulsively driven to social contacts, who cannot tolerate being alone. Compulsive sociability may also involve a sacrifice in creativeness, since in order to be creative the individual must be able to tolerate a certain amount of loneliness.

Weaning. In the case of weaning also, severe traumatic circumstances may arise. If the child is suddenly changed from one type of food or mode of feeding to another, it may go on a hunger strike which the parents obstinately oppose, saying "It will eat when it gets hungry enough." Indeed it will, but in the meantime it may have learned some of the fears or the apathy already listed. If parents punish the child for its refusal to eat the new food a genuine conflict is created which in turn will have its consequences. There seems hardly anything valuable that an infant can learn by punishment under such circumstances, and parents should take the greatest pains to avoid this.

Colic and recurring hunger. The child with colic is also a sore trial to itself and its parents. One of the simplest circumstances producing "colic" is that the infant has eaten too much and must regurgitate some of the food or the gases which its digestion pro-

duces. Once it has been laboriously walked or patted into parting
with food or gas it may be hungry again. Unimaginative parents,
not understanding that hunger has innocently recurred, will fail to
feed the child. If the mother does feed it, the child may overeat
again and the cycle of gastric tension, vomiting, and hunger may
recur. However, until an infant learns to make its gastric distress
anticipatory and thus to check itself while eating, there is no way
of avoiding these circumstances. The sequence overeating, gastric
distress, vomiting, and recurring hunger seems more likely to occur
with children fed on schedule since they will get much hungrier
while waiting for the scheduled moment of feeding and are more
likely to overeat.

If parents lose their tempers and punish the young child at any
phase of this awkward kind of learning to eat just the right amount,
severe conflict concerning feeding may ensue. If the infant is
punished before it is burped, the result may be that it has anxiety
attached to burping and regurgitating, and it is thus condemned to
bear gastric tension. If it is punished after regurgitating when it
is again hungry, anxiety responses will be attached to hunger
stimuli. Under these conditions punishment cannot teach the
infant anything that will help it along its road of development.
Nevertheless this unavoidable circumstance of colic is one to test
the character of the most devoted parents.

The foregoing discussion is by no means a check list of all the
things that a child can learn during the first year or so of life. For
example, in learning to crawl and walk the child is also learning
to fear bumps. It learns not to poke its head under the table and
then suddenly try to stand erect. It is learning a few words and
common commands. Those interested in the somatic development
of the child can consult Gesell (1940). Various specialists in pediatrics such as Spock (1946) have described the behavior problems
that are most frequent among young children in the home.

Secret learning of early years. What we have attempted to do
here is to show that the seemingly innocuous feeding situation can
be fraught with important emotional consequences. Outsiders
who cannot know what is going on in a home may see no reason
to suppose that the infant is learning anything at all. Yet observant
insiders may see the child becoming apathetic, apprehensive, learn-

ing to fear the dark, on the one hand, or becoming loving, sociable, and confident, on the other. It is this secret learning of the early years which must be made the object of scientific research. We are firmly of the opinion that anything that can be sensed can be scaled and thus that apathy, sociability, and fear can be scientifically treated if we but trouble to study the child in the home—where these habits are being learned.

Early conflicts unlabeled, therefore unconscious. The young child does not notice or label the experiences which it is having at this time. It cannot give a description of character traits acquired during the first year of life nor yet of its hardships, fears, or deep satisfactions. What was not verbalized at the time cannot well be reported later. An important piece of history is lost and cannot be elicited by questionnaire or interview. Nevertheless, the behavioral record survives. The responses learned occur and may indeed recur in analogous situations throughout life. They are elicited by unlabeled cues and are mutely interwoven into the fabric of conscious life. The fact that different children learn different things during this period undoubtedly accounts for some of the variability between children which is often attributed to innate factors.

2. Cleanliness Training Can Create Conflicts

If the child has come safely and trustfully through the early feeding and weaning experience it may learn for the first time in its cleanliness training that the culture patterns lying in wait for it have an ugly, compulsive aspect. No child may avoid this training. The demands of the training system are absolute and do not take account of individual differences in learning ability. The child must master cleanliness training or forfeit its place in the ranks of socially acceptable persons. Freud describes the culture's task as building within the personality of the child the psychic dams of loathing and disgust (Freud, 1930, p. 40) for urine and feces and particularly for the latter. The attempt to construct these inward barriers immediately puts the child in a conflict situation.

Observation of children within the home indicates that children begin with the same naïve interest in their feces and urine that they have in the other parts and products of their bodies. Development of the ability to grasp and finger objects makes it possible for the young child to handle and play with fecal material. The morning will arrive in every nursery when the astonished parents will observe their beloved child smearing feces over his person, his hair, and his immediate environment with gurgling abandon.   This may be the first occasion for sharp, punishing exhortations, for angry dousing, for the awakening of anxiety in connection with fecal materials.   On pain of losing the parents' love and so exposing itself to the high drives and tensions which occur when they do not support it, and on further pain of immediate punishment, the child must learn to attach anxiety to all the cues produced by excretory materials—to their sight, smell, and touch.   It must learn to deposit the feces and urine only in a prescribed and secret place and to clean its body.   It must later learn to suppress unnecessary verbal reference to these matters, so that, except for joking references this subject matter is closed out and excluded from social reference for life.

Difficulty of cleanliness learning.   Cleanliness training is difficult because culture must work a reversal of a strong innate connection between a cue and a response.   The swelling bladder or bowel produces a strong drive stimulus which at a certain strength releases the urethral sphincter or touches off the evulsion response in the anus. To meet cultural demands this sequence must be rearranged. The connection between bowel stimulus and the evulsion response must be weakened.   The child must learn to suppress the evulsion response to the bowel drive-stimulus alone.   It must then insert other responses in the sequence.   At first it must learn to call to the parents.   It must later learn to insert walking, unbuttoning, and sitting on the toilet chair while it is still suppressing the urgent evulsion response.   Only to a new pattern of cues—the bowel stimulus, the cues of the proper room, the sense of freedom of clothes, the pressure of the toilet seat on the child's thighs—may the evulsion response occur without anxiety.

In short, this response occurs not only to the pressure of the primary drive involved but also to the complex stimulus pattern just named.   If one can once get the child to order the responses correctly, the strong tension reduction produced by defecation will reinforce the responses to the pattern of cues enumerated.   The real problem, therefore, is getting the child to suppress the naïve evulsion response and to insert a considerable series of responses into the sequence before evulsion.

We do not revel in the details of this analysis but offer the detailed analysis because we believe it is impossible to understand the difficulty of the learning involved unless one sees all the new units which must be learned. For instance, buttoning and unbuttoning is a difficult habit for small children to learn and may hold up the perfect learning of the sequence for some time. The child, however, is not really trained until it can carry out the whole sequence by itself.

Learning without verbal aids. The difficulties which produce conflict in this learning arise chiefly from the fact that the child must accomplish it in a period of life when it has to learn mainly without verbal aids, that is, by trial and error. Learning cleanliness control by trial and error is a slow and vexing business. The child must learn to wake up in order to go to the toilet, though sleep seems good. It must learn to stop its play even when social excitement is strong. It must learn to discriminate between the different rooms of the house—all this by crude trial and error. In this case, "trial" means urinating or defecating in an inappropriate place, and "error" means being punished for the act so that anxiety responses are attached to the cues of this place. In the trial-and-error situation this must be repeated for each inappropriate place—bed, living room, dining room, kitchen, "outside."

The function of this training is to attach anxiety responses to the defecation drive so that they win out over the immediate evulsion response. These anxiety responses also motivate and cue off the next responses in the series, such as calling to the parents, running to the bathroom, unbuttoning the clothes, and the like. When accomplished by trial-and-error means, this training necessarily takes considerable time, perhaps several years in all, in which child and parent are under severe pressure.

Strong emotions aroused in cleanliness training. Learning cleanliness is no mere behavioral routine. It arouses strong emotions— perhaps as strong as are ever evoked in the child again. Anger, defiance, stubbornness, and fear all appear in the course of such training. Fear may generalize to the toilet itself and excite avoidance responses in the very place where the child is expected to "go."

Unable to discriminate between the safe and the unsafe place, the child may try "not to defecate at all." This behavior is perfectly automatic, but it may seem willful to the parents, and they may particularly resent the final loss of control after the protracted attempt to inhibit defecation. Once hit on, this response would be strongly reinforced and tend to become habitual since the drive reduction after prolonged withholding would be much more intense than after a normal period of withholding. When "losing control," instead of deliberately relaxing, is strongly rewarded, the habit of "losing control" should become anticipatory and thus prolong the problem of cleanliness training. In other words, great strictness at early ages may block rather than advance the child in his cleanliness learning.

Learning to escape from sight of parents. The child may become, from the parents' standpoint, furtive by the following means: When it is punished for a cleanliness error by the parent, anxiety is attached to the sights and sounds produced by that parent. In order to escape that anxiety the child may attempt to escape from the parental presence and attempt to keep to a minimum the amount of time it spends near the parent. This state of affairs has the disadvantage that the child is escaping from one of its natural teachers. It may learn to speak less well than it might because it simply does not remain near those people who could teach it to speak. Infliction of punishment may also arouse anger toward the inflicting agent. The child may attempt struggling with the parents, biting them, or slapping at them and, in turn, be punished for this behavior. Thus, an anger-anxiety conflict is learned.

Excessive conformity and guilt. Again, the child may get the impression that it is pursued by an all-seeing, punishing guardian and may try making as few responses as possible—and certainly not innovating any novel responses. Its conclusion on the basis of punishments received may be that unless a response is known to be correct it should not be risked. Thus may be laid the characterological basis of the excessively timid, conforming individual. Similarly, the child may not be able to discriminate between parental loathing for its excreta and loathing for the whole child himself. If the child learns to adopt these reactions, feelings of unworthiness, insignificance, and hopeless sinfulness will be created—feelings which sometimes so mysteriously reappear in the psychotic manifestations of guilt.

Advantages of verbal aids. From this discussion it will be clear that the trial-and-error method of early training, with its many punishments, has much more risk attached than training carried on at a time when the child can be verbally aided to hit on the right sequence of responses in a few early trials. Once the child has acquired the words "living room," "kitchen," "bedroom," and "outside," a single punishment trial, if properly conducted, can attach anxiety to all these cues at the same time and so spare the brutal repetition of punishment. If the child has already learned to call for help when it needs help, it can much more easily learn to call for aid when it needs to defecate. If it has learned to stop various activities to the word "stop," it is much easier to get it to check the evulsion response when this is occurring to its innate stimulus. If certain promises of the parents already have reward value attached to them, the child can be aided to make the right responses by being promised simple rewards. If the child already attaches anxiety to certain instructions of the parents, these instructions can have some of the same effect as repeated, direct punishments.

In this case also the reinforcement of the act of defecation itself will fix the correct series of responses into place. This will happen whether the course of the training has been stormy or smooth. However, in the case of the smooth, verbally aided learning there is much less danger of arousing furious anger or of creating maladaptive habits such as retention of feces and loss of control. Extremely strong anxiety reactions do not occur and feelings of excessive worthlessness are less likely. The end result is the same so far as mere cleanliness training is concerned. The difference lies in the fact that the later, verbally aided method of getting out the response has much less risk of violent side reactions and character distortions.

Freud's Superego. The foregoing analysis employs the thoughts and sentences of Freud reworked from the standpoint of behavior theory. The course of cleanliness training is unlabeled and unconscious. Any one of us may have been through a stormy period of this kind and yet have no recollection of it. The results may show themselves in our symptoms, our most deeply embedded "character" traits, in our dreams, in our intuitive presuppositions about life, but they will not show themselves in our verbal behavior. The record of this training will be found in no man's autobiography, and yet the fate of the man may be deeply influenced and colored by it.

The first broad strands of what Freud calls the Superego are laid down at this time. Anxiety reactions, never labeled, are attached to stimuli, also unlabeled. When these stimuli recur later the anxiety reactions automatically recur. The resulting effect Freud has called the "Superego" or unconscious conscience. When unconscious guilt reactions are severe, the personality is suffused with terror. It is hard to say whether a morbid conscience is a worse enemy of life than a disease like cancer, but some comparison of this kind is required to emphasize the shock produced in the witness when he sees a psychotic person being tortured by such a conscience. Enough is known now to convince us that we should make the humble-seeming matter of cleanliness training the subject of serious research.

3. Conflicts Produced by Early Sex Training

Sex-anxiety conflicts seem frequently to be involved in neuroses arising in civilian life. The recurrent appearance of sex as a conflict element does not seem to be due to the fact that sex is the strongest of human drives. At their highest levels, pain, hunger, and fatigue certainly outrank it. Many strong secondary drives such as anxiety, ambition, and pride can also be stronger than sex. Sex seems to be so frequently implicated because it is the most severely attacked and inhibited of primary drives. Even though relatively weaker, sex can exert a strong pressure which produces great activation in the organism and great misery if blocked for long periods. In no other case is the individual required to wait so many years while patiently bearing the goading drive.

Source of first sex conflict—the masturbation taboo. Erection of the penis can be observed in male infants as a reflexive response to interrupted feeding or to urethal drive pressure (Halverson, 1938). At the age of a year the child is able to grasp an object quite perfectly. The sensitivity of the genital and the ability to prehend make masturbation possible. It seems likely also that there is some kind of reward associated with masturbating. On the basis of his observations, Kinsey *et al.* (1948) believes that small boys acquire the capacity for orgasm long before they become able to ejaculate; similarly an experiment by Sheffield, Wulff, and Backer (1950) demonstrates that sexual responses short of ejaculation can serve to reinforce learning in the albino rat. It is certainly a fact that, if unchecked, children do learn to masturbate and that they sometimes obstinately persist even when quite severe sanctions are applied.

The sight of a child masturbating evokes intense anxiety in the adults of our culture and they promptly apply sanctions, ranging from persistently removing or jerking the child's hand away from its genital to slapping and spanking it. The result is to set up in the child the same sex-anxiety conflict which the adults have. As in other cases, masturbatory conflicts established in the first years of life are invariably unconscious. A vague negative feeling, a tendency to withdraw, an unease is established at the act, sight, or thought of masturbatory behavior. These conflicts differ for different individuals in many ways and for many reasons. Some individuals may be caught in the act more often than others; some may be punished more severely than others; some may have stronger innate sex drive than others. Some may have had more time to learn the habit before being caught and punished and may thus have a stronger appetite for this behavior than other persons. Some may, so to say, scare easier than others because they already have strong anxieties established in the cleanliness-training situation. Such anxieties generalize easily from urethral to the genital stimuli. Often both are called "nasty" and the cue produced by the common verbal response helps to mediate generalization of fear. In this case it is easy to train the individual out of the masturbatory habit, since the fear does not have to be learned but only generalized to the sex stimuli.

Parents don't notice effects of taboo. The imposition of a masturbation taboo can have important effects on the child's life. There may be immediate and direct changes in behavior of the kind to be described as a "bed phobia" in Chap XI. When behavior changes occur it seems quite surprising that parents do not notice them as results of conflict over masturbation. The fact that they do not so notice is, however, easily explained. Intimate as their contact is with the child they may yet be very poor observers of cause and effect. Most of the young child's emerging life is mysterious to parents anyway. They may further have particular avoidances against noticing matters and connections which arise in the sexual sphere. Likely, they believe themselves to have been sexless in childhood and can do no less than believe the same in respect to their children. Whether correctly evaluated by parents or not, the masturbatory taboo is the first of the important sex taboos, and it sets up a sex-anxiety conflict in each of us.

Sex typing of personality. The sexual development of the child cannot be understood without understanding the forceful training in sex typing which it receives. The unspecialized or less specialized human being, the infant, is identified as boy or girl and its relationship with others is defined in terms of sex type. Sex typing is a strictly conventional arrangement that varies from society to society (Mead, 1949). Our own society is strongly organized around sex specialization of personality. This begins with male and female names, clothes, play patterns, toys, and continues throughout life by defining specialized sex roles for man and woman. The ultimate love object of the child is defined as a member of the opposite sex. The nascent sexual reactions of the child are directed toward stimuli of the opposite sex. The child is led to expect eventual sex rewards from persons of the opposite sex.

The taboo on homosexuality. Training in sex typing has the indirect effect of imposing a vigorous taboo on homosexuality. Homosexual objects are not presented, are treated by neglect or, if need be, vigorously condemned. The errors children make while learning sex typing are the source of much amusement to adults. The little girl declares she is going "to marry mommie" when she grows up or the little boy states he will marry his admired older brother. Children are carefully corrected and trained into making the appropriate distinctions. Furthermore, it seems probable that parents, already sex-typed, help to develop this turning toward the opposite sex by themselves "favoring" the child of the opposite sex.

Students of sexual abnormalities have suspected that the failure to define sharply the sex type is a factor in producing perverse sex adjustment (Henry, 1948). Thus, if a boy child were ardently desired, the parents might fail to impose sharp feminine sex typing on the girl who actually arrived. Or, in the opposite case, a mother who prefers her son to remain her "baby" may make him effeminate when she should be emphasizing his masculine character. Such inversions of social sex typing cannot directly produce a sexual perversion since sex responses must be attached to same-sex cues before a perverse sex appetite can exist; but they might tend to confuse the child about what its socially expected sex goals were and thus contribute to deviation.

After sex typing has been imposed and well learned, the child is in about this net position: masturbation has been tabooed, and it cannot give itself sex rewards by this means; sex behavior between siblings has been suppressed; on the other hand, a new channel, though a long one, has apparently been opened through the fact of sex typing. The child is vaguely led to expect something rewarding in the general direction of the opposite sex. These two circumstances set up the situation of the Oedipus complex.

How fear is attached to heterosexual approach responses. The anxiety which adolescents, and often adults, show at the prospect of heterosexual contact must be explained. It does not arise by chance. It arises rather in the family situation which is the child's most important early learning situation. The first definition of sexual responses is learned in relation to parents and siblings and only later transferred to others. Freud calls this the Oedipus situation.

We will illustrate from the case of the boy child, where the matter seems to be clear, and rehearse and paraphrase the familiar facts discovered by Freud. The boy child turns to his mother in fact or thought in the hope of getting sex rewards when he can no longer get them by himself. He expects sex rewards partly by generalization (Miller, 1948*b;* von Felsinger, 1948) of expectation of reward—that is, by analogy to the many rewards the mother has already given him—and partly from the fact that by sex typing he has learned to expect sex rewards from a woman and his mother is the woman at hand. Doubtless some of the anxiety already learned in connection with masturbation generalizes to the sex impulse when it begins to show itself toward family women.

A new source of anxiety appears, however; that is, fear of the father. The five-year-old boy knows his father is the head of the house, the symbolic source of punishments and discipline. He also knows that his father is the husband of his mother and has some unique relationship to her. This rivalry of the father does not exist merely in the boy's mind. It is often made very concrete in the father's behavior. The father may complain that the little boy sleeps in the mother's bed when he is already "too old" for such behavior. The father may object to the fact that the child or children sop up so much of the mother's time and leave so little to him. The father may impose certain restrictions about entering the parents' room which leave the child with a mystery on his hands. Whenever the male child makes emotional demands on the mother, the father may become more critical of him in other and more general respects, saying that the boy talks too much, that he does not work enough, and so forth. If the boy reacts with fear toward his father as a rival, it is because the father, consciously or unconsciously, is acting in a way that seems fearsome and rivalrous. The child is usually unable to discriminate between opposition on ground of sexual leanings and that evoked by its other claims on the mother. The whole thing may be played out as a kind of dumb show. The heterosexual strivings of the boy toward the mother may be behaviorally real and active but not labeled in the boy's mind. On the other hand, the opposition of the father, though active and effective, may be oblique and unconscious.

Often the mother herself rejects the claims of the boy. She has anxiety at any overtly sexual responses from the child, stops fondling him, and may suddenly and inexplicably change from being loving and approving to being horrified, disgusted, and disapproving.

In this case there is less need for the father to be harsh and hostile. But if the mother does not reject and does not clearly show her separate loyalty and adherence to the father, a great burden is placed upon him to maintain his control of his wife. The mother, for example, may use the seeming need of the child as a way of escaping from her husband and from the sexual conflicts which she has in regard to him. She may favor and cozen the son while avoiding her husband, and unconsciously this may seem to the father like a genuine kind of preferment. The father may then react by very actively arousing the boy's fears.

Specific genital anxiety. If the boy's motives are sexual, the increased threat from the father produces anxiety which is directly attached to the sexual motives and interpreted as a sexual threat.

This is one way in which castration anxiety may become an important factor in the boy's life even though the father never threatens castration in so many words.   The boy has learned that the punishment often fits the crime.

There are other and less ghostly sources of the castration threat. Very often it has been specifically associated with the masturbation taboo—*i.e.*, that if the boy plays with his penis, the penis will be cut off.   The threat may appear in the fables of childhood which are told so eagerly.   One of the authors as a six-year-old boy was permitted to participate in an after-dark session of older boys. They were telling the tale of how Bill Smith, a prominent citizen of the town, had come home and surprised his wife in bed with her lover.   Smith thereupon pulled out a spring-bladed jackknife (demonstration of length and viciousness of same by boy telling the story) and proceeded to unman the lover.   Such a story does not remain, however, as a mere "fable."   It is taken to heart and has the effect of teaching straight-out castration fear to sex motives.

The castration idea may occur in still another way; that is, as an inference from the lack of penis in the girl.   The parents do not explain the different nature of the girl's genital.   The uninstructed boy may assume that the girl once had an external genital but has been deprived of it, perhaps as a punishment.   There is no doubt that this inference is often made.   The authors have repeatedly heard it in those in-family situations where children are first questioning their elders about sexual matters.   It is further surprising in the history of adults how often the idea of bodily damage occurs in relation to sex "sins."   Castration fear has been shown clinically to be connected with fears of bodily damage, especially in the cases of heart and brain, to aversion to crippled people, and to avoidance of women in their genital aspect.   Castration fear is frequently escaped by approaching the bachelor girl (who has no husband or father at her side) or by recourse to women of lower class or racial status (whose normal protectors are not allowed to function).

In any case, and engendered by whatever of these several means or combination of them, the sex conflict takes a new twist when it is worked out within the family.   Anxiety which was once attached only to the masturbation impulse is now attached to the heterosexual approach situation.   If this anxiety is made very strong it can pro-

duce a certain relief in the intensity of the conflict.   This is the so-
called "resolution" of the Oedipus complex.   When anxiety is
greatly dominant over approach tendencies, the conflicted individual
stays far from his goal and but few of the acquired elements in the
sexual appetite are aroused.   Thus, that part of the intensity of the
conflict which is produced by appetitive sex reactions is missing, and
the conflict is therefore lessened.   However, this conflict should
and does recur when the individual is placed near his goal object and
cannot easily escape, as frequently happens in adolescence.   Then
again the full strength of the sex reactions is pitted against the terror of sexual injury.   Marriage evidently seems to some adults a
similar situation—that of being held close to a feared goal—and they
make the blind escape responses which would be expected.

Heterosexual conflict not labeled.   If the prior intimidation of the
person has been very great, and if the mother's stand is correct,
much less fear need be imposed by the father.   If sex appetite is
weak rather than strong, there is much less pressure from the child's
side and less anxiety need be imposed to counteract it.

All these events are but poorly labeled at the time they occur.
The culture is niggardly about giving names to sexual organs,
sexual feelings, or the fears attached to them.   The child is therefore not able to make a logical case for itself and, so to say, "put
it up to the parents."   Furthermore, repression sets in in two
ways: Children are frequently forbidden to talk to others about
their sexual reactions.   Such sentences or thoughts as do occur tend
to make the conflict keener both by arousing sex appetites and by
cueing off the anxiety attached to them.   The child is pained when
it tries to think about sexual things and relieved when it stops.
The result is repression.   This repression has one unfortunate consequence for science.   When the individual is later interviewed he
is not able, promptly and freely, to give account of these matters.
The renaming and mental reestablishment of these bygone events
can thereafter only be made through the weary work of psychotherapy.

Science is not the only loser.   The individual himself has lost his
opportunity to use higher mental activities in solving the conflicts
involving sex and authority.   There are many ways in which the
person can be victimized.   A sexual perversion may lurk behind the

blank surface of repression. The individual may never again be able cheerfully and amiably to accept a measure of authority exerted over him. Acute anxiety may be attached to his heterosexual impulses and when the time comes that society expects, almost requires, that he marry, he may be unable to do so. Even though he is able to get over the line into marriage, he may find the years of his marital life haunted and poisoned by constant, unconscious anxiety. In this case, the individual has automatically generalized to all women the anxiety proper only to the incest situation. He has failed to discriminate, as a free mental life would enable him to do, between the tabooed sexual feelings and objects of childhood and the relative freedom permitted to adults. To every authoritarian figure in his life he generalizes the intense anxiety that he once experienced when attempting to rival his father in the sexual field. Only when higher mental processes are restored can the individual make those discriminations which allow him to proceed freely and constructively with his life as an adult.

4. *Anger-anxiety Conflicts*

At this point we are more interested in the connection between angry emotions and fear than we are in the problem of how angry feelings are aroused in the child. We assume, however, as before (Dollard *et al.*, 1939) that anger responses are produced by the innumerable and unavoidable frustration situations of child life. In the frustration situation, new and strong responses are tried out. Some of these have the effect of inflicting pain on other people. Society takes a special stand toward such anger responses, generally inhibiting them and allowing them reign only in a few circumstances (self-defense, war, etc.). Many of these attack, or "put through the act," responses produce strong stimuli, and these we recognize as the emotion of anger. Lift the veil of repression covering the childhood mental life of a neurotic person and you come at once upon the smoking responses of anger.

Patriarchal code on child's anger. Parents intuitively resent and fear the anger and rage of a child, and they have the strong support of the culture in suppressing its anger. Direct punishment is probably used much more frequently when the child is angry and aggressive than in any other circumstance. More or less without regard to what the child is angry about, fear is attached to the stimuli of anger. The virtuous chastisement of the rebellious child is an age-old feature of our patriarchal culture. According to the old Connecticut Blue Laws, a father could kill a disobedient son (Blue Laws of Connecticut, 1861, Section 14, p. 69). Even though this code was never exercised in this extreme in recent times, it shows the complete freedom to punish which was once culturally allowed parents. As the domestic representative of the patriarch in his absence, the mother is free to punish children "in their own interest."

How fear is attached to anger cues. We have already noted the situation of early cleanliness training as one tending to produce angry confusion in the small child. At earliest ages the cultural practice seems to be that of extinguishing anger rather than punishing it; that is, the child is segregated, left to "cry and thresh it out." However, parents' motivation to teach the child cleanliness training is so strong that they frequently also use punishment, especially in the case of what they interpret as stubborn or defiant behavior. Anxiety responses therefore become attached not only to the cues produced by the forbidden situation but also to the cues produced by the emotional responses which the child is making at the time. It is this latter connection which creates the inner mental or emotional conflict. After this learning has occurred, the first cues produced by angry emotions may set off anxiety responses which "outcompete" the angry emotional responses themselves. The person can thus be made helpless to use his anger even in those situations where culture does permit it. He is viewed as abnormally meek or long-suffering. Robbing a person of his anger completely may be a dangerous thing since some capacity for anger seems to be needed in the affirmative personality.

Other frustrations producing anger. The same state of affairs can prevail and be additionally reinforced as a result of the frustrations occurring in the sex-training situation. If the child is punished for masturbating it may react with the response of anger. The parent may not notice the provocative circumstance but see only that the child has become mysteriously "naughty." Its naughtiness may be punished and the connection between anger and fear be strengthened.

Parental rejection or desertion may likewise produce anger in the child. If the child feels secure only when the parents are present, it may react with fear when the parents leave or when they threaten to leave again. When the parents return, the child may make excessive claims, want unusual favors, "be clingy." To these demanding and possessive gestures on the part of the child the parent may react with unintelligent punishment, thus again teaching the child to fear.

The new tasks involved in growing up impose many frustrations on the child. Giving up long-standing privileges may arouse rage. Being forced to try out new responses, such as putting on its own clothes or tying its own shoe laces, can anger the child. If it screams, lunges, slaps at the parent in these circumstances, punishment is the almost inevitable answer, and the connection between anger and fear is additionally strengthened.

Sibling rivalry. Rivalry between siblings is a constant incitement to anger, and such rivalry occurs in every household, without exception, where there are siblings of younger ages. The occasions for rivalry seem innumerable. Siblings may compete for evidences of parental love. If the parent disappoints a child, that child may "take it out" on the luckier brother or sister. Younger children may anger older ones by being allowed to assume too quickly privileges which the older have long waited and worked for. Older children may tease and torment younger ones in retaliation. Sometimes the younger child is resented merely for existing and for having displaced the older one and alloyed its satisfaction in being the unique child.

The younger children may enjoy privileges which the older have been forced to abandon and thus create some degree of unconscious resentment. Younger children may tyrannize over older ones by too freely playing with or even destroying their toys and precious objects. Parents should intervene and prevent such behavior but often they do not, and the older child revenges himself in roundabout ways. Younger children may resent the privileges enjoyed by the older and attempt to punish older siblings for their greater freedom. These angry displays result in punishment of the one or the other child by the parents—and sometimes of both. The younger children tend to "catch it" more from the older, and the older children more from the parents. Though parents may mitigate these angry relationships between siblings by just rules which are honestly enforced, there seems no way to take all the hostile strain out of such relations.

Mental limitations. Small children confront an unintelligible world. Many of their frustrations result from this fact. They do not have the mental units to be patient and foresightful. They do not know how to comfort themselves while waiting. They cannot live in the light of a plan which promises to control the future. Since so much is frustrating to them that is later bearable, they are especially prone to anger. They want to know "Why isn't the circus here today?" "Why do I have to wait 'til my birthday to get a present?" "Why does Daddy have to go to work just when it's so much fun to play with him?" Living in the present and being unable to reassure themselves about the future, young children resort to anger at these inevitable frustrations. Adults experience the hostile or destructive behavior of young children as a nuisance, do not understand its inevitability, and frequently punish aggressive responses.

Devious aggression. If anger must be abandoned as a response in a frustrating situation, other responses will be tried out such as pleading for what one cannot take by force or submitting to frustrations which can only be worsened through opposition. Devious forms of aggression are particularly likely to occur in this case. The individual can be punished for direct anger responses but it is much harder to catch him at roundabout aggression. He may learn to lie in wait and take revenge by hastening and sharpening punishment which his opponent has invoked in some other way. Gossip, deceit, creating dangerous confusion about agreements and life relationships may all be indirect modes of angry reaction.

Anger conflict unlabeled. As in the case of sex-anxiety conflicts, the anger-anxiety conflict is likely to be poorly labeled. Verbal skills are at a low level when much of this training is going on. Repression of the language describing anger-anxiety conflicts may occur because conflict is thus, momentarily at least, reduced. As a result, the individual cannot, in later life, be selectively angry, showing anger in just those social situations in which it is permitted and rejecting anger where it is not.

The overinhibited person. Inhibition of anger may occur in two different degrees. The overt, or some of the overt, responses of direct aggression may be inhibited. Some such inhibitions must occur if a child is to live in our culture. The process may, however. go farther and the emotion of anger itself be throttled. If the response-produced drives of anger evoke intense fear, the individual may be incapable of a normal life. The victim loses the core of an affirmative personality. He may be unable to compete as is demanded by our society in school or business spheres. He may be additionally shamed because he cannot bring himself to fight. He may depend unduly on others, waiting for them to give him what is everyone's right to take. Such a child cannot be a self-maintaining person because he cannot produce any anger responses at all, let alone those which are "legitimate and proper."

Since many outlets for anger are permitted adults which are not permitted to children, the person who is overtrained to inhibit anger may seem childish in that he is still following the age-graded code of childhood and is unable to embrace the freer standards of adulthood. One of the chief tasks of psychotherapy, in the case of unduly inhibited persons, is to enable them to name and describe their angry feelings so that they may extinguish undue fear and begin to learn a proportionate self-assertiveness.

Frustrated Mobility Aspirations Produce Aggression

There is little doubt that adults can be in conflict concerning their mobility strivings and that these conflicts can lead to pathological results in behavior (Ruesch, Loeb, *et al.*, 1946). The conflict could be described somewhat as follows: In order to be strong and safe, or stronger and safer, the person wants to identify with and possess the symbols of a social group above that of his original family. In order to make this transition, however, certain prescribed routes must be followed. The person must have a talent which brings him in touch with and makes him useful to the group into which he wants entry. This talent could be intellectual, could be a facility for making money, could be beauty, could be an exceptionally loving and understanding personality. If an individual has the wish to change position but does not have such a talent or does not enjoy it to a sufficient degree, he may find it impossible to make the transition. He may find himself unable to establish the contacts which will enable him to learn the rituals of behavior of the superordinate group. He may gradually come to know that, though "the promised land" is in sight, he will never enter it. Meanwhile the group he is trying to leave punishes him for being "different" and the group he tries to enter rejects him as presumptuous. The realization, conscious or unconscious, that his campaign has failed may serve as a severe frustration and produce varying types of aggressive and compensatory behavior. The resentment of the person who fails of mobility is likely to be severely punished and thus to create an acute anger-fear conflict.

Mobility conflicts which are unconscious. Except in one circumstance, which we shall come to in a moment, it does not seem likely that conflicts such as the one just described are engendered in early childhood. The conflict may nevertheless be unconscious. This unconsciousness of the elements of an adult conflict can arise because the mobile person gets little help from his society in labeling his behavior. He is not told what he is trying to do, and he has no clear understanding of what the techniques are. If he hits on the means of mobility, it is, from his point of view, a matter of luck or accident. He is ordinarily not permitted to think that different social classes exist because the social beliefs which protect the class system forbid this recognition. Usually the mobile individual sees himself only as rising in some value such as "wealth" or occupation but he does not realize that his real mobility will be founded on a complex set of behavioral adaptations and changes in taste and outlook. Usually, therefore, the mobile person does not know what is happening to him while it is happening, does not know how he failed if he fails, and does not know until "afterward" how he succeeded if he succeeds. This is a set of conditions which is bound to baffle and to arouse a confusion of angry, rebellious, apathetic, and submissive responses.

Children of a mixed-class marriage. The one circumstance that we can see under which difference in social class can have an effect on a small child is the case where the child is born of a mixed-class marriage. If the mother is superordinate, she might in some ways "look down" on the father, apologize for him, and limit his usefulness as a model to her male child. Such a mother may be unduly "ambitious" for her children, attempting to speed them over the landscape of childhood instead of allowing them to find their natural pace through it. She may get satisfaction in imposing early cleanliness training because it seems to her like a guarantee of the future precocity of the child. She may inculcate the sex taboos strongly because she feels that the "goodness" of the child in this respect will keep it out of "bad company" and aid its development in the schools. She may handle its angry tendencies severely in the hope of making it amenable and yet urge it to highly competitive performance outside the home. One would predict that this kind of family training would give a special coloring to the circumstances which ordinarily produce conflict in small children (Davis and Havighurst, 1947; Warner, 1949, pp. 70–72).

A child in a class-stable family with parents matched from the class standpoint would not ordinarily discover in the early years of life that there is any group "above" its parents. During the formative period these parents would play their august roles, majestic in their competence and authority so far as the child could see. It would only be later in life, perhaps first during school days, that the child would learn that there are any people who look down upon it or its parents. Undoubtedly such knowledge would have some kind of effect on the career of the child, but we cannot say what the possible outcomes might be. We can be sure, however, that the evaluation put on the self and the family by the surrounding society will be a fact of importance in the developmental history of every child.

SUMMARY

Conflict itself is no novelty. Emotional conflicts are the constant accompaniment of life at every age and social level. Conflicts differ also in strength, some producing strong and some weak stimuli. Where conflicts are strong and unconscious, the individuals afflicted keep on making the same old mistakes and getting punished in the same old way. To the degree that the conflict can be made conscious, the ingenuity and inventiveness of higher mental life can aid in finding new ways out of the conflict situation. This applies to all emotional dilemmas, to those which survive from early childhood and to those which are created in the course of later life.

High drives produced during the nursing period can have disturbing side-effects. The child first faces severe cultural pressure in the cleanliness-training situation. At this time intense anger-anxiety conflicts can arise. Similarly, in the discipline of the masturbation habit and of heterosexual approach tendencies, the sex-anxiety conflict is regularly created in all of us. In some it has traumatic intensity. When the elements of this conflict are unconscious, they can have an abiding effect on life adjustment in the marital sphere. The culture takes a harsh attitude toward the angry and hostile behavior of children and regularly attaches anxiety to it, usually by direct punishment. Anger can be aroused in any of the situations of childhood where frustrating conditions are created. Conflicts centering around social class and mobility are known, especially in families where the parents have different social aspirations for the child.

Not all conflict arises through the pitting of primary drives one against the other, as in the case of hunger vs. pain. It is possible to have severe conflict based on one primary and one strong learned drive. This is exemplified by the sex-anxiety conflict. It is further possible to have severe conflict when two strong learned drives are involved—as in the case of anger-anxiety. In later life many of the strong learned drives, some quite remote from their primitive sources of reinforcement, can produce painful conflicts. "Ambition" can be pitted against "loyalty." The wish to be truthful can be arrayed against "tact." Wishes for social advancement may be deterred by the fear of appearing vulgar and "pushy." Many of these complex learned drives have never been effectively described in terms of the reinforcing circumstances. We do know, however, that when they compete they can plunge the individual into a painful state.

We must admit that we do not know the exact conditions under which the common conflict-producing circumstances of life generate severe conflicts in some and not-so-severe conflicts in others. We know that the conditions and factors described here *do* occur in those who later turn out to show neurotic behavior. It may be that the circumstances of life are not really "the same for normals and neurotics," that this sameness is an illusion based on poor discrimination of the actual circumstances. Therefore it may actually be that some individuals have much stronger conflicts than others. It may be that some are less well able to use higher mental processes than others and are therefore less well able to resolve traumatic tension. It may be that some are more "predisposed" than others in that they have stronger primary drives, or stronger tendencies to inhibition, or in other unknown respects. It is quite likely that the provocative circumstances of later life which precipitate neuroses are more severe in some cases than others; or that some are exposed to just those circumstances which for them excite neurotic behavior but that others are luckier and do not come into contact with just those adverse conditions which would set them off.

We must also say that the data available are subject to several severe faults. Much of the data is from clinical case histories and may be damaged by various flaws in reporting and by inability to report. There may also be, and probably are, various kinds of sampling errors. Neurotic people may come from "a different basket." We have not been able to study the matter experimentally to see just which factors differentiate neurotic persons from their normal controls. Many fundamental measurements needed, such as those concerned with the strength of anxiety and other learned drives, cannot yet be made. This qualification has, however, a positive side. We do the best we can with the data we have but affirm the lacks in our data and the need for rigorous time-consuming longitudinal studies. We do not yet have a science of child rearing (Dollard, 1949) and until we do our sketches of the trauma-producing years of childhood are bound to be rough.

CHAPTER XI

HOW SYMPTOMS ARE LEARNED

PHOBIAS

In a phobia acquired under traumatic conditions of combat the relevant events are recent and well known. Such cases provide one of the simplest and most convincing illustrations of the learning of a symptom.

The essential points are illustrated by the case of a pilot who was interviewed by one of the authors. This officer had not shown any abnormal fear of airplanes before being sent on a particularly difficult mission to bomb distant and well-defended oil refineries. His squadron was under heavy attack on the way to the target. In the confusion of flying exceedingly low over the target against strong defensive fire, a few of the preceding planes made a wrong turn and dropped their bombs on the section that had been assigned to the pilot's formation. Since not enough bombs were dropped to destroy the installations, the pilot's formation had to follow them to complete the job. As they came in above the rooftops, bombs and oil tanks were exploding. The pilot's plane was tossed violently about and damaged while nearby planes disappeared in a wall of fire. Since this pilot's damaged plane could not regain altitude, he had to fly back alone at reduced speed and was subject to repeated violent fighter attack which killed several crew members and repeatedly threatened to destroy them all. When they finally reached the Mediterranean, they were low on gas and had to ditch the airplane in the open sea. The survivors drifted on a life raft and eventually were rescued.

Many times during this mission the pilot was exposed to intensely fear-provoking stimuli such as violent explosions and the sight of other planes going down and comrades being killed. It is known that intense fear-provoking stimuli of this kind act to reinforce fear as a response to other cues present at the same time.[1] In this case the other cues were those from the airplane, its sight and sound, and thoughts about flying. We would therefore expect the strong drive of intense fear to be learned as a response to all of these cues.

When a strong fear has been learned as a response to a given set of cues, it tends to generalize to other similar ones (Miller, 1950). Thus one would expect the fear of this airplane and of thoughts about flying it to generalize to the similar sight and sound of other airplanes and thoughts about flying in them. This is exactly what happened; the pilot felt strongly frightened whenever he approached, looked at, or even thought about flying in any airplane.

Because he had already learned to avoid objects that he feared, he had a strong tendency to look away and walk away from all airplanes. Whenever he did this, he removed the cues eliciting the fear and hence felt much less frightened. But, as we have already said in Chap. V, a reduction in any strong drive such as fear serves to reinforce the immediately preceding responses. Therefore we would expect any response that produced successful avoidance to be learned as a strong habit. This is what occurred; the pilot developed a strong phobia of airplanes and everything connected with them.

Similarly, he felt anxious when thinking or talking about airplanes and less anxious when he stopped thinking or talking about them. The reduction in anxiety reinforced the stopping of thinking or of talking about airplanes; he became reluctant to think about or discuss his experience.

To summarize, under traumatic conditions of combat the intense drive of fear was learned as a response to the airplane and everything connected with it. The fear generalized from the cues of this airplane to the similar ones of other airplanes. This intense fear motivated responses of avoiding airplanes, and whenever any one of these responses was successful, it was reinforced by a reduction in the strength of the fear.

When all of the circumstances are understood, as in this case, there is no mystery about the phobia. In fact, such things as the avoidance of touching hot stoves or stepping in front of speeding

---

[1] For a similar analysis of other combat cases, see Dollard (1945).

cars usually are not called "phobias" because the conditions reinforcing the avoidance are understood. Our contention is that the
laws of learning are exactly the same, although the conditions are
often different and much more obscure, especially when the fear
is elicited by the internal cues of thoughts or drives.

Fear aroused by drive to perform a punished response. The way
fear can be elicited by the temptation to perform a forbidden act
is illustrated in the case of a four-year-old boy who showed a sudden
and prolonged flare-up of extreme resistance to going to bed. Previously the little boy had only shown the normal reluctance. Suddenly this became greatly intensified. He protested at having to
leave his toys, asked for extra bedtime stories, came down repeatedly
for drinks of water, was found sitting at the head of the stairs, expressed various fears of the bedroom that were hard for the parents
to understand, and had to be put back to bed as many as fifteen or
twenty times in a single night.

The parents realized that their child was seriously disturbed but
could not figure out why; they were baffled and annoyed. At first
they thought that the main interest of the child, who was an only
child, was staying up with adults. As they took increasingly firm
measures to keep him out of the living room so that they could
lead a semblance of a normal social life, they found him sleeping
in strange and uncomfortable places such as the threshold of the
entrance to the bedroom, in the hall, and even on the stairs. It began to appear that his real motivation was to avoid his bed. Occasionally he would go to sleep wearing two pairs of pants in spite of
the fact that it was the middle of the summer in a hot Midwestern
city.

The parents tried everything they could think of but nothing
seemed to help. Finally they took him to a clinic. There the following facts were gradually pieced together. The mother had had
a much younger brother who was severely punished for masturbation during his infancy and so she had resolved that she was never
going to treat her own children like that. She began by giving this
child complete freedom in this respect and then gradually made him
understand that he could masturbate only when he was alone or in
his own house without strangers being present. The trouble about
going to bed began shortly after a new maid was hired. The mother

remembered that the afternoon before the trouble started the little boy had reported to her that the maid had said he was nasty and had slapped him "like she slaps her own little boys." Because the maid seemed so gentle and affectionate the mother had doubted this, and in the face of these doubts the little boy had guessed that he had imagined it. Later the maid was observed to tell the little boy that he was nasty when she found him fingering his penis and was privately told to ignore this kind of behavior. The symptom had faded away somewhat during the week the maid was absent to take care of her sick mother and flared up again when the maid returned.

On the advice of the psychiatrist at the clinic, the mother made it perfectly clear to the child that the maid was not to punish him for masturbating; she dramatized this by making the maid apologize to him and say that she was wrong in calling him nasty. After this the extreme resistance to going to bed suddenly disappeared, with only a few minor recurrences that were easily met by further reassurance. There was also a marked improvement in the child's cooperativeness and happy, independent spontaneity.

In this case it seems fairly evident that punishment and disapproval from the maid had attached fear to the response of masturbation. The child seems to have been more strongly tempted to masturbate when he was alone in bed. Thus the fear was aroused in bed. (It is also possible that some of the punishments were administered in bed, but unfortunately we have no evidence on this point.) Whenever the child approached the bed or was told to go to bed, his fear was increased; any response that took him away from bed was reinforced by a reduction in the strength of this fear. He learned a variety of such responses. Putting on the two pairs of pants probably also tended to reduce the fear of masturbating in bed, not by physical escape but by covering up the penis. When the fear of masturbation was reduced, the motivation to perform all of these responses (*i.e.*, symptoms) was removed. Freedom from this source of anxiety and conflict also improved the child's general mood.

It will be remembered that Mrs. A's phobia seemed to be caused by the anxieties and sexual conflicts aroused by the temptations that she encountered when she left her solitary room.

Origin of response. When the fear-provoking stimulus is clearly circumscribed (like a hot radiator), the avoidance response that reduces the fear often occurs immediately with relatively little trial and error. Apparently it is either an innate response or is learned early in life and quickly generalized to new situations containing the similar element of a localized fear-provoking stimulus. In cases in which direct avoidance is physically or socially difficult (like dealing with the school bully), the individual may show considerable trial and error, reasoning and planning. Once the responses producing successful avoidance are elicited by any one of these means, they are reinforced by the reduction in the strength of fear and quickly learned as strong habits.

Origin of fear. In phobias, the origin of the responses of avoidance and the way they produce the reinforcing reduction in fear is usually quite clear. The origin of the fear is often obscure, stemming from the childhood conflicts about sex and aggression that were described in the preceding chapter. Further research is needed to enable us to describe in terms of rigorous behavior principles and social conditions all the detailed steps intervening between infancy and adulthood.

How fear is transferred to new cues. Theoretically one would expect the strong fears involved in phobias to transfer to new cues in a number of different ways:

1. *Primary stimulus generalization.* When a person learns to fear one situation, he should also tend to fear other similar ones. Stimuli more similar to the original traumatic ones should elicit stronger generalized fear. This is called a *gradient of generalization.*

2. *Higher-order conditioning.* After strong fear is learned as a response to certain cues, they will serve as learned (*i.e.,* secondary) reinforcing agents so that any cues that consistently precede them will acquire the ability to elicit fear (Pavlov, 1927).

3. *Secondary, or response-mediated, generalization.* When the fear is attached to response-produced cues, any new stimulus that becomes able to elicit the response producing these cues will arouse the fear they elicit.[2] For example, a young man may have fear attached to the cues produced by the first incipient responses of sex-

---

[2] In this case the fear would be classed as a *mediated learned drive.* It will be remembered that such drives were discussed in Chap. VII.

ual excitement. Then if a previously indifferent girl is labeled "sexy," she may arouse incipient responses of sexual excitement which in turn elicit fear.

When a response produces the cues eliciting the fear, any increase in the drive motivating that response will be expected to cause it to generalize to a greater variety of stimulus situations.[3] In other words, when the young man's sex urge increases, he will be expected to find a wider variety of situations sexually exciting and, hence, frightening. Conversely, when his sexual motivation is low, only the most provocative situations will be exciting and, hence, frightening. In short, the variety of situations feared will be expected to vary with the strength of the drive motivating the response mediating the fear.

Extinction of phobias. If a response to a given cue continues to be repeated without reinforcement, it gets progressively weaker. This is called *extinction*. It will be remembered that such experimental evidence as we have seems to indicate that the internal "response" of fear follows the same laws in this respect also and is subject to extinction. In the case of a strong fear, however, this extinction may proceed so slowly that it is scarcely noticeable within 200 trials, as was shown in Fig. 6. In this case, if only a small sample of behavior were observed, one might easily be led to the false conclusion that no extinction was occurring.

In some cases the extinction of phobias can be noticed. For instance, the pilot in the first example was somewhat less afraid of airplanes several months after his traumatic experience. Similarly, a young man with a moderately strong fear of high places gradually lost this fear when he was strongly motivated to participate in mountain climbing and gradually exposed himself to a series of increasingly steep heights.

In other cases, the fears involved in phobias seem to be enormously resistant to extinction. It will be remembered that the following variables are known to increase resistance to extinction: a stronger drive of pain or fear involved in the original learning; a

[3] As was pointed out in Chap. IV, Brown (1942) and Beach (1942) have shown that the generalization of overt responses varies with the strength of the drive motivating them. We assume that internal cue-producing responses follow the same laws as these overt responses.

larger number of reinforced learning trials; intermittent, or so-called partial, reinforcement; the generalization of reinforcement from other similar situations; the similarity of the phobic situation to the original traumatic one; the variability of the cues in the stimulus situation; and, as will be seen, the subject's memory for the original circumstances under which the fear was learned. Phobias also tend to be preserved because subjects usually manage to avoid the phobic situation and so do not receive many extinction trials.

As long as the subject can avoid the cues that elicit fear or that evoke the internal cue-producing responses eliciting fear, he will be expected to experience no fear. Thus the pilot in the first example was not afraid as long as he could stay completely away from airplanes, and the little boy in the second example was reasonably unafraid when he was safely away from the bed. If the social conditions allow successful avoidance of the fear-provoking situations, all that will be noticed is a blank area in the person's life. But as soon as he is forced to go into the phobic situation, strong fear will appear.

To summarize, in phobias the responses of avoidance and their reinforcement by a reduction in the strength of the fear is almost always quite clear. The origin of the drive of fear may be obvious or obscure; it often traces back to childhood conflicts about sex and aggression. Fear can be exceedingly resistant to extinction. The more exact determination of the factors that affect this resistance is a problem with important therapeutic implications.

COMPULSIONS

It is well known that if a compulsive response, for example excessive hand washing, is interrupted by a command or physical restraint, the subject experiences a marked increase in anxiety; he reports that he just feels awful. As soon as the compulsion is resumed, the anxiety disappears (Fenichel, 1945, pp. 306–307; White, 1948, p. 277). Thus it seems clear that the compulsion is reinforced in exactly the same way as the avoidance response in the phobia and the responses of turning the wheel, pressing the bar, or pulling of the handle in the experiments described in Chap. V. In fact, a phobia of dirt, which leads the subject to remove visible dirt by

washing, may shade over by imperceptible degrees into hand washing where the subject fears dirt even when the hands seem clean,
or where he does not know what he fears.

While the existence of the fear, guilt, or other drive motivating
compulsive responses usually becomes obvious if the patient is forced
to stop performing the compulsive response, the source of this drive
is often quite obscure. Frequently a hand-washing compulsion must
be traced back to childhood conflicts in which cleanliness training
produces an abnormal fear of dirt or sex training results in a strong
fear of venereal disease.

The responses involved in compulsions may be the result of more
or less random trial and error but often are ones that have already
been learned in other more or less similar situations. For example,
the mother who arouses anxiety in the child by criticising him for
dirty hands teaches him to wash his hands when they are dirty.

Similarly, the anxiety-reducing effects of a particular act, such
as hand washing, are often due to social training. Then the act of
washing the hands may have a direct reassuring effect because it
has been so frequently associated during childhood with escape
from criticism for having dirty hands. Stated more exactly, the
cues produced by the act may elicit responses that inhibit fear. In
other cases the effect may be more indirect; the function of the act
may be to elicit thoughts that are incompatible with the ones eliciting the fear. For example, the thought "I have washed my hands
so they must be clean" will be incompatible with the one "Perhaps
my hands are contaminated."

In other instances the compulsive act may have an anxiety-reducing effect because it serves as a distraction. Keeping the hands busy
with an innocent response may help to keep them out of anxiety-
provoking mischief. In the case of Mrs. A, concentrating on counting heartbeats served to distract her from sexual thoughts that
aroused anxiety.

Usually the compulsive act produces only a temporary reduction
in the anxiety. After a relatively short time, the anxiety starts
to increase again so that the patient is motivated to repeat the
compulsive act. In the case of Mrs. A, the primary drive of sex was
a constant motivation for sexual thoughts. As soon as she stopped
counting, these anxiety-provoking thoughts tended to reappear.

Thus she had a compulsion to continue counting whenever she was not completely preoccupied with some other distracting and innocent activity.

In conclusion, the drive-increasing effect of interfering with compulsions and the drive-reducing effect of performing them is usually clear-cut. The origin of the fear (or other drive) and the reason why a particular compulsive act reduces it is often not obvious and must be tracked down or inferred.

HYSTERICAL SYMPTOMS

Our analysis of how hysterical symptoms are learned will start with a case of war neurosis where the causation is relatively recent and clear. This is case 12 reported by Grinker and Spiegel (1945b, pp. 28–29). The patient had been directing the firing of an artillery platoon under great danger and with heavy responsibilities. After the acute phase of battle, he was lying on the ground exhausted when three shells landed nearby and exploded, blowing him off the ground each time. He was somewhat shaken up but otherwise fit. Half an hour later he found that he could not remove his right hand from his trouser pocket, having almost complete paralysis. He did not report sick and stayed with his company regaining some strength in his arm but still suffering partial paralysis. Then he was sent to the hospital, where he was calm and cooperative and had no anxiety, tremor, or terror dreams.

His condition was not organic (*i.e.*, it must have been learned) because under pentothal narcosis he was able to move his arm in all directions with ease. With reeducation and a short series of therapeutic interviews the condition cleared up. When it became obvious, however, that he was fit to return to his unit, he developed frank anxiety and tremor in both arms. The anxiety now appeared directly in relation to his battle experience and had to be dealt with as a separate problem.

Reinforcement vs. adaptiveness. In this case it is obvious that the symptom of a paralyzed arm served a certain adaptive function in that it kept the soldier out of combat. More general evidence that escape from combat is involved in reinforcing the symptoms of war neurosis is given by the fact that they vary with the requirements of the combat task.   Thus aviators are likely to turn up with disturbances in depth perception or night vision, symptoms that are peculiarly suited to interfere with flying, while paratroopers are likely to have paralyzed legs (Grinker and Spiegel, 1945a, pp. 103–104).

For the more rigorous type of theory that we are trying to construct, however, merely pointing out the adaptiveness of the symptom is not enough; the reinforcement should be described more exactly.   In the case of the soldier with the paralyzed arm, the eventual hospitalization and escape from combat could not have been the original reinforcement because it occurred only after the symptom was firmly established.   The original reinforcement must have occurred while the symptom was being learned.   Furthermore, we know that, in order to be effective in strengthening a response, reinforcement must occur soon after it.

In this case the drive is fear and the origin of the fear in combat is quite clear.   Since the fear was not experienced as long as the symptom persisted but reappeared as soon as the symptom was interrupted, it is apparent that the symptom reduced the fear.   But a reduction in the strength of fear is known to act as a reinforcement.   Therefore, the symptom of partial paralysis seems to have been reinforced by the immediate reduction that it produced in the strength of fear.

The symptom of paralysis produced this reduction in fear because the patient knew that it would prevent his return to combat. As soon as the patient noticed that it was difficult to move his hand, he probably said to himself something like "They won't let me fight with a paralyzed hand," and this thought produced an immediate reduction in fear.   Though the fear reduction probably was mediated by a thought, its reinforcing effect on the symptoms was direct and automatic.   In other words, the patient did not say to himself anything like "Since a paralyzed hand will keep me out of combat, I should try to have a paralyzed hand." In fact, when such a patient becomes convinced of the causal relationship between the escape from fear and the symptom, a strong increase in guilt counteracts any reduction in fear.   The reinforcement is removed and there is strong motivation to abandon the symptom.

Malingering. Now we can see how the hysterical symptom differs from malingering. In malingering, the guilt attached to thoughts of performing a response in order to escape from a responsibility, such as combat, is not as strong as the fear of the responsibility. Therefore the subject is able to plan to perform a response in order to escape. In hysteria, the response is made directly to the drive, such as fear; in malingering, it is made to the verbal cues of the plan. Therefore we would expect hysterical symptoms to vary with the drive and malingered ones to vary with the plan. Perhaps this is why, as Grinker and Spiegel (1945*b*, pp. 47, 95) report, hysterical symptoms are relieved by drugs such as pentothal (which according to us, Chap. XXIII, operate by reducing the drive of fear) while malingered ones are unaffected. It can also be seen that only responses that are under verbal (*i.e.*, voluntary) control can be involved in malingering, while any response that can occur may be reinforced as an hysterical symptom. In fact, the more plausible the response seems as an involuntary organic defect, the less likely it is to arouse guilt.

Origin of response. Phobias involve the exceedingly natural response of avoidance, and compulsions usually involve common responses. Often the responses involved in hysterical symptoms are much more unusual. Thus there is more of a problem concerning how the response occurs and is available for the initial reinforcement. Often symptoms have an organic basis at first and then persist after the organic basis has been cured (Grinker and Spiegel, 1945*a*, pp. 111–112). This seems to be a way of getting the response to occur so that it can be reinforced. Aviators' symptoms resemble diseases that often occur in fliers—pseudo air emboli, air sickness, and so forth (Grinker and Spiegel, 1945*a*, p. 57). As we noticed in Chap. V, many symptoms appear to be responses that are relatively normal to the drive of strong fear. In spite of these suggestive facts, the factors determining exactly which symptoms will occur are still somewhat of a mystery. For example, does allowing children to escape from school for certain kinds of pains or mild illnesses predispose them to the use of pseudo illnesses to escape from difficulties in later life?

To summarize, in hysteria the reinforcement, or primary gain from the symptom, is often relatively clear; the drives involved may be unclear at first, and the factors determining the occurrence of a particular response may be quite obscure.

A Civilian Case

The roles of drive and reinforcement in the learning of an hysterical symptom may be further illustrated by the case of Mrs. C,[4] a thirty-five-year-old married woman with an hysterical paralysis of the legs. This case clearly illustrates the point that the direct removal of a symptom (without treatment of its cause) produces an increase in drive and throws the patient back into a severe learning dilemma.

From the case history it is obvious that Mrs. C had a strong fear of sex. She had a stern, middle-class mother who "belted" her regularly and severely to make and keep her a "good" girl. As a child she swore that she would never marry and only later in life did this resolve change. When she got married, it was apparently as a means of escape from the constant punishment at home. She states positively that she had no information on intercourse or conception until her marriage. Immediately after her marriage, Mrs. C woke up with terror dreams, the content of which was that she was pregnant. She had a specific aversion to the sexual act and said she "felt nausea every time my husband touched me." In the light of these and other facts we believe that the sex anxiety of this patient was excessive.

Shortly before her hysterical symptoms appeared, her already strong fear of intercourse was increased. In the course of 15 years of married life Mrs. C was pregnant four times and had three living children. Her sexual anxiety was evident throughout the course of her marriage but became worse after the last, painful pregnancy. As a result of her fear, she attempted to avoid intercourse. The records state that she granted it to her husband only once or twice a month and then only after tears and entreaty by her husband. She said that she yielded from "pity."

[4] The case record was courteously made available to us by Dr. B. H. Moore, Associate Clinical Professor of Psychiatry, Institute of Human Relations, Yale University, New Haven, Conn., and Dr. Erich Lindemann, Director, Psychiatric Outpatient Department, Massachusetts General Hospital, Boston, Mass., who are, of course, not involved in any theoretical use which we make of it in this book.

After the fourth pregnancy, she concluded that she should not have any more children because a "doom" hung over them. She justified this on the grounds that a paternal aunt had been in a mental hospital. Although she had known this fact for years, it had never played a role in her thinking about the children until this time. Then she developed a morbid fear of pregnancy.

After the fourth pregnancy with its nausea and discomfort, Mrs. C experienced a certain amount of edema, and it is reported that her legs felt "weak, wobbly and trembled." It may be that this physical weakness helped her to learn her symptom. It is possible that when she noticed that her legs were not normal, she thought to herself "this will prevent intercourse," a thought which would be expected to reduce her anxiety and reinforce the incipient symptom. Unfortunately the details of the development of her symptom were not carefully observed so that we cannot be sure exactly how it was learned. It is known, however, that she was shortly brought to the hospital with her legs in an acute spastic condition. She was unable to flex her knees, to walk, or to stand. According to our analysis, this symptom must have been reinforced by the reduction in anxiety that the condition produced by making intercourse impossible. At the time she was brought in, her anxiety level was low; she accepted the symptom and displayed that *belle indifférence* of which Charcot spoke (Freud, 1925, Vol. 4, p. 94).

The doctors proved that the symptom was not organic. The signs of organic paralysis were not present, and the limbs were freely movable when the patient was under the influence of pentothal. The patient, however, was highly resistant to any explanation of her symptom on the basis of emotional factors. She said it is something "organic, inwardly, not emotional."

Had Mrs. C been willing to try psychotherapy, perhaps her abnormal fear of sexual intercourse could have been reduced so that she would no longer have been motivated to perform the symptom. Unfortunately this was impossible. The only alternative seemed to be to force Mrs. C to try walking. This was done. The doctors helped her to stand, used mild pressure to bend her knees, and convinced her that it was physically possible for her to stand and walk.

Once Mrs. C was convinced that her symptom was not organic,

her sense of duty to her husband and children forced her to try walking and to resume the normal duties of her life.   Apparently Mrs. C's conscience was too strong to allow her to enjoy an intentional escape; the reinforcing reduction in anxiety which showed itself as *belle indifférence* was dependent on the belief that the symptom was forced on her and beyond her control.

The fact that the symptom had been producing the kind of reduction in anxiety and conflict that would be expected is demonstrated by the increase in drive that occurred after its removal.   Mrs. C was angry at her doctors and suffered an attack of rage at one of the nurses on the very night that she was first convinced she could walk.

The increase in drive motivated the kind of trial and error that almost certainly had occurred and failed to solve her problem before the symptom was learned.   When she was released from the hospital and returned to her home, she tried a series of new escape responses.   She first considered divorce, but this measure threatened to produce still new conflicts—moral scruples and fears of loss of financial support for herself and children.   She went to live with her sister, using the rationalization that she was not yet strong enough to run her own house.   This means of escape kept her out of contact with her husband but created problems with her sister's husband and family, so she eventually had to come home.   After she came home, Mrs. C refused intercourse with her husband and avoided all occasions when it might occur.   Of course, this created problems with him but not sufficiently severe ones to make her willing to risk sex relations.   Finally she sought and received contraceptive advice but then did not actually make use of it. Evidently her fears were attached to the sex act as well as to pregnancy, since she was not willing to use contraception to avoid pregnancy while accepting sex relations.

In this case the motivation for the symptom is clear.   The fact that it allowed the patient to escape an anxiety-provoking dilemma is clear, but the details of the reinforcement and learning were not observed.   After the symptom was removed, it is clear that the patient was put back into a high state of motivation and a severe learning dilemma.

REGRESSION

When the dominant habit is blocked by conflict or extinguished through nonreward, the next strongest response will be expected to occur. In an adult this often is a response that was reinforced and learned as a strong habit during childhood. When this happens, it is called regression. The more strongly the earlier habit was reinforced in the past (fixation), the more likely it is to be the next strongest one and hence to recur. Similarly, the more weakly the adult habit is established the less interferences will be required to reduce its strength below that of the childhood one. As Sears (1944) has pointed out, all the foregoing propositions have been confirmed by experimental evidence on simple overt responses. Evidence from clinical cases (Freud, 1925, Vol. III, pp. 447–448, 453–454) seems to fit into the same pattern.

According to our hypotheses the internal cue-producing responses that are responsible for specific goal-directed behavior and the drive-producing responses that are responsible for learnable drives follow the same laws of learning as overt responses. Therefore, we would expect them to be subject to regression in exactly the same way as overt responses. This deduction has not yet been tested experimentally, but clinical evidence suggests that exactly this sort of thing occurs. For example, evidence cited by Fenichel (1945, p. 381) suggests that when a man's genital sexual appetites are inhibited, he may regress to the earlier learned responses of hunger appetite.

In many cases what has worked once will work again, so that the habit dynamics responsible for regression tend to produce adaptive behavior. It is only when the conditions have radically changed, as with the age-grading of the child, that the earlier responses are maladaptive and the shift is likely to be called regression. Usually what happens is a compromise between the earlier habits and the responses that have been learned in the current situation so that the regression is by no means a complete copy of earlier patterns.

Where the type of response that is acceptable in a child is strongly disapproved in an adult, a regression in learned drives and anticipatory goal responses will motivate behavior that elicits

strong anxiety reinforced by current social taboos. It may, therefore, be necessary to correct the regression (or failure to progress)
before adaptive responses can be firmly established.

DISPLACEMENT

When the dominant response is prevented from occurring, the
next strongest one will occur. As we have seen, when this other
response owes its strength to the fact that it was reinforced during
an earlier stage of the person's development, the process is called
regression. But it is also possible for a response to be strong
because of generalization. In this case the process is called displacement. A more rigorous analysis of displacement has been
presented elsewhere (Miller, 1948b); some of the main conclusions
may be summarized here.

Prevention by absence or by conflict. In the simplest case the
subject learns to respond to an original stimulus object and then
the responses to that object are prevented by its absence. In this
case, the responses will be expected to generalize to other similar
objects, with stronger responses being elicited the more similar the
new objects are to the original one. For instance, a girl who has
learned to love a given man but is prevented from continuing this
by his death, which she accepts without any persisting conflict,
will be expected to be attracted to other similar men and more
strongly attracted the more similar they are to her original sweetheart.

The situation is more complex when the direct response to
the original stimulus is prevented by a conflict. For example,
the girl may have first learned to love her father, but with any sexual
feelings toward him being inhibited by the incest taboo. In this case
the responses involved in the inhibition will be expected to generalize
also. It is obvious that there are two main possibilities:

1. The inhibiting responses may generalize as much as (or more
than) the responses that they inhibit. Then the original responses
will be just as inhibited in the new displacement situation as they
were in the original direct one.

2. The inhibiting responses may generalize less than the ones
they inhibit. Then the original responses will be less inhibited

in the new situation than they were in the original one. This is illustrated in Fig. 9 in which the smaller amount of generalization of the inhibiting responses is represented graphically as *a steeper gradient of generalization*.

On the basis of theory (Miller, 1948*b*) which has been confirmed by experiment (Miller and Kraeling, 1950) we know that the second of these possibilities is the one to be expected, at least under certain circumstances. Apparently this is the mechanism that is responsible for the clinical phenomena of displacement.

Deductions. A number of deductions can be made from this type of analysis. We have already seen that when the direct response to the original stimulus object is prevented by the absence of that object, we would expect the strongest responses to be elicited by the most similar object available. Different results will be expected, as can be seen from Figs. 9 and 10, when the direct responses to the original stimulus object are inhibited by conflicting ones. In this case the strongest response should occur to stimuli that have an intermediate degree of similarity to the original one. Thus the girl in our previous example would be expected to prefer a suitor who was not completely similar to, but not completely different from, her father.

Increasing the strength of a drive raises the height of the whole gradient of generalization (Brown, 1942). It can be seen from Figs. 9 and 10 that increasing the strength of the fear motivating the conflicting responses will shift the point of strongest displacement in the direction of stimuli that are less similar to the original one eliciting the direct response. It will also decrease the strength of all displaced responses, and if the inhibition is strong enough, no displaced response will occur.

Similarly, as can be seen in Fig. 11, increasing the strength of the drive motivating the direct response to the original stimulus will shift the point of strongest displacement in the direction of stimuli that are more similar to the original one eliciting the direct response. The strength of all displaced responses will be increased and the range of stimuli that can elicit such responses will be widened.

As far as we know, all the foregoing deductions seem to fit in with the clinically observed facts.

Drive generalization. So far we have been dealing with generalization from one external stimulus to another. If it is assumed that the internal patterns of stimuli produced by different drives are not completely distinctive, one would expect a certain amount of generalization to occur also from one drive to another.[5] This conclusion is supported by experimental evidence (Miller, 1948*b*;

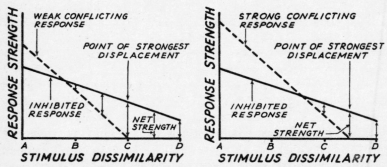

FIG. 9. Displacement produced by greater steepness in the gradient of generalization of the conflicting response (assuming linearity). It can be seen that displaced responses can occur and that the strongest displaced response will be expected at an intermediate point, C in the diagram on the left. Increasing the strength of the conflicting response weakens the strongest displaced response and causes it to be elicited by less similar stimuli, those between C and D in the diagram to the right. Although straight lines were used in order to simplify these diagrams, Fig. 10 shows that the deductions are not dependent upon the assumption of linearity. (*From Miller, 1948b.*)

von Felsinger, 1948). Thus it is not surprising that the child who has learned to approach his mother for food when hungry should tend to make similar approaches when motivated by sex.

Response generalization. Up to this point our discussion has been concerned with stimulus generalization. An analogous type of generalization occurs on the response side; after a specific response has been reinforced, it is found that other similar responses also

[5] A similar deduction can also be made from Hull's (1943) postulate 7, which states: "Any habit strength is sensitized into reaction potentiality by all primary drives active within an organism at a given time, the magnitude of this potentiality being a product obtained by multiplying an increasing function of habit strength by an increasing function of drive."

become stronger (Beritov, 1924; Hilgard and Marquis, 1940, pp. 184, 185). This is called response generalization. We may tentatively apply the same assumption to response generalization that we used with stimulus generalization, namely that the strength

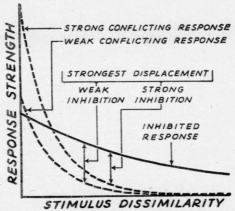

Fig. 10. Effect of strength of conflicting response upon displacement (assuming that gradients of generalization are negative growth curves). Increasing the strength of the conflicting response weakens the strength of the displaced responses and causes the point at which the strongest displaced response is elicited to be moved to stimuli which are less similar to those originally eliciting the direct response. Figure 9 shows that these same effects will also be produced by linear gradients; the only difference is that when the gradients are curvilinear the conflicting responses are above zero strength at the point at which strongest displacement is elicited.

The equations for these curves have the form $Y = ke^{-ax}$. The particular values chosen for this illustration were: slopes, $a = 1.25$ for both conflicting responses, and 0.25 for the inhibited response; x intercepts, $k = 2.5$ for the inhibited response, and 6 for the strong and 3 for the weak conflicting response. (*From Miller, 1948b.*)

of the generalized inhibiting response falls off more rapidly than that of the responses they inhibit. Then, as Whiting and Sears (1949) have pointed out, when the original form of the response is inhibited, some generalized form may not be inhibited. They have used this assumption to deduce the kinds of behavior that children should show in playing with dolls in certain projective test situations.

Reinforcement of displaced responses. We have seen that the origin of displaced responses lies in the mechanism of generalization. But in order for them to persist they must be reinforced. Many displaced responses are reinforced because they encounter greater social permissiveness. Thus the girl whose father is taboo is

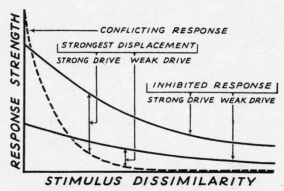

Fig. 11. Effect of strength of drive upon displacement (assuming that gradients of generalization are negative growth curves). By raising the height of the whole gradient of generalization, an increase in the strength of the drive that motivates the inhibited response will increase the strength of the strongest displaced response and cause the points at which the strongest displaced response is elicited to be moved in the direction of the stimuli more similar to those that originally elicited the direct response. The second of these effects is the only one of those illustrated in these diagrams which would not be produced by linear gradients.

The equations for these curves have the form $Y = ke^{-ax}$. The particular values chosen for this illustration were: slopes, $a = 0.25$ for both inhibited responses, and 1.15 for the conflicting response; x intercepts, $k = 5$ for the conflicting response, 4 for the inhibited response with strong drive, and 1.5 for the inhibited response with weak drive. (*From Miller*, 1948*b*.)

allowed to marry another man. It should be noted, however, that when a generalized act is completely adaptive it is often not referred to as displaced.

Displaced responses could also be reinforced by the generalization of a learned reward. For example, if a person often succeeds by responses of aggression in overcoming the frustrating resistance of others, the successful performance of these responses of aggression would be expected to acquire some rewarding drive-reducing value of its own. This could serve to reinforce the expression of aggression against scapegoats. To date, this is only a theoretical possibility, however, because the operation of generalized learned rewards has not been studied in complex situations of this kind.

Finally, it is possible that the responses involved in displacement can be reinforced by providing the subject with an anxiety-reducing explanation. For example, a man may be sexually excited by his wife but prevented from action by anxiety attached to sexual responses toward her. This conflict may produce a great deal of tension and frustration. He has a strong feeling of discomfort and irritation as he sits in his home. As a result of the types of training that were described in Chap. IX, he will feel uneasy as long as he has no explanation for such an obvious aspect of his behavior so he will be motivated to think of an explanation. Whenever thoughts even remotely related to his sexual conflict occur, they increase his anxiety. But if he hits upon the explanation that he is irritated at the noisy children, this reduces his anxiety about the unexplained behavior; it also tends to eliminate anxiety-provoking thoughts related to the sexual conflict. Because he has learned to feel angry at people who are labeled as being to blame, this explanation tends to direct his annoyance toward the children.

RATIONALIZATIONS AND DELUSIONS

The preceding example could also be described as a rationalization. According to our analysis a rationalization involves the following steps: Social training of the type described in Chap. IX produces a need to have a logical explanation for obvious features of one's behavior and plans; the person tends to feel uneasy in the presence of any behavior that is illogical or unexplained. In some instances, however, the true explanation would provoke anxiety, guilt, or some other drive. Thus the person is motivated to find *some* explanation but to avoid the true one. When he happens to hit upon a rationalization that meets cultural standards of sensibleness, it is reinforced by a reduction in anxiety about unexplained behavior. Furthermore, if some of the sentences that would constitute a true explanation have been tending to come into the subject's mind and elicit anxiety or guilt, the alternative sentences in the rationalization tend to block them out and hence remove the anxiety or guilt that they elicit. When this occurs, it serves as an additional reinforcement.

According to our hypothesis, a delusion is only quantitatively different in that (1) the problem of finding a socially acceptable explanation is more difficult, and (2) much stronger anxiety or guilt is involved. The reduction of this strong drive is a strong reinforcement for the performance of the delusional sentences. Whenever these sentences are interfered with, the strong drive reappears as a powerful motivation for the response of saying or thinking those sentences. The delusional sentences are, therefore, dominant over the competing responses evoked by social or self-criticism. The strength of drive and reinforcement accounts for the "fixed" character of the delusion.

HALLUCINATIONS

In connection with phobias and displacements we have already made use of the principle that increasing the strength of the drive raises the entire gradient of generalization, increasing the strength of all generalized responses and the range of stimuli that will elicit them. We have also found it useful to advance the hypothesis that internal cue-producing "responses," including images and perceptions, follow the same laws, including the principle of generalization, as do external responses. By putting these two together, we find that we have the nucleus of a theory for the influence of drive on perception. In extreme cases this might produce hallucinations.

According to our hypothesis, images and perceptions are cue-producing responses and should be expected to follow the same laws as other responses. They seem to be modifiable by experience, subject to inhibition by competing perceptions and images, etc.[6]

[6] The fact that part of the organization of perceptual responses may be determined by innate factors does not prevent them from being modifiable by learning or differentiate them from overt responses. Certain features of the organization of overt responses are also determined by innate factors, for example, the coordination involved in the stepping, balancing, and other postural reflexes (Fulton, 1949), but these can be modified by learning and indeed form an important basis for our learned motor skills.

If perceptual responses are also generalized in the same way as overt ones, we would expect them to be more likely to be elicited by stimuli more similar to the original stimulus object. This seems to be the case; one is more likely to make the mistake of perceiving one object when a different one is really there, the more similar the two objects are to each other. Furthermore, we would expect that the stronger the drive motivating a given perceptual response, the more it should generalize to other dissimilar stimuli. This also seems to be true; for example, experiments (Atkinson and McClelland, 1948) show that hungry subjects are more likely than satiated ones to perceive a somewhat ambiguous stimulus as a food or something related to eating. Similarly, a small boy frightened by going through the woods alone at night may perceive a gnarled tree to be a dangerous beast or the gleam of moonlight on a bush to be a ghost. When the same boy is less afraid because his father is with him, he is more likely to perceive the same objects correctly as a tree or a bush.

Ordinarily the generalized incorrect perceptions occur only to objects that are either quite ambiguous, and hence do not elicit any strong competing responses of their own, or else are relatively similar to the correct one. It can be seen that as the drive increases, however, the perceptual responses will become stronger and occur to a wider range of cues. Such exceedingly wide generalization of strongly motivated perceptual responses may be one of the sources of hallucinations. Motivated by an extremely strong drive the patient may generalize his perceptual responses to stimuli that are so dissimilar that the normal observer does not respond to them as a conceivable source of the hallucinatory responses.

Perceptual responses can be modified by learning. The scientist who is skilled at looking through a microscope perceives many things that are not noticed by the novice. Similarly, if one wears prisms that invert the field of vision and then takes them off, the world appears to be distorted as a temporary aftereffect of this experience (Stratton, 1897). When a "perceptual response" is entirely the product of a learned association, it is called an image. If the word "lightning" evokes a "response" faintly resembling a zigzag flash, this is called an "image." Ordinarily images are much weaker than perceptual responses to external cues. But experimental evidence indicates that if the external cues are very weak, subjects are unable to distinguish between a perceptual response and an image (Perky, 1910).

Overt responses become stronger when the relevant drive is increased. There is some evidence that images are influenced by drives (McClelland and Atkinson, 1948). It seems possible that increasing the drive might strengthen an image (*i.e.*, "perceptual response" elicited as a result of learning) enough to make it able to compete with incompatible responses elicited by external cues. This could be another factor involved in the production of hallucinations.

Striking evidence that the truly hallucinatory images involved in dreams are also influenced by motivation has been secured by Holmberg (1950). He studied a society, the Siriono, whose members were frequently exposed to severe hunger, and found that an unusually large proportion of their dreams was about hunting, eating, and other activities related to food.[7]

Finally, it will be remembered that we have reason to believe that children receive special training in discriminating between the "make believe" and the real, in perceiving accurately, and in responding to external cues rather than to images when the two are in conflict. If this is indeed learned, it should be unlearned when the balance of reinforcements is radically changed. Whenever paying attention to external cues is consistently painful so that the subject is reinforced by a reduction in fear of some other strong drive every time he shifts his attention from the external to the internal response-produced cues, he should learn to pay attention to the latter. Such learning would predispose him to hallucinations. It

[7] The fact that drives seem to be one of the determining factors in hallucinations and dreams, of course, does not mean that they are the only factor involved. For example, a borderline state of sleep normally is necessary for dreams. We do not know whether this effect of sleep is produced by stimulating the centers responsible for images, by releasing these centers from general physiological (*i.e.*, unlearned) inhibition from other centers, by differentially depressing the centers responsible for the learned habits of discriminating between images and external cues, or by some other process. The same is true for the effects of drugs. It is even possible that the balance between the excitation and inhibition of different centers can be modified by conflict or learning and that such a change plays a role in susceptibility to hallucinations.

should be noted, however, that for the members of our society, the drive aroused by paying attention to external cues will have to be exceedingly strong; otherwise its reduction will be more than counteracted by the strong anxiety aroused by seeing and hearing things that logically should not be there and that others report are not there.

It is interesting to note that in other societies where the social training is less against and more for reporting hallucinations they seem to occur much more frequently (Murdock, 1934, pp. 258, 279).

PROJECTION

The mechanism of displacement depends upon a psychological principle, *i.e.*, generalization. This gives a certain amount of unity to the phenomena. The mechanism of projection (*i.e.*, attributing one's own motives to others) seems to depend on a variety of social conditions of learning. For this reason, the phenomena are not so simple and unitary.

According to our analysis, the fact that members of our society tend to react in the same way to similar situations is one of the origins of projection. People tend to react in the same way because they are highly similar as biological organisms. Furthermore those people who frequently associate with each other usually come from similar social backgrounds and thus have been subjected to similar conditions of learning. Therefore each individual learns to expect his associates to react in the same way that he does; he learns that it is useful to judge others by himself. For example, the host who is cold may think that his guests are probably cold, verify this, and then build a fire in the fireplace.

Social interaction provides another origin of projection. When one is friendly, he is likely to behave in a way that elicits friendly behavior and feelings in others. When others are friendly, they are likely to elicit friendly behavior and feelings in you. Conversely, anger and aggressive behavior is likely to arouse anger in the other person and motivate "tit-for-tat" counteraggression. People thus learn to be on their guard against others toward whom they are hostile. Furthermore, if someone hates you, he is likely to make you miserable so that you hate him.

Cooperative behavior is more likely to succeed when individuals with similar desires get together. This reinforces seeking others with the same motives. Often a leader gets an idea and sells it to others.

A child who is caught in some mischief is likely to be punished somewhat less severely if the original instigation came from some-one else. There is still more likelihood of being rewarded by escape from punishment if everything can be blamed on someone else.

All of these circumstances, and probably many others, tend to cause the individual to think that others are motivated in the same way that he is. Freudians have noted that there is often a "kernel of fact" in the motivation attributed to someone else and have sup-posed that the "projector" could detect such unconscious motivation in the other person. But this behavior is usually called projection only when the others are not obviously motivated in the same way. Often in projection the individual not only labels others' motives incorrectly but also fails to label his own correctly. Such behavior is reinforced by the reduction in anxiety that occurs when the blame is shifted to the other person. Different ways in which the process of projection can work are illustrated by the two following examples.

The first of these is the case of Mrs. A. She had intense anxiety about any verbal expression of sexual desires. On several occasions as a small girl she had "been taken advantage of" by older boys or men. Later she frequently went into situations where she was likely to be taken advantage of. Instead of any thoughts about having sexual desires of her own, she was afraid that the man wanted to do something to her.

According to our analysis, being taken advantage of reduced this girl's fear of sex because it meant that she was not to blame. She was able to get some satisfaction in those situations that she was not able to get otherwise. These experiences attached learned reward value for the sex drive to the cues of being alone with a man in a provocative situation and to the cues produced by the thought "he wants to take advantage of me." This learned reward value reinforced the responses of going into those situations and thinking those thoughts. Since such intense anxiety had been attached to labeling her own sexual desires, any thought that she wanted the man to make advances was repressed by the mechanism to be described in more detail in the next chapter. Such a thought might have kept her out of the sex situation entirely. The thought "he wants to do something to me" also helped to provide an explanation for some of the behavior and to keep anxiety-provoking thoughts about her own desires out of her mind. This was an additional source of reinforcement for that thought.

The second example is a man who had a somewhat paranoid reaction to one of his professional associates. As we analyze the case, it went something like this. The subject was homosexually excited by this particular associate.[8] The incipient homosexual responses and thoughts aroused intense anxiety and were repressed. Because of the conflict, the subject felt miserable whenever he was in the presence of the other man and better whenever he avoided him. He reacted to this state of affairs with thoughts such as "I don't know why but I don't like him!" But as long as there was no rational explanation for this behavior, he felt uneasy. In previous situations the dislike had often been mutual and involved aggressive and discriminatory acts on the part of the other person. The thought that the other person disliked him and was persecuting him occurred and was reinforced by the reduction in anxiety it produced through providing a logical explanation.

Since aggression is more acceptable as self-defense, the idea that the other man was to blame also reduced the subject's anxiety about his aggressive tendencies; it tended to justify and strengthen his hate.

But the persecution itself was a fact that required logical explanation. To achieve it, the subject was motivated to find reasons and hit upon the satisfying idea that the associate envied and feared his superior intelligence. Furthermore, the thought of hate tended to eliminate any thoughts of love because of the logical incompatibility of the two, and the emotional responses of hate may also have had some tendency to inhibit the appearance of incipient homosexual feelings. Inhibiting these responses reduced the anxiety they elicited and thus produced additional reinforcement for the

[8] The relationship between repressed homosexuality and paranoia was first pointed out by Freud (1925, Vol. III, p. 448).

thoughts and emotions of hate. Finally the frustrations involved in the homosexual conflict may have been yet another source of aggression.

REACTION FORMATION

A person who is motivated to do something he has learned to disapprove or fear may respond with thoughts, statements, or behavior of the opposite kind. This is called reaction formation. It appeared as one of the features in the preceding example. The subject responded to frightening stirrings of homosexual love with the thought "I hate him!" Because of social training in excluding logical contradictions, the thought "I hate him" tended to eliminate the anxiety-evoking thought "I love him" and was reinforced by the consequent reduction in anxiety.

Often the denial of the intent to perform a forbidden act and the concentration on the thought of performing the opposite act will be expected to help suppress the tendency to perform the forbidden act. With less tendency to perform the dangerous act, the subject will be less frightened. Such fear reduction will reinforce concentrating on thoughts opposite to the temptation. Furthermore, the denial of the intent to perform a forbidden act is the type of thing that has been reinforced by escape from punishment in the past. Thus this denial will tend to reduce guilt.

For example, as a little girl Mrs. A hated her mother but was severely punished whenever she expressed her anger in any way. When she apologized by saying that she really loved her mother and by acting like it, the punishment was terminated. In this way, she learned to substitute statements of love for statements of hate. Years later, when she started to hate her mother-in-law, this aroused intense anxiety that could only be reduced by protestations of love. The mechanism was discovered through the fact that Mrs. A most protested her love just at the time her mother-in-law was treating her in a very nasty way.

It seems possible that the responses involved in reaction formation are favored by the fact that our verbal training produces an especially strong association between words that are antonyms. This is demonstrated by experiments on word association (Woodworth, 1938, pp. 343–355). In word-association tests, antonyms, such as "hate" for "love" and "hot" for "cold," are relatively frequent. Furthermore, if subjects are instructed to respond with antonyms, they can do this faster than any other type of controlled association.

ALCOHOLISM

A variety of experimental results shows that alcohol produces a reduction in fear.

Masserman and Yum (1946) trained hungry cats to perform a complex series of manipulations to secure food. After this they gave the cats electric shocks at the goal until they consistently refused to manipulate the apparatus. Then, they found that getting the cats drunk with mild doses of alcohol would cause them to resume manipulating the apparatus to get food. In interpreting the results they describe the persistent refusal to manipulate the apparatus as "a neurosis" and say that the alcohol "disintegrated those relatively complex 'neurotic' patterns and permitted relatively simple goal-oriented responses to supervene."

Conger (1949) designed an experiment to test the assumption that the behavior observed by Masserman is essentially a simple approach-avoidance conflict and that the effect of alcohol is to reduce the fear motivating avoidance. First he tested hungry rats in a simple approach-avoidance situation. He trained them to approach the distinctively lighted end of an alley to secure food and then threw them into an approach-avoidance conflict by giving them electric shocks at the goal. Five minutes after a control injection of water the rats would not approach the food-shock end of the alley; five minutes after one of alcohol (1.5 parts to 1,000 of body weight) they ran up to get the food.

Having determined that results could be secured in a simple situation, presumably not involving any complex habits, he performed a second experiment to determine whether the alcohol strengthened the approach habits based on hunger, weakened the avoidance habits based on fear, or modified both. He trained one group of rats to approach the lighted end of the alley for food and a *different* group to avoid the lighted end of the alley to escape shock. The strength of the tendencies to approach or avoid was measured by having the animal wear a little harness, temporarily restraining it, and measuring how hard it pulled. Half the animals in each group were tested when mildly drunk and half when sober. The alcohol produced little if any decrease in the pull of the hungry animals toward food and a marked decrease in the pull of the frightened animals away from the place where they had been shocked on previous trials. Since the same responses of running and pulling were involved in both groups, it seems reasonable to interpret the difference as indicating that the alcohol reduced the strength of fear without markedly affecting hunger.[9]

If, as these experiments seem to indicate, alcohol produces a reduction in the strength of fear, we would expect this to reinforce the response of drinking when frightened. This deduction is confirmed by the results of Masserman and Yum (1946). Before being frightened at the goal, normal cats regularly preferred plain milk to milk containing five per cent alcohol. After the cats had been frightened, forced to take mild doses of alcohol, and had their fear and conflict relieved by its intoxicating effects, they developed a preference for the five per cent solution of alcohol. Finally, during a series of trials in the apparatus without punishment, all signs of fear were extinguished and the preference for alcohol disappeared. In this experiment the response of drinking alcohol seems to have been reinforced by the reduction of fear or conflict produced by fear.

Cross-cultural data analyzed by Horton (1943) give further support to the hypothesis that the drinking of alcohol is reinforced by a reduction in fear. He analyzed 56 different primitive societies that had access to alcohol and had been studied well enough to provide adequate data. For each society he made separate ratings of the amounts of insobriety reported and of the subsistence hazards that presumably would evoke anxiety. When these two ratings were

---

[9] Since the avoidance animals, when sober, pulled harder than the approach ones and less hard when drunk, the difference could not be an artifact of unequal units of measurement in different parts of the scale. Since the approach habit was learned in a considerable number of trials over several days while the avoidance habit was learned very quickly in a few trials on the same day, it is possible that the differential effects of alcohol were due to the differences in the age of the habit or distribution in training rather than to the differences in the drives involved.

compared, the amount of insobriety was found to be reliably related to the degree of subsistence hazard.[10]

SOME GENERAL THEORETICAL PROBLEMS

Reinforcement of Maladaptive Symptoms

In the case of alcoholism and many other symptoms, the long-range result may be a great increase in the patient's misery. Such symptoms obviously are extremely maladaptive. In such cases an explanation of the symptom in terms of a general principle of adaptiveness or adjustment breaks down. When an attempt is made to salvage the principle by describing these symptoms as an abortive attempt at adjustment, this tends to obscure the real problem which is to specify the conditions under which adaptive behavior will occur and those under which maladaptive behavior will occur.

In dealing with maladaptive symptoms the superiority of the more exact and nonteleological principle of reinforcement becomes evident. Where the increase in misery is delayed, the principle of reinforcement can easily handle the problem; where an apparent increase in misery is immediate, a clear dilemma is posed for a strict drive-reduction interpretation of the principle of reinforcement. This clear dilemma should stimulate investigators to further work that will discover either that unsuspected factors are operating or that the principle of reinforcement needs revision. In either event the result will be a gain in our fundamental knowledge.

It will be remembered that immediate reinforcements are more effective than delayed ones. This principle is called the *gradient of reinforcement*. One aspect of the principle is that the effectiveness of a reward is reduced the longer the reward is delayed; the other aspect of it is that the effectiveness of a punishment in attaching fears to the cues produced by performing a response is reduced the longer the punishment is administered after the performance of that response.[11] In short, the immediate effects of a moderate reduction

[10] This study would have been more convincing if separate raters, unaware of the purpose of the study, had independently made the ratings of insobriety and of anxiety-provoking subsistence hazards.

[11] For experimental evidence on the first aspect, see Hull (1943) and Spence (1947); for evidence on the second, see Miller (1944, p. 441) and

in drive can be stronger than those of a much greater increase in pain that occurs long afterwards. Thus the strengthening effect of an immediate weak reinforcement on a symptom such as drinking may be much greater than the deterring effect of a much stronger but delayed punishment, which often also occurs in the presence of a considerably different set of cues.

Although reward makes a response more likely to occur and punishment usually makes it less likely to occur, the two are *not* simple opposites. As has already been pointed out, it is the *end* of the punishment, or the removal of the cues eliciting the fear, that strengthens whatever response is occurring at that time. Since the response terminating the punishment or fear is usually incompatible with the one leading to the punishment, the strengthening of the former usually tends to eliminate the latter. Under special conditions, however, it is possible for these two responses to be identical. For example, taking dope can produce punishing withdrawal symptoms which in turn are relieved by taking more dope. Under such circumstances one would expect punishment to reinforce the responses leading to it and thus create a vicious circle. Experiments in which somewhat analogous results were produced have been reported by Gwinn (1949) and Miller (1950).

When the painful effects of a symptom are delayed, they present no problem for reinforcement theory. Masochism, compulsive unpleasant thoughts, anxiety dreams, and other symptoms that seem to produce an immediate increase in drive present more of a problem. Our principles allow for two main theoretical possibilities. One is that they are responses that previously have been strongly reinforced in such a way that they require a long time to extinguish. The other is that the subject is not able to give a correct report of the true situation. An increase in fear, guilt, or some other drive may actually be occurring. This drive may be correctly labeled and reported by the subject. But at the same time, or possibly just before, there may have been a much greater reduction in some other drive that is unlabeled and unreported. This unconscious, unreported reinforcement may more than balance the punishing aspects of the experience.

Mowrer and Ullman (1945). Mowrer and Ullman specifically apply their results to the problem of the reinforcement of maladaptive behavior.

Take the example of a mother afflicted by fears that her small child might die. She may be in intense conflict between strong resentment about the many ways the infant severely interferes with her life and the anxiety and guilt that this resentment produces. Because labeling this conflict would increase her guilt, she does not think about it. Then when something causes her to think that maybe her child will die, she may experience an immediate and strong feeling of relaxation and relief that is not labeled as such, quickly followed by a weaker fear that is labeled. In this case the relief will reinforce the thought of the child's death, making such a thought more likely to recur. Since the socially unacceptable source of reinforcement is not reported while the socially acceptable fears are, the case might superficially seem to be an exception to the principle of reinforcement by drive reduction.

In other cases it is possible that the symptom does not produce the fear but follows it, producing some reduction in the fear but not reducing it to zero. Then the residual fear may be mistaken for the result of the symptom.

Other instances might possibly be accounted for by a different hypothesis. In our society there is a custom crystallized in the legal principle that a man cannot be placed in double jeopardy for a given misdeed. Thus children tend to relax and feel less afraid after they have been punished. Ordinarily the fear of punishment is not as bad as the punishment so the net effects are negative and the child continues to try to avoid punishment. If the fear is based on previous severe punishments that were given when the child was small and helpless and were much more traumatic than the present one, it seems possible that it could be considerably more painful than the present punishment. Such a fear that is out of all proportion to the consequences is called a disproportionate or unrealistic one. In such cases it seems possible that the relief following the punishment might reinforce seeking punishment, or perhaps even administering it to one's self.

It is interesting to note that this mechanism would only be expected to work in cases where the fears are unrealistic. People with such fears are often called neurotic and are the ones who seem to seek punishment.

To summarize, when the painful aftereffects of symptoms are considerably delayed, they do not pose any problem for reinforcement theory. Symptoms with an immediate painful effect pose a definite problem. Until detailed investigations of possible reinforcements have been made so that such symptoms are better understood, we will not know whether they fit our theory or are instructive exceptions that will force radical alterations and improvements in it.

What Drives Can Produce Symptoms?

Theoretically any strong drive can motivate symptoms and the reduction in that drive can reinforce them. We have mentioned the example of hunger influencing the dreams of the Siriono. The particular drives that become strong will be expected to vary with the physical and cultural conditions of the environment. With middle- and upper-class adults in a technically proficient society like ours, most of the potentially strong primary drives, such as hunger and thirst, are kept at a relatively low level and hence are not usually responsible for producing neurotic symptoms. Sex and aggression, though seemingly weaker biologically, are subject to more social restraint and hence likely to build up to greater strength. Furthermore the verbal responses to these drives are likely to be repressed by punishment, and, as we shall show, this fact favors the appearance of maladaptive behavior that is likely to be called symptomatic.

In certain sections of our society the striving for social mobility and various symbols of prestige is an exceedingly strong drive that is often frustrated. Furthermore it is not quite polite to discuss the status system and one's own ambitions frankly. In the light of these conditions, it might be profitable to investigate more carefully the possible role of frustrated striving for status in the production of symptoms.

One of the most important drives of all is fear, or "anxiety" as it is often called when its source is vague or obscured by repression (Freud, 1936). There are three main reasons why fear is so important: because it can be so strong, because it can be attached to new cues so easily through learning, and because it is the motivation that produces the inhibiting responses in most conflicts. Throughout this book we emphasize the role of fear, or anxiety.[12] This is partly because of its indubitable importance. It is also possible that it is overemphasized because the way it is learned and the effects that it produces are clear-cut and experimentally documented. The general form of the theory would not be changed, however, by substituting another drive for fear.

In some cases symptoms may be motivated by a single drive, for example, fear in the case of the airplane phobia. Sometimes the drive is high because it is physically impossible to perform the responses that would reduce it. This is the case with the Siriono who are frequently hungry because their techniques for getting and preserving food are poor. In most cases in our society, however, it is physically possible to perform the drive-reducing responses. In such cases the high drive must be the product of a conflict that prevents the performance of the drive-reducing responses. Then there must be some drive to motivate the other responses in the conflict. Thus when a person is afraid, it is profitable to ask why he does not simply avoid the fear-producing cues. Unless the possibilities of escape are physically absent, the person must be forced into the fear-provoking situation by other fears (avoidance-avoidance conflict) or lured into it by the goals of other drives (approach-avoidance conflict); he must be motivated to perform the dangerous responses that arouse the fear. Similarly when the sex drive is excessively high, one must look for the conflict that is preventing the responses that would reduce this drive.

When the dominant responses to two strong drives are incompatible so that there is a conflict, it sometimes happens that some of the less dominant responses to the drives are compatible. These responses are the ones that are likely to occur, and if one of them tends to be elicited by both of the drives, the summation of these tendencies makes it more likely to occur. Similarly, any response that will produce some reduction in both drives will be more strongly reinforced than one that produces an equal amount of reduction in only one drive. Symptoms often are compromise responses that are

---

[12] It will be remembered that we advance the hypothesis that other socially learned drives, such as guilt, shame, conformity, and the desires for power and status, may be composed of a considerable element of fear.

produced by both of the drives in a conflict. For example, a child with a compulsive tendency to tickle one hand with the other in bed may be getting a slight erotic gratification from the tickle and at the same time be reducing fear by keeping his hands away from his genitals.

Factors Determining Which Symptom Will Occur

The chief factors that determine which response (and hence, which symptom) will occur have already been mentioned in other contexts. As a clarification and review they are brought together in the following list:

1. *Drives and cues—their innate hierarchy of responses.* As a result of the innate wiring diagram of the organism, each drive has a tendency to elicit somewhat different responses. Usually a drive tends to elicit a considerable variety of responses and has a stronger tendency to elicit some of them than others. The responses to a given drive may be arranged in a hierarchy starting with the responses that are most strongly elicited and working down to those only weakly elicited. This hierarchy is different for different drives, although the exact listings have not been worked out in detail. Similarly, different cues, or patterns of cues, may innately favor the occurrence of certain responses. Therefore, the probability that a response will occur in a given situation is a function of the innate hierarchies of the drives and cues that are present.

2. *Drives and cues—responses previously learned or generalized to them.* The innate hierarchy of responses to drives and cues can be modified by learning so that a response that was originally weak to a certain pattern of drives and cues becomes much stronger. These effects generalize to other similar patterns of drives and cues. Thus the probability that a response will occur in a given situation is a function of the subject's past experience in it and in other more or less similar ones.

3. *Incompatibility of competing responses—the structure of the situation.* When there is a conflict between responses to different drives and cues, the incompatible responses will be expected to tend to cancel each other out so that compatible, compromise responses are likely to occur. Often the incompatibility of responses is determined by the structure of the stimulus situation. Thus a child in

a narrow street will be expected to respond differently to two threatening dogs when they are both behind him than he will when one is behind and the other in front. Similarly, the response to two threatening dogs, one behind and the other in front, will be different in a narrow corridor from what it would be in an open field.

4. *Reinforcement—drives and environmental conditions.* The preceding three factors determine the likelihood that a response will occur at a given time. Once it has occurred, it will be more likely to be repeated if it is reinforced and less likely if it is not. Reinforcement depends, on the one hand, on the drives that are present and, on the other, on the conditions in the physical and social environment that allow drive reduction to occur.

Symptoms Not Directly Learned: Psychosomatic Effects

There are two main kinds of symptoms: (1) those that are learned responses to a state of high drive, and (2) those that are innate physiological reactions to a state of high drive or to some consequence of a learned response. Up to this point we have been chiefly concerned with the first type; now we shall say a few words about the second.

It will be remembered that Mahl (1949) found that chronic anxiety produced an increase in stomach acidity and an increase in the rate and variability of the heartbeat of his dogs. Similar symptoms are also observed in human anxiety cases. Because of their nature, it seems highly likely that these reactions are innate direct physiological accompaniments of fear and hence do not have to be learned or reinforced. In fact it is entirely probable that they are not directly subject to modification by learning, *i.e.*, that as long as the fear is maintained at a constant level, their strength as a reaction to it cannot be strengthened by reinforcement nor weakened by extinction. Likewise, other psychosomatic symptoms may be direct physiological effects of high states of drive.[13]

Though such symptoms are not learned responses, they may be the indirect products of learning. One possibility is that the drive producing them is a learned one. Thus in Mahl's experiment the chronic fear, originally elicited by a strong electric shock, was

[13] For descriptions of such symptoms see Alexander and French (1948); Dunbar (1943); Saul (1944); and Weiss and English (1949).

learned as a response to the buzzer and cage that were associated with the shock. After training of this kind, the buzzer and cage (without shock) acquired the ability to elicit fear, which in turn produced an increase in stomach acidity. Similarly, reacting to an insult with anger is a learned response, but the anger in turn produces unlearned reactions, such as an increase in blood pressure.

There is another way in which the physiological responses to chronic strong drive could be an indirect product of learning. The drive producing them may build up to a great strength and remain there for a long time because the responses that normally would reduce it are prevented by learned taboos. Thus a young man who is sexually excited by a prolonged period of petting but is prevented by learned fears from going further and having an orgasm may suffer from severe pain in the region of the genitals.

Finally, a conflict that is the product of learning may produce certain unlearned effects, such as fatigue, or a learned response may produce physical effects, such as the sores and scars that can be produced by picking at a point of minor irritation on the skin.

The distinction between these two types of symptoms does not have to be absolute. A given symptom may be especially likely to occur to a specific drive because it is high in the innate hierarchy of responses to that drive but subject to gradual modification under conditions favorable to learning. Such a symptom will be still further strengthened if the environmental conditions are such that it is reinforced and weakened if the environmental conditions are such that it is not reinforced. We know that it is possible for a great variety of muscular and glandular responses to be learned and that some learning can occur even at a subcortical level (Morgan, 1943), but there is still much work to be done before we have a complete and definitive list of responses that are learnable and reactions that are not.

Facts That Fit Our Hypothesis

Now that the learning of specific symptoms has been discussed, some general facts may be reviewed that tend to confirm our hypothesis.

Often the conditions of learning are such that the first response to occur is not reinforced. Then it is extinguished and is replaced by other responses. Thus the early stages of learning frequently are characterized by variable behavior that is called trial and error. If symptoms are learned in the same way that other responses are, we would expect the first stages of this learning often to be characterized by variable behavior. Then, with more time for practice, the symptoms that produce the greatest amount of reinforcement should be strengthened the most and thus become dominant. As this occurs the behavior should become less variable. In combat neuroses where the early stages of symptom formation can be observed, this is exactly what is reported by Grinker and Spiegel (1945b, p. 1). They say: "A most pronounced characteristic of the cases seen early in their illness is the profusion in which new symptoms appear and disappear. As time goes on, without treatment, a more stabilized syndrome crystallizes."

Outside of combat, patients are not likely to be carefully observed during the early stages of the development of symptoms. In fact, our psychiatrists and clinics select for treatment only people with well-marked symptoms; hence we do not see patients in the early stages. It should be profitable to try to observe this phase and study the more normal responses that occur first before the subject is driven to symptomatic behavior. Thus we might gain more information about the details of the learning of symptoms. At present we know almost nothing about the symptoms that temporarily appear but are extinguished by nonreinforcement. For example, a recent widower with three young unmarried daughters developed heart symptoms and also quarreled with a succession of housekeepers so that each of them left. One after the other the daughters returned, but only long enough to find a new housekeeper. After a period during which the heart symptoms failed to induce any daughter to devote her life to caring for him, they disappeared. The man rose from his bed, found an attractive widow, and remarried within a year. Unfortunately these transient symptoms were not studied in any detail; we have no idea how many others like them may come and go.

If the progression from an initial profusion of variable symptoms to fewer constant ones is the result of differential reinforcement, as our theory demands, then we would expect these later symptoms to be harder to eliminate because they had received more rewarded practice. This is apparently exactly what happens; Grinker and Spiegel (1945b) report that treatment of war neuroses becomes more difficult as time goes on.

If the symptom is learned by reinforcement, we would expect any additional reinforcements that are received to increase its strength and make it harder to eliminate. This expectation is confirmed by the well-known fact that secondary gains, such as pensions, that are dependent upon a symptom make it harder to get rid of that symptom (Fenichel, 1945, pp. 126–127).

If a symptom is reinforced by drive reduction, we would expect it to tend to make the patient feel better and interrupting it to make him feel worse. As has already been pointed out this seems to occur. The *belle indifférence* so characteristic of the hysteric appears to be an example of drive reduction. Similarly there are many reports of patients feeling worse after a symptom is interrupted. This whole problem needs to be investigated in greater detail. It would seem profitable to try to devise some measure of the drives, such as the galvanic response or blood pressure, for fear and excitement and to make careful studies of the relationship between the measure and the symptoms.

If the symptom is reinforced by drive reduction so that interrupting it causes the drive to mount, we would expect this increased drive to motivate the learning and performance of new symptoms. Thus treatment that is aimed only at eliminating specific symptoms by such means as hypnosis or physical punishment should tend to be followed by the appearance of new symptoms. As is well known, this is indeed the case (Brenman and Gill, 1947, pp. 52–66; Freud, 1924, Vol. II, pp. 350–351).

If a symptom is a learned response, eliminating the drive motivating it should stop its performance; the symptomatic responses should drop out just as drinking does when one is no longer thirsty. This also seems to be the case. The reduction in the anxiety about returning to combat that comes with the end of a war is known to produce a dramatic improvement in many cases of war neurosis (Grinker and Spiegel, 1945a, p. 191).[14] Similarly, therapeutic pro-

---

[14] The fact that the end of the war does not cure all such cases requires explanation. In some cases the fears may not be elicited by verbal cues and thus do not disappear when thoughts about returning to combat are

cedures aimed at finding better ways of reducing the drives seem to be the most successful (Shoben, 1949, p. 372).

Finally, it is known that once a given response has been strengthened by reinforcement, it is easier to relearn that response. Thus a patient who has had certain symptoms and been cured should be more likely to have those symptoms reappear if the drives motivating them reappear. The return of the symptom should be especially likely if its removal did not involve pitting incompatible responses against it, as is often the case when the symptom is interpreted, but rather was produced by temporarily removing the subject from the conflict-producing situation. Again, these deductions seem to be confirmed by the clinical evidence (Menninger, 1948, pp. 149–152; Masserman, 1946, pp. 132–135).

---

eliminated by the news of the end of the war; in others recovery might arouse guilt, precipitate difficult problems of adjustment to a new way of life, or cause the loss of a pension or other special privilege. In any event, it would be instructive to make a careful comparison, guided by learning theory, of cases that are cured by the end of the war and those that are not.

CHAPTER XII

THE UNCONSCIOUS: HOW REPRESSION IS LEARNED

In his discussion of the unconscious, Freud (1925, Vol. IV, p. 134) says: "Now, too, we are in a position to state precisely what it is that repression denies to the rejected idea in the transference neuroses—namely, translation of the idea into words which are to remain attached to the object."

According to Freud, then, the repressed, or unconscious, is the unverbalized. It is not quite so simple as that because other representatives (we would call them cue-producing responses) are involved in conscious mental life, but the verbal ones play by far the most important role (Freud, 1925, Vol. IV, p. 135). As Watson (1925), Sears (1936), Guthrie (1938), Shaffer (1947), and others have pointed out, this is exactly what would be expected in terms of behavior theory. We shall attempt to develop this hypothesis in terms of the psychological principles and social conditions of learning and to fill in some of the details needed to make it a useful part of our theory.

Experiences That Never Were Verbalized

According to our hypothesis, drives, cues, and responses that have never been labeled will necessarily be unconscious. One large category of this kind will be experiences that occurred before the child learned to talk effectively. Since the effective use of speech develops gradually and may not be established for certain categories until long after the child has learned to say "mama," the period during which major parts of social learning are unconscious extends over a considerable number of years and has no set boundaries. As has already been pointed out, this is why so many early childhood conflicts are unconscious.

Even after childhood, certain aspects of life are poorly labeled. For example. many of the finer details of motor skill remain unverbalized throughout life. This is a major source of difficulty in trying to teach anyone to play golf or to fly an airplane. This lack of verbal description and control, however, applies only to the details of the movements; the larger functional units, usually described in terms of end results, such as walking faster or lifting the arms, can be described in words and elicited by them.

More important for our purpose is the fact that the same guilt and fear that motivate repression in neurotic patients tend to cause a general social deficiency in the labeling and discussion of factors such as sex and aggression. For example, the average parent teaches the small child a name for all the important parts of its body, but only a few give it a simple name for its sex organs. In fact there is even a certain amount of mislabeling: "childhood is the age of innocence," "brothers love each other," "nice girls don't like that," and "we don't have any class distinctions in Jonesville."

The Mechanism of Suppression

The mechanism of repression can best be understood after a brief discussion of a somewhat similar mechanism, suppression, that is a much more familiar part of everyday experience. A group of people are engaged in pleasant conversation at a party. Somehow the topic is introduced of people who have recently had strokes or heart attacks. Quite a few cases are known by different members of the group. This is a painful subject; it raises the general level of anxiety of everyone present. Finally someone says, "How did we ever get on this gruesome subject? Let's talk about something else!" The topic of conversation is changed and everyone feels relieved. According to our principles, the reduction in anxiety should tend to reinforce the responses of making the suggestion and changing the topic of conversation. In general, this seems to be true; people tend to learn to avoid unpleasant topics of conversation.

There are apparent exceptions and it would be worthwhile to study these. Sometimes the reinforcement for talking about something unpleasant obviously lies in an invidious comparison with those who are unfortunate; at other times it may involve the indirect expression of aggression or factors such as those already discussed in the previous chapter under the heading of how a symptom may be reinforced in spite of being maladaptive.

The process of avoiding painful topics can be highly self-conscious and verbalized as it was in this example and is when one reminds himself not to talk to Mr. X about politics or tries to put the thoughts that prevent sleeping out of one's mind by counting sheep. In this case the process is called suppression.

The same thing also tends to occur automatically. For example, there was a good deal of discussion in intellectual circles about the atomic bomb immediately after the war. This topic tended to arouse anxiety. Under present conditions of world politics, there seemed to be no practicable way to reduce this anxiety by making and following through any plan of action. Thus the anxiety persisted until the topic of conversation was changed. Often the change occurred inadvertently, without any verbal statement or thought about the desirability of change. Nevertheless the reinforcing effect of the reduction in anxiety was automatic so that the change tended to occur sooner and sooner until the atomic bomb was crowded out of many people's conversations and thoughts.

When one is slightly worried or tense, sports, reading, and recreation help to crowd the painful thoughts out of one's mind and thus tend to produce a reinforcing reduction in the painful drive. For example many people read in order to relax before going to bed and are more likely to read when they feel particularly anxious, nervous, or guilty.

Where changing to a new subject is a response to a verbal suggestion, as it was in the first example, another verbal suggestion can elicit a change back to the old subject. Many of the more automatic habits of changing the subject can also be reversed by motivations that are under verbal control. Thus a soldier may strongly dislike to discuss his combat experiences and have learned the habit of not thinking about them but can be made to talk about them if he wants to please the interviewer.

The Mechanism of Repression

Repression is similar to suppression except it is much more strongly motivated and is automatic; that is, the patient does not say "I want to repress this." Because it is not under the control of verbal cues and is so strongly motivated, it is not within the patient's power to revoke. The patient may try to remember but be unable to, just as someone who is afraid of high places may try to jump across a narrow gap at a great height but may involuntarily come to a halt at the brink. According to our analysis, repression is the symptom of avoiding certain thoughts; it is reinforced by drive reduction in exactly the same way as the symptoms that have already been discussed.

Some of the clearest examples of repression are the amnesias of men with combat neuroses (Grinker and Spiegel, 1945a and 1945b). In these cases the therapists know the events have recently occurred and often can learn the specific conditions from the man's comrades. They also know that the patient cannot remember these events; often they see him struggling hard to try to fill in the gaps. Finally they know that the amnesia is functional rather than organic because the patient can be made to remember by pentothal and psychotherapy. Incidentally, this differentiates amnesia from malingering, which is not affected by pentothal (Grinker and Spiegel, 1945b, pp. 47, 95, 110). In the light of these facts, there is no doubt about the reality of repression in such cases.

We would analyze the learning of this repression in the following way: During combat the soldier is being stimulated by many external cues. He is also producing internal cues by his perceptual responses, his labeling of the salient features of what is going on, and his thoughts about what he is doing. The traumatic conditions in combat attach strong fear to all these cues. This fear generalizes to other similar cues, and the stronger it is the wider it generalizes.

Later when the soldier starts to think about what happened, his memories, or, to speak more exactly, his thoughts and the images they provoke, are cues similar to the ones that were present in combat. Hence these thoughts and images evoke extreme fear.

As soon as the soldier stops thinking about his experience in combat, the cues eliciting the fear are removed and the fear is reduced. This marked reduction in the strength of fear strongly reinforces the response of stopping thinking. In mild cases this produces a disinclination to think and talk about combat; in severe cases it produces a complete inability to think or talk about the experience.

We would expect the response of stopping thinking to tend to become anticipatory like any other strongly reinforced response. Therefore the patient should tend to stop thinking, or veer off onto a different line of thought, before he reaches the memory of the traumatic incident. He should learn to avoid not only thoughts about the fear-provoking incident but also the associations leading to those thoughts.

Because their previous social training has produced a strong motivation to be oriented and label things accurately, patients tend to be uneasy when they are unable to remember and give a complete logical account of their experiences. Therefore the drive motivating repression has to be quite strong before its responses can overcome those of labeling and remembering.

Since stronger fears generalize more widely and perhaps also are transferred farther by higher-order conditioning, they stop a wider range of cue-producing responses. The milder cases lose a relatively few memories directly related to combat; the fairly extreme cases lose a large number of memories; and in the most extreme cases, all responses of thought, perception, and speech are stopped so that the patient is in a complete stupor.

The extreme cases are particularly instructive. Just as would be expected from our analysis, the progressive reappearance of the cue-producing responses more directly associated with combat is accompanied by a progressive increase in fear. To quote Grinker and Spiegel (1945b, p. 10): "In a stage of stupor, the patient is quiet, and with the gradual recovery of speech some slight signs of anxiety appear, such as tremor and startle reaction to noises. As a rule, the recovery of the forgotten experiences is attended with increasing anxiety, and the memory of the actual traumatic event produces intense anxiety."

Such patients can often be observed struggling to remember and produce a logical account for themselves. Often they report that this struggle makes them anxious, produces headaches or dizziness so that they have to stop trying. When an interviewer motivates them to try harder, they report symptoms of distress, especially when they seem to be on the verge of remembering. Similarly, when the memories are revived by pentothal (by a process that will be described in Chap. XXIII), they elicit strong fear. In short, the immediate result of removing repression, like the interruption of any other reinforced symptom, is an increase in drive. This is exactly what is demanded by our hypothesis.

Stopping Thinking as a Response

Repression is somewhat harder to understand than other symptoms because we are not used to considering the stopping of thinking as a response. We cannot point to it and study it in the same way that we can examine overt responses.

Yet to stop talking is obviously a response. Everyone has had the experience of catching himself just in time before blurting out something he would have regretted saying. It is possible to learn either to stop talking about certain limited subjects or to stop talking altogether in some situations. According to our hypothesis, stopping thinking is a somewhat similar response. We do not know to what extent there is any mechanism for producing a generalized response of stopping thinking analogous to the way that clamping the jaws together and keeping the lips closed can stop all talking, but we do know at least that it is possible for a given thought to be crowded out by others. In fact, it seems to be impossible to have two different thoughts in the same modality of imagery at exactly the same time.

It is interesting to note that one of the frequent symptoms of extreme combat anxiety cases is an interference with speech that may run from complete muteness to hesitation and stuttering (Grinker and Spiegel, 1945a, p. 84; and 1945b, pp. 4, 5). Similarly, the sufferer from acute stage fright is unable to speak. Many animals tend to stop vocalizing when frightened, and it is obvious that this tendency is adaptive in preventing them from attracting the attention of their enemies. In the light of this evidence one might suspect that the drive of fear has an innate tendency to elicit the response of stopping vocal behavior. Because of the close relationship between talking and thinking and because of normal examples of the mind going blank during extreme fright, one might speculate that the drive of fear also has an innate tendency to stop thought. This would greatly facilitate the learning of repression by making the response of stopping thinking more likely to occur so that it could be reinforced by a reduction in the fear that had been elicited by the thoughts.

How Children Learn to Fear Certain Thoughts

Under the conditions of severe combat it is easy to see how intense fear can get attached to the associated web of words and images that comprise the memory of a traumatic event. Under normal circumstances, most adults are able to avoid such severe conditions. As we have said before, small children are so extremely helpless and dependent that they can sometimes be subjected to conditions that are as frightening to them as the traumatic conditions of combat are to adults. A number of these conditions may attach strong fear, guilt, or disgust to certain words and thoughts.

Many children are punished for saying certain "nasty" words. This punishment can be direct and obvious, as in slaps and spankings, or indirect and subtle, as in an implied disapproval or threat to withdraw love and support. With the helpless and dependent infant such threats can be a great deal more frightening than they are for the relatively resourceful and independent adult. Anyone who has seen the panic of a small child who has lost his mother knows how terrorizing that experience can be for certain children. Apparently various statements of disapproval that threaten loss of love and support sometimes can evoke similar strong fears.

Fear is also attached to words and sentences when a child is punished for announcing his intent to perform forbidden acts. In our society openly stated defiance and intentional wrongdoing is much more severely punished. This general attitude of our culture is crystallized in laws that make a premeditated crime more serious than an unpremeditated one.

In addition parents may imply punishment by their general attitude. The effects of this, and also of other unknown conditions, are illustrated in the report of a neurotic patient, Mrs. A:

With my mother I could never discuss anybody's being pregnant. She wouldn't say they were pregnant. She'd say, "Oh, she's *so big*"—and she'd say it as though she were hitting me. It felt to me like she was hitting me. The way my mother would talk about pregnancy was sickening. It was something wrong—can I use the word—it was something *dirty*. Once when a girl had a miscarriage, she talked about it—I didn't want to listen to it!

We have discussed how fear can get attached to words spoken out loud. Experimental evidence indicates that fear attached to a word spoken out loud will generalize to the thought of that word. Miller (1950) presented the letter "T" and the figure "4" to a subject who was required to pronounce them aloud when he saw them. The "T" was always followed by a shock and the "4" never, until the subject learned to respond to the "T" with a large conditioned galvanic skin response, presumably indicating fear, and to the "4" with a much smaller one. After a discrimination had been established during an unpredictable sequence of presentations, the subject was presented with a series of dots and instructed to think "T" to the first one, "4" to the second, and so on alternately. The results are shown in Fig. 12. Large galvanic responses appeared after the dot eliciting the thought of "T" and small ones after the dot eliciting the thought of "4." In other words, the involuntary conditioned galvanic responses, which the subject did not know he was making, generalized from the cues produced by pronouncing the words aloud to those produced by thinking them. This would seem to indicate a considerable degree of similarity between the cues produced by saying and thinking the same words.

In the light of this evidence we would expect the fears that are attached to saying forbidden words and announcing the intent to perform forbidden acts to generalize to thinking these words and thinking about performing these acts. These generalized fears would be expected to be somewhat weaker than the original ones. With enough experience of being punished for the words and acts but not for the thoughts, a discrimination should be learned and further weaken the fears attached to the thought. But if the fears are so strong that the thoughts are repressed, the thoughts will not occur so the fears attached to them cannot be extinguished and no discrimination can be learned.

Fears can be attached to spoken sentences and generalized to thoughts; they can also be attached directly to thoughts. For example a child may have a "bad" thought just before he performs an act that is immediately punished. In this case the punishment

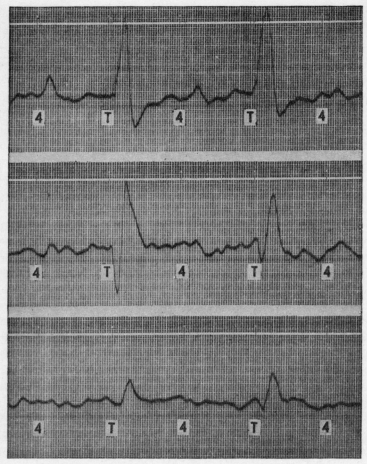

Fig. 12. The generalization of conditioned galvanic skin responses from words pronounced aloud to thoughts. The subject was presented with T followed by an electric shock and 4 not followed by shock in an unpredictable order. He named each symbol when he saw it. After a discrimination had been established, the subject was presented with a series of dots and instructed to think 4 when he saw the first dot, T when he saw the second, etc. These are his galvanic responses to presentations 1–5, 11–15, 21–25. (*From Miller*, 1950.)

will reinforce fear to the cues produced by the thought as well as to those involved in the physical performance of the act.

Often the child is not caught in the act and the punishment is delayed. In such cases the parent usually tells the child what he is being punished for and the child listens and thinks about it while receiving the punishment. Thus the fears are attached to the thought as well as to the deed. In fact, according to our analysis, this is the only way short of physically rehearsing the crime that a delayed punishment can be made effective.[1]

Sometimes parents, with their superior intelligence and experience, can tell what a child is likely to do before he says or does anything obvious. Thus they may warn the child when he has an evil thought before he has made any gross overt response. Such warnings attach fear to the thought and help to break down the discrimination between thoughts on the one hand and spoken words and acts on the other. To the small child it is as if the parents could read his mind.

As a way of stopping tabooed acts before they get started, our society specifically tries to attach anxiety to evil thoughts. This is represented by the religious doctrine that bad thoughts, bad words, and bad deeds are equally punishable. It seems likely that this culture pattern exerts a strong influence on the training of the conscience of the child. Unfortunately we do not have the detailed direct observation that would be required to give a rigorous account of this process in terms of our theory.

Theoretically a number of factors could influence the strength of the fear attached to thoughts and memories by the conditions we have been describing. The innate capacity for strong responses of fear may vary with the structure and physiology of the individual much as the capacity for a strong grip or a long jump. Early experiences can establish strong dependence on the parents that will

---

[1] After such punishment, the thought of performing the response may either evoke fear directly or evoke the thought of punishment which in turn evokes fear. Thus when the child thinks about and starts to perform the punished act he feels afraid. This motivates resolving not to perform it and stopping, which removes the thought producing the fear so that the resolve to stop and the response of stopping are reinforced by a reduction in the strength of the fear.

make any threat of non-cooperation on their part more terrifying. Early experiences can establish a generalized response of anxiety to most of the cues in the environment. Then any new experience will summate with the anxiety and produce stronger fear just as a strange noise at night frightens one more if for some reason he is already apprehensive. Some children may be punished more severely or inadvertently subjected to more severely traumatic situations. Finally, the punishments or other traumatic events may happen to occur in such a way that they hinder forming the discrimination between thoughts on the one hand and spoken words and acts on the other.

When a fear is weak or the discrimination between thoughts and deeds is good, normal prudence in spoken statements and overt acts will be motivated and reinforced along with perhaps a reluctance to think certain thoughts. When the fear is extremely strong and the discrimination poor, repression will be motivated and reinforced. Between the two there will not be a sharp dichotomy but a continuum.

Importance of Mild Repression

The milder forms on this continuum, where the person can think or remember but tends not to, are also important. For example, the fear aroused by thoughts of death or injury may motivate and reinforce the tendency to avoid planning adequately for these contingencies. Insurance salesmen are used to meeting resistance on this score. Other common examples are forgetting to carry out an unpleasant task such as answering a long-delayed letter or totaling up the budget when one suspects that the expenses may be exceeding the income. Even a scientist may have his reasoning interfered with by the tendency to avoid facts or topics that raise anxious doubts about his theories. Recognizing this, Darwin formulated his famous rule: "That whenever a published fact, a new observation or thought came across me, which was opposed to my general results, to make a memorandum of it without fail and at once . . ." (Darwin, 1898, Vol. I, p. 71).

Finally, as we have already pointed out, the same fear that tends to motivate repression in children motivates adults to be reluctant to talk. The adults do not teach the children good labels or drill them in good explanations in the first place; this initially defective verbalization is likely to be further damaged by repression.

How Repression Can Prevent Seeing Connections

If a subject tends to avoid thinking about certain facts, he is less likely to see a connection between them.   There is another mechanism, however, which would be expected to produce a stronger effect of this kind.

If a response is reinforced whenever two or more cues occur in combination but not when these cues occur separately, the response will tend to be elicited by the combination but not by its separate elements (Pavlov, 1927; and Hull, 1943).   This is called *patterning*.   Thus where the social conditions are such that punishment or other fear-provoking circumstances are associated with a particular combination of thoughts but not with the two separately, we might expect the patient to be able to respond with each separately but be specifically motivated to avoid the combination.

Sometimes the conditions of the incest taboo and family life seem to produce a result of this kind, although the situation is complex and admittedly mixed with other factors.   The small boy may have tender feelings and respectful thoughts toward his mother and sister because they take care of him.   At the same time any obviously sexual responses toward them are strongly punished and labeled "nasty."   By the mechanisms we have been describing, the fear of these responses also gets attached to sexual thoughts directed toward the mother and sister.   At the same time the tender feelings and respectful thoughts are a part of the stimulus pattern.

As we have already seen in our discussion of displacement, the inhibiting tendencies motivated by fear seem to generalize less widely than the responses that they inhibit.   For this reason a small boy may have less anxiety about having sexual phantasies or even displaying sexual behavior toward girls that are quite different from the mother and sister.   As was shown in Chap. X, these phantasies may be strongly reinforced by accompanying masturbation or in other ways.   Frequently the girls will be of a lower class or even of a different race labeled as "not to be respected" or even "nasty" by the parents.   Furthermore the label "nasty" may tend to be transferred by the cues produced by the sexual thoughts and responses. Finally, the sexual thoughts and responses will often not be subject to punishment in this context.

The net result of this situation is that the pattern of cues produced by sexual thoughts and feelings in combination with tender feelings and respectful thoughts is associated with punishment while the pattern of cues from sexual thoughts and feelings in the absence of tender thoughts and feelings or in the presence of disrespectful thoughts is associated with less punishment and is followed by sexual reinforcement. As a result, the boy can have either tender feelings and respectful thoughts toward a girl or else sexual thoughts, but the combination arouses anxiety. This motivates and reinforces responses incompatible with one or the other parts of the combination. It becomes difficult or impossible for the boy to think of the same girl in both ways. This is a fairly common phenomenon in our culture; Freudians (*e.g.*, Klein, 1948, p. 308) call it the "split imago."

In still other cases the fear motivating and reinforcing a tendency toward repression may be attached more specifically to the statement of the causal relationship. A superficial analysis of the function of language makes it clear that a sentence put together in such a way as to state two facts in a causal relationship serves as a different cue eliciting different courses of action (or other sentences) than one that states the two facts without causal relationship. The exact details of perception and patterning involved in a complex example of this kind are not yet known, but the general fact is obvious. It is also apparent that some of the social conditions of punishment in our culture are such that anxiety is attached to precisely such a causal relationship or intent. Thus a child is less likely to be punished if he is angry and performs no destructive acts or if he performs a destructive act inadvertently without a hostile intent; he is more likely to be punished if he performs a destructive act *because* he is angry. Thus it is not surprising that a patient may be able at one time to label a hostile feeling and at another time to label a destructive act but be specifically motivated to avoid seeing the connection between the two. In terms of our analysis, "seeing the connection" will arouse strong anxiety and denying it will be reinforced by a reduction in the strength of this anxiety.

What Drives Can Motivate Repression?

Theoretically any strong drive that is elicited by response-produced cues, and thus reduced when the responses producing those cues are stopped, could motivate and reinforce repression. It can be seen that it would have to be a learnable drive because as far as we know response-produced cues, at least those involved in language, have no innate tendencies to arouse strong drives. Since fear is an exceedingly strong drive that is readily attached to new cues by learning, it plays an important role in repression. Some other learnable drives are guilt, pride or shame, disgust, and the desire for independence.

There is some evidence that extremely hungry or thirsty people may under some circumstances tend to suppress the appetite-arousing, or in other words tantalizing, thoughts of food or water (Carlson, 1916, p. 136; Franklin, Schiele, Brozek, and Keys, 1948).

While other drives theoretically could, and perhaps do, motivate repression, we believe that fear and its derivatives, such as guilt, probably are the most important because they seem to be much stronger than the others. For example, the strength of emotion in a dream in which one's pride is hurt is quite different from the terror experienced in a vivid nightmare.

Three Different Types of Repression of a Drive

The three different ways in which repression may intervene in a drive sequence are illustrated diagrammatically in Fig. 13.

1. *Inhibition of responses labeling the drive.* In this case the drive would be present but unlabeled. For example, a person may be sexually excited without expressing this in appropriate words or may even mislabel the state as nervousness or something else. Similarly a person may be actually afraid but not admit it even to himself. In this case the ridicule and shame of being a coward provides the motivation and reinforcement for failing to label or for mislabeling the fear.

2. *Inhibition of responses producing the drive.* If the drive is response-produced, and according to our hypothesis all learnable drives are response-produced, it should have all the properties of a response. One of the properties of a response is that it can be

inhibited by stronger competing responses. Thus it should be theoretically possible for the response producing a drive, such as fear, to be inhibited, in which case the drive itself would disappear (Miller, 1950).

There is some evidence that this sort of thing does occur. For example, if a person with a given level of sex motivation is brought

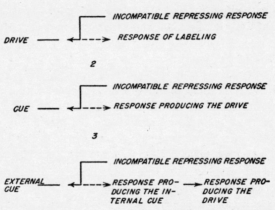

FIG. 13. Three different places at which repression can intervene in a drive sequence: (1) inhibition of responses labeling the drive; (2) inhibition of responses producing the drive; (3) inhibition of responses mediating the drive.

into a sexually exciting situation, certain internal and external responses occur, one of the most obvious of which is tumescence. These responses, in turn, produce a considerable increase in sexual motivation. If the person is then strongly frightened, this will inhibit the responses producing sexual excitement (for example, produce detumescence) and thus markedly reduce his sex appetite. Similarly disgust can spoil the appetite for a particular food.

Since learned drives are just beginning to be studied in the laboratory, we do not have a great deal of definitive experimental evidence on the possibility of their inhibition by competing responses. One experiment by Pavlov (1927, p. 30), however, suggests that even the presumably innate fear of painful stimuli can be inhibited by other learned responses. He used electric shock, cauterization, and pricking of the skin as conditioned stimuli for feeding. Starting very hungry dogs with mildly painful stimuli and working up to strongly painful ones, he observed that the original defense responses and also the physiological signs of fear disappeared. To quote him:

Subjected to the very closest scrutiny not even the tiniest and most subtle objective phenomenon usually exhibited by animals under the influence of strong injurious stimuli can be observed in these dogs. No appreciable changes in the pulse or in the respiration occur in these animals whereas such changes are always most prominent when the noxious stimulus has not been converted into an alimentary conditioned stimulus.

Similarly Jones (1924) eliminated a child's fear of a rabbit by first showing the rabbit at a distance when the child was eating and then gradually bringing it nearer until the child ate with one hand and petted the rabbit with the other. Apparently the responses reinforced by eating tend to be somewhat incompatible with fear so that they can be used to inhibit it.[2]

3. *Inhibition of responses mediating the drive.* In the case of mediated learned drives the responses producing the drive are not attached directly to external cues but are attached to the cues produced by other responses. For example, a given situation might not immediately elicit anger until the person said to himself something like "Why he is insulting me!" Then the thought of the insult would elicit the anger. This might even occur sometime after the incident was over. In such cases the inhibition of the mediating responses (*i.e.,* those that produce the cues that elicit the drive-producing ones) will eliminate the drive. Thus in some cases stopping thinking about insults can tend to reduce anger. Similarly stopping thinking provocative thoughts can help to relieve sexual excitement.

It can be seen that the second and third types of repression are different from the first in that the drive itself tends to be weakened. In the first type the drive itself is present at full strength, though unlabeled and unreported. Such unlabeled drives will be expected to function as unconscious motivations for symptomatic behavior.

---

[2] According to one theory (Miller, 1950), the extinction of fear may be produced by the reinforcement of stopping being afraid.

The three types of repression are paralleled by three types of suppression. Before such suppression can work, however, the proper incompatible suppressing responses must be attached to verbal cues and be strong enough to override the responses they are suppressing. This is discussed in more detail in Chap. XXX.

Unconscious Reinforcement

According to our hypothesis, all reinforcements have a direct automatic strengthening effect on immediately preceding responses. Thus the primary effect of a reinforcement is always unconscious. In addition to this primary effect, it is possible for a reinforcement to have other effects that are mediated by verbal responses. Thus, after a good deal of social training, a boy who is mowing the lawn in order to earn a dollar may be tempted to quit but may think, "I must finish or else I won't get paid the dollar that I need." As has already been suggested, the remote effects of reinforcement are mediated by verbal and other cue-producing responses.

There are several different degrees of verbalization of reinforcement:

1. The nature of the reward and its relationship to the response may be labeled, as in the example of the boy mowing the lawn.

2. The reinforcement may be mediated by verbal responses but unlabeled, as in the case of the soldier who felt much less frightened when he noticed that his hand was paralyzed. In such a case it might even be possible for the soldier to report that he felt less anxious without being able to label the causal relationship between this reinforcing event and the response of paralysis.

3. The drive and its goal response may be unlabeled, or the drive may be labeled but the goal response and the fact of drive reduction may be unlabeled and unreported. Examples of this kind have already been given in the discussion of how a symptom could be reinforced in spite of the fact that it apparently produced an increase in the strength of the drive.

How Responses Become "Unconscious" with Overlearning

Often during the early stages of learning, each detail of a complex task is elicited by a verbal cue. Sometimes the verbal cues are directions that are given by an instructor and rehearsed by the student; at other times they are the product of the student's independent reasoning and thought. Thus the person who is just beginning to learn to drive is likely to guide his behavior by detailed verbal directions such as "first put in the clutch, then press the starter and gas, then shift into low, and then slowly let out the clutch." Because his verbal responses are functioning in this way, he is unable to carry on a conversation or to plan for emergencies that may be developing ahead.

While he is practicing, the correct responses elicited by verbal cues are also occurring in the presence of the external cues in the situation and the kinesthetic cues produced by preceding responses. With more practice they get attached to these cues so that the verbal ones can gradually drop out. Since the direct responses are faster, they tend to anticipate, or short-circuit, the verbally mediated ones. Furthermore, as the responses related to each detail of driving drop out, there is less tension-producing conflict with other responses such as talking to companions or thinking about the best route or emergencies that may be looming ahead. After the verbal cues have dropped out, we are likely to refer to the habits as automatic or unconscious.

The fact that the verbal units have been learned as an original part of the performance make this type of "unconscious" behavior quite different from the early childhood habits that were learned without ever having had any verbal components. The fact that there is no strong drive motivating responses incompatible with the verbal ones is also an important difference between this type of "unconscious" behavior and that produced by repression. Thus, when the verbal units have dropped out during overlearning, it is usually relatively easy to recover them if they are needed, though one may experience some difficulty in recovering the appropriate labels and directions when one tries to teach a novice something that one has learned long ago. Finally, it is usually only the details that have become automatic; the larger functional units such as starting, speeding up, or passing another car, remain under verbal control.

Where strong drives are involved, however, we would expect them to motivate and reinforce strong habits of direct response to the external cues. If such habits of quick, direct responses become strong enough, they may be able to override the responses mediated by verbal cues. Then the response will no longer be under complete verbal control. This tends to be the case with the response of pressing on the brakes; it is motivated by fairly strong fear in dangerous situations and strongly reinforced by a reduction in the fear as the danger is avoided. That is why it may be difficult for a passenger to prevent himself from pressing on the floor boards when some grave danger suddenly looms ahead.

Two Functions of Verbal Responses

Two different usages of the word "unconscious" parallel the two main functions of verbal and other cue-producing responses. There are two functions of words: (1) they are responses which can be attached to specific cues; and (2) they produce cues which can elicit specific responses. The first of these functions is involved when words are used in labeling and description; it includes a person's public report of how he feels, what responses he is making, and his private thoughts about how he is feeling and what he is doing. The second of these functions is involved in responding to commands and directions from others, and to the commands and directions that one gives to oneself.

Ordinarily the word "unconscious" is used to refer to the absence of the first, or labeling, function of verbal responses. Without this function, the second one is also impossible because the verbal responses must occur before they can serve as cues to elicit instrumental or emotional responses.

The presence of the first function (label as a cue), however, does not necessarily ensure the occurrence of the second, namely, an appropriate instrumental or emotional response. The appropriate response may never have been learned to the verbal cue or it may be overridden by stronger responses to other cues. Thus a person may be quite frightened in a situation that he labels as perfectly safe. He may not have learned responses inhibiting fear to the cue of the word "safe," or the fear elicited directly (i.e., without verbal mediation) by the cues in the situation may be so strong that it overrides the responses elicited by the word "safe." Such a response is also often called "unconscious," even though the person may subsequently be able to report the occurrence of the response and the drives and cues involved.

It can be seen that specifying exactly which function is present or absent is potentially a much more accurate way of describing behavior than merely referring to it as conscious or unconscious.

The Superego, or Conscience, Is Partly Unconscious

Some of the strongest moral sanctions of our society seem to function directly without the mediation of verbal cues and sometimes even without the labeling of what is involved. Thus Freud (1933, p. 99) has pointed out that large portions of the Superego (*i.e.*, conscience) are unconscious, and Sumner and Keller (1927) have emphasized the unconscious force of the mores. Some of these responses may be unconscious because their strong emotional components were learned before the child could talk and think clearly. In other cases the responses may have been originally elicited by verbal cues but have been so strongly motivated and reinforced that they became strong direct responses to nonverbal cues; thus they are elicited directly and automatically much like the pressing of the floor board by the passenger in the car. The fact that the fundamental mores are not subject to debate may be yet another reason why they tend to be established as direct responses to situational cues so that it is hard to override them by verbally mediated responses. In yet other cases the verbal components may have been repressed because of the fear they evoked.

The following example illustrates the unconscious force of the Superego. A Southern girl who had moved into a Northern liberal social group learned to accept intellectually the idea that Negroes should be treated as equals. When she went to the Savoy Ballroom and saw a Negro man dancing with white women, she did not say or think "This is terrible." But she reacted directly to the sight in front of her with strong emotional responses of disgust. This surprised her. She labeled and reported her strong emotional responses of disgust but was unable to control them by reasoning. In this case the deficiency would seem to lie not in the absence of labels learned from her new friends but in the fact that the strong disgust was elicited directly by the cues in the situation and that strong responses incompatible with disgust were not attached to the new labels.

Functional Differences between Conscious and Unconscious

We have assumed that cue-producing responses, and especially verbal ones, play a crucial role in the higher mental processes. Therefore, we must expect the absence of these responses (or the overriding of the responses they mediate by stronger direct responses) to make an important difference in behavior. To the extent that verbal and other cue-producing responses are missing, either because they have never been learned or because they have been lost through repression, we must expect all of the higher forms of adjustment described in Part III to be missing. It should be remembered, however, that repression is usually limited to certain areas or topics. Therefore, the deficits will not be expected to be general, but will be limited to the functions of the particular cue-producing responses that are lost. For example, a professor may be quite logical and ingenious in the criticisms he expresses of his students; his only defect may be that he fails to label his statements as cruelly aggressive and hence fails to anticipate their demoralizing effect.

Some of the chief deficits to be expected when cue-producing responses are lost by repression will be briefly reviewed.

As a result of social training, distinctive names are given to similar stimulus situations that should be responded to differently. These distinctive labels help discrimination. When they are prevented from occurring by repression, the person should be more likely to respond to the crude sensory similarity of the situations and hence show more primary stimulus generalization.[3] According to our hypothesis this primary stimulus generalization is responsible for displacement. Therefore, there should be more displacement in the unconscious.

When the same label is attached to two distinctive stimulus situations it gives them a certain amount of learned equivalence, or in other words mediates secondary stimulus generalization. Social

[3] An experiment by Birge (1941) that demonstrates the role of verbal labels in transfer and discrimination also shows that this function is dependent on the actual occurrence of the labeling response in the training and test situations.

training and individual experience cause the person to refer to functionally equivalent situations with the same name or phrase. Loss of these cue-producing responses will be expected to decrease the amount of learned (*i.e.*, secondary) generalization and thus cut down on socially sophisticated types of transfer of training. Similarly, the great economy of verbal learning, which stems from the fact that learning a single appropriate label or sentence can mediate the transfer of a large number of different responses, will be lost. In short, there should be more primary and less secondary generalization in the unconscious.

Through their capacity to mediate learned drives and rewards, verbal and other cue-producing responses enable the person to respond foresightfully to remote goals. They free him from the control of stimuli immediately present in the here and now, provide a basis for sustained interest and purpose, and are the basis for the capacity for hope and reassurance. With their removal all these capacities should be lost.

Verbal and other cue-producing responses are the basis for reasoning and planning. The proper definition of a problem is an essential part of reasoning and planning. Interferences with labeling will be expected to prevent the patient from stating the problem at all or cause him seriously to misstate it. The fact that cue-producing responses are not limited by the conditions of the immediate environment and can work backward from the goal enables them to produce solutions to a problem that would be extremely unlikely in the process of instrumental trial and error. In the absence of cue-producing responses, the unique advantages of reasoning and planning should be lost.

Verbal responses are one of the chief means of getting help from others. The inability to give a complete report to them and to react properly to their words will seriously limit the patient's ability to get help from friends who have not been specially trained in decoding mute, unconscious behavior.

Many of our more sophisticated types of social training are in terms of words and sentences. We are trained to put words and sentences together in ways that are logical, to be consistent, and to avoid contradiction, etc. Also, much of our social training to be fair and self-critical, to distinguish between the make-believe and the real, and to be self-controlled is mediated by verbal responses. To the extent that the verbal responses are repressed, all these capacities should be impaired.

According to our hypothesis, the fact that small children are much less able to use language in all the foregoing ways is one of the reasons why their behavior is so different from that of an adult. Thus the general effect of repressing certain verbal responses should be to make the corresponding aspects of behavior much more childish.

All these expectations follow as necessary deductions from our theory. They also seem to be substantiated by the clinical data, fitting Freud's (1925, Vol. IV, pp. 118–120) description of the difference between unconscious and consciously determined behavior. According to him the unconscious is distinguished by characteristics such as less discrimination and more displacement, urgent reaction to the immediate present, neglect for the future, timelessness, amorality, lack of reasoning, lack of conformity to the rules of logic, and lack of avoidance of inconsistency or contradiction. According to Freud the attributes of the unconscious may be summarized as primitive and childlike. The therapeutic effect of removing repression is dependent on the far greater adaptiveness of conscious behavior.

Distinctions among Repression, Suppression, Overt Inhibition, and Overt Restraint

A serious misunderstanding of the goal of therapy often arises from the tendency of the general public to identify repression with all forms of restraint. Thus freedom from repression is confused with complete license. We are now in a position to clear up this misunderstanding and lay the basis for a rational policy by pointing out the proper distinctions.

Repression refers to the automatic tendency to stop thinking and avoid remembering. It is not under verbal control; the patient is not helped by being told or by telling himself to think. Its chief consequences have just been described. It eliminates the possibility of planned action but not the direct, unreasoned responses to drives and cues. Sometimes it may help to eliminate certain learned drives, but the primary, unlearned ones are unaffected.

Suppression also refers to stopping thinking and avoiding remembering. As long as it is operating its consequences are similar to those of repression, but since it is elicited by verbal cues, it can be highly selective and easily reversible and can show all the adaptive subtleties of the higher mental processes.

Overt inhibition will be used by us to refer to the prevention of instrumental responses by strong conflicting responses that are not under verbal control. Thus a patient is sexually inhibited when he is unable to perform normal sexual responses. Because the same social conditions are likely to produce both repressions and inhibitions, repressions that stop thinking are likely to be correlated with inhibitions that stop action. Similarly the reduction in the fear that motivates one is likely to relieve the other. Whenever the conditions for learning or unlearning them are different, however, they will be expected to vary independently. Thus, it is often observed in the course of psychotherapy that a person may have "insight," *i.e.,* have the correct sentences to describe his behavior, but may still be "sick," *i.e.,* be unable to make the responses that would relieve the misery of conflict.

Overt restraint will be used by us to refer to the prevention of an instrumental response by conflicting responses that are under verbal control. Since restraint is under verbal control, it can be much more highly selective and readily reversible and can show all the adaptive subtleties of the higher mental processes. Since suppression and restraint are both under verbal control, they are likely to be correlated. Furthermore, the suppression of provocative thoughts often aids in restraining undesirable acts.

The goal of therapy is to cause the patient to unlearn the crude responses of repression and inhibition, especially when they are out of line with current social conditions. For these crude responses he learns to substitute the much more discriminative ones of suppression and restraint. Since these are under verbal control, they have all the advantages of the higher mental processes. The result is not an escape from the mores of his group. To attempt this escape would almost certainly be maladaptive. In fact the foresight that comes with the removal of repression may help the patient to be on his guard and to exercise socially useful restraint.

CHAPTER XIII

THE INTERACTIONS AMONG THE BASIC FACTORS INVOLVED IN NEUROSIS

Now that the main factors involved in neurotic behavior have been discussed separately, some of the most important interactions among them can be summarized. These are illustrated diagrammatically in Fig. 14.

Let us begin with fear, guilt, and the other drives that motivate conflict and repression. Since fear seems to be the strongest and most basic of these, we shall simplify the discussion by referring only to it.

In the neurotic, strong fear motivates a conflict that prevents the occurrence of the goal responses that normally would reduce another drive, such as sex or aggression. This is called overt inhibition. It is produced in the following way. The cues produced by the goal responses (or even first tentative approaches to the goal) elicit strong fear. This motivates conflicting responses such as stopping and avoiding. The reduction in fear, when the neurotic stops and retreats, reinforces these conflicting responses.

Because the conflicting responses prevent the drive-reducing goal responses from occurring, the drives (such as sex and aggression) build up and remain high. This state of chronic high drive is described as misery. At the same time, the high drives tend to evoke the approaches (or other incipient acts) that elicit the fear. Thus the neurotic is likely to be stimulated by both the frustrated drives and the fear. Finally, the state of conflict itself may produce additional strong stimuli, such as those of muscular tension, which contribute to the misery.

Fear or guilt also motivate the repression of verbal and other cue-producing responses. The fact that certain thoughts arouse fear motivates stopping them, and the reduction in fear reinforces the stopping. Repression is similar to overt inhibition except that it

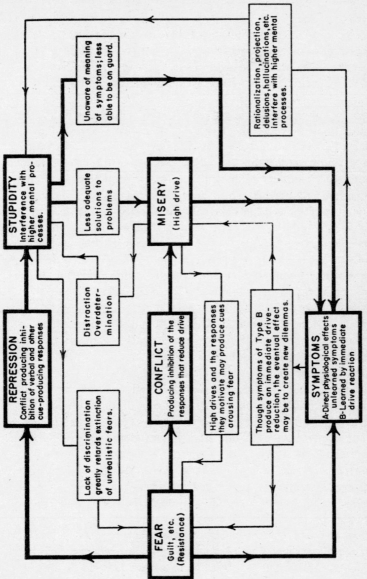

Fig. 14. Schematic diagram of some basic factors involved in neuroses. Arrows indicate "produces" or "tend to contribute to." Heavy arrows indicate major causal sequences; lighter arrows, subsidiary ones.

is a conflict that interferes with thinking instead of one that interferes with acting.

Since the verbal and other cue-producing responses are the basis
for the higher mental processes, the repression of these responses
makes the neurotic stupid with respect to the specific function of
the responses that are repressed. One of the functions of the cue-
producing responses is to aid in discrimination. When they are removed by repression, it is harder for the patient to differentiate
the situations in which he has been punished from similar ones
in which he has not. Interference with such discriminations greatly
retards the extinction of unrealistic fears and thus helps to perpetuate the vicious circle of fear, repression, stupidity, lack of discrimination, and persistence of unrealistic fear.

The stupidity in the areas that are affected by repression also
tends to prevent the neurotic from finding adequate solutions to
his problems and to cause him to do maladaptive things that contribute to his state of high drive or, in other words, misery. At
the same time the misery tends to interfere with clear thinking and
thus contributes to his stupidity. The high drives make it harder
for him to stop and think. They overdetermine or, in other words,
motivate certain thoughts so strongly that they occur in inappropriate situations. They produce preoccupation that distracts him
from thinking clearly about other matters.

Both the fear and the drives that build up when their goal responses are inhibited by fear tend to produce symptoms. Some
of these are unlearned physiological effects of the chronic state of
high drive. Others are learned responses that are reinforced by
the immediate drive reduction that they produce. These symptoms
may be motivated by either of the drives in the conflict, but they
are often compromise responses that are motivated by both drives.
Similarly they may be reinforced by producing a partial or complete reduction in either one or both drives. Where more than one
conflict is involved, the symptom may have still more sources of
motivation and reinforcement. Other things equal, the response
with the most sources will be most likely to occur as a symptom.

Though the immediate effect of the learned symptoms is a partial
reduction in the strength of the drive, the long range effects, as in
the case of alcoholism or a phobia that prevents a man from going

to work, may be to create new dilemmas that contribute to the fear, guilt, and other high drives. The unlearned symptoms, such as stomach acidity, also may create new dilemmas that increase the height of the drives.

The fact that repression has impaired the patient's ability to think intelligently about his problems is also an important factor in the production of maladaptive symptomatic responses. Repression often prevents the patient from labeling the cause of his symptoms and makes them seem something utterly mysterious and uncontrollable. Because he has not labeled the impulses involved, he is less able to be on his guard. He is also frequently prevented from thinking clearly about the consequences of his symptoms. At the same time, some of the symptomatic responses (such as rationalization, projection, delusions, and hallucinations) may seriously interfere with the higher mental processes and contribute to his stupidity.

This is a general sketch of the most important factors in neurotic behavior. In specific cases the relative importance of the different factors can vary greatly with the original conditions of learning, the current social conditions, and the individual's innate capacities, such as those for drive, response, and the higher mental processes.

Various kinds of differences in conditions and capacities can occur. For instance, a person may have a strong repression of angry thoughts and inhibition of aggressive acts that spreads to all competitive situations. But through special social conditions of inherited wealth or fortunate occupational opportunities he may be able to avoid all competitive situations. In this case he will suffer relatively little fear, conflict, or misery; all that will be observed is the symptom of excessive meekness. If, however, the social conditions change radically and demand a display of aggression in a fiercely competitive situation, he will suddenly show strong fear, conflict, and misery, which in their wake may bring additional symptoms, rationalization, and other forms of stupid, maladaptive behavior.

To cite another example, a soldier may come out of combat with an amnesia. As long as the amnesia persists, no other factor than repression may be apparent. If the repression is weakened, however, he will begin to show acute fear and conflict between the responses motivated by fear and by loyalty.

For a while, fear, conflict, and misery may be the dominant factors. Then under this high motivation, he may learn an hysterical symptom that is reinforced by a reduction in his fear of returning to combat. With the fear and consequent conflict and misery reduced, the symptom may become the sole obvious feature of his case.

Attempts to demonstrate that the symptom is functional will meet resistance, however, and show that the patient is motivated to repress labeling the connection between the symptom and escape from combat. He may be very hard to convince, unreasonable and stupid on this particular point.

When he is forced to see the connection, his increase in guilt cancels out any reduction in fear, removes the reinforcement, and motivates him to abandon the symptom. This shows that repression played an essential role in the maintenance of the symptom. As the symptom is lost, fear, conflict, and misery will return as major active factors.

PART V
THE NEW CONDITIONS OF
THERAPEUTIC LEARNING

CHAPTER XIV

PREVIEW OF MAIN FACTORS IN THERAPY

The conditions of the patient's earlier life have created his neurosis. Before contrasting these conditions with the newer ones of the therapeutic situation we will attempt a sketch of the common effects on patients which these older conditions have produced. In the typical patient, his friends and relatives have given up the attempt to help him. Perhaps his physician has also thrown up his hands. The patient himself is becoming hopeless. He has suffered long and tried many cures. All have proved vain. The patient's friends and family have stopped listening to him—he has complained too long, never able to explain himself. The environment has proved hostile to the expression of his drives, and he fears prudish rejection and gossip if he tries again. Furthermore, he fears criticism of his thoughts if he speaks them out. He feels that people expect him to be unbearably good in thought and act. He has also suffered a series of wounds to his self-esteem. He finds his own thoughts confusing and sometimes menacing. He has lost confidence in his ability to use his mind. He has been humiliated by his many failures to solve real life problems; he has been forced to attempt to adapt in marriage, school, army, or business and has failed. He senses the contempt of others at these failures. No one understands him and he does not understand himself.

The normal person uses his higher mental processes to solve emotional and environmental problems. When strong drives arise, he learns the responses that reduce these drives. The neurotic has failed to solve his problems in this way. Since he has not learned to solve his problems under the old conditions of his life, he must have new conditions before he can learn a better adjustment. What are these new conditions?

Therapy: New Conditions and Main Factors

As the chief conditions of therapy and the most important effects that they produce are described, it will be seen that these conditions contrast in certain crucial respects with those of the neurotic patient's previous life.

In the therapist the patient finds someone with prestige who pays favorable attention, listens sympathetically, and holds out hope by having enough faith in an eventual cure to attempt treatment. The therapist shows exceptional permissiveness; he encourages the patient to express feelings in speech (but not in direct action) in the therapeutic situation. He does not condemn and is exceptionally able to tolerate the discussion of matters that have caused the patient's friends to show anxiety or disgust. The therapist's composure tends to be imitated by the anxious patient and thus has a reassuring effect. When the patient has always received severe disapproval, the therapist's calm accepting silence is experienced as a great relief and a striking intervention.

In addition to permitting free speech, the therapist commands the patient to say everything that comes to mind. By the free-association technique the therapist sets the patient free from the restraint of logic. The therapist avoids arousing additional anxiety by not cross-questioning. By encouraging the patient to talk and consistently failing to punish him, the therapist creates a social situation that is the exact opposite of the one originally responsible for attaching strong fears to talking and thinking. The patient talks about frightening topics. Since he is not punished, his fears are extinguished. This extinction generalizes and weakens the motivation to repress other related topics that were originally too frightening for the patient to discuss or even to contemplate. Where the patient cannot say things for himself, the therapist helps by attaching a verbal label to the emotions that are being felt and expressed mutely in the transference situation.

The therapist helps the patient to discriminate. First he helps to locate the problem by ruling out false hopes of miracle cures and by subtle means of emphasis. He points out the important difference between thoughts and actions. He contrasts disproportionate fears and actions with the realities of the situation. He brings out the contrast between the helpless past conditions of childhood, in which the fears were learned, and the present social conditions of the adult.

As the fears motivating repression are reduced by reassurance, extinction, and discrimination, and the patient is urged to think about his problems, mental life is greatly intensified. The removal of repressions restores the higher mental processes, which in turn help with further fear-reducing discriminations, reasoning, foresight, hope, and adaptive planning.

The patient begins to try better solutions in real life as fears are reduced and planning is restored. Some of the fear reduction generalizes from thinking and talking to acting. Becoming clearly aware of the problem and of the unrealistic basis of the fear serves as a challenge to try new modes of adjustment. As these new modes of adjustment are tried, the fears responsible for inhibitions are extinguished. When the new responses produce more satisfactory drive reduction, they are strongly reinforced. The reduction in drive and the extinction of fear reduce the conflict and misery. As the motivation behind the symptoms is reduced, they disappear.

In addition to permissiveness, to skill in decoding conflict, and to the ability to aid the patient to label and discriminate, the therapist has skill in "dosing" anxiety. Others have tried to punish the symptoms or force the patient to perform the inhibited act. Both of these methods tend to increase the fear and the conflict. The therapist concentrates on reducing the fears and other drives motivating repression and inhibition, or in other words on analyzing "resistance." He tries to present the patient with a graded series of learning situations. He realizes that the patient must set his own pace and learn for himself; that it is the patient not the therapist who must achieve insight. He does not try to force the patient into any preconceived mold but helps him to develop his own potentialities in his own way within the limits imposed by our culture.

Each of the processes that we have just described goes on bit by bit with the others, and all interact. As fears are reduced by reassurance and extinction, the most lightly repressed thoughts begin to occur and may help the patient in some discriminations and problem solutions. As more strongly repressed and inhibited responses appear, the cues that they produce elicit new and intense fears which must be eliminated by further extinction and discrimination. All these processes will be discussed in more detail in subsequent chapters. Although they go on simultaneously and interact, they must be separated for the purpose of exposition.

Our account will necessarily be schematic and simplified. It is hard to do justice to the great richness, variety, beautiful intricacy, and lawfulness of the phenomena.

CHAPTER XV

SELECTING PATIENTS WHO CAN LEARN

Out of a great deal of experience, psychoanalysts have developed a number of useful rules for selecting patients who can benefit from psychotherapy. Some of these rules are summarized in text books (Fenichel, 1945, pp. 573–581; Alexander and French, 1946, pp. 96–106); many of them are taught in special seminars or transmitted from master to apprentice during supervised practice in therapy. If psychotherapy is learning, these should be rules for selecting patients who can learn under the conditions of therapy. It should be possible to deduce similar rules from a knowledge of the principles of learning and the conditions of therapy. When the rules are logically related to the principles and conditions, it should be easier to remember them and, what is more important, easier to adapt them to new situations.

According to our principles, the following considerations should be important in selecting patients who can learn. These seem to agree quite well with the rules derived from empirical experience and classical analytic theory. In discussing each of them separately, one has to assume that the other factors are equal. Most of the rules are relative matters so that the final prognosis depends on the sum of the various pros and cons.

A learned, not organic, disorder. Sometimes it is possible for learning to compensate for a deficit produced by organic factors, but in order for the disorder itself to be unlearned it must obviously be one that is the product of learning. Thus learned (*i.e.,* functional) disorders will be candidates for psychotherapy while organic ones will not. Sometimes the symptoms will be of mixed origin so that it will be difficult to decide whether psychotherapy will be effective. In case of doubt, organic factors must be ruled out by a thorough medical examination before psychotherapy is attempted.

Motivation for therapy. Motivation is important for learning. Because psychotherapy must overcome conflict, and this inevitably arouses fear, it requires strong motivation. From this point of view, the prognosis is good if the patient is extremely miserable because his misery will motivate therapy, and it is bad if he is self-satisfied. It is good if the patient has enough motivation actively to seek therapy on his own, and it is bad if he must be dragged in or sent by others. Similarly, it is a good sign if the patient is willing to make sacrifices to get treatment and a bad one if he is not.

Other things equal, the more disadvantageous the symptoms are, the stronger the motivation for therapy should be. Some symptoms, such as perversions and drug addictions, are exceedingly effective in reducing drives. Thus the patient has less motivation for therapy and the treatment of such symptoms is exceedingly difficult. The prognosis is improved, however, the more pressure the patient's environment puts on him to abandon these symptoms and the more trouble they cause him. As a measure of his motivation and a way of increasing it if necessary, the patient should be willing to agree in advance to try to resist the drug or perverse habit whenever the therapist thinks this is necessary for the treatment.

Reinforcement of symptoms. The more strongly the symptoms are reinforced the harder it will be to get rid of them, and hence the poorer the prognosis. Symptoms that produce an immediate great reduction in the drives involved in the neurotic conflict will be strongly reinforced even though their delayed effect may be an eventual increase in misery. The strong immediate reinforcement from relatively rapid drive reduction is another reason why drug addictions and perversions are difficult to treat. Secondary gains, such as financially important pensions or compensations in the case of an hysterical paralysis, may also help to reinforce the symptoms and reduce the motivation for therapy. In this case the reinforcement is mediated by thoughts about the pension, but the causal relationship between these thoughts and reinforcement of the symptoms is not labeled by the patient.

Potential rewards for improvement. The prognosis for therapy should be more favorable "the more the patient has to live for," or, in other words, the more rewards he will receive for improvement.

These potential rewards allow the therapist to increase motivation by holding out realistic hopes, and as they are achieved, they reinforce greater effort and consolidate specific gains. Conversely, if the patient's personal capacities and social conditions are such that it will be impossible for new habits to be rewarded, therapy cannot succeed.

Factors such as good physical health, youth, beauty, intelligence, education, or special skills, a good professional position, a good social-class position, wealth, and a good marital partner or prospects increase the possibility of reward and hence are favorable; their opposites decrease the possibilities of reward and are unfavorable. Therefore the prognosis is bad when the disorder is the product of unfavorable environmental conditions that are irrevocable. For example, we would expect it to be difficult to secure lasting cures of combat neuroses if the patients have to return to severe combat immediately upon getting well. Similarly, extremely strong objections to birth control are a disadvantage in a patient who has a sexual maladjustment growing out of conditions making childbirth dangerous or further children a severe economic liability.

Prerequisite types of social learning. The type of psychotherapy that we are describing (essentially the psychoanalytic technique for adult neurotic patients) was devised to remove repression and thus restore the higher mental processes. Certain minimum units of social learning are required before it can be used; it does not provide the conditions for giving the fundamental types of training that the small child receives in the family. Patients with basic deficits in this training will therefore be poor prospects.

Since treatment is carried on by talking, the patients must have a certain minimum ability to use and respond to language. Thus, ignorance or lack of intelligence are handicaps.[1] The technique has to be modified in dealing with young children who are not yet able to use language effectively; it is not applicable to the feebleminded.

---

[1] We are assuming that anyone who has enough intelligence to use language effectively in the therapeutic situation will have enough learning ability for the other aspects of therapy. Therefore having enough intelligence to learn is not mentioned as a separate requirement.

In addition to use of language *per se,* the patient must have had the general training in trying to be reasonable that was sketched in Chap. IX. In other words, the patient must have higher mental processes to restore, and the better these are (or in psychoanalytic terms, the stronger the Ego), the better his prospects for recovery and continued learning on his own when repressions and inhibitions are removed. The person with strong adaptive behavior in certain areas of his life shows that he has these general elements to build on. For this reason severe conflict limited to one area is more favorable than general retardation of the whole development. The more different units of social skill the patient has to learn, the harder his task will be. This task will be especially difficult whenever the conditions for the type of learning that is missing are sharply age-graded. Then the patient may not have the chance to make up what he lost when he was younger. These lacks are apparent in the social sphere—dialectal speech, poor manners, lack of ease in social situations. Perhaps some of them could be made up if the therapist sent the patient to a "charm school."

The conditions for learning some of the fundamental habits essential to the conscience, or Superego, seem to be sharply age-graded. Apparently in our culture it is hard to supply the first units of conscience training once the individual is beyond the strong dependence and the rigorous controls of childhood. Certainly the therapist does not ordinarily control the immediate powerful rewards and punishments that are needed to supply this deficiency. Thus patients, such as criminals and psychopaths, whose basic difficulty is the lack of a conscience, are not suitable for this kind of therapy. Such patients must be discriminated from those who have learned good moral habits but rebelled against them after intense conflict.

Previous adjustment. The patient with a long history of neurosis that started when he was young and continued with no free periods is more likely to have missed valuable units of social skill that will be hard to make up. Furthermore, the early onset and continuous tenure of the neurosis suggest that the motives behind it are strong; in any event the patient will have had more time to practice the bad habits involved. Thus, this is an unfavorable sign. Conversely if the patient has had considerable free periods of good adjustment, he is more likely to have learned useful skills. The later onset and the free periods are likely to mean that the motivations behind the neurosis are weaker and that the bad habits have not been practiced so much. Since the patient has already experienced some of the important rewards, it will be easier for the therapist to arouse the anticipatory goal responses involved in hope and to keep the motivation for therapy high.

Habits specifically interfering with therapy. Any habits that interfere with the responses necessary in the therapeutic situation will make the treatment harder and the prognosis poorer. For example, the psychotic is often unable to listen or to talk reasonably and thus needs to be treated by other methods. Similarly, extreme suspiciousness will interfere with talking to the therapist, listening to what he says, and trying out new responses. Extreme pride, especially when it is an overcompensation for a feeling of weakness or dependence, will tend to prevent the patient from coming to therapy and cooperating after he arrives. He is humiliated by the very fact of temporary dependence on the therapist; it frightens him to be in need of help. Finally, indications that the subject is extremely passive or tends to give up easily will be on the negative side because such tendencies will interfere with the determined trying out of new responses during therapy.

Practical considerations not directly related to learning. Other factors, such as the need for hospital care or restraint, for protection from the danger of suicide, etc., are very important in the selection of patients, but they are in a different category and will not be discussed here.

The Selection of Mrs. A as a Patient

When Mrs. A, the patient who was described in Chap. II, came to the therapist, he had to decide whether to accept her. His decision to accept her rested on these facts:

She was neurotic. Her difficulties (phobias, compulsions, etc.) were the kind that are usually produced by learning. A thorough physical examination revealed no organic defects.

She was intensely motivated. She sought treatment on her own initiative. She was extremely miserable because of the painful anxiety she was suffering and because of her troublesome symptoms.

Although the symptoms brought a few secondary gains (she could not be expected to hold a job, and she received some sympathy), their disadvantages were far greater. Her fear of going out by herself confined her to a lonely, drab two-room apartment and prevented her from going shopping or to the movies. The sympathy of her friends and husband had worn thin; in fact, her husband was so fed up with her illness, which he thought was nonsense, that he threatened to get a divorce. The drives that were blocked by conflict were high. She was so desperate from her failure to solve her own problems that she was afraid she would go crazy.

This patient's prospects of reward for improvement were in general excellent. She had recently made a favorable marriage, having a good husband with fine vocational prospects. She was beautiful, which improved her chances for a successful marital and social adjustment. On the other hand, the fact that she came from a lower social class than her husband gave her the handicap of poor grammar and a deficiency in manners and the social graces. Being past the age at which such things are usually taught and having an unsympathetic mother-in-law instead of a sympathetic mother as a teacher, she would have some difficulty repairing these deficiencies and winning complete acceptance in her new family. However she was young. This meant that she had had less time to practice bad habits and had enough time ahead of her to practice, perfect, and be rewarded for the new responses learned during therapy. She had no children and was therefore not heavily committed. She was not quite as intelligent as the usual psychoanalytic patient but was well within the range of the general population.

She had an adequate conscience and was not criminal. Those acts that bordered on delinquency, such as hitchhiking with truck drivers, seemed to be products of her intense conflict rather than signs of a complete lack of responsibility. In fact, her conscience was too rigid rather than too weak.

She had a strong desire to be reasonable and was able to talk and listen. She was neither psychotic nor overly suspicious. Unfortunately she was somewhat dependent and passive, looking for sympathy and expressing the desire that the doctor provide the cure by drugs or some other means. But when told that the success of the therapy would be strictly up to her, she seemed to be willing to make a courageous try.

Her neurosis was neither long standing nor continuous. Her worry about her heart began only a few months before she came to the psychiatrist. Until her worry about her heart began, she had been able to meet the problems of daily life passably well. This meant that she had had less time to practice all the bad habits involved in a neurosis and more time to learn the good habits necessary for psychotherapy and daily living. Furthermore her neurosis did not interfere with all areas in her life; she was able to make a good adjustment in those areas outside of her neurosis. This gave an additional indication that she had many of the habits necessary for social adaptation and that the motivation behind her neurosis was not maximally strong.

She was not a suicidal risk and did not need hospital or other institutional care.

In view of the patient's high motivation and excellent prospects of reward, the fact that she seemed to have the habits that are prerequisite for therapy, and in the absence of any strong contrary factors, the chances seemed to be good that she would be able to learn under the conditions of therapy.

CHAPTER XVI

FREE ASSOCIATION — PERMISSIVENESS
AND THE COMPULSION TO UTTER

Repression interferes with the neurotic's higher mental processes and prevents him from using these effectively in solving his emotional problems. This repression was learned in a social situation in which fear, shame, or guilt were attached to certain spoken words and generalized from them to thoughts. In therapy a new type of social situation is created, the opposite of that responsible for the learning of repression. In this new type of social situation the patient is urged to say whatever comes into his mind and to be especially sure to resist suppressing those words that he finds himself afraid, ashamed, or reluctant to say. As the patient says words that provoke fear or shame, the therapist does not punish him or show any signs of disapproval; he remains warm and accepting. In this way, the fear, shame, and guilt attached to talking about tabooed topics are extinguished. This extinction generalizes from speaking to thinking. It also generalizes from the painful but not completely repressed topics that are discussed to similar topics that could not be discussed because they were repressed. As the drives motivating repression are weakened by such generalization, it becomes possible to talk about those additional topics that had been weakly repressed, and another cycle of extinction and generalization is initiated. Thus repression is gradually unlearned under permissive social conditions that are the opposite to the punitive ones under which it was learned. This is the general outline of the procedure; the specific steps will now be discussed in more detail.

New conditions permit new learning. We may ask why does the patient not unlearn repression for himself and shake off its hampering effects alone? The answer seems to be that the ordinary conditions of social life favor the learning of repression and favor maintaining it in those who have already learned it. Unless some new circumstances can be brought to bear on the problem, the patient will continue to live his distorted life until its end without relief from neurotic tension.

The therapeutic situation which Freud hit upon after considerable trial and error (Freud, 1924, Vol. I, pp. 253–254) is arranged so that anxiety can be steadily weakened by extinction. As anxiety is reduced, the repressed sentences gradually become articulate. This situation is different from that of childhood in that it is vastly more permissive of free speech and free naming of emotional factors. The constricting conditions of childhood learning are reversed.

Free Association: the Compulsion to Utter

The first of the new conditions of learning imposed on the patient is that of free association. Under the rule of free association the patient is required to say everything that comes to mind immediately, to resist and abandon the etiquette of the ordinary conversation. He is not to reject any thought whatever, be it trivial, personal, embarrassing, obscene, aggressive, or fanciful. The patient is to try hardest to say that which is most difficult. He is to resist the ordinary constraints of logic, and he is not to try for a connected narrative account. If imageal responses occur, he is to describe them since they may be the cues to which emotional responses are attached by primitive mechanisms. In short he is to say immediately what comes to his mind, using his voice to describe what occurs on the stage of the mind much as a radio announcer might give a play-by-play account of a game to his unseeing audience.

The rule of free association is not a mere invitation to speak freely. It is an absolute obligation which is the foundation of the therapeutic situation. It is a compulsion which has some of the rigor of any compulsion. This rule defines the "patient's work" which is to drive ruthlessly through to the pronouncement of sentences which may evoke sickening anxiety. The rule is a force which is applied against the force of neurotic fear. Without it, and unless he follows it, the patient will remain fixed in his neurotic habits and cannot recover the free use of his mind.

Even if he wished to, the therapist could not elicit the relevant information by questioning because he does not know what questions to ask. At the outset the therapist is baffled himself. Furthermore, the patient must *volunteer* information, *i.e.,* he must take the risk of saying what he must say in the face of whatever hampering forces there are. Only thus can extinction of fear occur.

The effect of the rule is to motivate the patient to talk. The intense energy of the neurotic conflict must be put *behind* the work of the therapy. The therapist must discover what the patient's difficulties are and must surmise how the neurotic responses are motivated and rewarded. Looking to the future, he must estimate what motivations and rewards are available for establishing new habits and what conflicting responses stand in the way of these habits. The information needed to form these judgments can come only from the patient.

The patient invariably finds the therapeutic situation surprising— "different" from what he thought it would be. This is natural since the patient inevitably thought it would be like the suppressive situations of his past. It is different in another respect also. The patient has not realized how much of the burden of therapy would be placed upon him. He does not understand the nature of psychological treatment and has little belief in it. He had hoped for a quick, and often passive, cure. He learns, not always with pleasure, that no drugs, surgery, or other physical measure will be helpful.

Free association is not free and easy. Free association is in some respects not aptly named. Certainly it is far from "free and easy." At times and recurrently, the patient finds it very hard work. As he loyally follows the rule he finds mysterious opposition arising within him. He finds that same fear arising which was present when he last tried to talk freely to himself, that is, in childhood. Anxiety reappears at the slightest cues of the forbidden sentences. Habits of suppression also tend to be activated and the patient is inclined to dodge the rule by "private assumptions" that such-and-such matter surely could not be relevant.

Such was the case in the first four hours of the treatment of Mrs. A. These hours were marked by reiteration of her symptoms, by

pleadings for advice, and by silent periods. Each of these manifestations prevented her from getting ahead with her task. On
the fifth day it appeared that Mrs. A was limiting herself to a
narrow area, *i.e.,* "things connected with my illness as I define
them." Mrs. A rehearsed her litany of symptoms and then came
again to the end of her line of thought, saying, "I've told you everything that happened in the last four months." The therapist again
explained the rule of free association and asked her to make no
exceptions to it: nothing was to be left out because it referred to
events before the last four months (when the neurosis became
evident), because it seemed to her unconnected to the illness, or for
any other reason. In short, Mrs. A was to exercise no censorship
and to say what came to her mind. Although Mrs. A followed the
rule with ever better success, she showed the expected tendencies
to repression and suppression whenever a new fundamental theme
was hit upon.

We must not conclude from this discussion that the course of
psychotherapy is one continuous anxiety attack provoked by the
effort to state the forbidden. The rule of free association, though
rigorously stated, is gently and gradually taught. Though therapy is
bound to bring some discomfort, the patient will pause for many a
breather. He will hit on some lines of association of a highly
hopeful and encouraging character. He will find comfort in seeing
some of the dread memories of the past in the proportionate light
of adult reason. The situation is so arranged that, despite stormy
moments, the patient does not dread every hour. Anxiety reduction is intended to be gradual and the amount of anxiety which
the patient is asked to bear, bearable.

New Benign Conditions: Permissiveness

We now turn from the rules of the psychotherapeutic situation
to the nature of the situation itself. From the patient's standpoint,
the novelty of the therapeutic situation lies in its permissiveness.
He is allowed a good turn to talk. His statements are received by
the therapist with an even, warm attention. The therapist is understanding and friendly. He is willing, so far as he can, to look at
matters from the patient's side and make the best case for the
patient's view of things. The therapist is not shocked by what he

hears and does not criticize. The frightened patient learns that here is a person he can really talk to—perhaps the first such person in his life. These permissive circumstances are genuinely new, and they have their great effect. The fears evoked by free communication are gradually extinguished through lack of punishment. If the situation were not so designed, if acid comments and horrified surprise greeted the patient's statements, no extinction of fear, and therefore no therapy, could occur.

Generalization to the therapist. Therapy occurs as part of a relation to another human being. The therapist acts as a focusing stimulus in the therapeutic situation. He is similar to real-world persons whom the patient has known and yet some of his behavior is markedly different from that displayed by other persons in the patient's past. The therapist attempts to define himself as a stimulus as little as possible. Nevertheless, he immediately evokes two types of reaction from his patient which indicate that he is a very important stimulus. Since he is a human being, similar to those who have punished the patient in the past, a great deal of anxiety is immediately and automatically generalized to him. Were this not so, psychotherapy could not occur. On the other hand, the patient views the therapist as a specialist and accords him the prestige of his specialist's role. To the therapist as a specialist, the patient generalizes responses of trust, confidence, optimism. In this role the therapist acquires immediately the capacity to reassure the patient. This capacity to be reassured is generalized from other authoritarian figures and specialists who have, in the past, aided the patient to solve difficult problems.

Therapist not prude, judge, or gossip. Freedom from fear of punishment is a highly permissive circumstance. Thus, the therapist discriminates himself from a variety of frightening human beings, such as the prude, the judge, or the gossip. If necessary, the therapist will indicate that the patient need have no fear of "shocking" him. He is accustomed to viewing the trials, strivings, and failings of others with compassionate neutrality.

The therapist may need to discriminate himself from the judge who listens, evaluates, and condemns. As Hanns Sachs put it in a lecture at the Berlin Psychoanalytic Institute (in 1932), the therapist does *not* act like the bailiff who must warn his prisoner, "What you say may be used against you." The wisdom of this aspect of the therapist's role is evident when we consider how hard it is to get at the truth, say in a court of law, when the defendant resists through fear of punishment.

The patient usually comes to the therapeutic situation with a lively fear of gossip. The therapist may reduce this fear by assuring him that information given will not be passed on. Then the therapist must make good on this assertion—a matter of considerable delicacy in hospitals and clinics where records must be kept. Despite these assurances of reversal of conventional attitudes, the patient will have to "learn" to trust the therapist in the actual situation. Such trust is not automatic but is slowly built up as the patient risks confidences and finds they are not punished.

How the Therapist Rewards Talking

Talking despite anxiety, talking while anxious is "the patient's work." He must be kept at this work if therapeutic results are to occur. Like any other habit, talking while anxious must be rewarded strongly enough so that the net balance of reward is in favor of talking, else the patient will remain silent or will hit upon lines of sentences which do not produce anxiety. This behavior often occurs for shorter or longer periods of time.

The most obvious reward for talking is the full, free, and exclusive attention of the therapist. The therapist is a good listener— sometimes, the patient feels, too good a listener. Usually the patient has a strong need for such attention. He has complained about his difficulties until he has exhausted the patience of his environment, and others have become tired of listening. To such a starved person, the permissive attention of the therapist comes as a new and striking reward. To have others give real thought to one's problems is a frequent precondition of help; the therapist's attention, therefore, makes the patient more hopeful and reduces anxiety at being isolated.

Therapist's acceptance of past. As noted above, the therapist listens, accepts, does not condemn. The patient has been used to being interrupted, judged, and often condemned. The therapist takes the view that what is past had to happen. The patient understands this acceptance as forgiveness which, in a sense, it is. But it is no routine forgiveness based on the supposition that the patient, once forgiven, will go forth and make the same mistake again. The therapist accepts the past because he must do so in order to understand it. Without understanding the past, the future cannot be changed.

Mere catharsis not effective. In this connection we state that we do not accept the "catharsis doctrine" of psychotherapy. This doctrine seems to say that merely telling someone else of one's sins or mistakes will have a therapeutic effect. We would not expect such therapeutic effect from mere recital. If the recital is followed by condemnation and punishment we would not expect the effect of confession to be therapeutic. The patient is not relieved by a confession if he is·told at the end "What an awful thing to do!" Catharsis should work, according to our hypothesis, only under permissive conditions. Its essential features seem to be two: confession followed by nonpunishment may lower guilt or anxiety; being forgiven reduces a sense of isolation and indicates acceptance into the circle of cooperative human beings. Being forgiven also makes it possible for the patient to hope for reward if he tries a new solution.

Therapist's understanding and remembering a reward. Another powerful reward for the patient's work is that the therapist *understands* what the patient is saying. He understands the communications in their literal, obvious sense and often much more deeply, seeing relations between apparently separate acts. In the past the patient has had much trouble in getting his points across; neither he nor anyone else has understood his behavior very well. The patient shows a justifiable annoyance if the therapist is stupid or unable to understand the patient's native tongue.[1]

In this connection, having the therapist remember what the patient has said in the past is one of the most effective guarantees of good listening. Mr. Earl F. Zinn, one of our finest therapists,

---

[1] Dollard remembers his first control at the Berlin Psychoanalytic Institute. Dr. Max Eitingon had secured for him a German patient. Dollard's German, though deemed sufficient for the purpose, was far from overlearned to the point where easy communication was possible. The German patient was correspondingly annoyed whenever the therapist failed to grasp the fine points of a statement.

remarked on the great importance of having the patient feel himself to be "in the therapist's thoughts" even when the interview is not occurring. Zinn mentioned a case where such an indication on the part of the therapist had converted an apathetic patient into one zealously doing the patient's work.

Therapist's calmness and sympathy rewards talking. To have the therapist speak in a calm manner about matters of intense importance to the patient gives marked reward. The therapist is not frightened or appalled by the patient's problems; his manner indicates that he has seen such, perhaps worse, before. The patient's shame or anxiety will be greatly reduced if he is able to assume the therapist's attitude toward his own problems.

The therapist may occasionally reward by direct expressions of sympathy or approval if the patient has had an especially trying time or endured unusual suffering in the effort to carry out his part of the work. But the therapist is careful and niggardly with his approval. He gives no loose sympathy. He tries to place his rewards directly after those actions of the patient which have the best chance of forwarding the therapeutic work. He knows that, to a degree at least, the patient must suffer to learn and that there is no way in which this suffering can be entirely abolished.

Therapist speaks tentatively, does not cross-question. The patient comes to therapy with justified fears that he will be asked to bear more than he can stand. The life situations which have precipitated his symptoms have usually done just this. The therapist therefore does well not to justify any such fears. For example, if he must label unconscious drives or point out unseen connections, he does so tentatively, thus permitting the patient to feel free rather than trapped. He suggests that such-and-such is possible, may be the case, etc. If the patient is alarmed, the therapist does not press.

Furthermore, the therapist does not cross-question his patient. The patient doses himself with the amount of anxiety he can stand at that time. He is not exposed by cross-questioning. Such questioning might punish free association by evoking unbearable embarrassment or fear. In therapy, the patient is able to push his thinking up to his limit without granting himself the margin of safety which he would soon find he needed if he were exposed to interrogation.

The therapist, on his part, must learn to wait and hear his patient out, letting him say what he must say when he is able to do so. The therapist must therefore learn to endure stopping on many a hot trail and failing to complete a factual picture that seemed almost obvious. The patient likes a man who takes his time.

Discrimination between Thinking and Acting

Thinking and acting are for most people so closely joined that the patient frequently fears the same punishments for thinking that would attend the action represented by the thought. The therapist can therefore loosen up the thinking process by making the discrimination between thinking and acting. He points out to his patient that while an act can produce a stimulus to other people and hence evoke punishment from them, the thought produces a stimulus only to the thinker. Therefore merely thinking of punishable courses of action cannot be dangerous since no one can catch him at it. However, since forbidden acts can be and often are punished, the patient should distinguish carefully between thinking and acting. The therapist can guarantee that the patient will not be punished for anything he thinks or says in the therapeutic situation, but he cannot guarantee "no punishment" if the patient throws off restraint and acts. Patients who "fly into action" must be restricted for the time of the therapy to behavior in the verbal and mental spheres. The therapist is trying to remove *repression* of mental activity and not restraint of antisocial acts.

Restriction on acting out. In the same connection the patient is frequently required to delay important actions until an advanced stage of the psychotherapy. Thus, the patient is asked not to change his marital status, not to seek revenge, not to change his job or otherwise to unsettle his significant life relations. The point is that precipitate actions are likely to be prompted by neurotic motives and may produce punishing consequences which are irreversible. The course of psychotherapeutic work turns up a variety of formerly repressed motives, and these are wisely held in check

until the work of undoing repression is relatively complete. This
suppression of precipitate action may at times be felt as a severe
strain by the patient and at other times as a great relief. In the
latter case he realizes that the taboo on action may save him the
punishments attending hasty or unwise behavior.

In early stages of therapy, patients frequently gabble to outsiders
thoughts which are appropriate only to the therapeutic situation.
There are two dangers in this behavior. Such communications
may shock and repel those who do not have the therapist's training
or motivation. Furthermore, these communications constitute a
kind of escape from the therapeutic transaction. The patient
obeys the fundamental rule but in respect to someone else than
the therapist. Such a mock compliance may reduce the patient's
motivation to bring the same material into therapy and so serve to
withhold needed information from the therapist. Therefore it is
sometimes necessary to ask patients to limit "therapeutic" conversation to the therapeutic situation.

How Anxiety Attached to Sentences Is Reduced

The goal of the benign conditions we have been discussing is
"freedom of thought," that is, to make the patient free within his
own mind to consider every possible alternative course of action.
This is a different goal from that of freedom of speech. Speech
cannot be free under all circumstances. It must be guarded in the
light of the various conditions of associative life (*i.e.,* before
children, before women, before strangers, before enemies, etc.).
When *thought* is free, conscious anticipation of punishment and
reward replaces repression and maximum freedom to act adaptively
is gained.

How is freedom of thought achieved in the therapeutic situation? The answer to this question from the standpoint of behavior
theory is clear. The patient must pronounce the forbidden sentences
while being afraid. This is why it is important that the patient
should generalize a certain degree of fear to the therapist and that
the therapist should not indiscriminately reduce fear. If the patient
is not at all afraid, no therapeutic result can occur. As the patient
timidly and reluctantly produces sentences in the face of his fear, the
benign situation already described has its effect. Punishment does

not occur and the fear attached to the formerly forbidden sentences is not reinforced. The patient, just to be sure, may repeat the dangerous statement and again find no punishment follows. Gradually his fear of talking about matters formerly forbidden is extinguished.

The patient is not yet free to think, but the step from talking to thinking must be a short one. The extinction effects which are first attached to talking out loud generalize swiftly to "talking without voice" (thinking). At this point, the patient has achieved his valuable freedom to think.

Fear of real dangers not extinguished. Naturally the patient does not extinguish anxiety to every possible sentence which he can make. To take extreme cases, he is not allowed to be without fear when he is planning murder, incest, or criminal behavior. This discrimination must be made quite clearly by the therapist. The therapist can, so to say, promise nonpunishment for certain activities—those which were once punished but are now no longer forbidden—but the therapist cannot tamper with life's realities. He cannot let his patient, for instance, think that apprehension, trial, and conviction may not follow upon murderous thoughts which lead to murderous acts. The therapist must therefore correctly interpret the real world and its danger signs. He can diminish only those fears which are already out of date in the sense that they are no longer followed by punishment in the actual conditions under which the patient lives. Here again the immense importance of the sociological conditions of the patient's life is evident.

Behavioral view of testing the therapist. In the beginning of therapy the patient's reluctance to talk is not based on rational fear, *i.e.*, on the likelihood of punishment in the real, current world The patient fears—he knows not why. This reluctance to speak is an inevitable event in the course of therapy. In the patient's repertory of forbidden sentences there are some which have strong anxiety attached and others where the anxiety is much weaker. Initially the latter responses appear first. The patient proceeds, as it were, by easy stages, from peccadillo to sin. Technically expressed, he makes his first verbal extinction trials on material with small anxiety attached. As this anxiety is extinguished and the extinction effects are generalized to other cues producing anxiety, he is able to make sentences which evoke stronger anxiety. Thereupon the cycle of fear, extinction of fear, and generalization of extinction effects is repeated. Seen from the outside, this automatic process looks like "testing" the therapist.

For example in the case of Mrs. A this testing behavior was very clear during the seventh hour of treatment. She told the psychiatrist how, as a child, she had snooped in her mother's bedroom while her mother was away, that she had stolen 15 cents from her first-grade teacher, that she once tried to snitch some candy from a store, that she broke a window with a rock on the way home from school, and she once accidentally-on-purpose set a fire in her grandmother's house. The therapist showed no alarm or shock at these disclosures and did not condemn Mrs. A.

It was soon evident that she had really been testing the therapist for she shortly found something much more important to say. A few minutes after the end of the session, Mrs. A came back to the psychiatrist's office and made an important confession. She said, "I have something to tell you. Should I tell you now or wait 'til the next hour?" The therapist encouraged her to say it then and there. Mrs. A continued, "Well, this is very difficult—my brother took advantage of me when I was a child. I never told anyone—not even my husband. You won't tell anyone, will you?" The therapist assured her that he could not tell anyone since he was expected as a professional man to protect the confidences of his patients. It can be seen that any alarm on the therapist's part at an earlier disclosure might have blocked the patient from giving the facts about the seduction.

Reassurance can reduce fear. Although extinction is the fundamental mechanism, there are other ways in which the patient can receive reassurance. For instance, the stimuli of the serene and sympathetic therapist can directly provoke reassurance reactions in the patient. Again, the patient may imitate the verbal and other attitudes of the therapist and thus evoke reassurance reactions in himself. Finally, the patient may reassure himself by making the verbal responses which directly inhibit anxiety, such as telling himself, "This evidently is not as bad as I had thought."

Whenever reassurance occurs under these varied conditions, the reassuring value or anxiety-reducing value must already have been attached to the pertinent cues through prior learning. For instance, if the stimuli of the therapist directly reassure the patient, he must already have learned to quiet down when being helped by a specialist.

Extinction of fear helps creativeness. As the extinction and inhibition of fear responses go on, the patient gets an ever-increasing sense of freedom and creativeness about his mental life. He begins to be conscious of a new power in dealing with the world around him. The sentences that he is trying to unbind from fear are not trivial or irrelevant. They refer to some of his most important needs and motives. Without freedom to think, the patient is helpless in many areas of his life; with it, he gains new powers of choice and self-direction.

Free Associations are Lawful

The watching therapist is repeatedly struck by the fact that free associations are not chance associations. They are bound and necessary. The responses which occur first should be the ones with the strongest algebraic sum of "motivation for" minus "motivation against." As motivation-against is reduced by extinction of anxiety, all the necessary repressed sentences can occur. The impression of something lawful and inevitable is just as clearly gained from this material as from watching the heavenly bodies. The difference is that we know the laws governing the heavenly bodies very much better than we know those governing the human mind.

How Free Association Helps the Patient Recover Lost Memories

In one of his most valuable papers, Freud (1924, Vol. II, pp. 366–376) speaks of different types of remembering which are evoked in the patient by the course of free association. He mentions four types: intelligible verbal memories, fragments of verbal memory, screen memories of early childhood, and "repetition compulsions." Evidently Freud has greatly broadened the concept of remembering and in a manner which is suitable for behavioral analysis.

Behaviorally seen, there seem to be seven different ways of recalling the past. They are: *intelligible verbal statements* which describe the past; *isolated verbal fragments* where fear has broken up correct patterning; *screen memories* of childhood, which are elided, condensed, misaccented verbal statements; *emotional responses* which appear in behavior when old cues are activated; *instrumental responses* which are attached to verbal or emotional cues; lost *symptoms* which reappear when the cues to which they were attached are reactivated; and finally *dreams*, which are stimulated by the revived cues of the past. All these responses are in a certain sense "remembering" since they give information in present times about the responses, conflicts, and life circumstances which prevailed in the past. They are useful, as will be shown, because they help give that knowledge of past conditions of life which makes it possible to discriminate between the past and the present.

At the moment we are interested in how the conditions of free association permit these memory responses to emerge when they have been latent for so many years. Somewhat oversimplified, the process appears to be this: as the patient endures anxiety and produces sentences which have been repressed, these sentences produce cues for many new sentences. The new sentences in turn produce cues for still others. When fear appears as a response to new sentence units, it must be extinguished and the effects of extinction generalized. Once each roadblock of fear is passed, the new sentences and other responses which can emerge are multiplied. The patient experiences these events as a flood of memories and "insights."

More than that occurs, however. The cues of the once-forgotten sentences have yet other kinds of response connected to them. The patient confronts the enigmatic "screen memory" which recurs persistently and yet seems to lead nowhere. It must be decoded like a dream. Meaningless shreds of memory recur. Some of the old sentences evoke emotional responses and these "well up" from the past. In some cases instrumental responses are attached to the cues produced by these emotions as when the patient feels an inexplicable compulsion to strike his therapist. Together these emotions and instrumental responses constitute the "repetition compulsion" described by Freud. Symptoms which once reduced childhood stresses reappear by the same mechanism. Verbal descriptions of forgotten dreams recur and, on occasion, the dreams of childhood are redreamed during the course of therapy. In each case these are viewed as responses to the cues produced by reactivated memories or emotions. It is not always possible for the patient immediately to label the emotional responses which occur; they appear, tucked into the stream of response, in ways not intelligible. The study and utilization of these emotional reactions is part of the subject matter of transference and will be further discussed under this heading. For the patient, the course of free association does more than create enigmas; it produces a great clarification concerning his past, an attempt at understanding and evaluation, and often bitterness, woe, and remorse. For the therapist, it produces some of the most essential data on which he builds his concept of the patient's life and his plan of therapy.

How the Therapist Recognizes What Is Repressed

The patient frequently needs help in identifying distortions of his mental life and the therapist must be able to give this help. But before he can do so he must construct a rational account for himself. The technique is this. He is trained to listen attentively to the patient, noting all evenly, and failing to impose *a priori* hypotheses. His goal is to have a complete and rational verbal account of the patient's life. In the ideal case the therapist has no tendency to repress any of the elements of the patient's verbal account nor the emotions which may be evoked by these. He has within himself the learned drives to give a complete account, to be logical, to judge appropriateness of response. These drives are aroused by the cues of incompleteness or inappropriateness in the patient's account; he will sense that the stimuli alleged should not provoke a certain kind of response or that there is "something missing" in the account. He will then ask himself what response would be appropriate or what the missing link of thought could be. The therapist may suddenly feel that a given anecdote does not "make sense" and will ask himself what would have to be true if it were to be sensible.

As he tries to answer these questions for himself he hits on hypotheses about the patient's motivation and behavior. Frequently these hypotheses refer to what is repressed, those motives which are present and active but inexpressible. Summed up and taken together these queries and hunches constitute a theory of the patient's life; they become part of the therapist's plan of campaign of conducting the therapy. The therapist, so to say, plays the patient's tune softly on his own piano and listens for gaps, disharmonies, sour notes, and failures to end the music. The therapist listens at once to the patient and to the sentences that dart into his own mind concerning the patient's account of his behavior. In the best case these sentences which the therapist can make, but which the patient cannot make, describe that which is repressed in the patient's mental life.

Blocked associations as pointers. Although the foregoing is the most fundamental activity, there are many additional aids and helps. For instance, blocked lines of association act as pointers. The therapist notes the places where the blocking occurs and asks himself what "should" have come next. Such blocking can occur through a fearful withholding or through repression. In the case of the former, the patient must overcome his fear and speak what he knows; repression can best be attacked by following to the letter the rule of free association.

Significance of the blank mind. "Nothing coming to mind" indicates repressive activity. The patient who has been starved for years for a chance to speak and who has his whole life behind him suddenly cannot think of anything else to say. Since the therapist knows that this is impossible in a free mind, he assumes that repression is at work, *i.e.,* that the patient has something to say but unconsciously dares not say it. In this case, the therapist may merely insist that the patient can talk and urge him to proceed, or he may attempt to stimulate the patient by interpretation. In the latter case, he might ask, "Have you had any thoughts about me, my office, or our association?" Frequently this move on the therapist's part will bring the patient to state that he had personal or critical thoughts regarding the therapist which were the reason for his reluctance to talk. The patient fears particularly to alienate the therapist by criticism and thus run the risk of losing his help and support in dealing with the neurosis. However, any strong motive of which the patient is deeply ashamed can cause silence. Repression falls alike on the description of the motive and on all other sentences lest they might lead to it.

Patient B spent almost a month in therapy during which nothing important happened and the treatment was at a standstill. Considerable parts of every session were spent in resistant silence. The patient insisted that he had no thoughts at all. At the end of this difficult period of waiting, he finally brought out some sentences which indicated strong fear of homosexual motivation within himself and some real evidence for the existence of such motivation. Thereafter his ability to communicate was remarkably freed for a time. The silent "spots" dropped out and much new information was brought forward.

Failure to deal with common areas of response. If the patient fails to talk about a common area of response, the therapist may infer that there is some conflict in connection with this area. If a married person, for instance, is in the therapeutic situation for three months and does not mention his sexual life, the therapist will sense something "peculiar" about this omission. The therapist argues that the matter of sex response would be bound to come to mind in a free discussion during this period of time. If this did not occur, it was because the discussion was not free and repression or withholding was somehow operating.

Dreams. Dreams also may point to repressed material; in fact, they have been called by Freud the "straight road" to unconscious mental life (Freud, 1924, Vol. I, p. 268). As already noted, dreams are private, imageal responses which produce cues. These cues are what are "seen" as the dream. Since they are private responses they are less likely to have strong anxiety attached to them and are likely to be "franker." For example, early in Mrs. A's treatment, she had a dream which portrayed her as being married to her foster brother. This dream pointed to an incestuous wish which Mrs. A could not express in a more direct way at that time. Later it was learned that she had had sex relations with this brother.

Slips of the tongue. Slips of the tongue and other errors sometimes attract attention to repressed material. Mrs. A said that her husband had once agreed to meet her in downtown New York and then failed to appear at the agreed-upon time and place. "He left me *strangled* there," she said. Her intent was to say "stranded" but her strong feelings of anger and fear entered and caused the slip. At the time this slip occurred, however, she was not able to express resentment of her husband directly. It seemed to the therapist that the slip condensed the following thought: "He neglected me, left me stranded; I could have strangled him for this; had I tried he would have strangled me."

Stereotyped failures may point to repressed. Stereotyped outcomes of life dilemmas may also indicate a conflict area. Repeated divorces, for instance, may point to severe sexual anxieties which become attached to each wife in turn and ultimately drive the husband away. Once out of the committed sex situation, anxiety is reduced and sex approach tendencies become dominant, thus leading to another marriage. The girl who would like to marry but always finds some serious fault with the actual man who presents himself is suspect by the man in the street as well as by the psychiatrist who asks, "Is she perhaps afraid to marry?" The man whose friendships with other men always begin with great intimacy and run through an inevitable course to neglect and termination shows another type of "stereotyped outcome." The therapist would like to know, "Does he perhaps discover that he likes his new friend too well and does he fear that the relationship might become more than friendship?" With some such hypothesis the repeated breaking off may become intelligible.

In the case of Mrs. A, repeated seductions pointed to an area of conflict. In speaking of these seductions Mrs. A always said, "He *took advantage* of me." This might have been a mere fashion of phrasing the matter but proved not to be so. Mrs. A was stating that she had had sex relations but denying that she had had any responsibility for such relations. There was a hint in this disclaimer, which proved to be a fact, that Mrs. A's "conditions of love" included the condition that she should not be responsible herself for sexual activity but should have it forced upon her. It turned out that the problem of assuming responsibility for her own sexual feelings was central in Mrs. A's life.

Why Psychotherapy Takes Time

It must be evident now why therapy takes time. The patient's work is hard work. Continually facing anxiety is painful and exhausting. One can see in every psychiatric out-patient clinic persons who once introduced to psychotherapy, will plead for electroshock or any form of somatic intervention rather than continue facing the anxieties produced by free association.

If the patient is allowed to choose his own pace in therapy, he will choose a slow pace and, as a result, extinction of anxiety attached to verbal responses is a slow affair. The therapist can best advance the proceeding by holding the patient as closely as possible to his work, insisting upon the fundamental rule; but if severity forces the patient to face more anxiety than he can bear, the therapist runs the risk of driving the patient out of the therapeutic situation.

Culture Limits Therapeutic Learning Situation

We are reminded in this connection that psychotherapy, as it is now developed, depends in part on the social circumstance of the private practice of therapy. If the relationship is to exist, the patient must come and pay. Many strong drives and rewards cannot be used because the mores forbid. The conditions inside the therapeutic situation cannot be so productive of misery that the patient abandons therapy. Therapy should be speeded up under circumstances where the patient is more "under control," as perhaps in the Army. Drugs may aid in more rapid access to unconscious conflicts. Psychological tests may serve to orient the therapist more quickly in regard to such conflicts. Following our principles it would seem that any circumstance which will aid the patient to address himself more ardently to his work of talking despite anxiety should speed up therapy.

Mrs. A's Case Illustrates Main Points

During the first few hours of the treatment, Mrs. A spoke mainly about her symptoms. She came rapidly to the end of lines of thought, then lapsed into silence or demanded advice. She insisted that she could think of nothing further to say—even though she had said nothing at all about her personal life and feelings and had not mentioned her marriage. Free communication was resumed when the therapist pointed out her dependent attitudes, i.e., that she had learned to depend on others to make decisions for her, to do her thinking for her, and that she had transferred these expectations to the therapeutic situation.

This permissive interpretation (abundantly justified by facts of the life history) encouraged Mrs. A to talk more freely. She began to speak of more significant, more personal topics. She told first of her resentment against her foster mother, then of her minor misdeeds as a child; finally, as the expected thunderclap of disapproval never came, she ventured to confess some early sexual and aggressive activities.

This slow broadening of topics shows the gradual, progressive effect of extinction of anxiety. At first Mrs. A was reluctant to talk about anything that might bring disapproval. She was "afraid people would laugh at me." She tried talking about an almost but not quite harmless topic and found that she was not punished; then bit by bit she extended the range of her topics until she felt free to talk about even the most personal matters— her menstruation, her sexual deeds, her social inadequacies, her abhorrent reaction to erotic advances from her husband. When cases like that of Mrs. A can be recorded and reproduced with breath-by-breath fidelity, the account given here of the effect of new conditions of learning on mental life will gain greatly in power to convince.

CHAPTER XVII

TRANSFERENCE: GENERALIZED RESPONSES IN THE THERAPEUTIC SITUATION

The therapist is seeking data to make a construction about the patient's life. The patient gives some of these data directly in verbal form. The phenomenon of the transference gives other and new information which the patient cannot give directly. During the course of therapeutic work the patient transfers, or generalizes, to the therapist many strong emotional responses. A large part of these responses have never been labeled, so the patient cannot speak about what he is feeling. The patient fears, hates, pleads, but is not aware that he is doing so. These unwitting reactions are called "transference." They provide important data because the therapist can label the reactions correctly though the patient cannot.

In his daily work the therapist is most aware of those transferred reactions which obstruct the progress of therapy. As it is used technically in Freud's (1924, Vol. II, pp. 312–322) sense, transference means such repressed emotional reactions as *either* aid or impede therapy. We feel that this usage is still too narrow. It can be shown that all kinds of responses of which the patient is capable can generalize to the therapeutic situation. Thus, all the patient's verbal habits generalize—and where would therapy be without them? All the responses attached to such verbal responses can also generalize. All types of instrumental responses can generalize— the patient can come to the office of the therapist or write a check without special training! Similarly, all kinds of emotional responses can generalize. For instance, the patient can be consciously grateful to, or unconsciously angry at, the therapist. Though in a general theory of higher mental life it is important to notice this wider type of generalization, it remains true that the most important and informative responses to the therapist are the unlabeled emotional responses. They are the ones whose occurrence brings critical new information.

Transferred behavior in everyday life. The ordinary social presumption is that the responses of an individual are appropriate to the cues which excite them; that is, if a man is angry, he has been provoked; if a girl is in love, someone has been making love to her; if a person is frightened, he has reason to believe that danger threatens. In developing his technique of psychotherapy, Freud introduced a presumption of an opposite kind, *i.e.*, that many responses of the patient are transferred to the therapist and not, in the ordinary sense of the word, earned. In the situation of free communication which Freud set up, he had excellent opportunity to observe that anger, love, or fear may appear in the absence of what, in ordinary life, would be considered adequate stimuli for them. These responses he viewed as transferred and called "transference."

Transferred responses are not in any way unusual. They are everyday phenomena. A tennis player, meeting a new opponent, transfers his habits—good and bad—to this opponent. These responses will include more than his repertory of strokes. He may show his characteristic anger at losing, his intense competitiveness by playing better when he is at a disadvantage, or his "fear of success" by losing inexplicably just when the match is in his grasp. Such idiosyncrasies of top-flight players are well known to close followers of the sport.

Similarly, our immediate likes and dislikes of other persons in the ordinary course of life are transferred responses. Without knowing it themselves, strangers may present us with cues to which we immediately generalize love or hate. Sometimes these reactions persist, but often they are changed and we fail to understand how we could at first sight have "fallen so hard" for Jones or how we could have disliked so fine a person as Smith. Ordinarily, we pay little attention to these reactions, counting ourselves lucky when they win us a strong friend and charging it off to "life" when someone appears instinctively prejudiced against us.

In psychotherapy, the case is different. Therapists notice these transferred reactions because they are part of the essential information which is needed to aid the patient. However earnestly he may try, if the patient does not know that he is capable of a certain kind of emotional reaction he may never be able to tell the therapist about it. He may be able to "reveal" himself only by having the reaction and directing it toward the therapist. The mildest patient will, for this reason, frequently surprise himself at the responses and emotions of which he is proved to be capable.

Therapist as a Vague Pattern of Stimuli

Though the therapist tries to keep his personality as vague as possible, he is still another human being and his presence creates a social situation similar to those in which the patient has often been punished or rewarded. The therapist is someone in authority and has potentially the power to punish and to reassure. He is, further, an expert who has the right to specify conditions of work and to indicate what lines of activity are likely to have favorable and unfavorable outcomes. Once the patient is involved in the work, the therapist must urge the patient on to a task that is partly painful. He must support correct labeling on the patient's part and bafflingly withhold his consent from errors. He helps to keep the patient at his task until the end (always unknown to the patient) is reached.

The stimuli of the therapist make him similar in many ways to the teachers, parents, and age-graded superiors of the patient, which fact makes it easier to generalize to the therapist the very same responses which were learned in interaction with the authoritarian figures of earlier life. Though the therapist cannot keep himself perfectly ambiguous, he avoids the excesses of self-revelation. He "provokes" the patient's responses only through a formal and well-defined situation. He accepts what is generalized to him in his role (Parsons, 1942) as therapist but otherwise provokes response as little as possible.

Generalization is automatic. In the therapeutic situation the patient generalizes those responses which the stimuli of the therapist evoke. Every therapist knows intuitively the lawful consistence with which patients respond to him and how sharply they differ from one another. Generalization is automatic; both the good and the bad, the helpful and the obstructive habits are transferred. Both primary (that the therapist is an adult male) and response-mediated (that he is an expert) mechanisms of generalization play an important role. Naturally, once responses are transferred to the therapist, their resistance to extinction will depend on conditions of the therapeutic situation.

Transferred responses weaker. Like all generalized responses, transferred responses are weaker when attached to the therapist than they were when attached to their original stimuli. The dependence and helplessness often manifested in therapy can never be as intense as it was when first learned as a habit. The patient is too well aware of the many respects in which he is capable and has indeed learned other counterhabits, such as to be up and doing, which can be evoked by the therapist to oppose the dependent trends.

Transference reactions interwoven with others. Furthermore, transference responses may be interwoven with other and later-learned reactions. They may be defended by adult-style rationalizations and combined with adaptive behavior patterns. For example, a rage attack, which is essentially an infantile manifestation, may serve to frighten others away from goals that the patient wants; and, upon reflection, he may maintain that it is indeed a valuable means of reaching such goals.

Generalized Habits Facilitating Therapy

Many highly adaptive habits are immediately transferred to the therapist and the therapeutic situation and, were it not for these, therapy could not be conducted at all. The patient transfers his training in being "sensible," that is, in matching his sentences with environmental events. He shifts also his training in being self-critical, that is, a tendency to label his own behavior correctly and not to be satisfied with agreeable but delusive labels. Particularly valuable is his training in giving an intelligible account of himself. He tries for a complete and orderly narration which will give the therapist the facts, and he is correspondingly rewarded at "being understood." Saying "I don't understand that," therefore, becomes an important stimulus which the therapist can produce to activate the patient to further explanation. The patient tries also to be logical, a habit which he generalizes from his prior life. He is uncomfortable when his sentences do not "add up," that is, when they suggest inconsistent courses of action or when they predict a plainly ludicrous course of behavior. When the therapist says that something is not logical, the patient can be motivated to new efforts.

The patient has been trained also to resist unreasonable fears. If an expert says that a certain response is safe, the patient expects himself at least to try though he be afraid. The patient further transfers his long-learned habits of rehearsal to the therapeutic situation. He is thus enabled to listen attentively and to borrow new verbal response sequences from the therapist. The patient's imitative habits are also transferred. They enable him to be quieted by the therapist's calmness and motivated by his concern. In the past, the patient has learned to respond to reassurance from experts and these relaxing responses are put at the therapist's disposal by generalization. Most important of all, in many ways, is the fact that the patient has a large repertory of judgments on which responses are appropriate to what cues. He has learned when sorrow, anger, fear, laughter are common and expected, and when they are rare or out of place. To the judgment of inappropriateness, the patient has learned to be motivated. The therapist can count on having this motive at his command. When the therapist questions a response connection, the patient can be relied on to attempt to inhibit inappropriate responses and to attempt to find the correct ones.

The prestige of the therapist as a specialist may create immediate hope in the patient since he has learned to trust specialists and to be comforted when they take a matter in hand. If the therapist has a "big name" in the field, such responses may be intensified. The patient may have a well-supported confidence in "science" and have strong habits of doing what he is told when scientists give the instructions. If this were not so, patients could hardly be gotten to accept the novel and strenuous conditions of psychotherapy. "Confidence in science" means that the patient is used to trying to do what he is told to do even when he does not understand all the reasons behind it.

Usefulness of wish to please therapist. The patient regularly brings to the therapeutic situation a motive to please the therapist, though this will differ in strength from patient to patient. This motive has in it elements of love, dependence, hope, and gratitude. The motive can be greatly strengthened by evidence of the therapist's permissiveness, understanding, concern, and fairness, *i.e.*, by reducing anxiety and by giving evidence of skill. It is highly important to do everything possible to strengthen this motive because it is the main force which keeps the patient in a situation which is bound to have many disagreeable aspects. But, in the first instance, "the motive to please" is generalized from similar sentiments felt toward parents and other authoritarian figures. It can be strengthened by having the therapist play the role of the good and intelligent mentor. This motivation is immediately put to work. In response to it the patient tries to follow the new conditions of the therapeutic situation; he makes his first uncertain struggles to do "the patient's work" of thinking in spite of anxiety. Since the patient's task is one involving considerable uncertainty, he needs to have a lively motive to trust the therapist. He must struggle along toward an unknown goal, depending on the therapist's assurance that if he will try responding in the required direction he will eventually escape misery.

There are undoubtedly many more such useful habits to identify. It may be that some of the variability in the outcome of therapeutic work depends on the strength with which such habits exist within the patient and are generalized to the therapeutic situation. If the "logical" training of the patient is poor, a potent weapon is struck from the hands of the therapist. The therapist may be called upon to give, during the course of therapy, training which should have been acquired by the patient in childhood. This may prove impossible. A better understanding of these positive transferred habits would undoubtedly enable us to predict the outcome of therapeutic attempts more accurately.

Immediately Generalized Obstructive Responses

At first glance, the relation of patient and therapist is a peaceable-seeming, almost intellectual affair. How then can it happen that such urgent and ugly responses as those of sex, anger, fear, and distrust come forward? There seem to be at least two different ways in which these strong and obstructive reactions can occur: some interfering reactions are immediately generalized to the vague stimuli of the therapeutic situation; others appear only after work is started and are evoked in the course of interstimulation between patient and therapist. Both types of reaction are necessary and inescapable. They provide essential information but much time is required to get this information.

Fear and dependence. Some obstructive responses are immediately generalized to the therapeutic situation and occur without the patient's having become directly involved in this situation. Only the most general stimuli of the "new situation" seem to evoke these responses. The most common and important of these immediate reactions is fear. The patient has had harsh training to fear his thoughts on many topics. At the outset he cannot believe that he will not be punished for thinking freely. He strongly and blindly generalizes his fear. Another reaction frequently seen by therapists is that of dependence or helplessness. When there is a strong or competent person around, the patient is accustomed not to exert himself. He is, rather, accustomed to asking for and demanding help and to feeling bitter resentment if that help is not forthcoming.

Mrs. A proved to be a case of this type. She manifested early in the treatment an excessively dependent attitude. Some signs of dependence are to be expected in every patient because they are appropriate to the situation of a person turning for help to someone more skillful. But Mrs. A's dependence went beyond this reasonable degree. She cast her burden entirely on the therapist and relied on him to do the work. Her first words during the second hour point this up nicely: "Aren't you going to suggest anything? I told you everything Friday." Having said "where it hurt," Mrs. A expected the therapist to outline a course of behavior, give her instructions to meet all eventualities, and generally to take over. When the therapist could not comply, she kept reiterating her symptoms, pleaded for advice, and then quickly came to the end of lines of thought and lapsed into silence. If the therapist would not help her, she could not, she felt, help herself.

These helpless and dependent attitudes are frequently transferred directly from the parental figures to the therapist. And it was further known in Mrs. A's case that her upbringing had been exceptionally severe and limited. It seemed possible that she was *afraid* to have a thought of her own. The therapist therefore asked her: "Do you feel helpless now because your mother never let you use your mind? As a child you didn't have much practice in making up your own mind. It seems that even now you don't dare take the risk of thinking for yourself by speaking out and saying what you really think." The therapist was making a discrimination between the inhibiting situation of childhood and the more permissive conditions of the therapeutic situation and indicated that Mrs. A could now venture to have a mind of her own. Mrs. A reacted to this interpretation with considerable relief and, after trying out her new freedom and finding she was not punished, she was able to speak much more freely.

False hopes of cure. The false hopes of cure which the patient brings to the therapeutic situation clearly show their origin in former experience. The patient expects from the psychiatrist the same behavior that he had learned to expect from other doctors. This was exemplified in the case of Mrs. A. She came to the therapeutic situation with hope for a quick, magic cure. This expectation was almost certainly generalized from her previous experience with physicians. She had learned that you tell a doctor what your symptoms are—where it hurts—and then he tells you what to do. She therefore quickly recited all her symptoms—her concern about her heart, her nausea and loss of weight, her fear of going out alone. Then she said, "That's all; I have told you everything," and sat back waiting for the doctor to provide a simple cure. The therapist had to explain to Mrs. A that psychotherapy is different from medical treatments. He pointed out that in order to help her he would need to know a great deal more about her. Her job was to talk, to do the patient's work. However, the discrimination between this and other types of treatment was not easily set up. Mrs. A kept pleading for advice throughout the first several hours of the therapy. She expected the usual prescriptions, rules, and instructions.

In the case of Mrs. A the problem of overcoming the false hopes of cure was intensified because of her dependence. But such hopes seem to present a problem quite generally, and the therapist's first task is to clear the ground of them. The patient must know that he will not be made well by a pill, by the best intentioned advice, by commands or reassurance, but only through new self-knowledge and the learning of new skills.

It seems worthwhile to identify this kind of a transferred response, *i.e.*, one which occurs immediately and blindly almost without regard to the personality of the therapist and before the patient has become seriously involved in therapeutic work. It is obviously a direct transfer of habits learned in other dealings with authoritarian persons.

Behavioral Analysis of Dynamics of Transference

A discussion of the obstructive responses evoked in the course of therapy involves a knowledge of the dynamics of the transference. This discussion will therefore be briefly postponed while the variables involved in transference are discussed.

Why should the therapist, who after all is only trying to help the patient in a professional way, be the recipient of intense emotional reactions? The matter is mysterious until one realizes that the therapist invites these reactions and sets up the very conditions which are bound to bring them forth. He cannot fail to set up these conditions, and he cannot fail to deal with these emotions once they are aroused.

If we picture a series of persons designated by the words *rival, boss, therapist, teacher, minister,* we can clarify the matter. The patient is thought of as reacting to all five. Rival, boss, teacher, and minister all maintain the social sanctions intact. They are the kinds of people who have punished the patient in the past for various sayings and misdeeds. Tendencies to approach them are present but these tendencies are opposed by strong tendencies to avoid.[1] They set up no special conditions but follow the old policy, "Let the patient beware." With the therapist, the case is quite the contrary. He too evokes the initial avoidance but he sets up special circumstances to deal with it. He enjoins free speech, and, when it is forthcoming, rewards it. Is it surprising that communication is freer and that a more intense emotional relationship springs up between patient and therapist?

The matter should also be viewed in a more technical way as a

[1] We are using "approach" and "avoid" as convenient general categories to describe the two aspects of a conflict. Thus "approach" is meant to include all the responses (*e.g.*, love, aggression, etc.) that the patient is motivated to make toward the therapist, and "avoidance" is meant to include all the responses (motivated by fear, guilt, etc.) that are in conflict with those of approach. See also Chap. XXII.

change in net strength of approach reactions to the therapist. Initially the patient generalizes both elements of approach-avoidance conflicts to the therapist. As free association continues under permissive conditions, the anxiety attached to speaking about forbidden matters is gradually extinguished. These extinction effects are generalized to the fears which provoke avoidance in the emotional conflicts. As avoidance is weakened, the formerly inhibited emotions gain in net strength. They are generalized to the therapist with this increased strength and thus surprisingly appear in relation to a professionally neutral person. Surprise lasts only while we see the matter from a distance. Close up it appears that the therapist is not behaving neutrally; he has invited transference reactions by setting up conditions which produce them.

In a typical case the patient talks tentatively about disappointment in the therapist. Unpunished, he brings out his complaints more clearly. As he talks, angry feelings attached to his words are aroused. Finding that he can talk freely, his fear of feeling freely is reduced. As fear is reduced, his angry feelings become stronger. His reproaches gain in strength and he shows in voice and posture that he is more deeply mobilized emotionally. Now the therapist has evoked a full-blown transference reaction. If he has done nothing to earn anger, he will be able to deal with it as a generalized reaction. He will further be able to put his analysis of the reaction to work in the patient's service. (In the case of the four other types of persons mentioned above such a reaction cannot occur because the first words and gestures of protest are opposed by anxiety within the patient himself and never get "under way.")

This process was very clear in the case of Mrs. A. As she was slowly brought to a limited freedom in talking about her sexual life it became evident that she had been repeatedly seduced since childhood. It became apparent also that she was afraid the therapist would seduce her as so many other men had done. This fear of course interfered with the progress of the treatment, and therefore the therapist asked Mrs. A, "Is there something here that frightens you? I wonder if you are afraid that I will 'take advantage' of you?"

Mrs. A answered: "No . . . no. . . ." (Mrs. A began to cry.) "If you were ugly I think I would be afraid. . . . When you say that it makes me tremble and shake. . . ." (A silence of five minutes followed.) Mrs. A broke the silence by telling how she saw the man next door (to whom she was sexually attracted) in her dreams.

In the next hour when Mrs. A again became blocked, the therapist said, "Our talking here about sex must frighten you—and it must also arouse sexual desire in you." Mrs. A's response confirmed the interpretation of the previous hour.

"No," she said, "it just makes me afraid. I know you would not take advantage of me. There are people in the waiting room, and your secretary is in the outer office. I knew if you did try to take advantage of me, I could run out the door." (It was apparent that Mrs. A had considered the possibility carefully, a long time before.) The therapist said that of course as an ethical therapist he would not seduce her, but there was also another good reason for not doing it. It would simply be another case of someone else taking the responsibility for her own sexual activities and so could teach her nothing that she did not already know all too well. He pointed out that what she really needed to learn was to take responsibility for her own sexual feelings and to find gratification in situations where *she* was responsible.

Obstructive Responses Evoked in the Course of the Work

During the course of his prior life the patient has hit upon various ways of escaping from anxiety situations, especially when these are provoked by his own thoughts. He brings these escape reactions into the therapeutic situation, and when they appear they have the effect of warding off a continuation of the essential work. These responses are automatically evoked by the anxiety stimuli produced in the course of talking. They frequently give the therapist the impression of devilish ingenuity, but they are not purposive or ingenious except in the sense that the patient has already learned many ways of escaping anxiety-provoking thoughts.

Stopping talking. Stopping talking is the commonest of these avertive responses. Being silent is an effective way of escaping talking out loud about anxiety-provoking matters. Even though the patient goes on thinking the sentences which produce anxiety, it may be that this anxiety is considerably less than when he makes the same responses out loud. The "thought" response may be weaker, produce a weaker stimulus, and therefore evoke less anxiety. The patient has presumably learned to be mute in many situations where talking would only make matters worse, and he tries out this response in the new therapeutic situation. The therapist makes a continuation of the "silent" response impossible by interpretation. The interpretation is useful if it evokes new motivation to continue in the patient. He assures the patient that he cannot have a blank mind, that thoughts will come to his mind, and that when they come he must utter them. Or the therapist gives a clue as to what such thoughts might be, thus both urging and giving the patient permission to speak the dangerous thoughts.

Leaving. A second well-learned response to a social situation which is producing anxiety is to leave it. This is a means often taken. The considerable number of patients who break off brief psychotherapy is especially evident in out-patient clinics. The fact seems to be that the patients leave when the going gets tough, that is, when they hit upon a line of sentences which produce severe anxiety. In the favorable case—the well-handled case—the positive relationship to the therapist inhibits leaving. The forces holding the patient in the situation must be stronger than those prompting him to leave. Such positive factors include the patient's wish to get well, his wish to please the therapist and do well, the rewards which the therapist is able to administer in the therapeutic situation, and the new plans which the patient hits upon which are successful. Those unfamiliar with the situation of therapy should realize, however, that these forces are often too weak to hold the patient in the situation and as a result he makes his well-practiced response of running away.

Obfuscation. A third type of interruptive response is that of obfuscation. Many patients have this response down to perfection, and indeed it appears frequently enough in ordinary life. The patient has learned to avoid anxiety dilemmas by obscuring or confusing issues. He may argue about theoretical points which have little to do with the matter at hand. He may stress small points of error instead of the massive truthful facts of the situation. He may engage in intellectual quibbles. Very often he pursues irrelevant lines of association, being careful not to hit on anything that is not safe. Frequently also he will talk in repetitious circles, repeating the well-known and not bringing up anything novel. He may even argue in the latter case that this behavior testifies to the fact that there is nothing more to say. In such cases, the therapist must carefully point out the escape value of these various tactics and again urge the patient to address himself to his proper work. The various learned drives to be sensible, intelligible, and logical can be evoked to incite the patient to continue his task.

Anger evoked by fear. Many people have learned to pick a quarrel when frightened. Anger and the responses they make to anger may get them out of the fear situation, or may at least take attention from fear cues, which temporarily has the same effect. They now transfer this mechanism to the therapeutic situation. When free association produces responses which evoke fear, the fear cues in turn evoke anger. Such patients may criticize the therapist unfairly, borrow every scrap of hostile comment that they can find about him, and seize any occasion to belittle him. The therapist must bear these responses, identify them, and turn them to therapeutic use.

Fear evoked by anger. In other cases, fear is dominant. The first news that the therapist gets that his patient is angry is a strong demonstration of fear. He must decode this reaction and identify the sequence of responses. Several mechanisms can operate here. In the one case, weak or transitory anger cues evoke fear responses. These cues are conscious but they are disregarded by the patient. In the other, and frequent, case, strong but unlabeled anger cues are present and these too evoke fear. The therapist then observes his patient suddenly become frightened when there is no apparent cause. His knowledge that anger (and other punished emotions) can evoke fear is one of his most useful tools of thought.

Dependence. In some cases a pair of linked attitudes is transferred to the therapist. These may take the form of an ambivalent reaction. Thus, a dependent patient may generalize great "love" to the therapist—a love which is really a claim on him. When, then, the therapist is unable to respond to this claim, the frustrated patient becomes hostile. Naturally the therapist cannot be blamed for eliciting this kind of reaction. He can only attempt to get the patient to decide whether it is a reasonable and fruitful attitude, and, if it be judged not so, to return to his work.

Transference responses occurring in line of duty. In the formal course of any therapeutic situation there is bound to be some transitory resentment of the therapist and the therapeutic situation. In the course of his duty the therapist encourages the patient to bring up anxiety-provoking thoughts and, on occasion, to embark on anxiety-provoking courses of action. The painful thought or course of action is felt as a frustration; if the patient has learned to react with aggression to the stimuli of frustration, some of this anger will be vented on the therapist.

In the case of Patient B, encouraging him to name and confront his fear of sex relations with his wife produced first anxiety, then anger. Since it was the therapist's interpretation which was the means of provoking the anxious thought "Am I afraid of doing sexual things with my wife?", Mr. B was resentful. If the interpretation eventually leads to reducing the basic emotional conflict, the patient will accept these inevitable and momentary increases in anxiety and hostility. But he cannot know at the moment whether or not the offensive interpretation will have this benign eventual effect; the other drives of the immediate situation should keep him at his work despite these deterrents.

Therapist's Mistakes Produce Appropriate, Not Transferred, Reactions

The therapist must be careful not to give real reason for the emotional reactions of the patient. He must not provoke anger or make any personal use of the sex responses which occur. If the therapist is hasty, stupid, cruel, or uncontrolled, he will earn real emotional reactions from his patient. We hope, and believe, that this is never done by reputable therapists. Since the patient is likely to be frightened by any of these traits in the therapist, and since this fear will be real, the therapeutic work is bound to be impeded or ruined by such actions of the therapist. Real fear cannot be dealt with by the psychotherapeutic methods described here. If the therapist in an inadvertent moment makes a hasty or stupid mistake, he had best honestly admit it to his patient and let it be seen as a deviation from the standards of behavior he holds for himself. If he is unable to do this or if the deviation is too gross, the therapist had best transfer his patient—and himself recur to psychotherapy.

Transference Not a Duel

The therapist is under stress in accepting, identifying, and using transferred reactions for the ends of therapy. Though informative, transference emotions are often obstinate and difficult to deal with. They interrupt the smooth growth of effective labeling. Therefore the transferred reactions must frequently be considered as resistant. The emotions themselves may be so strong that they overpower the line of verbal responses that the patient has just been making; or the verbal responses produced by the emotions may have the same effect. In either case, effective labeling is interrupted.

The therapist is frequently inclined to feel that there is something diabolically purposive in these emotional interruptions, that the patient is somehow cunningly "resisting" him. He should refuse to accept such a view of the phenomenon. He should, instead, understand that the emotional responses in question are generalized *automatically* to the therapeutic situation because the strength of avoidance reactions to unconscious emotion has been reduced. It is particularly important that the therapist should not imply that the patient is purposely producing these reactions, else he will confuse his patient and possibly give real cause for a feeling of injustice. The therapist's task is to identify these responses as transferred and find out how they arose.

Transferred reactions not "iffy." Transference is a real battle. The emotional reactions transferred to the therapist are not iffy or imaginary. The patient feels them as coming from his deepest soul and feels his whole body and personality mobilized behind them. He tends to believe that any reactions which *feel* so real to him must be proportionate to the situation in which they occur. The therapist's task is to prove to him that they are not. Even though he is dealing with such emotional dynamite, the therapist need have no fear providing the patient has no power over him in real life. This is one of the reasons why it is not advisable for an instructor to analyze the chairman of his department or for a minor consultant to accept the chief of his clinic in therapy. The therapist's reactions can hardly have the desired neutrality or objectivity if he has any other relationship to the patient than that specified in the therapeutic situation, *i.e.,* being paid for his skill. In such a case, the patient is really not safe since he runs the risk that exterior motivation will cause the therapist to do things that he should not do or to fail to do things that would be in the patient's interest.

In the case of angry or sexy reactions, these are always to some degree adapted to the current situation. The drive to be "reasonable" shows itself here. The angry patient will take advantage of any evident failings of the therapist. The therapist may be mocked for his baldness or fatness, for his poor teeth, for the fact that he is a foreigner or an ethnic. The therapist must learn to regard such criticisms as automatic defensive responses on the part of the patient inevitably aroused in the course of the therapeutic work. If he allows himself to become angry, he plays into the patient's hands in that he permits the patient to fix attention on irrelevant matters instead of on the psychological work at hand. Incidentally this is easier said than done. The clever and angry patient will invariably nip the therapist where the skin is thinnest. The therapist needs the strong support of his theory to continue reacting properly when thus attacked.

We emphasize, however, that psychotherapy is no mere intellectual exchange wherein patient and therapist serenely discuss the behavior of the former in historical terms. The patient is, and must be, really roused. The emotions involved in the basic neurotic conflict must appear, at least in limited degree, within the therapeutic situation itself. The therapist who treated Mrs. A had good reason to know the genuineness of transferred emotions. In the twelfth hour, Mrs. A announced that she had decided to go for a visit to her husband's family. She tried to get the therapist to support this plan and to assure her that if she only managed to defy her "bounds" phobia and get on the bus alone she would be completely cured. "If you would only encourage me," she pleaded. The therapist refused to take the responsibility for the decision. Mrs. A snapped back at him, "You are making me worse. You are not trying to help me at all. I had good intentions of going to see my in-laws; now I can't do it." (Mrs. A began to cry.) Then she flashed, "I think you are just experimenting on me." The therapist disregarded this taunt and explained that Mrs. A would have to decide about the trip for herself. But she persisted in the question, "Should I go to see my family? Can't you give me just a little advice?" Thus, when the therapist had to frustrate Mrs. A's dependent demands she became genuinely angry and accused him of being merely a cynical experimenter without real concern or feeling for her.

In other cases, emotions of shame at past deeds appear and show the patient cringing away from the therapist as though he would inevitably condemn. Erotic emotions appear in dreams and associations which involve the therapist's person, his wife, his receptionist, and others related or presumed to be related to him. The patient shows at the same time a lively fear of rejection. Vengeful feelings appear at the thought of neglect of the patient or damage done by others and in each case the patient generalizes his fear of punishment to the therapist.

Transference Reveals the Never-labeled

If the therapist had only the free-association data to go on, he might neglect to study and identify the never-labeled emotional responses. These responses, not having been labeled or having been mislabeled in early life, have never been tied in with the system of verbal responses and cues. The patient therefore cannot give an account of them. He can only show them. Hence the transference provides the therapist with a route to the most deeply "unacknowledged" or the patient's emotional reactions. By producing these reactions in the therapeutic situation he can attach verbal labels to them and thus eventually learn to control them. To paraphrase Alexander and French (1946, p. 21), the emotional reactions occur first and the labeling afterward.

First identify generalized responses. When the patient feels strong emotional responses toward the therapist these must first be identified. The patient may be angry or sexy without knowing it. Then the fact that they are generalized to the therapist from other persons in the patient's life must be established. The question may be asked, "Is there any sufficient reason for your being angry at me?" If not, the anger must have been found useful by the patient in the past in a similar dilemma and generalized to the therapist. At this point the patient must bring to bear an already acquired skill, namely the ability to judge what responses are appropriate (conventional) to what stimuli, and what not.

If the reaction can be shown to be without foundation in the therapeutic situation a further question arises. If generalized, "From whom? When?" When the patient puts himself these questions, he may be led to bring up significant items of history and may find himself in a better position to identify the circumstances under which the generalized responses were learned. When blocked by privation before, he was often successful in escaping by getting angry. Fearful of carrying on his part in the therapeutic task, he tries getting angry in the therapeutic situation. If such a response can be clearly identified, the acquired drives to be reasonable and logical are mobilized and tend to drive the patient back to his task of free association.

There is one exception to the rule that transferred responses are routinely identified. The therapist gratefully accepts the transferred responses which act as a positive force in the therapy and does not until the end identify them (Freud, 1924, Vol. II, pp. 365; 383–384).

Never-labeled responses point to obscure past conditions of learning. As the transferred responses unroll in the course of therapeutic work, they show what the patient has learned in his past experience. The patient *can* make only those responses which he has learned and *has to* produce them when the stimuli are appropriate. Even though the patient mutely makes emotional responses in the tranference, it is often possible to infer what the conditions were under which these responses were learned. They can therefore provide a basis for inferences about what the earliest conditions of the patient's life actually were. He who fears "never getting enough" must have learned this painful attitude in a situation of privation. The man who reacts with immediate defiance to any type of authoritarian control must have adopted this attitude as a defense against excesses of force and authority. He who is eternally suspicious must have been betrayed. If the patient fears to make the sentences denoting sexual acts, he must have been punished for such thoughts and expressions. We have noted that patients will sometimes react with horror to sexual thoughts who yet insist that no one has ever talked to them of such matters.

Recalling the patient to his task. Intruding emotional responses may stop the forward movement of therapy. They will be temporarily reinforced by anxiety reduction if they succeed in doing so. If the therapist does not know how to recall the patient to his proper task, such responses may persist and may end therapeutic progress. Failure to understand transference manifestations is one of the commonest sources of failure for the amateur in psychotherapy. The first therapists lost many patients in this way, and inexperienced therapists still do.

In the case of the quibbles already discussed, the therapist may get the patient to resume his proper work in the following way: He calls attention to the connection between anxiety cues and the occurrence of quibbling. He asks the patient to notice that when free association produces anxiety the patient automatically turns to quibbling. If this is true and when the patient is convinced, the acquired drives to be logical and to get ahead with the work impel the patient to return to free association. The anxiety produced by calling quibbling an escape is greater than the reduction in fear produced by escaping the anxiety-provoking thoughts. Thus the reinforcement for quibbling is removed. At the same time the patient is motivated to stop quibbling.

Transference produces emotional responses for labeling. Labeling can occur most effectively when emotional responses are actually occurring. Contiguity is an important condition in connecting response and cue. Thus the verbal response "I am angry" is easiest attached to the cue of an angry emotion when the latter is present and strong. The therapeutic situation by permitting emotional responses to occur sets up the condition under which labeling can occur. As emotions are named or labeled, these names become part of the patient's thoughts and can be used in forecasting and planning behavior.

Therapy Limits Generalization

Transference reactions that occur early in the therapy are likely to be indiscriminate and wide. In the end, the patient has been taught to transfer more adaptively and discriminatingly, to treat the therapist for what he is—a specialist in mental life and behavior and not the mother, father, sweetheart, enemy, or sex partner of the patient. By studying and labeling his emotional reactions the patient also gets a greater degree of control over them. Known emotional responses can be controlled while unknown emotional responses may appear at unexpected moments and break up good plans and intentions.

Frustration due to Real-life Dilemmas

If the patient's demands in the therapeutic situation are excessive and are not met, as in the case of Mrs. A, the therapist may be the target of angry reproaches. Here the clarifying intellectual work of therapy may show the patient clearly that he is living under painful or obstructive real-life conditions. He may, for example, be in a "social-class trap" unable ever to reach his high social goals. The patient's wife or husband may really be stupid, once the generalizations of the past are clearly separated out from the appropriate reactions of the present. The patient must then face the pain of living with an inferior person or the conflict involved in getting a divorce. In other words, the process of confronting reality may bring painful vistas, and this pain is to some extent charged up to therapy and the therapist. If the proper positive motivation is preserved in the therapeutic situation, however, such pains will be borne.

Advantage of protected situation of therapy. As Freud remarked, there is one great advantage to the therapeutic situation from the standpoint of the patient. His blundering, confused emotional reactions can be expressed in therapy without the price which is often exacted from him in real life. He has a chance to learn, in a protected situation, to know himself and how he really feels. He is prevented by rule from acting on the sudden whims or impulsions which occur during the course of therapy. The intelligent patient will see that he is far better off in this secure situation than he was before when working out his neurotic trends in his daily life and suffering the real consequences of them.

SUMMARY

Strong emotions occur during the course of therapeutic work. They are directed at the therapist and are felt by the patient to be real. They occur because the permissive conditions of therapy weaken repression and inhibition and thus increase the net strength of inhibited tendencies. These tendencies generalize more strongly to the therapist than to others just because the avoidance responses to him are less strong. These responses are ones which, having been long inhibited, have frequently never been labeled. By labeling these emotions while they are occurring, the therapist makes it possible for them to be represented in the patient's reasoning and planning activity. Frequently these responses block therapeutic progress. By identifying them and showing that they are generalized, the therapist mobilizes the learned drives to be reasonable and healthy, thus helping the patient to return to his project of self-understanding. Generalization of emotional response is not only useful but inevitable; it is not purposive and should not be thought of as a duel.

CHAPTER XVIII

LABELING: TEACHING THE PATIENT TO THINK ABOUT NEW TOPICS

We have said that the neurotic is "stupid" in the areas where his emotions are in conflict. This stupidity is, however, relative and exists only by comparison with his mental powers in areas free of conflict. The stupidity is evident only to an outside observer; the neurotic person does not *feel* stupid. He knows he is miserable but he does not suspect the nature of his emotional conflict.

We are reminded of a pertinent anecdote concerning the death of Gertrude Stein. It seems that she came out of a deep coma to ask her companion Alice Toklas, "Alice, Alice, what is the answer?" Her companion replied, "There is no answer." Gertrude Stein continued, "Well, then, what is the question?" and fell back dead (Gregg, 1949, p. 280). The neurotic person also does not know the answer and, furthermore, he does not know there is a question. Eventually the therapist will supply the question and, if need be, the answer.

The neurotic is a person who is in need of a stock of sentences that will match the events going on within and without him. The new sentences make possible an immense facilitation of higher mental processes. With their aid he can discriminate and generalize more accurately; he can motivate himself for remote tasks; he can produce hope and caution within himself and aid himself in being logical, reasonable, and planful. By labeling a formerly unlabeled emotional response he can represent this response in reasoning.[1]

[1] *Warning.* While behavior theory provides us with a point of view of great utility, we are well aware that our equipment for analyzing labeling is still very imperfect. It is certain that we will overemphasize what we understand best. We are likely also to neglect or underemphasize aspects of the matter which we do not understand. Future research will enable us to see the matter more clearly and, in the meantime, we will do our best to clarify it.

It acquires a "voice" within the individual. The unknown response does not appear as a surprising element in a plan which had disregarded it. Occasions for action can be foreseen and judged in advance as to suitability. For example, the individual is forewarned as to whom he likes and dislikes so that he can try to avoid close contacts with people he actually dislikes and who might otherwise provoke him to unexpected outbursts of anger.

Close integration of free association, transference, and labeling. Any separation of free association, transference, and labeling is bound to seem and to be artificial. The work of free association and the study of transferred emotional responses tell the therapist where labeling is needed. As already indicated, free association points to repression through blocks in lines of association, slips, dreams, stereotyped outcomes, and other evidences. Similarly, the pantomime of transferred behavior presents the never-labeled emotional responses.

How the Therapist Knows What to Say

As the patient's verbal responses unroll, the therapist rehearses them. In other words, he listens to the patient. If the therapist has emotional responses attached to the sentences he rehearses, these emotions occur—constituting the basis of sympathy or empathy. If the patient's account is incomplete, a learned drive to complete it is excited in the therapist. In fact, this is the mechanism by which, from a behavioral standpoint, the therapist gets into action. If the patient's account is contradictory, a tendency to resolve the contradiction is aroused in the therapist. With his greater mental freedom, he may be able to resolve it at once within his own mind and be able to say what the logical account should be. He may or may not immediately announce his solution to the patient. Or he may note the contradiction, be unable to resolve it, and "set it aside" as a problem for later solution.

If the patient is acting under strong emotional stimulation but has no label, the therapist will tentatively label the emotion within his own mind. If the patient has sentences without having the appropriate emotions attached, the therapist notes this (often dangerous) sign. If the patient fears without reason, the therapist rehearses the fears and supplies the consolation to himself. Depending on his strategy, he may give such consolation then or withhold it.

If the patient lags, the therapist thinks the sentence which arouses learned drive within himself, and communicates it to the patient—and so on throughout the range of behavior possibilities. The therapist sees the missing connections, makes the discriminations and generalizations, sees the hidden forces of the dream. The whole transaction must go on in his mind. He may use the construction gained in several different ways, *i.e.*, to verify an innovation of the patient's, to select and repeat a chosen part of the patient's statement, or to announce a novel verbal unit which the patient cannot hit upon—but the therapist must have a correct construction or he cannot perform his function.

How the Therapist Notes Gaps and Defenses

The therapist often had occasion to point out gaps in Mrs. A's account of her life. For instance, she said that when plans were being made for her wedding her mother had favored a big wedding and her sister had insisted on a small one. Mrs. A said nothing about what her own wishes in this important matter had been. The therapist asked, "Didn't your wishes count for anything? Didn't it matter what *you* wanted?" The patient's account was obviously incomplete since it did not show a reasonable self-assertiveness.

Similarly, at another time, Mrs. A told how her brother had bossed her around and once even slapped her face after he had returned from Army service. She expressed no resentment toward him. The therapist asked, "Didn't that make you angry?" (Something is obviously lacking in the response repertory of an adult who does not resent physical punishment.)

An example of an inappropriate response occurred in one of the last hours of treatment. Mrs. A wept almost continuously, although nothing she said was sad enough to call for weeping (according to the therapist's rehearsal). The therapist asked, "Why are you crying? Isn't there something you should say and don't want to say?" Later in this hour Mrs. A confirmed this interpretation by saying, "It seems that I don't want to talk about something and then I want to cry." She thereupon ventured on a new line of thought. In psychoanalytic terms, the crying served as a defense. In the language of learning theory, crying was rewarded because it enabled Mrs. A to avoid anxious thoughts. When the therapist pointed out that crying was a way of avoiding talking, he was trying to evoke all of Mrs. A's motives to continue the work despite fear. In the above examples, the therapist labeled fear of anger and fear of talking.

When the Therapist Should Intervene

The therapist should intervene only when he begins to have some rough construction as to what is repressed. This construction is built from observation, hints, gaps, emotional reactions, and other signs already discussed. The creation of hypotheses inevitably takes time. Even if he wished to, the therapist could not immediately announce to his patient everything the latter needed to know. Further, the therapist should not intervene until the patient ceases to make progress by himself. The therapist should give no help that is not urgently needed. Finally, knowing that his intervention may create stress, the therapist should take into account what the patient can bear at the time.

Successive Approximation in the Therapist's Hypotheses

The therapist's earliest hypotheses about dynamics are usually much less accurate than later ones. He should be constantly refining his hypotheses to get as good a fit to the facts as possible. He can hit on correct surmises sooner if he has a knowledge of psychodynamic principles and wide experience. It is of great advantage to the therapist to know what the most likely areas of repression are. If he knows, for instance, that sexual and hostile wishes are likely to be repressed, he can more quickly fill in, at least tentatively, the gaps in the patient's account and can more readily decode the patient's mute transferred behavior. The skillful therapist, however, does not make interpretations on mere hunches. He waits until he has strong evidence for his hypothesis before he supplies a label, points out a transferred response, or teaches a discrimination. If the patient is to be convinced, the evidence must be convincing. The fewer ill-founded notions the therapist utters, the greater his authority when he does speak.

Three Ways in Which the Patient Can Learn New Verbal Responses

Apparently there are at least three ways in which the patient can acquire new verbal units. First, he can hit upon them by himself in the course of thinking out loud, with silent verification by the therapist. Second, certain of his responses can be strengthened by selective repetition on the part of the therapist. The therapist notes and repeats some things the patient says but neglects others. Third, the patient can acquire new responses by rehearsal from the therapist. The therapist can provide labeling when it is missing in the account that the patient gives. Only the last has traditionally been called "an interpretation."

What Is a Novel Verbal Response?

Novelty in the case of a verbal response does not consist merely in learning a new word or sentence. The patient may have many words in his vocabulary which he "knows" in a technical sense but which are but loosely and vaguely connected to specific cues. The patient knows that these words are English words and can recite them but cannot use them appropriately and discriminatingly. We therefore regard connecting the word to the right cues as being a genuine element of novelty. If a word but vaguely used in the past is pinned exactly to the correct emotional or environmental cues during the course of therapy, we feel free to call such a word a "new" verbal response. For example, the patient may use the word "angry" to label the behavior of others and even to label his own behavior in some situations. But the defect may be in labeling anger directed toward his wife, *i.e.*, those cues have no label. Novelty consists in giving the cues a label. Similarly, a neurotic soldier may correctly label everything about his fancied disability except the intense reduction of anxiety which it brings. The cue produced by sharp reduction in anxiety does not have the verbal response "I'm not afraid any more" attached. We emphasize, in this connection, that a single missing unit in a verbal series may seriously distort an account of behavior. In the foregoing case, unnoticed reduction in fear may strongly reinforce the sentence "I'm really sick."

Novelty in this case would consist in labeling fear reduction and connecting this label to others which correctly described the course of events. Thus the patient may himself discover the correct use of a word he already knows, the therapist may emphasize a weak connection by repetition or he may connect the vaguely known verbal response to new and significant emotional or environmental cues. In any of these cases the element of novelty is present.

Method I: The Patient Himself Hits on Verbal Novelties

The situation of free association helps the patient himself to create verbal novelties in a number of different ways. In the first place it puts upon him the compulsion to verbal experimentation and holds him to considerable periods of practice at the new skill. This experience is likely to be the first of the kind he has had. The therapist selectively encourages this freedom and fails to reward falling silent or thinking in routine ways. Further, as the patient hits on new lines of thought, the new verbal cues evoke anxiety responses. Such fearful reactions are gradually extinguished in the permissive situation of therapy. The patient speaks with reluctance or fright and finds that no punishment follows. Thereupon the patient "gains confidence"; that is, extinction effects generalize from the cues of sentences which have not been punished to other incipient sentences to which fear is attached. Both enforced experimentation and extinction of fear tend to create a new habit of "freedom of thought" which helps the patient to hit on verbal novelties. Some of these novelties constitute solutions to his problem at the mental level. It could be said of psychotherapy, therefore, that it tends automatically to make the patient more intelligent.

Furthermore, as the patient wrests new sentences from the effects of repression, he gains more mental units with which to think and thereby increases his chances of accurate labeling, reasoning, and plan-making. In some cases the patient will know immediately that he has created a valuable new sentence because drive reduction (insight) occurs at once. In other cases, he refers his new construction to the therapist with the implied question "Is it correct?" The patient will say, "I must have been more disappointed than I realized that Christmas when I got a pair of shoes instead of a sled." Or, "I must have loved my mother very much or I wouldn't have been so angry at her when the new baby was born." Patients, once involved in the work, frequently hit upon inferences of this kind independently. In a case fragment contributed by Dr. Richard Newman,[2] a patient with a stomach-ache had learned that his pains in the head frequently occurred when he had certain angry thoughts. The patient expanded this idea analogically and said, "If a thought can cause pain in the head, maybe it can also cause pain in the stomach."

At the beginning of therapy the patient is likely to be very poor at original thinking. He has already done his best to extricate himself from his neurotic conflict by the use of his own mind and has failed. Toward the end of therapy, such original thoughts should be a more striking feature of the patient's mental life. After therapy, he will have to count on himself for all the plans necessary to adapt to life circumstances. The more of the essential work the patient can perform by himself during therapy, the more certain he is to be able to do what he needs afterward. The therapist should be careful not to deprive the patient of the pleasure of making his own discoveries.

Method II: Patient's Responses Strengthened by Selective Repetition

It is possible to have a marked effect on the patient's thinking even though the therapist never "tells him anything new." The patient will be saying a great many things. Some of these will seem more important to the therapist than others. If the therapist will merely notice those that he thinks important and neglect those he thinks not important, he can materially affect the patient's thinking. Method II is appropriate when the patient presents a number of different, confused, and jumbled facts and hypotheses. Since the therapist's attention is a strong reward, any one of the patient's thoughts that he chooses to notice is likely to be strengthened to its attendant cues. Such thoughts are more likely to recur than those which are neglected.

[2] Associate Clinical Professor of Psychiatry and Mental Hygiene at Yale University.

There are a variety of ways by which the therapist may notice and reward the sentences of the patient. He may say "Uhuh" to some sentences but not to others. He may include some matters in a summary of the patient's remarks which he makes ostensibly to clarify the matter for himself but actually to clarify it for the patient. But he may omit other matters from such a summary and thus "pass them by." The therapist may repeat what the patient has said in some cases but not in others. The effect of such selective intervention is to help the patient untangle his confused emotions and put his mental units into a useful order.

The rewarding effect of such notice is entirely automatic. The patient need not realize what is happening. As we pointed out previously, this was tested experimentally by Greenspoon (1950) who instructed subjects to "say all the words they could think of." Whenever the subjects said a plural noun the experimenter gave some expression of approval. ("Mmm-hmm!") It was found that the subjects began to give plural words to a reliably greater degree than singular words. Only a very few of the subjects "caught on" to the fact that it was the plural words which were being rewarded. This work seemed to show that such signs have reward effect and that such effect is automatic.

There is another way in which merely repeating a sentence of the patient's may have a teaching effect. The therapist may choose to repeat a sentence which is contradictory to something else the patient has said and thus, by calling attention to the contradiction, evoke in the patient the drive to be logical. Gaps in a story can be pointed out by repeating in a questioning tone an explanation which the therapist deems unsatisfactory.

Selective repetition, like every other device of the therapist, should be used sparingly. The therapist who treated Mrs. A tells us that he talked too much in the first hours with her. His talkativeness had the effect of encouraging Mrs. A's dependence and of blocking the train of free associations. If the therapist is chatty he can "talk the patient out of" giving him valuable information. When Freud said that treatment should go forward under conditions of privation, he meant, among other things, that the patient should get as little direct reward out of the treatment as possible (Freud,

1924, Vol. II, pp. 383–384; 396). The advantages of reflecting back and clarifying have been stressed by Rogers (1942).

Asking questions of the patient is a variant of this selective approach, provided that they are a request for clarification of material already introduced by the patient. The question functions then as a kind of hint. It says, "Look in this place" and thus narrows the area of search. Such limited questioning can be exemplified in the case of Mrs. A. "After I told you *that about my brother,*" Mrs. A once told the therapist, "my fears were much less." The therapist directed Mrs. A's attention by saying, "What about your brother? You have told me that he 'took advantage' of you but we don't know what it meant to you. How did you feel about it?" Thus the therapist encouraged Mrs. A to express her feelings about her brother. If let alone, however, Mrs. A would have glossed over this topic with the phrase "that about my brother."

Introduction to Method III: Rehearsal

Before discussing new verbal units learned by the patient by rehearsal of the therapist's sentences we will briefly refer to the mechanism of rehearsal itself. Rehearsal is matched-dependent imitative behavior in the verbal sphere. It is learned with considerable difficulty and over long periods of time in early life. In ordinary terms, it constitutes listening.

If a verbal response is strongly opposed by anxiety, acquiring it by rehearsal has great advantages over waiting to hit upon the same response oneself. Rehearsal causes the needed verbal response to occur in the patient while the relevant cues are present. The patient may never learn to label an emotion by himself because the label and the cues produced by the emotion never occur at the same time. By his comment and the patient's rehearsal of it, the therapist can make sure that the verbal response and cue and the emotional response and cue are occurring at approximately the same time. We have seen in the last chapter how careful the therapist was to label Mrs. A's sexual emotions, calling them sexual, when he was quite sure that they were active and that the emotional cue was present.

Rehearsal by paraphrase. The patient may, and frequently does, paraphrase the sentences of the therapist instead of rehearsing them exactly. Apparently the paraphrase has the same effect as the original sentences provided it is correct. An example of incorrect paraphrase (which we use with thanks) comes from a case of our colleague, Dr. Richard Newman. Dr. Newman's patient was suffering from a neurosis mainly caused by bottling up his feelings of anger toward his wife and business associates. His unverbalized anger was expressed only by indirect physiological action, *e.g.*, a pain in the stomach, headaches, a pain in the neck. The therapist tried gradually to have the patient recognize and label his hostile feelings so that he could deal with them intelligently. At the end of each hour, however, the patient would ask the therapist, "So when I begin to feel nerved up I should just forget it, huh, Doc?" The therapist had to explain again that the patient must not forget his hostile feelings. The patient's paraphrase was so different from what the therapist had intended that it seemed almost ludicrous.

Rehearsal is swift. Rehearsal need not be labored and conscious as when one whispers a phrase of a foreign language half out loud. One's own language, heavily overlearned, can produce cues which are less and less strong and distinctive as the language habit becomes more and more automatic. Nor does the patient need to give immediate evidence of rehearsal. Rehearsed sentences may take some time to "soak in." Indeed, the patient may say, "Yes, that's right," without really accepting and making use of the interpretation. The final test must be the effect on the further mental life of the patient.

Mrs. A seldom repeated out loud the new sentences that had been taught her, but the therapist's statements had their effect none the less. Evidence of this was her reference in later hours to interpretations that she had mulled over. For example, she said, "You know, I was thinking about what you said about getting excited when my brother took advantage of me. I don't think I did then, but when my uncle fondled me—I was excited then." Mrs. A is here giving a delayed reaction to an earlier interpretation. She is also shown creatively expanding and correcting the first interpretation.

Reward for rehearsal. Rehearsal, like any other habitual response, must be rewarded, and it is. Many statements of the therapist which are rehearsed provide secondary rewards, *i.e.*, inhibit anxiety and offer hope. Rehearsed responses frequently enable the patient to make discriminations which reduce fear and thus reward rehearsal. In the case of Mrs. A the therapist pointed out to her that she would feel somewhat worse before she felt better but in due course she would feel better. This assurance seemed to help Mrs. A to bear the anxiety that was aroused by confronting her problem.

Not only does a useful interpretation reduce tension directly but it also gives the patient the feeling of "getting somewhere." In the case of Mrs. A careful therapeutic work had at last enabled her to tell the therapist that her brother had "taken advantage of" her. The result of this admission was striking. She experienced immediate reduction in anxiety when she found that the therapist did not condemn her. Her heart symptoms disappeared along with a good deal of her fear. She came into the psychiatrist's office the next hour in a gay mood, announcing as she entered, "Well, I think we've got it licked." This remarkable result of telling the therapist an event from her past life did not fail to impress her. Mrs. A had received a convincing demonstration that listening to the therapist and following the rule could have a significant effect.

Real-life success in reducing conflicting drives will retroactively strengthen rehearsal. If as a result of therapeutic work the patient is able to make and carry out plans which do reduce emotional conflict, all responses attached to the therapist and the therapeutic situation are reinforced. Confidence in the therapist is strengthened, free association becomes easier, and habits of rehearsal become stronger.

Rehearsal can produce anxiety. Not everything that the patient hears from the therapist is agreeable. The patient may be called upon to rehearse sentences which produce sharp anxiety. Under such circumstances the patient would be expected to resist rehearsal. It is common under such circumstances for the patient to mis-hear or not to hear at all. For example, after the therapist had made an anxiety-arousing interpretation Mrs. A sometimes asked, "What did you say?" She had been unable to rehearse the sentences because her anxiety mounted when she rehearsed and only decreased to a bearable level when she stopped rehearsing.

Under such circumstances the attempt to repeat anxiety-inciting sentences may lead the patient to an irrelevant response, *i.e.*, start the patient off on a new line of thought. In the following quotation from Mrs. A we see her producing confused associations to a question which aroused anxiety. She said, "My husband and I both used to work together. I gave him my salary . . . Now I'm no longer happy about buying things. It doesn't seem that I want anything. I tried to go shopping the other day—I had to leave and go home. I was afraid something would happen to me—I don't know why."

The therapist asked, *"What could it be that would happen to you?"*

Mrs. A continued (irrelevantly):

Sometimes my heart beating—I think I'd do something silly when I was in the store. (*Pause.*) I keep seeing that apartment. . . . I used to like to be alone—to be quiet. When I was home last year I always had to be doing something all the time. I couldn't sit still and carry on a conversation with my parents. But I liked staying home at my mother-in-law's. I was happy when my husband was at home." (*Pause.*) "Isn't it awful to be scared of yourself?" (*Pause.*) "I wanted a family. I don't want it any more."

We see in this excerpt how Mrs. A would begin to develop a line of thought and then become anxious and start off on another topic. This behavior is all the more remarkable because Mrs. A can speak cogently when she is not under emotional stress.

At some times resistance to rehearsal can be extreme. We have known a patient to beg a therapist to stop talking, not to finish an interpretation that he had begun. In this case the therapist was raising the question as to whether or not the patient had masturbated and been punished for it in early childhood. Though the question seemed a natural extension of what had gone before, the patient reacted with intolerable anxiety.

The management of rehearsal is a delicate matter. It involves judging what is constructive and what is not and what the patient can and cannot bear. As usual, the therapist must keep the balance of rewards for listening and rehearsing stronger than the punishments inflicted by rehearsal. In practical terms, the therapist must be careful not to set the patient an impossible task. Correct management of the therapeutic situation is a high skill and the therapist well earns his fees if he performs his task correctly.

Method III: Teaching New Verbal Units

By teaching new verbal units we mean that the patient acquires such responses and that they are attached to the correct cues—emotional, environment, verbal, and instrumental. If the patient can hit upon these new units himself or if cautious repetition will serve to teach him, there is no need for the therapist to intervene further. However, the learning required is difficult. The patient may not spontaneously produce the desired sentences when emotional stimuli are active; or he may fail correctly to pair the verbal with the environmental event. Selective repetition may not have the opportunity to strengthen responses which the patient makes because the needed responses do not occur. In such a case, the therapist who does not actively teach new verbal units must content himself with inferior results. If the patient cannot make the required innovation in some manner, the therapist cannot help him by repetition or clarification. If the therapist is prevented by his theory from originating and offering verbal units at the appropriate time and place, he may have to be satisfied at the end of therapy with a patient who is still befuddled on important issues.

Does interpretation impede therapy? We believe that it can be highly in the patient's interest to have the therapist "prompt" him when he himself persistently fails to hit on the right verbal units. In fact, we do not see, in many cases of severe neurosis, how the therapist can get along without doing this. The therapist's interpretation says, in fact, "Could this be the emotion involved? Is it fear that is stopping you? Do your interests somehow conflict with those of your father-in-law?" If such notions are needed and the patient does not hit on them there seems no alternative to such interpretative prompting. If the patient is greatly in need of these sentences and if having them brings great relief, he will not feel that the therapist is unduly influencing him.

There may be a slight tendency in all patients to resist interpretation because of the feeling that they should solve all problems themselves and not accept help from anyone. This can be called a "drive for independence" which is taught by home and school in childhood. The child is discouraged from too easily running for help. Neurotic persons have such independent motives but they are usually of small effect compared to the misery which impels them to seek therapeutic aid. At least while the needed help is forthcoming, they are very appreciative.

We have repeatedly noted, however, a case in which interpretations are really resented and produce avoidant behavior on the part of the patient, thereby slowing down the progress of therapy. This is the case where a stupid or awkward interpretation produces strong fear or other shock reaction. The patient reacts with resistance exactly as if a cruel therapist had attached a grid to his patient's chair and given him a strong shock. It is too little realized that fear reactions of shocklike strength can be attached to the mere sentences which the therapist utters and the patient rehearses. Apart from such understandable circumstances, patients seem to welcome useful contributions to their verbal series.

There is one other case which should be rare in psychotherapy because such patients should rarely be accepted. This is the one where the patient is engaged in a desperate attempt to repress homosexual tendencies. Such patients, as a result of their conflict, may be especially restive at any attempt to influence them and quite intolerant of any "help." This follows because they interpret help as an attempt to subordinate them. Constantly on the alert lest homosexual tendencies get out of control, they must reassure themselves by claims of extraordinary mastery and independence. Similarly, if the would-be helper is a person of the same sex, his nearness may activate homosexual appetite and intensify the already existent conflict.

If the therapist knows his business and so does not inflict undue pain on his patient and if he avoids such cases as just described, he may safely feel that interpretation will forward the work of therapy when the signs indicate its use. He should under no circumstances put an absolute ban on its use, and, we believe, no good therapist actually does, whatever his theoretical protestations may be.

Detailed mechanism of learning new labels. Let us say now exactly what the teaching of a new verbal unit involves. Motivated by his misery and involved in the situation of psychotherapy, the patient is rehearsing such sentences as are provided by the therapist. Rehearsal thus gets the new verbal units tried out. The new response will be extinguished if it proves useless (a bad guess on the part of the therapist later to be recalled or corrected) and will be strengthened and confirmed if it is rewarded. Any label at all should be strengthened to some degree if it is plausible, since it will reduce the learned motive to have a name for everything. Such reinforcement will be transient, however, unless the label is correct and therefore useful, since the motive to label is only reduced by getting what proves to be the correct label. Labeling may be reinforced also if the label rehearsed has the direct property of inhibiting the responses which produce a learned drive, such as fear (as when the doctor says, "It's *not* cancer."). A label may further be reinforced if it is the means of providing a drive-reducing discrimination or generalization (rapidly learning a new telephone number so you do not have to call the operator for it). A labeling response may also be reinforced by irrelevant learned rewards (such as a therapist's misplaced praise). Labels may likewise be strengthened by the retroactive effect of primary-drive reduction, provided always that some mechanism for bridging the temporal gap is available (for instance, labels and descriptions of edible foods strengthened by hunger-drive reduction). This is a mechanism by which one always hopes to profit in the case of psychotherapy.

Verbal labels attached to various kinds of cues. By the means just described, verbal labels can be strengthened to any cues—emotional, environmental, other verbal, or instrumental. This process has already been described in the case of teaching the words "sex excitement" to the patient's strong but unclear sex emotion. The pairing of cues with concurrent emotional, environmental, instrumental, or other verbal stimuli is particularly useful because the verbal cue then becomes part of the environmental pattern. In this way reactions attached to the environmental stimuli can generalize to the verbal cue alone and be elicited by it. If the stimulus of the word "hot" is patterned with the sight of the radiator, the retraction response learned to the visual cues of the radiator and the pain of the burn can generalize to the verbal cues of the word "hot." The person can then stop himself from approaching the radiator by saying the word "hot."

Verbal responses can produce cues to which other verbal responses are attached. If I write, for instance, "Mary had a little lamb . . ." the reader will almost compulsively add the verbal responses which are connected to the terminal stimuli, *i.e.*, "its fleece was white as snow." If I say, "The bigger they come" the reader will likely fill in, "the harder they fall." These are cases of verbal response units tied to verbal cues. Finally, we teach the patient to add appropriate instrumental responses to the cues of the verbal responses he produces. If the patient says, "I intend to go home," we expect him shortly to perform the instrumental response of walking to his door.

These matters are illustrated in part in the case of Mrs. A. When Mrs. A came into therapy she let it be known that she was on good terms with her mother-in-law. Although she had actually been angry in situations where her mother-in-law was present, she did not know she was angry or that her mother-in-law was the target of this emotion. As the information came in, however, it turned out that the mother-in-law had administered a whole series of damaging status affronts to Mrs. A and her family. When the mother-in-law came to Mrs. A's wedding, she insulted Mrs. A's family by staying at the hotel and refusing to visit the family. Later, the mother-in-law advised her son about his life insurance without considering his wife's wishes. The mother-in-law described Mrs. A as "lazy." She refused to have Mrs. A visit her house when important status relatives were present. In short, she humiliated and insulted Mrs. A. Despite these affronts Mrs. A was outwardly meek and submissive.

Mrs. A repressed her hostility toward her mother-in-law, just as she had repressed her hostility toward her mother in childhood. This repression prevented her from recognizing it and from reacting appropriately to the social affronts. She did not recognize that her mother-in-law was competing with her for her husband's love (recognizing this, of course, involved recognizing her hatred for her mother-in-law). After Mrs. A was able to express resentment of the insults she had endured from her mother-in-law (when she found that the therapist encouraged her and did not take her to task for being angry) her anxiety about saying and thinking hostile thoughts was greatly reduced. She was able to discover that her mother-in-law was jealous of her. She was able to label her anger (make it conscious) and to recognize the social cue (mother-in-law) who evoked it. She was also able to put new demands on her mother-in-law.

A beautiful example of appropriate labeling came forward in a case well known to us. During the second hour of therapy the patient became excited, began to weep and tremble, to lose his breath, and to show other signs of marked perturbation. The therapist understanding the behavior as a transferred fear reaction to himself said, "You realize that you are having an attack of anxiety?" This interpretation tended to stop the hysterical behavior and the patient slowly "cooled off." The therapist had explained to this intelligent patient that he was having an attack of "unreasonable fear." A statement from an authority that a fear is unreasonable tended to inhibit anxiety in this patient who had learned previously to be comforted by such statements. Furthermore, it showed the attack to be an event known to the therapist—experienced before and presumably manageable. The idea that helpful skill was at hand was also comforting. The patient had not at all realized that his behavior was motivated by fear. Labeling the emotion "fear" helped to discriminate the current safe situation from a really dangerous one.

Similarly, the therapist had to deal with an exaggerated fear of death in the case of Mrs. A. He did this by contrasting her actual chances of dying soon with her morbid fear of death, saying, "You should live to be eighty, according to life insurance tables." The therapist did not, of course, think that his reassurance would remove her fear because he knew he had not touched the root of it. But, by showing in a striking fashion how unrealistic the fear was he hoped to make Mrs. A say to herself, "This fear is silly. Why should I have it? What am I really afraid of?" Such questions could, and did, lead to the discovery of what really caused the fear, *i.e.*, an intense anxiety attached to her sexual feelings and wishes. She felt she ought to die because she had been "so sinful" as to enjoy sex relations with her husband.

Ordering verbal responses as clarification. In addition to attaching verbal responses to emotional cues and pairing verbal cues with environmental cues, we have noted the importance of attaching verbal responses to other verbal cues. This is the department of linking or ordering verbal responses, in many cases responses already occurring in other connections. It is sometimes referred to as "clarification." The verbal responses in question must be ordered in a proper causal sequence so that the patient can, for example, say that he became sick *after* (and therefore because) he was not to be promoted. To have sentences that match the temporal order of events is thus of high importance. The patient should be able to say that his neurotic behavior began *after* the death of a comrade with whom he was somewhat rivalrous. If the patient's sentences are not correctly arranged in such causal or temporal order, it may be impossible for him to know what has happened to him in the past. The therapist attempts to aid the patient to get the verbal links fitted in correctly so that they truthfully describe what has gone on, both within and without him. Having such links correctly established enables the patient to plan sensibly and practically.

An example from the case of Mrs. A should make this matter clearer. One day Mrs. A told the therapist she had been frightened on the preceding afternoon as she was coming home from the house of a friend who lived in the country. Mrs. A had accepted a ride from a strange man who was driving a truck. They had struck up a conversation. She asked whether he was married. He volunteered that he was married but not devoted to his wife. He asked her, in turn, how old she was, if she was married, and so forth. She replied. Then she began to get frightened that he would "take advantage of" her so she invented an excuse to get out of his truck. Seeing an old woman on the sidewalk, Mrs. A said, "Oh, there's my aunt! I'll wait with her and take the bus."

Since the conversation between the truck driver and Mrs. A struck the therapist as having preliminary sexual implications, he asked Mrs. A whether she had been sexually aroused by the man. She denied this. "You did get into the truck, though," he pointed out, "and this exposed you to some danger. What made you get in it?"

In this case, the therapist did not have the evidence to press home his interpretation; he felt that Mrs. A had been sexually aroused and that she had half contrived the circumstance under which she could be "taken advantage of." Other evidence introduced later fully confirmed his suspicion. In this case, the therapist had hoped, by reordering the events and showing the part Mrs. A herself played in bringing about the danger situation, to help her from then on to make better guesses as to what effect her actions would have. Her ability to predict her behavior depended mainly on recognizing clearly and concretely the sexual wishes which were impelling her. She had many times before been seduced in situations like the one described above but had always afterward denied to herself (and the therapist) that she had in any way desired the situation or unconsciously arranged it.

Once Mrs. A had her labeling straightened out, she could connect the correct instrumental responses to the adequate verbal cues. In the case just recounted she could, for instance, ask herself if she was trying to bring about the "rape" situation and resolve not to get into the truck. She could instead, after this soliloquy, walk to the bus station and wait for the public bus. In order that labeling be really effective it must be connected to the instrumental responses which serve to get the person out of danger situations. The most complete verbal-mental account in the world is of no use unless the cues of the terminal verbal responses are connected to the actions which have an effect in real life.

Labels should be homely and convincing. Therapists should not try to teach patients the professional labels of the technician. As Freud has said (1925, Vol. III, pp. 60–61), the words that the patient already knows and has been using are always better, *i.e.,* they already have attached to them the emotional responses that are critical. If the patient is asked to learn a technical term the therapist will have to start in from the beginning and teach the patient to attach it to the correct emotional and environmental cues. Using the well-known words is therefore an economy in learning. In the case of Mrs. A the therapist occasionally fell into the error of using a technical word. For example, when he was trying to teach Mrs. A to discriminate between eliminative functions and sexual ones he spoke of "defecation" instead of using the common word. When Mrs. A asked what "defecation" meant, the therapist realized he had erred by choosing the technical term. It turned out that Mrs. A had several terms for eliminative activities and of these the therapist chose the one which aroused least anxiety.

Labeling should never be haphazard or theoretical. It should be useful on the face of it and should solve real problems. Both patient and therapist should recognize the importance of such real issues. For example, labeling Mrs. A's attitude toward sex as "fear" explained why her marriage was unsatisfactory and why she was so miserable; both she and the therapist recognized that her unhappy marriage and the phobic fears of her daily life were crucial problems. Finding correct labels in this area was what the patient came for.

Similarly, the depressed patient feels his depression as an unutterable misery. It is a real problem on which he desperately needs help. In one such case at a crucial moment the therapist said, "If you were really angry instead of indifferent when Jones insulted you, that would explain why you are depressed now. Anger, even though justified, may have aroused strong guilt within you, and it may be the latter which you experience as your depression." In this case, labeling the angry emotion and calling it legitimate helped make the self-punishing depression unnecessary. It is in such situations of intense pain and conflict that correct labeling has its strongest justification.

Stopping to think. In addition to learning new and correct labeling, the patient must frequently learn to "stop and think." Part of his trouble in the past may have been that he has had the habit of putting bad plans impulsively into effect. He must learn that good plans are rarely perfected without effort, and he must learn to stop and canvass his plans. Learned drives to be logical, rational, practical, and sensible should be attached to and aroused by the stimuli of conflict. Uneasiness about a prospective course of action should not be suppressed but treasured. Action should be stopped and attention focused on the doubtful plan. The patient must learn

when the going is rough, stop and think. Is there evidence for unlabeled emotional responses? If so, labeling must be completed. Do the sentences available correctly match environmental stimuli? If not, they must be made to. Are there inconsistent sentence elements in the plan? If so, they should be removed. Is the plan complete; that is, does it forecast a likely successful course of action? Does the plan indicate a specific and feasible set of "first things to do" once planning is accomplished? If not, the initial action responses must be indicated in the plan.

All this describes what we mean behaviorally when we speak of "stopping to think." Since stopping to think is effortful it will presumably be learned only by those whose "rushing into action" has been punished in the past. Just why mental activity is so effortful and expensive is not completely understood. In the light of the pride man has in his "reason," it is surprising how reluctant he is to think. The reluctance is understandable in those cases where thinking is blocked by fear, but perhaps there are also other factors.

Evaluation of the Three Methods of Teaching

Method I, that of allowing the patient to hit on new verbal units for himself, is obviously to be preferred. Indeed if Method I is possible to begin with, the patient is rapidly cured. When it becomes possible the patient can be dismissed. The advantages of Method I are obvious. When the patient makes a verbal response out loud, the therapist can be certain that it is being made, but when the patient is silently rehearsing, the therapist cannot be so sure. Responses made out loud are probably stronger and produce more distinctive cues than silent ones. When the patient hits on the unit himself, it is made in the presence of the correct cues and does not have to be learned to new situational cues, thought cues, or drive cues. Finally the patient can bear any response he makes himself or it would not occur. However, the patient may not be able to perform according to Method I. Relevant responses may be swamped by fear. The patient is sick just because his mind is lamed by repression, and he cannot use it freely to solve his problems.

Method II is advisable when the patient presents a number of different hypotheses and labels. The therapist gets the impression of confusion. Fear responses prevent the correct ordering or patterning of verbal responses and cues. The patient is creating some of the needed units, but he is unable to line them up in the right way. Here the method of selective repetition can be used advantageously. The therapist can help to order and connect, to focus attention on problems, to highlight and simplify. The advantages of Method II are those of economy and safety. Responses which have already appeared must be learned to new verbal cues (that is, in new connections) but do not have to be loaned to the patient by rehearsal. The patient is probably also better able to tolerate the new ordering since he has already produced some of the subunits for himself.

The difficulty with Method II is obvious—the fragments of response needed for effective ordering may not appear. They may be blocked by frightened resistance, or the patient may be preoccupied by transferred emotion. Such factors may make therapy so slow that it threatens to drag on forever, or may enable the patient to leave therapy without ever having recognized and dealt with anything more than his most superficial problems.

Method III should be used when the patient has no useful hypotheses or labels in areas which are nevertheless indubitably problematic. If the patient struggles, if time passes and he cannot help himself, the therapist much teach new verbal labels. He originates these in his own mind and speaks them to the patient. The patient tries them out by rehearsal.

There are several disadvantages of this method, even granting for the moment that the therapist always hits on the right labels. For one, the therapist is less certain that the patient is making the response when he is rehearsing than when he is speaking it out loud. The patient may be thinking of something else while the therapist is talking. For another, the silently made verbal responses are probably weaker and less distinctive than spoken ones. For another, the rehearsed responses must be generalized from the therapist's voice plus concurrent drive cues, thoughts, and environmental cues to the latter alone. Finally there is the danger of "interpretation shock" already referred to. The patient may find it hard or impossible to bear the emotional reactions bestirred in him by rehearsing the interpretation. The necessity of rehearsal may also frustrate weak independence wishes of the patient.

Despite all, the therapist must frequently teach new verbal units directly. Neither he nor the patient can afford to wait out the process of independent creation, in whole or even in part. Indeed, such creation may never occur at all. Risks attendant on interpretation must be run. These risks can be reduced by the skilled therapist-teacher who, as already shown, would always make novel interpretations in a provisional way. It should be remembered, on the positive side, that interpretations can be immensely useful and can provide the patient with just those units he needs to solve the deadly problems of the neurosis.

Filling the patient in on the verbal units he needs is, of course, a highly important undertaking. The attempt at logical analysis here given necessarily distorts the actual course of events. All ways of improving labeling will be used during the same therapeutic hour. Free-associative and transferred emotional responses are continuously being produced. The therapist is constantly rehearsing what the patient says and feeling within himself the learned drives to make the patient's account more complete and sensible. Labeling goes on inevitably in a cut-and-fit manner because the therapist's knowledge of repressed responses is always provisional. The patient fears his work of free association and sometimes the therapist's interpretations. The result is that the course of an individual therapeutic situation is slow and haphazard. The best hope of speeding therapy along now seems to be an utter clarification of the theory on which therapy is based. With such a theory the therapist will, at least, not waste time by mistakes. A clear theory, functioning as a set of self-instructions to the therapist, permits the best moves to be made with the utmost economy.

Emotional vs. Intellectual Learning

It must be clear from the foregoing that we are not advocating any mere intellectualization of the therapeutic process. The patient has a direct, new, emotional experience with the therapist. He extinguishes real fear, feels real anger, identifies real dependence, and tries out responsible action—all within the frame of the therapeutic situation. These experiences in the transference relationship constitute the "corrective emotional experience" of which Alexander and French (1946, pp. 22, 253) have written. Some of this learning can and does occur unconsciously, that is, without labeling. We believe, however, that the learning is more transferable, and therefore more efficient, when adequate labeling occurs.

Such a view of the matter makes it impossible for the therapist to hope for cure merely by announcing his own insights to the patient—a mistake that is characteristic of those not trained in therapy. The patient himself must have the emotional experience and must correctly label it. If the patient has only a collection of sentences not tied to emotional or instrumental responses, little immediate therapeutic effect may be anticipated, though some delayed effects may occasionally occur. If the patient is so frightened that he cannot listen, interpretation will have small effect. The therapist's interpretations must be timely, that is, must occur when the patient can listen and when the emotional response to be labeled is actually occurring. We believe, however, that the nature and use of adequate labeling has been too little understood, and so we have highlighted its role in the total therapeutic process. We emphatically do not take the stand that mere labeling can be important if it is not immediately linked with the emotional, instrumental, and other responses which are being manifested and *changed* in the relation between patient and therapist.

CHAPTER XIX

TEACHING THE PATIENT TO DISCRIMINATE: ROLE OF PAST AND PRESENT

One of the most interesting and important aspects of higher mental life is the way in which verbal cues can make *different* stimulus patterns seem *equivalent* and *similar* stimulus patterns seem sharply *different*. These properties of verbal cues play an important role in psychotherapy. Most generally stated, the problem is to keep the patient's behavior up to date, to keep it in accord with current conditions of life. In order to modernize the neurotic patient he must frequently learn to try out new responses appropriate to new conditions and, in order to get him to try out these responses, he must clearly see that the conflicts and repressions from which he suffers are not justified by the current conditions of reward and punishment. He must further learn that the conditions in the past which produced these conflicts are sharply dissimilar from those of the present, thanks to age-grading and often to original mistraining. He must notice that many of his current habits are similar to those which he had in childhood and were learned in childhood under childhood conditions.

As a result of noting these similarities and differences, the patient becomes convinced that his neurotic behavior is functionally obsolete, and this conviction gives him the courage, which he has not had, to try new responses. If he tries such responses and, if they are rewarded, the neurotic impasse is broken up and the patient begins to learn anew.

Similarity of Current Conflict with That of the Past

One of Freud's earliest and most important findings was the continuity of neurotic behavior from childhood into adulthood (Freud, 1924, Vol. I, pp. 242–243; 317–318). The emotional conflict and accompanying repression actually occurred in early years. But they became strikingly obvious only when the child left the protected situation of the family and attempted to assume the burdens of adult life (Fry, 1942, pp. 100–101).

The first task of the therapist is to identify the neurotic habits of the patient as they appear in daily life. Relevant evidence is provided by the free-association data and in the transference. Frequently this information is surprising to the patient. He knows well enough his rosary of symptoms but is astonished to note his abnormal dependence, suspicion, or fright. Thereafter, retrospective data often permit the therapist to follow the same habits backward through the life history and to find that they have existed as long as the patient can remember. The therapist is then able to help the patient identify these habits of childhood and to show their similarity to those of adult life. By picking out and naming "what is the same" in childhood and adult behavior, the therapist can put these habits into a common class or, as we say, give them an acquired similarity which they have not hitherto had.

The patient will perceive, for instance, the same patterns of response toward his wife that he had shown so much earlier toward his mother. In one case the following similarities appeared: the patient noticed that he expected the same dominance from his wife as from his mother, had the same passive wish to be seduced, the same murderous jealousy. The question arose automatically in this patient's mind whether responses so similar toward objects so dissimilar could possibly be adaptive.

The fact of continuity of neurotic habit from childhood to adulthood will shortly be discussed in terms of two of its aspects: dissimilarity of reinforcement conditions between childhood and adulthood, and failure of adult neurotic habits to match the permissive conditions of adult life. In the meantime we will discuss the striking effects of discrimination on anxiety and the utility of verbal cues in producing discrimination.

Reducing the Anxiety Arm of the Conflict by Discrimination

If the patient is in a sex-anxiety conflict, the anxiety pressure against the sex response must somehow be reduced before this response can occur. Unless rewarding sex responses do occur, the patient cannot escape the conflict.

The mechanism of extinction is always available for the reduction of the anxiety gradient. If the patient can be induced to try making a sex response while afraid and if he finds that he is not punished, extinction will do its work. It may, however, be very difficult to get the patient to "try" making the formerly punished and now inhibited sex responses if the anxiety gradient remains unchanged. It is at this point that the principle of discrimination can mercifully enter.

Discrimination is often useful because of the speed with which its effects can be produced. The patient can sometimes learn to make a sharp discrimination merely by learning two verbal responses each of which produces a distinctive cue. One stimulus context, for instance, can be labeled "past" and its dangerous circumstances enumerated; another stimulus context can be labeled "present" and the lack of threatening stimuli noted. If the dangerous and nondangerous stimuli are sharply contrasted, a reduction of anxiety can ensue.

We have had the opportunity to observe the striking effect of discrimination in the use of pentothal therapy with war neurotics. A patient under the influence of pentothal was discussing the alarming and horrifying circumstances of a combat mission. As he proceeded, his description had evoked in him a very intense fear response which was evident in facial expression, writhing, gestures, and all relevant signs. He was apparently reacting only to the sentences he was making and not at all to his safe situation in a hospital. Suddenly the therapist asked him, "Where are you?" The patient turned with a blank look to see his hospital bed and room, his American doctor, the sunlight of the Florida afternoon. He began to react to these stimuli and as he did so his anxiety rapidly faded. The therapist said, "I'm not Duke, the pilot. I'm your doctor." The patient who had given his doctor a role in the drama of the flight looked first with incredulity and then with dawning recognition. In this case, the doctor had forced him to make a discrimination between the phantasy of the flight which was producing intense anxiety and the secure conditions of his present life, thus sharply discriminating the circumstances of origin of the anxiety from the stimuli of the current situation. The discrimination operated to prevent generalization of anxiety responses from past to present cues and also gave the "safe" cues of the present situation a chance to inhibit anxiety. Our conviction is that it might have taken months of slow extinction practice in civilian life to produce so marked a reduction of anxiety.

The same effect, though not so sharp, can be perceived in civilian neuroses. Mrs. A was very much mixed up on the matter of eliminative and sexual functions. She had learned as a child that sex was dirty and that defecation was dirty. She tended to react with avoidance to the stimuli connected with either drive. This attitude was brought out clearly when Mrs. A said, "My mother would groan and moan when she was on the toilet . . ." and later, "Once I was lying in bed. My mother and father were having intercourse, and my mother was moaning and groaning. I asked her, 'Are you all right?' She said, 'Yes, and go to sleep!' "

The therapist pointed out to Mrs. A that sexual and eliminative functions had seemed alike to her, especially when her mother's behavior seemed the same in the toilet function and in intercourse. The therapist asserted that these two functions were really very different and tried to help Mrs. A to discriminate them sharply. Privacy, aversion, and suppression are appropriate responses to eliminative matters both in childhood and adulthood. Such reactions are not appropriate to sex behavior in adult life. Indeed, sex behavior must be shared and should be admitted to discussion among adults.

In the case of the eliminative and sex stimuli just discussed, some anxiety would remain attached to the sex response even when a sharp discrimination between the two stimulus patterns is made. Though discrimination will greatly reduce the transfer of abhorrence, it will not completely obliterate it. In this case, the extinction mechanism must, so to speak, "mop up" the residual anxiety. The person must try the sex response, with the now greatly reduced anxiety, and not be punished. At the same time, the rewards of a strong goal response in the sex sphere will begin to bind his habits to the concurrent sex stimuli.

Behavioral Analysis of Discrimination

As a swift reminder concerning the mechanism of discrimination, we point out that different responses can be attached to different raw (or primary) stimuli by differential reinforcement. Thus, children differ from adults in being smaller—a primary stimulus difference. Anxiety can be attached to the sex response to the cue of "children" but approach responses can be attached to the sex response to the cue of "adults." This distinction, incidentally, is one recognized in the law as well as in the mores.

Secondly, different verbal responses can be attached to more or less similar primary patterns of cues and can produce highly distinctive cue patterns. Thus, groups of people who are somewhat similar, but can be discriminated, may have the word "friend" attached to the one group and "enemy" attached to the other. The second group can then seem highly different and the two stimulus patterns are said to have acquired distinctiveness.

A third variant of the situation is possible. Withdrawal responses may *already* be attached to the cue produced by the word "enemy" and approach responses may already be attached to the cue produced by the word "friend." If such is the case, these respective withdrawal and approach responses will be evoked by members of the enemy and friend groups respectively. The two kinds of response are then said to be "mediated" by the verbal cues.

Paying attention, turning the head, listening intently are responses which can help to make cues distinctive. For instance, as an audience "subsides," the speaker's voice becomes a much more distinctive cue for each member. Paying attention to the separate elements in a cue pattern can also make these elements distinctive. Thus, the therapist can say, "Would you mind telling me that again?"—which implies that he wants to examine the statement more closely. This precaution may imitatively excite a similar tendency in the patient. He looks again to see if his account makes sense. If he is comparing two situations, he may start to "add things up," that is, to enumerate similarities and differences.

By merely failing to understand, the therapist may also direct attention to a problem area and evoke new discriminations. If someone does not understand, the patient has already learned that there is likely to be something confused, missing, or contradictory in his account. This excites the learned drives to have a complete account and to eliminate contradictions. "Failure to understand" is the essence of the Socratic method of teaching. To each answer of the student the teacher poses a further question which tells the student that there is something missing in his response and motivates him to continue responding. Patients and students who like to adopt rather than to innovate their own responses find this method quite annoying.

Response-mediated generalization. In the third type of situation described above, we said that a verbal response can produce a distinctive cue which can, in turn, give distinctiveness to a vague stimulus pattern. As was further pointed out, such a response-produced cue can also have a response attached to it. The child can, for instance, learn to distinguish a sharp from a dull knife by scrutinizing the edge of the knife or trying it on some resistant material. If the child learns the word "sharp" and its hand is slapped when it approaches sharp knives, the retraction response to the sight of the knife generalizes to the cue of the word "sharp." If the word "sharp" is then attached to yet other objects such as razors, the retraction response will generalize without differential training to the razor.

This view of verbal responses is of great importance since it enables the transfer of elaborate series of responses to new sets of stimuli by the mere device of teaching a word to which such sets of responses are attached. Thus, the enormous and dangerous trial and error of finding a safe way through a mined battlefield can be swiftly eliminated by a path marked out with a series of "safe" signs. In the last war, the soldier was trained to regard as dangerous, and hence to avoid, all manner of innocent-seeming things in a house which had been occupied by the enemy. Everything was "dangerous" because everything from the bedspring to the alarm clock might be booby-trapped. The common cue generalizing avoidance responses was "booby trap." Likewise, the word "normal" applied to a person makes him a member of a distinctive class and permits the transfer of appropriate habits of approach, discussion, and relaxation. To call a person "insane," on the other hand, not only makes him distinctive but mediates the transfer of habits of avoidance, fear, and unease.

From the "wolf's" point of view, the sight of a ring on a woman's finger may produce the response "married woman" to which the further verbal response "husband" is attached. To the cue of this response, in turn, anxiety is attached and approach tendencies to the woman are inhibited. If, however, a man learns the word "widow" in connection with the woman, anxiety may drop out and approach tendencies be restored.

Similarly, when the therapist told Mrs. A, "Enjoying sex with your husband is expected and permitted," the word "permitted" could serve as a cue for all the responses that had already been attached to it and would tend to make Mrs. A free to respond to sex activity as she had previously responded to other "permitted" activity. Furthermore, the word "permitted" might have directly attached to it the capacity to inhibit anxiety and so actually reduce sex anxiety toward her husband.

The therapist discourages many possible courses of action by making use of labels which evoke avoidance or hopelessness. The patient has learned not to try cures labeled "fake" by someone in authority since he has tried such in the past and not been helped. He learns to abandon false hopes of cure and false accounts of his disorder by having them labeled "false." The label directly evokes avoidant responses to the plan in question. If the therapist "doubts" that such and such a line of thought "will get us ahead" and the patient rehearses the statement, the avoidance responses attached to a course of action labeled "doubtful" compete with that course of action.

Responses attached to mediating cues must be learned separately. Wherever the therapist uses verbal cues to mediate responses he is taking advantage of what the patient has already learned. Unless the patient has already learned approach habits to the word "safe," the therapist cannot effectively make use of this word, and similarly for the other examples given above.

The long (and long-seeming) years of childhood are required to attach the correct emotional responses and habits to verbal cues. This all-important learning, without which no individual seems human, occurs largely within the family in the course of "teaching the child to talk." If the therapist finds that the patient cannot be motivated and reassured by ordinary verbal means, if the common verbal instructions do not have the correct approach and avoidance responses attached to them, the difficulties involved in therapy are grave. The therapist is essentially an operator in this field of language, exciting learned drives and administering learned rewards, eliciting adequate sentence chains to guide instrumental responses.

Generalization of learning. Once the therapist has established a discrimination in one situation he can count on a tendency to generalize the word producing the discrimination where it is pertinent. This is a great advantage since it enables the patient to carry on by himself the making of useful generalizations and discriminations which are initiated during psychotherapy. The therapist first used the word "excited" to label Mrs. A's feelings when she was seduced by her foster brother in childhood. Later, Mrs. A used the word to describe how she felt when, as a child, another little girl stimulated her sexually. In other words, Mrs. A generalized the label from the situation to which it had been applied by the therapist to another similar situation.

As is well known, extinction effects can also be generalized from one set of stimuli to similar sets. Mrs. A, for instance, found that the therapist permitted her to show much more independence during the treatment hours than she had been accustomed to. As her fear of having thoughts and demands of her own extinguished, she became more spunky and independent and expressed her feelings much more freely to her husband and others. Mrs. A had generalized from the therapeutic situation to other social situations: "If I can be more independent here, perhaps I can be more independent elsewhere" was the thought. The generalization, in this case, produced the attempt to behave more independently in situations where she had been inhibited. But the independent response in the new situations could persist only if rewarded.

Generalization of labels need not be left to chance; it can be facilitated by the therapist. Such labeling might follow the form, "Just as it happened that you were frightened at first in this situation but later found you could speak freely, it may also be that you can speak more freely in many situations where you are frightened on the outside." Such a sentence could mediate inhibition of fear and help to produce more independent behavior in a wide variety of circumstances where responses had formerly been inhibited.

Importance of Retrieving the Past

The present-day behavior of the patient has been learned under specific conditions in the past. We notice references to the past because we want to know exactly what these past conditions were. Knowledge of such conditions will prove that the patient could not have learned anything else than what he did learn. This knowledge may have marked reassuring value, since it permits the patient to escape from any sense of biological "doom" connected with his behavior. A clear picture of the past conditions has another advantage. It enables the therapist to contrast these sharply with current conditions of life, and if the latter are, as they usually are, much more permissive, the patient is encouraged to try again in areas where he has often failed. As Alexander and French (1946, p. 21) write: "By reviving the past emotional reactions . . . , we enable the patient to develop the power to differentiate between the original childhood situation and his present status."

Past conditions are reconstructed from many kinds of data. First and foremost are the patient's conscious memories. The bare facts as to sibling order, childhood illness, parental conflict, rivalry, in themselves give much information. Concentrating the patient's attention on the past will further expand the therapist's information (the fore-conscious). In the course of therapy, as anxiety about speaking and thinking is reduced, the patient may retrieve descriptions of the past which have been truly unconscious. Hints and inferences as to what is repressed (derived, for instance, by noting what the patient fears) may also give information on past conditions. The knowledge that a response is inhibited often suggests the circumstances necessary to create inhibition. Transferred responses, such as dependence or aggression, likewise point to the past and often imply the circumstances under which they were learned.

This attention to childhood conditions of learning is no empty ritual of the therapist. Clear definition of past conditions permits that contrast with the present which enables the therapist to prove that conditions have changed. The rival of childhood may have disappeared, but the patient still has his dangerous habits of rivalry. The wife may be in no way like the dominant mother, and yet the husband may still be expecting that combination of tyranny and indulgence which the mother gave. The sexual privation imposed on the child is not imposed upon the adult and yet the adult may sit frozen in marriage, unable to experience sexual excitement toward his spouse.

Conversely, the carefree conditions of childhood no longer prevail. The dependent gratifications of childhood are not available. The fluttery rush from pleasure to pleasure is not possible. The adult must be responsible for others. He must take painful thought. He must stop and plan. He must live more in his mind and less in his muscles, more in the future and less in the present. In this case, likewise, the circumstances of childhood which permitted a degree of freedom and irresponsibility must be contrasted with the more demanding conditions imposed by adulthood.

Evoking Past and Present Side by Side

Describing the past accurately constitutes a kind of "reliving" of the past. Making the old sentences which describe bygone events tends to evoke the emotion attached to these sentences and to the events they describe. This is a type of emotional behavior in the therapeutic situation which is different from the transference. It is more like the unshared nostalgia which an adult feels when he tries to describe his youth to a child. As old emotions are evoked by description, old habits are also activated, and as old habits and feelings reappear, the conditions which produced them are defined. This kind of reliving is of great advantage in therapeutic work because it enables the therapist, so to say, to lay the past and the present side by side. A description of emotions appropriate to present conditions can be presented more or less simultaneously with inappropriate emotions which have occurred as a result of past conditions. Experiments on easily controlled and independently observable external cues, such as tones of different pitches or objects of different weights, have shown (Woodworth, 1938, pp. 438–439; Andrews, 1948, pp. 330–338) that discrimination is much easier when the stimuli to be discriminated have temporal or spatial contiguity.

Throughout this book our assumption is that the internal response-produced cues involved in imagery and memory (1) obey the same laws as external cues and (2) are similar enough as cues to the external stimuli so that generalization occurs from one to the other. If this is true, one would expect that reviving memories, so that response-produced cues similar to those in the past are actually there in close contiguity to those of the present, should facilitate forming discriminations. Such facilitation should be greater the more completely all the response-produced cues functioning in the past were revived and brought into close temporal contrast with those of the present.

This deduction seems to be confirmed by the generally accepted clinical fact that it is helpful to recover memories of the past. It would suggest also that recovery of the past is not useful *per se* but only to the extent that past and present conditions are actually different and that the contrast between them is vividly made, either spontaneously by the patient or with the aid of the therapist. The identical reasoning applies to the formation of generalization. Thus, seeing the similarity between neurotic habits of childhood and adult life can be facilitated by comparing the cues produced in describing these habits—the same fear, the same feelings of helplessness, the same inhibited rage are evident.

Discrimination inhibits fear and produces hope. These considerations were beautifully exemplified in the case of Mrs. A. She had spent hours in miserable, frustrated, and hostile descriptions of the oppressive conditions imposed upon her by her foster mother. The therapist was able to point out that although in childhood her mother did not permit her to think for herself now she was expected to think for herself. In the therapeutic situation especially she was *required* to do so and to make her own decisions. The therapist could give no advice that would be applicable to all situations or that could cut the Gordian knot of her illness. She would have to find the solutions to her own problems; the therapist could only be a catalyst to her thought (a midwife to thought—to use an expression of Socrates).

The therapist made the contrast concrete. He said,

When you were a child, your mother didn't let you think for yourself. From what you've told me, I gather that she didn't let you have a thought of your own. You had to come right home from school so that you could do the household chores; you had to stay in the yard when you were playing. She beat you for anything or even for nothing at all. You relied on her to tell you what to do, because if you didn't, if you tried to do what *you* wanted, you got slapped down for it; if you didn't rely on her, you got punished.

But now things are different. You are an adult now, and you're expected to be independent and to think for yourself. In some ways, though, you're still acting as though you didn't dare to say what you think or to do anything without asking permission. I think you can be more independent than you are. Nobody will punish you *now* for standing up for your rights and expressing your own opinion.

In order to make discrimination as sharp as possible the therapist concentrates attention on every aspect of difference between the controlled conditions of childhood and those of the present day: the size of the patient which made him dependent then and competent now; the age of the patient which made him subordinate to authority then and relatively free now; the skills and mental resources of the patient which were meager then and are great now.

In Mrs. A's case, pointing out these differences had two important effects. The first was to inhibit fear of carrying out actions necessary to her health by preventing generalization of fear from childhood to present circumstances. The second was to create hope that there was a rewarding way out of her neurotic impasse. Mrs. A began to believe that her powers and resources were sufficient to deal with old conflicts even though they survived into present times. Her adult mind, developed despite conflict, could be the means of resolving dilemmas which had long been insoluble. As a result of noting differences her fear was reduced and she saw a hopeful way out.

Knowledge of Past Clarifies Present

At first glance the neurotic habits of the patient are likely to be as mysterious to the therapist as they are to the patient himself. What the therapist needs to know is: Why does this conflict have the form that it has? Only thus can past circumstances be com-

pared with present. Knowledge of the past often helps to answer
this question and to clarify the present-day problem. What seemed
at first mysterious seems obvious and necessary once the earlier
conditions of life are known.

Mrs. A's neurotic symptoms were at first quite unintelligible to
the therapist. Her life was filled with a continuous anxiety and
limited by phobic restrictions. The therapist was able to infer
from her immediate behavior that some kind of sex-anxiety conflict was involved. When the therapist learned that Mrs. A had
developed strong sexual appetites in early childhood (because
of seduction by her foster brother and other sexual activities)
and that she had also been given a severe, repressing sex training
by her mother, he understood why her neurotic conflict took the
form it did. The strong sex appetite along with strong sex anxieties
required Mrs. A to find gratification in situations where she would
not feel responsible for sexual activity, where (as she said) she
would be "taken advantage of." Her marriage had increased her
conflict by increasing her guilt at the prospect of betraying her
husband and had intensified her sexual anxiety. This formulation
of the problem defined for the therapist what his therapeutic
strategy should be. This strategy involved calling attention to the
vital nature of Mrs. A's sexual feelings and to the fear attached
to them. It further involved contrasting the vulgar and hostile
attitude of her mother with the more benign view of sexual matters generally held by adults and by her husband in particular.
She might hope for reward, not punishment, if she tried acting like
a responsible wife in the sexual sphere. Incidentally, the formulation stated here was not developed until the nineteenth hour of
treatment. Previous formulations had, however, approximated it.
Discovery of how adequate formulations can be hit on more quickly
would be a great advance in psychotherapy.

Reconstruction not a necessity. While highly advantageous,
we do not feel that the reconstruction of the past is an absolute
necessity for therapeutic advance. The therapist may be able to
set up a strong presumption that present-day neurotic habits have
been learned without being able to specify the learning conditions
in detail. He may be able to convince his patient that excessive
dependence, readiness to anger, or irrational fear must have been

produced in the same circumstances in childhood in which we see them produced in adults. He may be able to insist that present-day life conditions of the patient do not reward the identified dependence, anger, or fear. But it seems inevitable that such a reconstruction will have less convincing power than a clear identification of the past would have. Nevertheless it may suffice to make a distinction and to help reduce anxiety about new trials under present conditions. For bringing conviction that conditions have changed, there is nothing quite like holding the past and the present, one in each fist, so to speak, and looking closely at the one and the other.

Neurotic Habits Compared with Likelihood of Current Reinforcement

We have earlier referred to the importance of locating the patient's current conflicts and repressions and showing that they are continuous with those of the past. We now wish to emphasize another aspect of the matter, *i.e.,* the contrast between the patient's current habits of repression and inhibition and the opportunities for gratification which exist in his environment. The neurotic starves in the midst of plenty; a beautiful woman cannot love; a capable man cannot fight; an intelligent student cannot pass his examinations. In every case the contrast is sharp between capacity to enjoy and opportunity to enjoy.

The therapist must avoid dealing only with historical knowledge and must emphasize the current conflicts because the patient is sick in the immediate present. There are things that he should be doing, that others expect him to do, that he is not doing. Wherever behavior learned in the past is adapted to present-day reinforcement conditions, the therapist neglects study of such behavior because it constitutes no problem. The patient does not need to be "cured" of his adaptive habits.

Contrasting the patient's incapacities with the positive opportunities of his current world has a challenging effect. It mobilizes the drive to be sensible and to form a realistic mental picture of the world around him. The therapist's assurance that the environment is benign may have the capacity to inhibit existing anxiety. The learned drive not to fear the harmless, not to be a "sissy," is mobilized. As anxiety is weakened, the inhibited member of the conflict pair begins to excite action appropriate to it. The patient tries out being braver or sexier or more independent, or whatever response has been unduly inhibited.

The importance of the contrast between a habit of fear and the actual permissiveness of the environment is nowhere so clear as in the case of a married person who is sexually inhibited toward his spouse. Months may pass without conscious sexual excitement or sex response to the spouse even though every sanction of society favors such response.

Mrs. A was among those who feared the sexual life so easily attainable in her marriage. In order to contrast her frightened withdrawal with the realities of the case, her therapist once told her, "You were taught as a child that sex is wrong. You were frightened—they scared you about sex. *But you should not be afraid now.* You are expected to enjoy sex with your husband. In fact, sex is an important thing. It can help make your marriage better, help bind you and your husband together. It can make up for the annoyances of married life and make them bearable. Why should you be frightened about sex now when people expect you to enjoy it as part of marriage?"

The obvious goal of pointing to this contrast is to enable the patient to begin responding in a situation where she has formerly inhibited response through fear or despair. Behavioral changes must be made in the real world of the patient's current life. If benevolent changes are to occur, the patient must begin doing something new. The patient must be shown that it is safe to try out new responses and that the environment, far from being discouraging, is actually favorable.

According to our theory of the matter, the matter of "trying out something new" is quintessential to a therapeutic result. Mere verbal change will not suffice. The most complete description of the inner and outer world will be without value unless it leads to new, strong responses in the environment. The patient must be helped and encouraged through the awkward period of first attempts at new responses.

The importance of an accurate view of the current possibilities of reinforcement is brought out in one of the therapist's questions to Mrs. A. Mrs. A had been treated badly by her mother-in-law and had shown remarkable submissiveness under this treatment. At an appropriate time, the therapist asked, "You said your mother-in-law is like your mother. Aren't you acting toward her as you would toward your mother? Yet your mother-in-law is certainly not the tyrant your mother was, nor does she have the control over you that your mother had when you were a child." In this example we see the analysis of a generalized submissive response, the teaching of discrimination of past from present, and the comparison of the present reinforcement situation with current habits. Indeed, these three are intimately connected.

SUMMARY

Much of therapy consists of teaching the patient new discriminations. Some of these are achieved by directing the patient's attention toward relevant aspects of his environment or behavior. Some are achieved by contrasting the patient's present inhibitions with the lack of punishment in his present environment. Others are achieved by reviving memories of traumatic conditions of childhood, so that they can be contrasted with the different conditions of adult status. When the contrast is clear and immediate, the effect can be direct and automatic. Verbal responses play an important role in discriminations. They can help to revive memories of the past and to direct attention toward relevant details. They can function to make past neurotic habits seem similar to present ones but to make past conditions of reinforcement seem highly different from those of the present. They can also be the means of contrasting neurotic inhibitions of the present with real-life possibilities of gratification. Verbal cues can prevent generalization of anxiety from past to present. They can mediate responses inhibitory of anxiety. They can excite acquired drives which impel the patient to view the world realistically and to act intelligently. As anxiety is reduced by discrimination, reassurance, and extinction, new responses occur. When they reduce neurotic drives, these responses can be the basis of new habits which will permanently resolve the neurotic conflict.

CHAPTER XX

GAINS FROM RESTORING THE HIGHER MENTAL PROCESSES

This chapter will summarize and illustrate the therapeutic effects produced by removing repression, improving labeling, and thus restoring the higher mental processes. Before emphasizing the importance of these factors, however, it should be made perfectly clear that *significant therapeutic effects can also be produced in other ways without any improved labeling or "insight"* on the part of the patient. As has already been pointed out, we would expect the general reassuring and permissive attitude of the therapist to be able to produce a considerable reduction in fear. This reduction in fear should generalize from the therapeutic situation to the rest of the patient's life and thus reduce somewhat his conflict, misery, and motivation for symptoms.

An example of this kind has already been presented. When Mrs. A told about the times her foster brother had seduced her, she was reporting on an incident that aroused considerable fear and guilt but that had never been completely repressed. The therapist made no interpretation at that time. Nevertheless his failure to show any signs of anxiety, disgust, or rejection was a striking intervention that helped to reduce fear and guilt. In the next hour Mrs. A reported a marked reduction in her heart symptoms and that for the first time she had really been able to enjoy sex relations with her husband. The permissive attitude of the therapist had produced a marked therapeutic effect without any obvious removal of repression or improvement in labeling.

Furthermore, as has been pointed out, repression is not an all-or-none matter; the patient may be able to remember or think about certain things but have a strong disinclination to do so. Reducing the fear-motivating avoidance will not uncover any additional thoughts, but will enable the patient to use the thoughts he has more freely and flexibly. Thus the patient's behavior will become more intelligent and adaptive.

Why improved labeling is important. The gains that have just been described usually are not enough to produce a complete cure in a severe neurosis. They must be supplemented by the removal of repression, by new labeling, and by the consequent improvement in discrimination and the higher mental processes. There are two reasons why the recovery of a repressed memory is likely to be especially significant in therapy: (1) the fact that the patient is able to overcome the repression means that the fear motivating it has *already* been considerably reduced, and (2) the restoration of the ability to think about the events and impulses involved is a useful addition to the higher mental processes. The removal of a repression is thus both a sign that therapy has occurred and the cause for additional therapeutic effects.

According to our hypothesis, the higher mental processes are carried on by means of verbal and other cue-producing responses. Therefore the failure to learn the proper verbal responses, or their removal by repression, eliminates the possibility of the specific higher functions that the missing responses would have performed. Conversely, when the repression is removed or the missing labels are learned, the patient begins to get the advantages of using these responses in the superior types of adaptive behavior that the higher mental processes allow. The most important changes to be expected will be recapitulated with some brief illustrations.

Adaptive discriminations. One of the functions of verbal and other cue-producing responses is to make innately similar situations more distinctive and thus to cut down on the amount of primary stimulus generalization. This helps in the formation of adaptive discriminations, especially with respect to culturally emphasized differences. Such discriminations can reduce irrational fears. As was pointed out in the previous chapter, the removal of the repression that obscures the past helps the patient to discriminate by enabling him to contrast the childhood conditions responsible for establishing the fear with the quite different ones of his adult life. Even without recapturing past repressed memories, somewhat similar results can also be achieved by labeling the current situation accurately. Verbal labels and other cue-producing responses also help to cut down on the type of generalization responsible for displacement.

Effects of this type were evident in the case of Mrs. A. As the result of the cruel domination of her foster mother, who punished any form of independence or counteraggression, she was practically unable to express any form of anger. In fact she had learned to suppress her anger by protestations of love that would be described in analytic terms as a reaction formation. Since she could not label her foster mother as being to blame, her smoldering aggression generalized to other people who reminded her of her foster mother but did not frighten her so much. This generalized (*i.e.,* displaced) aggression came out in sudden, inexplicable, murderous thoughts. For example, once when she was washing dishes with a girl friend, she was frightened by the thought: "What if I picked up this knife and killed her?"

The therapist pointed out the difference between the childhood conditions, when she was helpless in the face of the cruel domination of her foster mother, and the current conditions of her life as an adult. As he directed her attention toward and helped her to label these differences, she became able to bear the thought of being angry. Once the drive of anger was labeled, it was possible to help her to make another socially important discrimination. While our society taboos irrational and unjustifiable expressions of aggression, it does permit a certain amount of aggression in self-defense or in response to unfair treatment by others. After this difference was pointed out, Mrs. A was able to get angry at the snubs that she received from her mother-in-law, who was from a higher social class, and to point out to her husband the unfair treatment that she was receiving.

With the source of the anger clearly labeled and the proper self-defensive measures taken, one would expect the irrational murderous impulses against friends to drop out. The patient did not report any more of these, but she also did not specifically report their absence. Thus, unfortunately, our evidence must remain unclear on this point.

Adaptive generalizations. Attaching the same label or other cue-producing response to different situations should increase the amount of secondary stimulus generalization and help the patient to respond adaptively to culturally emphasized similarities.

One of the symptomatic features of Mrs. A's behavior was that she got into situations in which she was likely to be seduced or raped. For example, she went out on drinking parties with single girls, hitchhiked with truck drivers, and went into secluded places alone with strange men. When she was in these situations, she was afraid that she would be "taken advantage of," and she sometimes was. The therapist pointed out to her the common element in these situations by saying: "You are seeking situations where you can have sexual gratification without feeling responsible." After this was pointed out to her, she became more cautious and generalized the caution to other similar situations. Thus, when the man downstairs was home in bed with a minor illness, she had an impulse to go in and visit him but said to herself, "No, I would just be giving him a chance to make a pass at me." Previously, she had indiscreetly told this man that she had sex problems.

Foresight, ability to motivate and reward self. The foregoing example also illustrates the use of verbal responses in anticipating danger and motivating foresightful behavior. After the patient was convinced of the correctness of the therapist's interpretation, she was motivated to be more careful in avoiding situations of potential seduction or rape. In addition to the learned drive of caution, verbal responses can mediate the hope and the sustained interest that is necessary for planning and carrying out long-range projects. Similarly, verbal and other cue-producing responses enable the patient to reward himself for achieving subgoals and to wait for delayed rewards. Thus in the early part of therapy, Mrs. A said: "If I wait for anything, I can't—I have to have it right then!" After she was able to think about sexual and other pleasures, she seemed to become more tolerant of delays. This may also have been because the drives motivating her behavior had been reduced.

Reasoning and planning. In order to reason and plan, one must be aware of the problem and have it defined correctly. At first Mrs. A was completely obsessed with concern about her heart. The question she asked the therapist was: "How can I forget about my heart—how can I stop worrying about it?" As long as her thoughts were directed exclusively toward this problem and thoughts about other problems were absent, there was no adequate solution. This problem, which was so stubborn and insistent at first, disappeared when she became able to talk more freely about sex and had some of this fear extinguished. As the fears that prevented her from thinking about her real problems were reduced and more adequate statements were supplied by the therapist, she asked herself a number of questions that came progressively nearer to the sources of her difficulties. First it was, "Should I go back home to visit?" Then it was, "Should I visit my old boy friend in New Jersey?" From these it shifted to "Why do I fear my husband? Do I have to leave him?" Eventually it became something like "How can I get along better with my husband?" When she became more aware of her problems she had a better opportunity to use reasoning and planning in solving them.

Utilizing cultural store of tested problem solutions. One of the problems she was able to give more thought to was the question of whether or not she wanted to have a child at that time. After her fear of thinking and talking about sex had been reduced, she was able to discuss it with her husband, while before treatment she had been too shy to mention anything like that to him. Having her problem better defined in words and being freer to think and talk about it, she was able to make better use of the cultural storehouse of techniques that have been learned by generations of trial and error, planning, and reasoning. For example, she got a sensible book on sex and asked the therapist about the various techniques of birth control.

Avoiding waste of contradictory behavior. After her conflicting desires were adequately labeled and she was encouraged to think about what she was doing, it was easier for her to detect logical contradictions and to avoid the waste of embarking on mutually contradictory courses of action. For example, she wanted to please her husband and make her marriage more satisfactory, but she also wanted to avoid her husband and escape from her marriage by visiting her old boy friend in New Jersey, perhaps getting some sexual gratification by "being taken advantage of" in a situation for which she did not have to accept responsibility. At first her motives for visiting her boy friend were only partially stated: "I wanted to see the evil that was in him and find why thoughts about him come between me and my husband." The "evil" mentioned was, of course, in her and not in her boy friend. Furthermore, the probable results of the visit were not clearly thought through. The inconsistency of this visit with her plan for trying to improve her marriage was not obvious to her; in fact, she had rationalized the visit as part of that plan.

The therapist stimulated further thought by a series of questions: "What *do* you want? What would you do if he told you he loved you?" Mrs. A protested that she just wanted to see "the evil that this boy was." Then the therapist asked: "Would you leave your husband and live with him?" Mrs. A replied "Oh, no!" Apparently the thoughts that these questions stimulated made her see that this plan was inconsistent with the one of trying to improve her marriage; in any event, she did not make the visit.

Behavior under social control. As the foregoing example shows, once the behavior is more adequately verbalized it is under better social control. In Mrs. A's case, the weakening of the repressions that prevented her from thinking about her sexual life and the weakening of the inhibitions that prevented her from responding sexually to her husband did not result in completely uninhibited or licentious behavior. Being able to take advantage somewhat more adequately of the culturally permitted outlet, she was less motivated to get into situations where she was likely "to be taken advantage of." Her improved ability to label her desires and think about what she was doing also helped her to foresee the danger of such situations before it was too late and to avoid getting into them.

Limitations to verbal control. This case also illustrates the limitations to verbal control of behavior. As long as words are attached only to other words without the proper emotional or instrumental responses, it does no good to say them. Furthermore, the nonverbal habits of responding directly to the immediate stimulus situation may be stronger than the emotional or instrumental responses elicited by words. Thus one may know that a fear is unreasonable but still be afraid or know what one should do but still be unable to do it.

When the therapist knew that the treatments would have to be ended soon because the patient and her husband were moving to another town, he tried to hasten the progress and accomplish all that he could by telling the patient more about her problems. For example, he tried to point out to her how important it is in marriage to be able to think about sex and to anticipate sexual pleasure. "When you are afraid," he explained, "you can't think about sex or talk about it. And that's unfortunate, because if you are able to look forward to sex relations with your husband, it makes your life so much better. This makes the work you do all day less burdensome and ties your life together."

The therapist's advice was not entirely effective because Mrs. A still had such a strong habit of thinking about sex as something crude and vulgar that she had to be caught somewhat off her guard, without thinking, before she could enjoy sex relations. This prevented her from anticipating it with much pleasure or enjoying preliminary love-making. Until fear and disgust were further extinguished as responses to thoughts about sex and were replaced by pleasant anticipatory responses, the therapist's advice and interpretations could not be very helpful.

Need for additional practice or working through. The reappearance of repressed responses may provide the basis for a better discrimination and thus reduce fear, but these responses also produce cues eliciting fear. The immediate net result of these two opposing effects may be in either direction. When the cues elicit strong fear, further extinction is needed. The patient may not get the full use of the restored verbal responses because he has to fight against strong tendencies to avoid them.

The same is true when the therapist supplies a new label; the labeling may elicit a strong fear that requires a considerable number of trials to extinguish. This is the basis for the belief by clinicians like Rogers (1942) that interpretation impedes therapeutic work. We recognize the force of this fact but feel that the opposing effects are often beneficial and must always be taken into account.

After a person has learned in one situation to label something correctly, such as an aggressive response motivated by anger, he may not immediately generalize the correct label to all other relevant situations. He may have to relearn the label in a number of somewhat similar situations before he has a habit that generalizes readily. It may be a considerable time before enough such situations occur for a skill in labeling to be acquired. The patient often must use a certain amount of mental trial and error (mulling things over) in order to fit the various units together and see all of their relationships. Finally, the patient must translate his thoughts and plans into action and get rewarded for carrying them through. As will be pointed out, much time may be required before the most favorable opportunities occur for action and reward.

All these factors tend to introduce delay into the process of therapy. But once the patient has been rewarded for starting to use his higher mental processes, he tends to continue to practice and acquire skill. Thus some of the benefits of therapy may occur a long time after the sessions with the therapist have ended, just as a chess player may continue to profit throughout his career by correct habits acquired from his first coach.

PART VI
CONFLICT

CHAPTER XXI

WHY CONFLICTS AND MISERY CAN BE
RELIEVED ONLY IN REAL LIFE

There are actually two dimensions or aspects to psychotherapy which are usually not clearly separated. The first one is the inside, or "talking," phase of therapy. This we have already discussed. During the "talking" phase repression is revoked; that is, the patient unlearns the anxiety responses which have been attached to various kinds of sentence making. New labeling represents repressed or disregarded stimulus aspects within the body and without as new emotions appear in the relation between patient and therapist. Verbal cues exhibit their wonderful possibilities of aiding in appropriate generalization, discrimination, and mediation of response. As anxiety attached to verbal units is extinguished, these extinction effects generalize to, and reduce, the fear motivating the inhibition of instrumental and goal responses.

Real-world Aspects of Therapy

The second aspect of therapy might be called the outside, or real-world, aspect. Freud (1924, Vol. II, p. 320) pointed out: "Actually it is quite unimportant for his cure whether or not the patient can overcome this or that anxiety or inhibition in the institution; what is of importance, on the contrary, is whether or not he will be free from them in real life." In order to be well, the patient must learn to make new responses. These must be rewarded and strong habits competing with anxiety must be built. This second, or performing, phase, in contrast with the "talking" phase of the treatment, is the subject of this chapter.

In this second phase, the patient must directly confront the distortions of his current life produced by neurotic inhibition. The past has helped to create his problem but only in the present can

331

it be solved. In order to aid, the therapist must have a realistic picture of how emotional conflict has disturbed the immediate life of the patient. Very frequently the patient has hidden from himself the nature of this actual current conflict. He complains about his sufferings and his symptoms, but he does not protest about his failure to solve the real problems he faces. The therapist helps the patient to identify his actual sociological difficulties.

For example, a young man came to therapy complaining of intense chronic anxiety and occasional alcoholic outbursts. A closer view of his problem showed that he was having an affair with his employer's mistress which caused him much fear. Further, he felt a sense of unmanly dependence upon his employer, felt himself too docile and agreeable. He had no idea, however, of the real current problem about which he should have been worried—namely, his incapacity openly and responsibly to fall in love. Inquiry into this real current deviation proved highly productive of insight and behavior change. Study of the past and the neurotic substitutes led inevitably to the study of the present and the actual behavior incapacity. The patient had previously believed himself capable of "loving" but had failed to notice that it was only in a covert and irresponsible manner.

Generalization of Habit from Therapist to Outside Persons

Few patients can afford psychotherapy indefinitely and but few therapists would grant perpetual help to such patients. The positive effects of the therapeutic situation must therefore be carried over into real life. The freedom to feel, think, and act which is developed in the therapeutic situation must be applied to real problems and real persons in the patient's life. The tendency to generalize responses made within the therapeutic situation to life without is observable in every patient. Mrs. A, for instance, had to try out—and did try out—being more self-assertive toward her mother-in-law.

This type of activity is often unnoticed from a theoretical standpoint and is passed over as a part of "working through" (Freud, 1924, Vol. II, p. 375). When seen from the standpoint of behavior theory, it is a most important condition of cure. Failure to generalize is also believed to be an important source of failure of therapeutic results. The therapist can call attention to this failure by noting that the patient is doing better "here" but not "out there." Attention is thus called to the real-world goals of therapy and the therapeutic situation is defined as a transitory learning situation which is only preparing the patient for his real trials and conquests. Loving, hating, or freedom from fear have only a small value if confined to therapy and the therapist. They can remake the patient's world if transferred and tested outside.

The mere fact of generalization does not guarantee that responses learned in therapy will continue to be performed outside the therapeutic situation. Generalization is a means of getting new responses tried out. Once tried out, a new response will be strengthened or extinguished depending on reinforcement conditions. If conditions are favorable, the generalized response can be strongly attached to outside cues. When Mrs. A tried being more assertive toward her mother-in-law, she found, in fact, that the mother-in-law "would take a good deal more off her" than Mrs. A had originally supposed. She was thereby rewarded for making conventional self-assertive demands.

If, on the other hand, the patient is punished for generalizing a response, this response will tend to disappear and generalization will be inhibited. This state of affairs is especially unfavorable when it occurs on one of the early attempts of the patient to behave expressively. For example, it was unfortunate that when Mrs. A tried to act more independently and assert herself more toward her husband he sometimes punished her for it. When she bought a toaster without consulting him (using part of her food budget to buy it) Mr. A refused to give her more money for food for the rest of the week. He declared angrily, "Well, if you've spent the food money, I'll eat bread and butter!"

If the patient is married to a neurotic partner, some degree of punishment for new responses is almost inevitable. As the patient becomes freer, his increasing freedom puts increasing demands on the neurotic partner. These demands provoke anxiety and counteraction by the partner, which punish the new expressive attempts.

Gains between sessions. The patient inevitably continues the mental work of the therapeutic situation between sessions with the therapist. He reviews the new information gained, rewards himself again with the comforting thoughts hit upon, and perseveres in the mental attack on his problems. This "running on" of therapeutic thoughts sometimes brings the patient new information. A good deal of "working through" inevitably occurs. Sometimes, hearing himself talk to others will stimulate the patient to new formulations. The work of practice and confirmation of the new sentences gained within therapy plays a momentous role.

Mrs. A exhibited this "working through" very clearly, especially in relation to the incident of her seduction by her foster brother. In the twentieth hour of treatment, the therapist said, "You were probably sexually excited by your childhood experience with your brother." We know that Mrs. A mulled over this interpretation between hours. During each of the next three hours she showed evidence that she had "gained something" by the interval of time between sessions. Each hour she recalled more of the details of the incident and each time she came closer to putting into words how she had felt when her brother had seduced her.

While it does not seem wise to demand that the patient conduct these exertions outside the therapeutic sessions, it seems reasonable to reward them when they do inevitably occur. Certainly it seems unwise to discourage them since such discouragement would increase the burden of the work to be performed directly between patient and therapist.

Patient Must Try Responses Never Performed in Therapy

It is not enough that the patient generalize emotional and verbal attitudes from the therapist to persons in his real world. Some of the responses necessary to make him well have been prepared for but never performed in therapy itself. These are the great actions of the patient's life in the spheres of love, work, and social relations. The anxiety attached to reasoning and planning with respect to these actions has largely been extinguished and inhibited by talking and thinking. The emotional conflicts, which make the patient miserable and cause the symptoms, still remain. These conflicts must be completely and permanently resolved for the best therapeutic effect to be secured.

Let us take the example of the *sex-anxiety conflict*. Anxiety must be weakened and sex responses must occur and be rewarded before this conflict can be resolved. The patient has learned to attach verbal units to the stimuli of the two members of the conflict. He has learned not to be anxious about talking about it. Extinction of fear of talking about sexual matters is generalized to the fear motivating the responses that inhibit sex. The inhibitory responses are weakened; at this point the sex responses can begin to occur. Some of these responses, such as incipient tumescence, produce stimuli of drive strength; others produce new cues, such as sexual thoughts which, in turn, tend to elicit learned drives of sexual excitement. Thus sex appetite is increased. This increase in appetite excites stronger sex responses and further tilts the balance of relative strength in the conflict in their favor. Sex responses can now begin to occur in real life. If the therapist is able to say that there is no danger in carrying out these sex responses (Why be anxious about having intercourse with your wife?), the drive to be reasonable and not to fear when there is no danger is invoked. This drive further weakens inhibitory forces and so relatively increases the dominance of sex responses.

It has been noted by Freud (1924, Vol. II, pp. 371–372; 1925, Vol. III, p. 302) that there are sometimes complications at this point. The increased strength of the sex drive (primary and acquired) may push the patient much nearer to the sexual goal. However, as the patient comes nearer, anxiety reactions are more strongly excited. It may therefore be that in the course of getting well the patient arrives, as it were, at a last minute anxiety attack after having shown much progress. This is the negative therapeutic reaction. Freud regarded this reaction as a very unfavorable sign. We cannot see from our theory why this should be so. The reaction is certainly unfortunate, but there seems no reason why the operations and forces which have impelled the patient so near the goal cannot, if continued, carry him across it.

The overeager therapist may experience such a reaction as discomfiting. He should resume his patient attitude, perform his role correctly and, realizing that the patient's behavior is automatic and inevitable, he should wait until the force of the sex drive breaks through the anxiety barrier and produces the drive-reducing sex responses. The occurrence of sex rewards will strengthen the units of the sex habit involved. If anxiety responses have been occurring along with the sex reaction and have been provoked by it, they will disappear along with the sex stimuli, and their disappearance will further strengthen the sex responses. If, on the other hand, the patient has learned to be anxious *after the event,* he may show some guilt after the break-through of sex response. Further, with the strength of the sex drive greatly reduced, the fear component of the conflict may become dominant for a while. These reactions must be patiently waited out. The patient will find this time that he is not punished afterward and fear will gradually be extinguished. The crucial fact is, of course, that novel responses must occur if new habits are to be formed. The responses that do occur will determine what those habits will be.

There are many ins and outs to this process of trying out new responses. For example, new fears may be aroused which could not occur until the new responses were tried. Mrs. A's phobia had the effect of keeping her off public conveyances and out of public places. She really feared to be approached, overwhelmed, and seduced if she let herself react to others in these situations. When this was pointed out to her, she realized for the first time that she did have within her strong and urgent sex reactions and the question was raised, "If you have such reactions, why not express them toward your husband?" Thereupon, a phobic reaction which she had already displayed toward her husband was intensified. Apparently the increased incipient sex responses toward her husband produced cues which elicited fear. The fear in turn motivated avoidance responses which were reinforced by reduction in fear. Consequently, she remembered how she hated to have her husband say anything sexy to her, how she hated to have him touch her, how she undressed shyly in the bathroom, put on her nightgown and fled to bed, so that he would not see her body With the help of the therapist she was now able to think about her sex feelings toward her husband, to notice her reserve and avoidance, and to ask herself if this was reasonable.

At this juncture, new defenses appeared. When Mrs. A began to feel sexually aroused by her husband, the thought of "this other boy" whom she had once gone around with before her marriage came to mind and "got between me and John." She wondered if she had done the right thing in marrying Mr. A. She wondered if she should not see "the other boy" again to test where her true affection lay. She was at the same time aware of increased attraction to her husband. In this time of conflict she would say, "I was in the car and wanted to sit closer to my husband. Then the thought of this boy came." These phantasies of the boy friend did not arouse much anxiety. After all he had safely gone out of her life. On the other hand, her husband was real and present. When she began to feel herself responding sexually to him she had intense anxiety. As a result she "escaped" to the phantasies of the boy friend, *i.e.*, they were reinforced by reducing the fear which sexual thoughts about her husband created. This behavior illustrates the Freudian mechanism of *defense* and shows that it can be subjected to a stimulus-response analysis. Thoughts of the former boy friend did appear in place of, and did defend against, sexual thoughts about her husband. In the absence of a detailed analysis in terms of motive, stimulus, response, and reward, the sheer fact of "defense" is all that could be noted; with this analysis available, the defense becomes intelligible in terms of a general theory of behavior. It is precisely the function of scientific theory to take such orphaned notions and give them a conceptual home.

Cut-and-fit nature of first responses. Much trial and error is bound to occur while the patient is making these responses in his real world. If his problem is excessive timidity he is likely to be successively over- and underaggressive. When he is less than legitimately self-assertive, he fails of his goal. If he is overaggressive, he is punished. Since the therapist does not know and cannot control the patient's real world, it is difficult to predict with great nicety just when reward and punishment will occur.[1] The patient must therefore use the technique of approximation and correction. He must try and succeed, try and fail in part, or try and learn that some of his new responses will not be tolerated at all. He is likely to be awkward until he acquires skill. The therapist knows this and "sits out" the period of trial and error. The patient, on his part, must take these risks. If he does not do so, he cannot learn the new habits which will stabilize his life.

---

[1] Opposed to this classic assumption is the belief of Alexander and French (1946, pp. 40, 47). They advise the therapist to try to control real-life conditions as by working through relatives or employer when the latter are generously cooperative.

Connecting verbal and instrumental responses. The importance of these new outside responses is not very clearly emphasized in Freudian theory.[2] Freud seemed to assume that they would occur automatically; if the therapist did his part of the work well, the patient's "life" would take care of the rest. The tendency which Freud assumed does indeed exist. Labeling of incipient motor responses makes them more likely to occur under favorable conditions. Nevertheless, such a tendency is not innate. The connection between verbal cues and instrumental responses is learned. If therapy is to have a real effect, the terminal verbal cues of the plan must be strongly connected to overt responses. The patient must go into action with his plan and try it out.

Where such a connection is weak, we speak of a condition of "apathy," one of the most baffling phenomena in therapeutic work. We also speak of "living in a dream world," or getting satisfaction out of phantasy only, and we recognize it as a malignant phenomenon. If the connection between plans and action is weak, the therapist's task is clear. He must get some "action" responses following upon the cues of plans, and this connection must be slowly rewarded and strengthened. Such strengthening is a true and sometimes necessary part of psychotherapy.

We might remark that this condition is the opposite of "rushing into action," in which case the patient has strong action responses attached to a large number of sentence cues or directly to external cues. In the latter case, the patient must learn restraint, *i.e.*, to inhibit instrumental responses while the work of reasoning and planning goes on.

We repeat here the truism that the trying out of new responses occurs continuously throughout therapy and not just at its end. There is no sharp split between the "talking" and the real-world aspects of the work. Indeed the therapist wants to see with his own eyes that the patient is able to generalize responses learned in therapy and is further able to try out instrumental responses suggested by the plans made in therapy. He has learned to fear leaving his patient with a brand new set of mental plans and no assurance that they can in fact be executed.

[2] Alexander and French (1946, p. 40), however, believe the therapist should stimulate these real-life trials by "timely directives and encouragement."

Importance of Life Conditions That Allow Strong Drives to Be Reduced

Psychotherapists have always known in a matter-of-fact way that the conditions of the patient's real life have an effect on the psychotherapeutic process. As has been pointed out, therapists exhibit this knowledge by rejecting many patients whose life conditions are exceptionally unfavorable. Control analysts will tell their apprentices, as Dr. Abram Kardiner told one of us, that "patients get well in life," thus pointing out that life conditions are an important and separate factor in psychotherapy.

Our theoretical analysis gives added emphasis to these life conditions. We believe that the misery and symptoms of neurosis are produced by high drives and that therapy consists of learning the new responses that will reduce these drives more adaptively. From our assumptions it follows that drive reduction is important for two reasons: (1) to reduce the misery and motivation for symptoms, and (2) to reward the learning and persisting performance of the new responses that constitute the cure. But the major sources of drive reduction for the patient do not exist in the limited therapeutic situation; the therapist cannot give the major rewards that the patient needs. Therefore it is inevitable that the patient must ultimately get these rewards and reduce his high drives outside the therapeutic situation, under the conditions of real life.

To emphasize this point let us briefly consider some of the most important innate and socially learned rewards. To begin with, it is obvious that the therapist cannot give the patient the primary sexual rewards that would reduce a high sex drive as a source of misery and motivation for symptoms. If the patient suffers from sexual inhibitions, he cannot be cured until he is able to overcome these in real life outside the therapist's office. Once he has done this, the powerful reward of sexual gratification will reinforce his new habits and consolidate his cure.

If the patient is married, the character of his spouse may have an important effect on the outcome of therapy. If the spouse is neurotic, the patient is much less likely to be rewarded for his own attempts at more adequate expression. In such a case, the therapist may recommend psychotherapy for the spouse but this is as far as he can go. The spouse may be resistant and there may be no way of altering her behavior. The patient may then be confronted with the serious choice of getting a divorce and finding a nonneurotic partner or of attempting to live a life of relative privation.

What is true of sex is also true of many of the other most important primary and learned rewards. One of these is money. The therapist obviously can not reward the patient's adaptive actions by payment, nor can he solve a patient's financial difficulties, if these are one of the sources of his trouble. Financial rewards, as far as the patient is concerned, are entirely in the control of people separated from the therapeutic situation. Likewise, the therapist has little direct real-life effect on the social-class aspirations of the patient. In the usual case, he cannot accept the patient into his personal clique and therefore cannot "socialize" with him or his family. This factor is not always important, since the patient and therapist are frequently class-matched, and the patient does not desire social support from the therapist. Nevertheless if the conditions of the patient's life are such as to frustrate aspirations for social mobility or even to threaten downward mobility, such conditions can have a marked negative effect on the outcome of therapy. In this case the patient ultimately must make in real life the responses that will improve his position. If the real-life conditions are so unfavorable that nothing the patient can do will have any effect, the therapist may have to sit helplessly by and see the effects of his hard work partly or wholly destroyed.

The therapist cannot give professional recognition, since this must be accorded by a whole group of colleagues. There is one limited sense in which he can aid the patient professionally. If the therapist be a famous one and the patient an apprentice therapist, merely being "taken" by such a teacher may have a favorable effect on the professional career of the student.

Religious beliefs may either impose barriers to the cure or facilitate it. Under some conditions married people will regard having more children as punishing, and such punishments are, of course, attached to the sex relations which produce the children. If the patient is not able to make use of contraceptives, for instance, it may be impossible for the therapist to decide whether the anxiety attached to the sexual impulse is earned or transferred; so he may never be able to state positively that such anxiety *is* unrealistic and hence urge the patient to attempt the feared sex response. Religious beliefs, on the other hand, may facilitate therapy in that they express common aspirations and realistic anxieties and thus help to keep the patient from escaping into a world of chaotic response where psychotherapy cannot reach him.

The result of all this is somewhat unpleasant as far as the psychotherapist is concerned. He can perform his work correctly and yet fail of a therapeutic result. He may help his patient to take better advantage of the conditions of life which do exist, but these conditions may yet be so unfavorable that nonneurotic habits cannot be reinforced. In this case at least the therapist need have no sense of guilt about his work. He should understand, and the patient should be made to understand, that life conditions are a factor of importance and that the therapist has little control over these conditions. He cannot be blamed for failure to produce results where he cannot control all the conditions affecting such results. He tries to select patients whose life conditions are favorable, but very often these conditions are obscure at the outset and emerge clearly only when the patient begins to react to them in novel ways. Check lists of such favorable and unfavorable circumstances should be invented. They would take a portion of the uncertainty out of the prediction of therapeutic outcome.

If life circumstances are potentially favorable, the patient can help to create and perpetuate them. The recovered husband may not tolerate a neurotic wife but may remarry a normal woman. A neurotic person who is able for the first time to offer normal rewards to the life partner is in a position to do something new and important as a result of the therapeutic work. The reward system can then become a truly social one, that is, one where the rewards of the two partners are mutual and reciprocal.

This fact of life was explained to Mrs. A, and it became, from her standpoint, the task of therapy to get herself into a state of mind where she could reward her husband. If she wanted love, attention, and security in the marital relationship, she, on her part, had to have a strong sexual tie with her husband, had to have and rear the children he wanted, and had to take care of the household and social tasks incident to her role as wife.

Therapeutic results are sometimes delayed through the operation of real-life circumstances. If the patient must wait for favorable conditions, he must be able to bear his misery until these conditions occur. He must bear primary drives until they can be reduced and attempt to deal with learned drives by emphasizing the hopeful aspects of the future. Likewise, "chancey" conditions of reward make therapeutic results unstable. If rewards are present for a time and are then indefinitely withdrawn, the individual will certainly relapse into misery. If the person is punished for attempting drive-reducing responses, inhibition and even repression may recur. We conceive of therapeutic results therefore as strictly related to and dependent upon the external conditions of reinforcement in the life of the person. Reinforcement for persistence in the face of discouragement (so-called, "partial reinforcement") may increase the resistance of learned drives to extinction (Miller, 1950).

WAR NEUROSES SHOW RELATION OF CURE TO CONDITIONS

In the case of the war neuroses we can see quite clearly how different types of "cures" are adjusted to different degrees of rigor of conditions. Some patients with psychoneurotic disorders could, with therapeutic help, readjust to one and some to others of these conditions. We will mention four such conditions.

Cure at the Front with Return to Combat

This was the most severe condition. The greatest danger, fatigue, and privation were involved. Some exhausted and depleted men could be returned to combat after enjoying sleep, good food, and comfort for a short time. Psychotherapy (in the military form of activating the patient's wish to do his duty and stay with his unit) strengthened the forces impelling return to combat.[3] Menninger (1948, p. 147) felt that with intensive treatment close to the front lines approximately 60 per cent of combat casualties could be sent back to duty.

[3] Case 14 described by Grinker and Spiegel (1945b, p. 31) is in point.

Cure in Foreign Zone

Some men who could not tolerate combat itself could accept foreign duty if it were offered instead. This duty had the advantage of enabling the Armed Forces to keep a specialist on overseas duty at a time when he was needed. From the soldier's standpoint, conditions were less rigorous in that fear, exhaustion, and food privation were greatly reduced or eliminated. Psychotherapy was used to reduce the soldier's guilt about leaving combat and being a "failure" while emphasizing the valuable service he could render if he remained overseas. The soldier still had to endure rigorous discipline, separation from home, and other minor privations.[4]

Cure in Zone of Interior with Military Service

Still other soldiers were felt to need much more drastic reduction of ominous circumstances if they were to be retained in military life. These were returned to the United States and assigned duties on bases here. In this case, the danger and privations of foreign service were eliminated and the soldier could reintegrate himself to a degree with his civilian family. Psychotherapy here had the same function as in the second case, namely, to reduce the soldier's guilt feeling about failure in combat and foreign duty, as by telling him that he had done a good job while he had held out, etc., and by emphasizing the value of his continued military work.[5]

Cure in Civilian Life

In many cases, neurotic soldiers were discharged directly into civilian life. Menninger (1948, p. 127) reports 256,134 men who were so discharged. In these cases it was felt that the men could not tolerate any of the hardships or restrictions of combat or military service already mentioned and, being of no further use to the Armed Forces, should be discharged. Psychotherapy, when it was available, played an important role in these cases. It helped enable the soldier to return completely free to civilian life feeling that he had done his best and that there was no stigma attached to

[4] Case 7 reported by Grinker and Spiegel (1945*b*, p. 18) is an example of this discharge to noncombat duty.

[5] Case 40 reported by Grinker and Spiegel (1945*a*, pp. 281–288) falls in this category.

his discharge. The soldier was encouraged actively to resume civilian family and work relationships—and, in the best cases, was trained to deal positively with any prejudice that might exist against him as a psychoneurotic soldier. Presumably, although this process is but slightly known, many of these soldiers stopped reacting with fear and resentment because the military stimuli for these reactions no longer existed. In many other cases, those with excessive fears quietly extinguished these fears through lack of reinforcement. Where psychotherapy was available it undoubtedly helped such soldiers to resume a positive civilian life and to avoid hospitalization as neurotic veterans.

In Guilt Cases Change of Conditions Did Not Cure

In some cases, complete relief from combat and military stress did not result in cure of the military neurosis. These cases seemed frequently to have been ones in which severe guilt reactions were involved. In addition to enduring fear and frustration, the patient had managed to use the military situation to work out a latent aggressive wish. A liked (but unconsciously hated) friend had been killed. Severe guilt reactions set in and the patient blamed himself for sins of omission. This kind of reaction would obviously not be relaxed by mere relief from military stresses. Where the best psychotherapy was available, these problems could be resolved by pointing out the aggressive wish, the depressive reaction to this wish, and by making a clear discrimination between such an unconscious wish and the actual social acts which bring about death. If the soldier had a clean conscience in the latter regard, he could usually accept his aggressive feelings as an inevitable concomitant of life and excuse himself on the ground that he "really" had not done anything to put this wish into effect. Removal of repression is obviously necessary in the course of effecting such a cure.[6]

Needed, Social Therapy?

The patient may expect more of psychotherapy than it can give. He may, for instance, hope that it will help him to marry a girl in a class group above his own or hope that it will be an aid in solving

---

[6] Grinker and Spiegel's case 17 (1945a, pp. 192–195) is a case of this kind. Psychotherapy had the favorable effect intended.

a mobility, ethnic, or caste problem. If a man who speaks poor English hopes to learn to speak correctly during psychotherapy, he will be disappointed. The therapist cannot, among his other pressing duties, stop to correct the patient's grammar. It may indeed be that such a change is impossible in adult life. If the person has not learned to speak or behave correctly in childhood, it may be difficult for him to learn as an adult. We are not contending that change is impossible because such habits are impervious to change but rather that the conditions of good teaching are often missing. Adult friends cannot be got systematically to correct one's manners or speech—such a relationship indeed is antipathetic to friendship. The mobile patient may not be able to find and associate with the people who could teach him what he wants to know—either by direct instruction or by serving as models for imitation. In such a case the psychotherapist may do his part of the work correctly and yet know that the patient will be frustrated.

This was the case with Mrs. A. Mobile through youth and beauty, she still retained many of the social habits taught her by the lower-class associates of her childhood. She lacked some of the skills and graces characteristic of wives in the A family. She wished ardently to be a correct and conventional wife, yet the therapist could not help her. The therapist felt, as anyone must, that something is lacking in our "psycho" therapy. Perhaps the resources of schools where speech, manners, "charm," and class traits are taught should, when needed, be added to those of the therapist.

A similar difficulty exists in regard to the age factor. Some patients come to therapy in their forties and after. They acquire for the first time the capacity to live a normal life. They may find it difficult, however, to meet marriageable persons since their ordinary acquaintances, themselves long married, no longer associate with marriageable people. Naturally, this difficulty is not insuperable, but its solution may require exceptional ingenuity and persistence. Similarly, older persons will find that the weakened primary sex drive of later years cannot be made the basis of the strong sex habits which would earlier have been possible. Psychotherapy cannot enable anyone to "begin over"—it can only help the patient to make the best of what is at hand.

Conflict Resolution Must in General Agree with Moral Standards

The members of a society punish deviation from their moral codes. Thus, if the neurotic person attempts a response not sanctioned by the mores, this response is likely to be punished and inhibition instead of extinction will be strengthened. The person who attempts an antimoral solution will find that he has exchanged an unconscious mental conflict for an open social conflict. Antisocial responses are sometimes reinforced since not all members of the society conform to the general moral standards.

The homosexual, for instance, is likely to find others who will share his sexual adaptation and reinforce homosexual responses. In this case he must nevertheless face the fact of social disapproval and the possibility of severe punishment. If he occupies an important place in the society, he runs the constant risk of losing his place. Since homosexual lovers are not bound together by legal codes, moral sanctions, economic ties, and the presence of children, they may find themselves losing such partners more easily than heterosexuals do. Such losses are necessarily painful and disruptive and leave the individual at loose ends. Many persons find it repugnant also to have to live a secret life and would be glad to be rid of the constraint which is involved.

Homosexuals who accept certain restrictions on their behavior seem to adjust better than those who do not. If they live in great cities they are less subjected to the daily scrutiny which might bring discovery. If they have firmly separated their professional adaptations from their sexual adaptations, they are less likely to disrupt their professional lives. If they observe the general sex taboo on relations with children, they will not arouse the moral horror of the community. Yet, it would seem worth a good deal of psychotherapy and reconditioning of emotional appetite to escape these real-world difficulties. In general, modes of sexual gratification and ways of getting wealth and seeking status must be in accord with the standards of the community.

We must notice nevertheless that there is often more "play" in social standards than neurotics dream of. The mores, being always in change, may be also to some degree in conflict. There is certainly marked variation by culture, some variation by nation, and some, though less, by region, as big city vs. small town. Class variations in moral standards are well known and have been beautifully exemplified in Kinsey's (1948) famous report.

Vague Social Hostility to Drive Life

Within any stable social system, however, these variations are usually of small comfort to the neurotic. Despite recent trends of tolerance and enlightenment, our society is far from having a truly positive attitude toward sexuality. We have not learned how to tame sex during formative years while preserving its full force for expression during years of marriage. The surviving climate is one of disapproval and nervous neglect. The expression of sex in conventional ways wins a certain reluctant assent but the person who is fearful because of early training is likely to perceive the reluctance and secrecy surrounding sex as signs of hostility toward it. Neurotic persons, alert for punishment, cannot discriminate between this social coolness and real danger. They find it hard to believe that the culture will tolerate behavior which it will not openly encourage. Society certainly tolerates private acts and thoughts much more than public acts and public discussion; public education on sexual matters is likely to be merely instrumental, oblique, and aseptic, omitting to note the importance and value of sex rewards in a good life. Hence there is little chance for the neurotic, outside of therapy, to get convincing evidence that something he fears to do will actually be tolerated. He will lack also the comfort of knowing that others share some of his own failings. The neurotic person must learn to tolerate this mildly hostile situation and to take full advantage of the opportunities permitted to him. He must, of course, see clearly the line between what the society will and will not "stand for" and keep on the right side of that line; but that is not usually his problem. His problem is the reverse one—to become expressive enough so that he can live constructively.

Drive-reducing Habits Must Replace Neurotic Habits

We have stressed the necessity that the patient make new responses toward the persons of his real world. We have emphasized that these new responses must be rewarded. When both these circumstances occur, the result is a strong habit. This strong drive-reducing habit must be attached to the very cues which once evoked the inhibitory response. In the sex-anxiety case, where the patient has once reacted to rising sex drive with strong anxiety, he must now react to this drive with habits of approach and consummation. Since consummation is impossible in the therapeutic situation, these habits are necessarily attached to persons outside therapy. When the transaction goes off correctly, the patient is thus freed from the therapist and the therapeutic situation. The neurotic conflict which drove the patient to therapy no longer exists. In its place is a positive adjustment to a person outside therapy. These positive habits usually represent the inhibited limb of the conflict. The patient shows an outgoing loving adjustment rather than a sexual inhibition, a useful self-protective or assertive habit rather than fear of his own anger.

Such positive habits can have a great effect on many aspects of daily life. Strong sex rewards can be attached to verbal cues; when such cues are produced in daily life, the secondary rewards attached to them will reward the effortful responses required by daily tasks. Rearing children, bearing privation and economic struggles can all be made easier if husband and wife give each other sex satisfaction. No lesser (and hardly any more difficult) goal should be held out to our young people than the achievement of a vital sexual relationship with the marriage partner.

Complications occur when the inhibited response is a response that is not tolerated by society. If it is a perversion that the patient fears to execute, the therapist must then confront his patient with the following choice: either the patient can attempt to execute the perverse habit in the face of constant social opposition or he can attempt to extinguish this appetite while building a normal sexual habit in its place. If the patient deeply craves a dependent relationship to life, the therapist must point out the conflict of such an attitude with adult standards of behavior and wait while the patient practices being independent. Such circumstances inevitably prolong the therapeutic relationship and test the motivations of the patient as well as the perseverance of the therapist.

Why Can't the Patient Try Out New Responses at Once?

Is the "talking" or "inside" part of the work really necessary? If the therapist can sense at an early time the nature of the patient's conflict why can't he simply tell the patient what that conflict is and why can't the patient try out the requisite responses? In some cases, indeed, this is enough. Inhibitory forces are but barely dominant. The person needs only a nudge to make the expressive action possible. In such a case, friends may say, "What you need is to get married," and the person, thus encouraged, is able to take the step. But these cases do not come to psychotherapy. Where a little environmental pressure is sufficient, it has almost invariably been applied and had its effect.

Where inhibition is highly dominant and repression is added to prevent rational attempts at solution of the conflict, the "talking" part of the work is imperative. Without relief from repression and practice on the higher mental processes the patient *cannot* try. Well-meant advice goes unheeded and may, indeed, provoke greater anxiety and recoil from expressive gestures. He who needs only a "kick in the pants" to get him over life's hurdles has already had it and profited by it.

Favorable life conditions are essential to the completion of therapeutic work but we do not wish to emphasize them disproportionately. Both psychological work and real tryouts under favorable conditions are required for the cure. Without the psychological work the needed new responses cannot be tried out. Without the real tryout and reward the conflict cannot be resolved.

When Is the Patient Ready to Stop?

Obviously the patient cannot leave the therapeutic situation until the baneful effects of repression are lifted. The weakening of fear at the verbal level generalizes also to the inhibitory limb of the conflict. We believe that the patient should not be allowed to stop until he is innovating new responses in his outside life and getting significant rewards for them. Within the therapeutic situation, he should be developing the mental components of those habits which will protect him from neurosis. As these outward directed habits are rewarded, outside rewards replace those of the therapeutic situation.

No therapist should content himself with mere knowledge or good intentions on the part of his patient. Behavior theory emphasizes the great importance of being certain that the groundwork of new habit is laid while the therapist still has some influence. Perhaps most therapists already instinctively follow this injunction of behavior theory. If so, they should continue to do what they are doing and put this condition of therapy yet more consciously and systematically into effect.

Alexander and French (1946, p. 36) have emphasized the sensible view that the patient knows he can "go it alone" when he has tried living without the therapist and found that he can do so. They advise "interruption" of treatment in which the patient can test himself. Such interruption should be of at least a month's duration. Periods of interruption may also increase motivation and clarify the problems awaiting solution. We believe that the principle applies to any psychotherapeutic work, brief or prolonged.

Graded Tasks

The ideal of the therapist is to set up a series of graded situations where the patient can learn. Thus he tries, as Hanns Sachs said, "to dose anxiety." Anxiety should be sufficient to propel therapeutic work but not so great as to make escape from therapy necessary. If a long and complex habit must be learned, the therapist should reward the subunits of the habit as they occur. It will be sufficient later to assemble them in the right order. At one point in a therapeutic sequence the therapist may have to reward masturbation so that the patient may experience the sexual orgasm for the first time. Similarly, thinking, coming as it does before acting, should be at one time rewarded even when no positive action follows. At a later time, the thoughts and relevant gross actions can be tied together. The patient should never face his complete dilemma at any one time. The therapist is therefore careful about directing attention to unconscious trends. Suddenly confronting a repressed tendency may have the same painful effect on a patient as would a strong electric shock—and the effect may last much longer. The goal is a bit-by-bit revelation, since the "bits" are all the patient can stand at any one time.

Some failures of therapy may be due to the difficulty in setting up these graded conditions. In order to grade the units of a task, the whole task must be conceived. This is just what is difficult to foresee in the case of psychotherapy. Different neurotic disorders pose different tasks. Theory to guide the therapist is fuzzy at many points. Therapists differ in clinical skill and hence in their intuitive ability to forecast outcome. Despite difficulties, however, the problem remains. Further time and research should be spent in defining the therapeutic transaction as a series of graded tasks.

CHAPTER XXII

THE DYNAMICS OF CONFLICT: THEIR
IMPLICATIONS FOR THERAPY

As our previous discussions have emphasized, the neurotic patient is in severe conflict. His higher mental processes are disturbed by a conflict between the motivation to remember and think and the responses of repression that prevent him from remembering and thinking. The goal responses that normally would reduce his high drives are blocked by conflicts with inhibiting responses. The drives caused by these conflicts produce misery and symptoms.

Since the therapist is trying to resolve these severe conflicts, his tactics should be based on a theoretical understanding of the dynamics of conflict behavior. Our analysis of conflict behavior here will repeat and assimilate into a tighter theoretical integration certain points that already have been made separately in different contexts; we will also introduce new points fundamental to the discussions in subsequent chapters.[1]

Basic Assumptions about Gradients of Approach and Avoidance

The following four assumptions are essential to our analysis of conflict behavior:

1. The tendency to approach a goal is stronger the nearer the subject is to it. This will be called the *gradient of approach.*

2. The tendency to avoid a feared stimulus is stronger the nearer the subject is to it. This will be called the *gradient of avoidance.*

3. The strength of avoidance increases more rapidly with nearness than does that of approach. In other words, the gradient of avoidance is *steeper* than that of approach. This will be illustrated in Fig. 15.

---

[1] The following discussion of conflict is based on a chapter by Miller (1944). which also summarizes the experimental evidence supporting this type of analysis.

4. The strength of the tendencies to approach or avoid varies with the strength of the drive upon which they are based. In other words, an increase in drive raises the *height* of the entire gradient.

Technical discussion of assumptions. Most of the experimental tests of the foregoing assumptions and of the deductions derived from them have been made in simple situations in which the subject approaches or avoids a goal or a feared object by locomotion through space (Miller, 1944). According to the theory, however, we would not expect these effects to be limited to the dimension of distance in space.

The gradients of approach and avoidance are derived from two more basic principles, namely, the gradient of reinforcement and the gradient of stimulus generalization. According to the gradient of reinforcement, the immediate effects of reward and punishment are greater than the delayed ones.[2] Since approach in response to stimuli nearer the goal will be more immediately reinforced than approach in response to stimuli farther from the goal, we would expect the gradient of reinforcement to produce a gradient of approach in the dimension of distance in space. The same should be true of avoidance. But the effect of the gradient of reinforcement should not be limited to spatial sequences; it should produce gradients in any reasonably short, regular, temporal sequences leading to reward or punishment.

According to the principle of stimulus generalization, the strongest approach should be elicited in the situation that is most similar to the one in which approach was rewarded, and the strongest avoidance should be elicited in the situation most similar to the one in which fear and avoidance were reinforced. The cues near the goal are usually more similar to those at the goal than are those farther away. Therefore the strong, immediately reinforced approach responses at the goal should be more likely to generalize to the cues near to the goal than to those far from it. The same thing should apply to avoidance responses reinforced by punishment. Thus the gradient of stimulus generalization should tend to produce a gradient in the strength of approach and avoidance in

[2] See Spence (1947) for an article suggesting that the gradient of reinforcement may be derived from the more basic principles of stimulus generalization and learned reward.

the dimension of space. But the effect of the gradient of stimulus generalization is not limited to simple spatial situations; it applies to all dimensions of qualitative stimulus similarity. Therefore we would expect gradients of approach and avoidance, respectively, to exist in any situation that involves regular sequences of cues that become progressively more similar to those present at the goal or point of punishment. We would also expect a gradient of approach when the subject had never been rewarded for approaching a given goal so that the tendencies to approach it were derived solely by generalization from other somewhat similar goals which he had been rewarded for approaching. The same thing should apply to the avoidance of situations similar to those in which the subject has been punished.

If we extend our analysis from primary stimulus generalization, based on the innate similarity of cues, to secondary generalization, based on the learned equivalence of cues, we would expect gradients of approach and avoidance to exist in culturally defined sequences. Take, for example, the sequence of attending a mixed social event, being introduced to a person of opposite sex, making a telephone call, having a casual date, having a more serious date, engagement, wedding ceremony, and married life. In such sequences the gradients in the strength of approach and avoidance responses would be the consequence of a complex series of mediating cue-producing responses.

Thus far we have been discussing the first two assumptions dealing with the existence of gradients of approach and avoidance. The third assumption states that the gradient of avoidance is steeper than that of approach. In simple situations involving approach that is based on hunger, and avoidance that is based on fear, this assumption has been found by Brown (1948) to apply to the dimension of spatial distance and by Miller and Kraeling (1950) to apply to the dimension of qualitative stimulus similarity. Furthermore, deductions based on this third assumption have been verified by experiments on conflict behavior in simple spatial situations (Miller, 1944) and by clinical observations of displacement (Miller, 1948b). These same articles suggest ways in which the greater steepness of the gradient of avoidance might be derived from more fundamental principles. Until these derivations have been tested, however, so that we know what factors are responsible for the greater steepness of avoidance, we cannot be certain that the assumption applies to all types of situations.

The fourth assumption, that the height of the entire gradient is raised by an increase in drive, has been verified with both approach based on hunger and avoidance based on electric shock for the dimension of distance in space (Brown, 1948) and for a dimension of qualitative stimulus similarity (Brown, 1942). It is so much in line with the general principles of behavior (Hull, 1943) that it seems quite likely to be generally applicable.

Extension of the simple spatial model to other dimensions. Both a theoretical analysis and such experimental evidence as is available lead us to expect our assumptions to apply to any situation in which the subject can be said to be coming nearer to a goal in space, time, or some dimension of qualitative or culturally defined similarity of cues. All the clinical evidence that we are aware of also strongly suggests the same conclusion. Since it is easiest to represent conflict in simple spatial terms, we shall draw our diagrams in this way and then use them as *models* for thinking about nonspatial situations. In the following discussion we are assuming (1) that the responses producing inhibition and repression follow the same laws as those involved in simple spatial avoidance, and (2) that the responses that are inhibited or repressed follow the same laws as those involved in simple spatial approach.

Approach-avoidance Conflict

The situation in which a person has strong tendencies to approach and avoid the same goal is called an approach-avoidance conflict. According to our assumptions, this is the kind of conflict that usually occurs between the responses of trying to remember or think about something and the responses of repression; it is also the kind of conflict that occurs when a neurotic is prevented by his inhibitions from achieving a goal.

The dynamics of approach-avoidance conflict are represented graphically in Fig. 15. It can be seen that at a distance from the feared goal the tendency to approach is stronger than that to avoid. Thus, when the subject is in this region, he should move toward the feared goal. As he gets nearer, the strength of avoidance in-

creases faster than that of approach because the gradient of avoidance is steeper than that of approach. Eventually he reaches a
point at which the strength of avoidance equals that of approach.

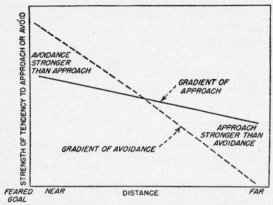

FIG. 15. Simple graphic representation of an approach-avoidance conflict. The
tendency to approach is the stronger of the two tendencies far from the goal,
while the tendency to avoid is the stronger of the two near to the goal. Therefore, when far from the goal, the subject should tend to approach part way and
then stop; when near to it, he should tend to retreat part way and then stop.
In short, he should tend to remain in the region where the two gradients intersect.

It is only for the sake of simplicity that the gradients are represented by
straight lines in these diagrams. Similar deductions could be made on the basis
of any curves that have a continuous negative slope that is steeper for avoidance
than for approach at each point above the abscissa. (*Figure adapted from
Miller, 1944.*)

At the point where the two gradients cross, he should stop.[3] Similarly, whenever the subject is too near to the goal, he should retreat, with the strength of avoidance falling off more rapidly than

[3] This going part way and then stopping, which is so characteristic of subjects in an approach-avoidance conflict, can be deduced only from the assumption that the gradient of avoidance is steeper than that of approach. If
the two were parallel, the tendency that was stronger at the start would be
stronger all of the way to the goal. If the gradient of approach were
steeper than that of avoidance, once the subject reached the point where he
started to go toward the goal, the relative advantage of approach would continue
to increase the farther he went. Thus he would never stop or turn back.

that of approach, until he reaches the point at which the two are equal, and consequently is stopped. Thus it can be seen that the subject should tend to remain trapped at an intermediate point where the two gradients cross. The situation should be one of stable equilibrium, like a pendulum which has a stronger tendency to return the farther it is pushed off center.

This is what occurs in experimental situations (Miller, 1944); the subject goes part of the way to the goal and then stops. If he is placed at the goal, he retreats and then comes part way back. The same thing is observed clinically: people in such a conflict seem to be unable to go forward far enough to reach their goals or away far enough to forget them. Thus Mrs. A was continually attracted sexually by men but, unable to achieve her goal of a successful adjustment in her marriage, she nevertheless did not want to leave her husband. As would be expected from our analysis, she frequently wasted effort by starting on projects that she did not want to carry through to their logical conclusion. The proposed visit to her former boy friend in N is an example of one such project.

Effect of increasing drive to approach. Figure 16 shows that the location of the point at which the gradients intersect, and hence the locus of the region where the subject remains, depends on the relative heights of the two gradients. When the motivation to approach is weak, the entire gradient of approach is low; thus it intersects the gradient of avoidance at a low point, far from the goal. In spatial situations, the subject will be expected to remain so far from the goal that he is not frightened by it; in nonspatial ones, he will not be motivated to perform responses that produce cues eliciting fear. Since both approach and avoidance are weak at the low point where the gradients intersect, the conflict between them will be weak.

Increasing the strength of the drive to approach will be expected to raise the entire gradient of approach. Figure 16 shows that this causes the point of intersection to occur nearer the goal and at a much higher point on the gradient of avoidance. Thus when the drive motivating approach is increased, the subject will be expected to move nearer to the feared goal, and when he is nearer, the cues there will be expected to arouse stronger fear motivating avoidance. Similarly, in nonspatial situations he will be motivated to perform responses producing cues eliciting strong fear. With the strength of both tendencies increased, he will be in a much more severe conflict.

This deduction holds only for the range within which the two

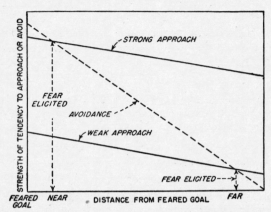

FIG. 16. How increasing the strength of approach in an approach-avoidance conflict increases the amount of fear and conflict elicited. The subject will be expected to advance or retreat to the point where the gradients intersect, *i.e.*, where the strengths of the competing tendencies are equal. Thus as the strength of approach is increased, he will move nearer the feared goal. When he is nearer the feared goal, the strength of both tendencies will be increased. Therefore, more fear and conflict will be elicited.

This deduction holds only for the range within which the two gradients intersect. If approach is increased until it is stronger than avoidance at the goal, the subject will advance to the goal. Then further increases in the strength of approach will not be expected to produce further increases in the amount of fear and conflict elicited. It is only for the sake of simplicity that the gradients are represented by straight lines in these diagrams. Similar deductions could be made on the basis of any curves that have a continuous negative slope that is steeper for avoidance than for approach at each point above the abscissa. (*Figure adapted from Miller,* 1944.)

gradients intersect. If approach is increased until it is stronger than avoidance at the goal, the subject will advance to the goal. Then, further increases in the strength of approach will not be expected to produce further increases in the amount of fear and conflict elicited. As the goal responses become completely dominant over inhibition, the amount of conflict will be reduced.

From the foregoing analysis it can be seen that if a person's inhibitions are so weak that he has practically reached the goal, increasing his motivation will cause him to reach the goal without much additional increase in fear. On the other hand, if the avoidance tendencies are strong enough to keep him far from the goal, increasing his motivation to approach it will produce a marked increase in fear and conflict. Since fear is such a strong drive (Miller, 1950), it is possible to establish conflicts in which no readily available increase in the motivation to approach will cause the subject to reach the goal.

Neurotic patients a selected group with strong avoidance. The most common reaction of the members of our society to an inhibited person is to try to increase his motivation. His friends, relatives, and associates urge him to try harder. The person whose avoidance tendencies are so weak that his conflicts can be resolved by increasing his motivation to approach does not reach the psychotherapist. Hence we have no idea of the frequency of such cases.

The person with a severe neurosis who does reach the psychotherapist is a specially selected case with extremely strong avoidance tendencies. Therefore, trying to increase his motivation to approach goals will only increase his fear and conflict. This increase in misery will tend to drive him out of therapy. This is indeed what seems to happen. Therapists have found that the first thing to do is to concentrate on reducing the fears motivating avoidance (*i.e.,* to analyze resistances) rather than to try to increase the motivation to approach the feared goal.

In later stages of the treatment, the fear motivating avoidance may be reduced to the point where the subject is able to approach near to the goal without undue fear or conflict. When this has occurred, we would expect increasing the neurotic's motivation to approach to be more likely to produce a good effect.

It should be noted that the tactics of reducing the fear and avoidance first rather than trying to increase the motivation to approach are based on a number of factors. First are the social conditions that cause the patients to be a specially selected group of people with strong avoidance. Next come the dynamics of the conflict situation. If avoidance is strong, increasing the motivation to approach will greatly increase the patient's fear, conflict, and misery. Finally there is the fact that the private therapist does not control powerful enough rewards and punishments to keep the patient in the therapeutic situation if it produces a great increase in misery.

If the therapist's control over basic rewards and punishments were increased so that it was much greater than that of the patient's friends and associates, the therapist might be able to succeed, where they had failed, in using the technique of increasing the motivation to approach. There may well be a limit beyond which this technique will not work under any circumstances. But the social conditions of therapy in our culture do not afford exact data on where this limit may be.

As a final note of caution, it should be observed that we would expect any marked changes in the social conditions responsible for the selection of patients to alter the relative merits of various strategies of therapy. If the expense and social stigma which tend to keep milder cases away from therapy were reduced, and especially if a program of mental hygiene were introduced for normal people with relatively weak avoidance, the technique of increasing the motivation to approach might be found to be more successful for this different type of patient.

Basis for the negative therapeutic effect. As Fig. 17 shows, when the avoidance is strong relative to the approach, the two gradients intersect far from the goal. The point of intersection is not only far away; it is also relatively low. At this distance the approach tendency is so weak that the subject is not strongly tempted to do frightening things. In spatial situations, the subject will remain so far away from the goal that he is not frightened; in nonspatial ones, the responses that would produce cues eliciting fear will be completely inhibited or repressed.

Extinguishing the fear of the goal or making it seem less dangerous by an improved discrimination or by reassurance will lower the entire gradient of avoidance. For the limits within which the two gradients intersect, this will produce a paradoxical effect. As Fig. 17 shows, when the gradient of avoidance is lower, the intersection moves nearer to the dangerous goal and occurs at a higher point on the approach gradient. Thus in spatial situations, the effects of the decrease in the "dangerousness" of the goal will be more than compensated for by the fact that the subject is lured nearer to it. In nonspatial situations, as the apparent danger is reduced the subject will be more strongly tempted to do things

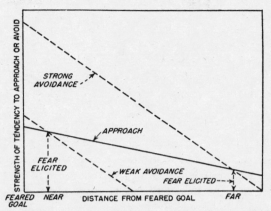

FIG. 17. How decreasing the strength of avoidance in an approach-avoidance conflict increases the amount of fear and conflict elicited. The subject will be expected to advance or retreat to the point where the gradients intersect, *i.e.*, where the strengths of the opposing tendencies are equal. Thus, with weak avoidance, he will approach nearer to the feared goal. When he is nearer to the feared goal, the strength of both tendencies will be increased. Therefore, more fear and conflict will be elicited.

This deduction holds only for the range within which the gradients of approach and avoidance intersect. If the gradient of avoidance is weakened so much that it no longer intersects the gradient of approach, the subject will advance to the goal and further decreases in the gradient of avoidance will decrease the amount of fear and conflict. It is only for the sake of simplicity that the gradients are represented by straight lines in these diagrams. Similar deductions could be made on the basis of any curve that has a continuous negative slope that is steeper for avoidance than approach at each point above the abscissa. (*Figure adapted from Miller, 1944.*)

which frighten him. Stronger fear and conflict will therefore be elicited.

This happened in the case of Mrs. A. First the reassuring and permissive attitude of the therapist produced a marked reduction in the amount of fear that she experienced. Then the fears motivating her inhibitions were reduced enough so that she was able to become more sexually responsive toward her husband and to become a more aggressive, less subdued person. As she was able to come nearer to her goals in these respects, she began to experience renewed fear and conflict, which produced a recrudescence of symptoms.

Returning to Fig. 17, it can be seen that if the gradient of avoidance is lowered enough so that it no longer intersects that of approach, the subject will be expected to advance all the way to the goal. After he has reached the goal, further decreases in the gradient of avoidance will not produce any additional paradoxical increase in fear and conflict. From this point on, fear and conflict will be reduced. This also seems to occur in therapy; the patient may show an increase in fear and conflict as he is approaching near to a new feared goal and a marked decrease after he has achieved it.

The application of the foregoing type of analysis to the therapeutic situation is complicated by the fact that a number of different goals and subgoals are usually involved. At any given stage of the treatment the patient may be at different positions in a number of more or less related approach-avoidance conflicts.

Finally, it should be noted that the increase in fear and conflict produced when the strength of approach is increased is dependent on the fact that avoidance is stronger nearer the goal. The paradoxical negative therapeutic effect is dependent on the fact that the strength of approach is stronger nearer the goal. Since the strength of avoidance increases faster than that of approach (the greater steepness of the gradient of avoidance), we would expect the former effect to be greater than the latter. This can readily be seen by comparing Figs. 16 and 17. Causing the subject to move a given distance toward the goal by increasing the strength of approach produces a much larger increase in fear and conflict than causing him to advance the same distance by reducing the strength of avoidance.

This deduction is confirmed by the experience of therapists. They find that the procedure of reducing the fear motivating avoidance is much less painful than that of increasing the strength of motivation to approach. That is the basis for the general strategy of concentrating on reducing the fear that motivates the severely neurotic patient's repression and inhibition.

Repression and appearance of symptoms. As has just been shown, when avoidance is strong relative to approach, the subject will be expected to remain far from the feared goal and to experience relatively little fear or conflict. For the limits within which the gradients cross, a reduction in the strength of avoidance or an increase in the strength of approach will cause the subject to come nearer to the feared goal or to start performing responses producing cues eliciting strong fear. Thus the result will be an increase in the strength of fear and conflict. This increase in fear and conflict will be expected to be especially great if the close approach to the feared goal was produced by an increase in the strength of the motivation to approach. According to our hypothesis, symptoms are produced by the strong drives involved in conflict. Thus we shall expect this increase in conflict to produce an increase in symptoms. This seems to occur; Freud (1925, Vol. IV, pp. 92–97) reports that symptoms are especially likely to occur when strong repressions and inhibitions are on the verge of breaking down.

Avoidance-avoidance Competition

The situation in which an individual is forced to choose one of two undesirable alternatives (either X or Y) is represented by Fig. 18. Let us suppose that the subject starts nearer to X. Since the strength of avoidance increases with nearness, the tendency to avoid the near evil, X, will be stronger than that to avoid the remote one, Y. The subject will be expected to go away from the nearer evil and toward the more remote one. But eventually he will be nearer to the other evil, Y. Then the tendency to avoid Y will be stronger, so he will stop and turn around. Thus the situation is one of stable equilibrium like that of a pendulum. Provided that there is no third way out, the individual will remain vacillating in conflict, trapped between the two sources of avoidance at the point where their gradients intersect.

If the avoidance of one of the alternatives is increased, that entire gradient will be raised. It can be seen that this will move the point of intersection of the gradients, and hence the region in which the subject will remain trapped, nearer to the other alternative. The intersection will not only be moved nearer to the other alternative but it also will occur at a higher point on both gradients. In other words, if the subject is between two frightening alternatives, increasing the avoidance of one will force him nearer to the other,

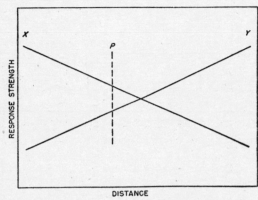

FIG. 18. Difference between approach and avoidance choices. This is a schematic diagram of the gradients to approach (or to avoid) two stimulus objects, *X* and *Y*. If the two objects elicit only approach, the individual started at *P* will be expected to go directly to *X*; if they elicit only avoidance, he will be expected to go away from *X* until he passes the point at which the gradients cross and then to turn back. It is only for the sake of simplicity that the gradients are represented by straight lines in these diagrams. Similar deductions could be made on the basis of any curves that have a continuous negative slope. (*Figure adapted from Miller, 1944.*)

and when he is nearer, stronger fear and conflict will be elicited.

Conversely, weakening the strength of one of the alternatives will lower the point of intersection and reduce the conflict. No negative therapeutic effect will be expected in an avoidance-avoidance conflict.

Finally, if the difference between the two alternatives is too great, the gradients will not cross and the subject will be driven past the weaker source of avoidance and out of the situation.

In the preceding deductions it has been assumed that the conditions are such that the subject must go toward either one or the other of the sources of avoidance. Frequently he is not limited in this way. For example, a man at a street corner who sees two people he wishes to avoid coming from opposite directions may avoid both of them by going down a side street at right angles to their line of approach. As soon as he starts in one direction or the other, the response of continuing will be a more direct avoidance than the one of turning back. Therefore the situation will be one of unstable equilibrium, and he will continue going in the direction he starts. Whenever such a compromise response is physically possible and is a part of the subject's hierarchy of habits, we will expect it to occur because it is motivated by both sources of avoidance. Unless completely hemmed in, the subject should escape from an avoidance-avoidance choice.

From the foregoing analysis it can be seen that the therapist who wants to try to force a patient toward a feared goal by increasing the disadvantages of the alternatives must be sure that he has covered all other possible means of escape, including escape from the therapeutic situation. If the patient is almost ready to accept a given alternative, he may be motivated to do this in order to avoid other consequences; but if he is a considerable distance from that alternative, driving him toward it by increasing his avoidance of something else will produce a marked increase in fear and conflict.

Why Pure-approach Competition Produces No Conflict

Figure 18 may also be used to represent the situation in which the subject is presented with a choice between two equally desirable goals, both eliciting only tendencies to approach. It is unlikely that the subject will be exactly at the center, the point at which the two gradients cross, and even if he is, slight fluctuations in the stimulus situation are likely to get him started in one direction or the other. It can be seen that, once the subject gets off center, the tendency to approach the nearer goal will be stronger so that he should start to approach it. After he starts, the tendency to approach will become progressively stronger the nearer he gets. Such a choice is a situation of unstable equilibrium like that of a pencil balanced on its point, which, as soon as it starts, has an ever-increasing tendency to continue falling and hence never reverses its direction. For this reason, we would expect choices between desirable alternatives to be easily made provided nothing but pure approach tendencies are involved. Experimental evidence and clinical observations (Miller, 1944) seem to confirm this expectation. Donkeys do not starve midway between two equally desirable stacks of hay, unless there are thorns, eliciting avoidance, concealed in the haystacks.

Double Approach-avoidance Conflict

Our analysis suggests that therapists should look for latent avoidance whenever their patients are having great difficulty making up their minds which of two apparently desirable alternatives to accept. The girl who cannot choose between two suitors may have concealed tendencies to avoid each of them. Sometimes the source of avoidance may be in the original ambivalence towards each of the goals. In other instances it may grow out of the choice situation which demands that the subject renounce one goal to accept the other. The subject may want to try to keep both. This is especially likely to be true if the two goals are qualitatively different so that one is not a complete substitute for the other.

Ambivalence that is not strong enough to prevent the subject from choosing a goal if it is the only alternative can introduce conflict into a choice between two such goals. This is illustrated in Fig. 19.

When the entire gradient of approach is stronger than that of avoidance, the subject will go completely up to the goal; the fact that he is somewhat ambivalent may not be immediately obvious. Such a situation is represented in Fig. 19A. Although the subject will be expected to reach the goal, the effect of the avoidance (increasing in strength more rapidly than approach) will be to produce a decrease in the net tendency to approach as the goal is neared. Instead of becoming more eager as he nears the goal, a person with latent avoidance would be expected to become more hesistant. According to our analysis, this effect is what makes distant pastures seem greener. More exactly, the old proverb should be rephrased: Distant pastures seem to have fewer thistles.

If the subject is presented with a choice between two goals each of which elicits latent avoidance, the situation might be mistaken for a pure approach-approach competition because of the fact that he will go to each goal when they are presented separately. As can be seen in Fig. 19B, however, the results to be expected are quite different. The strongest tendency will be to approach the more distant goal. But as the subject goes toward this goal, the other one will become progressively more distant until the tendency

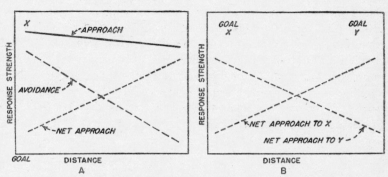

FIG. 19. Double approach-avoidance competition. In *A* is represented a single approach-avoidance situation with avoidance weaker than approach at the goal, so that the subject should go completely up to the goal. Subtracting the strength of the avoidance from that of the approach results in a net approach tendency which becomes weaker nearer the goal. In *B* the two net tendencies are represented in a double approach-avoidance situation. As the individual moves toward either of the two goals, *X* or *Y*, the net tendency to approach that goal becomes weaker and to approach the other, stronger. This should produce conflict.

It is only for the sake of simplicity that the gradients are represented by straight lines in these diagrams. Similar deductions could be made on the basis of any curves that have a continuous negative slope that is steeper for avoidance than approach at each point above the abscissa. (*From Miller, 1944.*)

to approach it is the stronger so that he will stop or turn around. The situation will be one of stable equilibrium like that of the pendulum.

Relationships between Fear and Conflict

According to the preceding analysis, pure approach-approach choices are easily resolved; conflict should appear only when avoidance is present. This suggests that whenever unexplained indecision and conflict appear, the therapist should look for concealed sources of avoidance. Since fear is one of the strongest sources of avoidance, he can often profitably ask: "What is feared?"

The relationship also works the other way. As has been suggested, the subject who is not physically restrained will soon escape from most fear-producing situations unless he is prevented by conflict. This conflict can be produced by other sources of avoidance that keep him away from the avenues of escape or by unsatisfied drives that motivate him to approach feared goals. Therefore, when unexplained fears persist, the therapist should ask: "What conflicting tendencies prevent the patient from escaping the fear-provoking stimuli? What frightening thing does he want to do?"

Other possibilities are that the fear is attached to a primary drive that the patient carries around with him or that it is attached to stimuli that are ubiquitous.

CHAPTER XXIII

A HYPOTHESIS CONCERNING ALCOHOL, BARBITURATES, AND LOBOTOMY

The old proverb *in vino veritas* expresses the folk knowledge that people will often say things under the influence of alcohol that they would not say when sober. They may also do things that they would not ordinarily do. Similarly, ever since the classic work of Bleckwenn (1930) and Lindemann (1931), it has been known that the intravenous injection of barbiturates can be used to produce a temporary remission in some catatonic patients and enable them to report information that they would not otherwise be able to give. During the war, medical officers effectively used one of the barbiturates, sodium pentothal, to speed up psychotherapy in a large number of cases of combat neurosis (*e.g.*, Grinker and Spiegel, 1945*a* and 1945*b*; Sargent, 1942; Horsley, 1943; Menninger, 1948, pp. 309–311). Barbiturates have also been used to speed up the treatment of civilian neuroses (Glueck, 1946; Freed, 1946; Adatto, 1949).

The psychological effect of alcohol and the barbiturates is often described as taking away the patient's defenses or reducing his anxiety. Thus Grinker and Spiegel (1945*b*, p. 136) say: "Through the artificial intervention of the drug the intensity of the anxiety is diminished; the pressure upon the ego is decreased. Accordingly, the potential ego span is widened."

In this chapter we shall attempt to formulate some of the details of this process more exactly in terms of learning theory. Our basic assumption will be that alcohol and the barbiturates produce a greater reduction in the strength of fear than they do in that of other drives. Thus they lower the gradient of avoidance more than that of approach. In this way they quickly but temporarily produce effects analogous to those from the gradual reductions in fear produced by the technique of psychotherapy

369

It is well known that these drugs also produce other effects, such as sleepiness and incoordination. They also seem to produce an increase in suggestibility, which may or may not turn out to be dependent on the reduction of fear. In this discussion we shall not be concerned with any of these other effects.

Experimental evidence on fear-reduction by drugs. Experiments on cats and rats show that alcohol produces a reduction in the strength of fear. These experiments have already been described in the section on Alcoholism in Chap. XI. It will be remembered that, when approach and avoidance were established separately in different groups of animals, alcohol produced a greater reduction in the strength of pull of the animals performing an avoidance habit motivated by fear than in those performing an approach habit motivated by hunger. Similarly, when both tendencies were present simultaneously in an approach-avoidance conflict, the alcohol caused the animals to resume going up to eat at the place where they had been frightened by electric shock.

Furthermore, normal animals did not prefer a solution of alcohol in milk to plain milk, but ones that were subjected to fear and conflict did. This suggests that the reduction in fear produced by the alcohol served to reinforce the response of drinking when frightened. Cross-cultural data suggest the same conclusion. When accessibility of alcohol is held constant, there is a correlation between the degree of subsistence hazard, presumably eliciting anxiety, and the amount of insobriety.

Though the effects of the barbiturates on fear have not been investigated as thoroughly as those of alcohol, the available experimental evidence indicates that they are much the same. Masserman (1943) reports that sodium amytal produces "mitigation of recently acquired neurotic patterns" in cats, and Miller and Bailey (1950) report that it causes hungry cats in a simple approach-avoidance conflict to resume going up to secure the food at the place where they had been frightened by mild electric shocks.

Results of the general reduction in the fear drive. If, as we assume, the drug produces a general reduction in the strength of the fear drive, we would expect it to lower the whole gradient of avoidance. The effects of this lowering of the avoidance should be exactly the same as those deduced in the preceding chapter. If the subject was able to come near to the goal before the administration of the drug, lowering the avoidance should cause him to come up to the goal and reduce his fear after he has reached it. The experiments on animals have demonstrated this result. If the subject was quite a distance from the goal, lowering the gradient of avoidance should cause him to approach nearer to it, at which point, paradoxically, more fear should be elicited.

These expectations are confirmed by the observations that Grinker and Spiegel (1945a and 1945b) report on the use of sodium pentothal in the treatment of cases of war neurosis. Before the drug is administered, some patients are suffering from mild anxiety and from an almost complete amnesia of their traumatic battle experiences. In such cases, the immediate effect of the injection is a reduction in anxiety. The patient seems less tense and he reports that he feels less anxious. At the same time, if he tries to remember or is motivated to respond by the commands of the therapist and by the presentation of cues similar to those involved in the traumatic episodes, he can begin to lift his amnesia. With the fear-motivating repression reduced, responses that previously were completely repressed can now occur. As some of these memories occur, they produce cues eliciting additional memories. But they also produce cues eliciting fear, which becomes stronger the nearer the patient approaches to the most traumatic incident. Thus the net result is a paradoxical increase in fear exactly like the negative therapeutic effect that has already been described.

Grinker and Spiegel (1945b, p. 80) give a characteristically vivid description of the effect:

The terror exhibited in the moments of supreme danger, such as at the imminent explosion of shells, the death of a friend before the patient's eyes, the absence of cover under a heavy dive-bombing attack, is electrifying to watch. The body becomes increasingly tense and rigid; the eyes widen and the pupils dilate, while the skin becomes covered with fine perspiration. The hands move about convulsively, seeking a weapon, or a friend to share the danger. The breathing becomes incredibly rapid and shallow. The intensity of the emotion sometimes becomes unbearable; and frequently, at the height of the reaction, there is a collapse and the patient falls back in bed and remains quiet a few minutes, usually to resume the story at a more neutral point.

According to our analysis, we would expect that patients whose repression was exceedingly strong or whose tendency to remember was relatively weak would keep so far away from thoughts of the traumatic incidents that they would experience relatively little fear before the administration of the drug. Since these patients would be starting farther out on the conflict gradients, the reduction produced by the drug would be less likely to bring them up to the point of remembering the most traumatic incidents. This seems to be the case; Grinker and Spiegel (1945*b*, p. 81) report:

Other patients, in whom there has been amnesia without much overt anxiety, become suddenly blocked in the account of their experience as they approach the moment of trauma. As the anxiety begins to appear in anticipation of the traumatic scene, they cease talking and resume their characteristic defenses; they don't know what happened next. At this point the therapist applies pressure, demanding, forcing the patient to proceed. More than one session of narcosynthesis may be necessary to uncover the trauma.

Reassurance and extinction while repression is weakened by drugs. According to our analysis, it is safest for the therapist to assume that the mere expression of a thought or emotion has little therapeutic effect *per se*. This seems to be confirmed by the experience of Grinker and Spiegel (1945*a*, p. 392) who report:

We have stated many times that the emotional expressions evoked under the influence of pentothal must be considered usually as an abreaction, which is rarely curative in itself but is the necessary beginning to the attainment of insight. . . . Abreactions spontaneously lived through under alcohol are nontherapeutic, as we have learned from our patients who, while drunk, explode terrific hostilities in neighboring bars.

If the mere expression of emotions does not dissipate them, how are therapeutic effects achieved?

Many of the cases of war neurosis accuse themselves bitterly of being cowards, weaklings, and failures. A strong motivation of this kind is readily understandable in the light of both their previous civilian and military training. Thus it seems reasonable to assume that, in addition to eliciting fear of combat, the memories of the combat situation and the expression of any fear of combat elicit strong guilt and fear of being stigmatized as a coward.

Similarly, the expression of hostility toward the army that is forcing him into such dangerous situations, toward officers, comrades, and even toward the enemy, might be expected to produce strong guilt. Such guilt and the fear of being called a coward would be additional strong motivations for repression. They would tend to prevent the patient from thinking over his problem rationally.

If the therapist, as a person with prestige and authority, condemned the expressions of fear and hostility that occurred when the fear-motivating repression was weakened by the drug, this would reinforce fear and guilt; we would then expect the uncovering of repressed memories and emotions to be without therapeutic value. Similarly, it may be conjectured that the unfortunate consequences of explosions of terrific hostilities in neighboring bars prevent any extinction of fear or guilt from occurring as the result of such episodes.

The therapist, of course, does not condemn. Instead he either calmly accepts the patient's expression of emotion or else actively steps in and reassures him. For example, the therapist may say that the patient was not to blame for his buddy's being killed, that it is natural for him to think that he is glad that his friend was killed instead of himself, that he was really exceptionally brave in withstanding the danger as long as he did, that he tried his best and was pushed beyond the breaking point. We would expect such reassurance, just at the time the patient is remembering the details of his experience and expressing his strongest emotions, to help to reduce his guilt, fear of failure, and fear of being called a coward.

Similarly, we would expect any other cues that cause the subject to stop feeling afraid or guilty while he is still remembering his experiences to hasten the extinction of fear and guilt as responses to those memories.[1] The cues in the safe hospital situation would

[1] According to our type of analysis (Miller, 1950) this is because the reduction in the strength of fear will reinforce the responses involved in stopping, or partly stopping, being afraid. Thus anything that reduces fear in the presence of the cues eliciting it will hasten the process of extinction. The reduction in fear that occurs after these cues are removed will have much less of an effect because the responses involved in stopping being afraid will occur in a different stimulus situation and have to generalize to the cues originally eliciting the fear. A similar deduction would also be made from

be expected to accomplish this result to some extent, and the therapist often intervenes by directing attention toward those cues. He may also intervene more directly. Grinker and Spiegel (1945*b*, p. 81) report:

Here the medical officer is called upon to play a variety of roles. When the patient becomes convulsed with the violence of the terror, he must step in as a protective and supporting figure, comforting and reassuring the patient, and encouraging him to proceed. If this is not done, there is a tendency for the initial protective reactions of stupor or amnesia to be re-established, and the patient makes no progress.

Discrimination while repression is weakened by drugs. In addition to facilitating extinction, the therapist helps the patient to discriminate between the dangerous situation of combat and the safe one of the hospital. It will be remembered that we have already advanced the hypothesis that one of the advantages of recovering memories of the past is that it allows the patient to contrast the conditions of the past with those of the present and to see the significant differences between them. This aids in the formation of discriminations that reduce the generalization of fear.

Exactly as in therapy without drugs, the therapist aids the process of discrimination by directing the attention of the patient toward relevant cues in various ways and by supplying appropriate labels. Here again Grinker and Spiegel (1945*b*, p. 85) give a vivid, insightful description:

As the patient crosses the threshold between the nightmare reality of his battle experience and the protected environment of the present, the medical officer has an unparalleled opportunity to strengthen the discriminating and appraising functions of the weakened ego. . . . It is the task of the therapist to aid in this process at the moment when the ego is still partially in strong contact with the battle experience and partially in contact with the protected environment of the present. The medical officer now emphasizes, in a firm but sympathetic tone, that the traumatic battle experience is over—finished, a thing of the past—and that it will not be repeated; that the incidental noises about the ward and the gunfire in

the theory of learning and extinction advanced by Guthrie (1935 and 1938). This same type of analysis can be applied to shame, guilt, and other learned drives.

the distance are not dangerous; that the patient's combat experience has terminated and he no longer has anything to fear.

Generalization from drugged to normal state. One of the difficulties in this kind of therapy is making certain that the effects will generalize from the drugged state to the normal one. This transfer is aided by using a drug, sodium pentothal, with relatively brief effects and by keeping the patient rehearsing his thoughts and memories while the effects of the drug are rapidly wearing off. Sometimes the patients seem to continue to do a considerable amount of spontaneous thinking about their experiences between sessions. In other cases it is necessary to insist that they try hard to remember, and even to repeat to them some of the things that they have said or done. It would be interesting to have more data on the ways in which the patients think over their experiences, rehearse and elaborate on what the doctor has told them, and use their restored higher mental processes in solving their emotional problems.

Change to noncombat duty. Quite naturally the thought of returning to combat is one of the strongest sources of fear. In order to effect a complete cure it usually is necessary to remove this thought and to produce a real change in the patient's conditions of life by assuring him that he will be assigned to noncombat duty. Thus Grinker and Spiegel (1945b, p. 89) say:

Therefore, after the psychiatrist has made his own decision, the patient is told as early as possible that he will not be sent back to combat. He is told it repeatedly, because it is seldom accepted as truth the first time. . . . It is important that the medical officer should assume an early and consistent policy on this point.

This reassignment to noncombat duty is similar to the drive reduction that civilian neurotics must achieve in their everyday lives outside of the therapeutic situation. According to our principles, it should be a necessary part of the treatment whenever the main cause of the neurosis was real dangers of combat that are likely to be repeated on reassignment to it. It should be less necessary if the neurosis was caused by an unusually traumatic experience that is not likely to be repeated or by an unrealistic guilt stemming from expressions of aggression or the death of a close friend.

Why drugs often do not work so spectacularly on civilian cases.
Although drugs do have a similar effect on civilian cases (Freed, 1946), the effects in general seem to be less spectacular and rapid. This may be because repression has been practiced for a longer period and is a stronger habit. The cases that do work seem to be those where the conflict is relatively evenly balanced. This suggests that the differential specific effect of the drug on fear may not be great enough to reduce the most intense fears without reducing the patient to a condition of stupor, a conclusion which is also indicated by the experimental work on animals (Miller and Bailey, 1950). Perhaps a combination of psychological, pharmacological, and physiological research could lead to a better understanding of the reasons for the differential action of the drug on the fear drive. This in turn might lead to the discovery or synthesis of a drug that would have a more powerful and specific effect.

In combat neuroses the therapist knows the general type of situation that has produced the disorder and often has a quite exact knowledge of the details of the traumatic situation. This enables him to tell the patient what he wants him to remember and to provide various cues that have strong tendencies to elicit the memories and emotions. The therapist dealing with civilian cases does not have this advantage. Perhaps it would be possible for him to make a systematic canvass of the types of situations known sociologically to be most likely to be involved, or to use the drug after he has located critical areas in the course of preliminary stages of therapy. In either event, he would have a larger number of incidents to cover than the therapist dealing with combat cases.

In the civilian cases, the contrast between the past and present may not be so obvious as the contrast between combat and the safety of the hospital. Here it seems possible that a gain could be achieved by systematically pointing out to the patient the differences between his dependence and helplessness in childhood, when the traumatic incidents occurred, and the different conditions of independence and freedom now that he is an adult.

The final and perhaps most significant difference suggested by our type of analysis is that the medical officer in combat has the power to produce a drastic change in the patient's life by assigning him to noncombat duty. The civilian therapist does not have similar control over the important conditions of reward and punishment in the patient's life. These conditions usually must remain the same while the patient extinguishes the fears motivating his inhibitions and learns the responses necessary to achieve the goals that will reduce his strong drives. This requires time.

Informal use of alcohol in self-therapy. It is obvious that many laymen use alcohol to achieve for themselves results somewhat similar to those that the therapist secures by using a barbiturate. As has already been pointed out, alcohol seems to produce a temporary, direct reduction in fear and conflict and hence in misery. For people who are suffering from fear and conflict, this reduction will be expected to reinforce the responses involved in drinking. Furthermore, if the fear motivating inhibition is only moderately strong, it should be weakened to the point where drive-reducing goal responses may be attempted and enjoyed. Results of this kind are commonly observed.

We would expect different results with people whose inhibitions are strong enough to keep them so far from the goal that they are experiencing relatively little temptation, fear, and conflict. The effect of alcohol should be to bring them nearer to the goal, increasing the strength of temptation, fear, and conflict without allowing them to secure the drive reduction of reaching the goal. Our theory suggests that such cases should not be reinforced by alcohol and should not learn to use it. In between the extremes described above one would expect people who would get enough immediate anxiety reduction to reinforce drinking but would become more anxious and miserable after they had time to advance toward the goals that they seek and fear.

It is our general impression that alcohol is more frequently used by the layman to overcome inhibitions than to overcome repressions. This is probably because the average man has never been taught to try to overcome repression, is not strongly motivated to try to solve his emotional problems by thinking, and is not trained in the techniques of doing this. It should be noted with caution, however, that under the conditions of everyday life it is much harder to observe the removal of a repression that prevents thinking than it is to observe the removal of an inhibition that prevents action.

We would expect the informal use of alcohol as a therapeutic agent to create certain difficulties. Since it produces a temporary direct reduction in fear and conflict, the person is immediately reinforced for drinking and may merely learn to drink himself into a pleasant stupor. Furthermore, in the absence of a therapist to guide his activities, he is less likely to stop to think or form better discriminations, and more likely to rush directly into action. Since alcohol reduces realistic as well as unrealistic fears, some of the actions may lead to unfortunate results. Even where the results are favorable, the alcohol is readily available and the person controls his own dosage. Therefore he is likely to continue to lean on it as a prop and fail to face and extinguish the fear involved in trying to perform the responses when he is without inebriation. Finally, although alcohol seems to have a greater effect on fear, it is a general depressant. With all his motivations reduced, the person will not achieve such strong reinforcement.

Because of the selective factors involved, it is hard to evaluate the effects that are achieved in spite of these disadvantages. The cases most likely to be brought to our attention are those who fail to achieve permanent therapeutic effects through the transient or moderate use of alcohol. Instead they become addicted because of the temporary release and suffer from severe long-range disadvantages. We have no good way of knowing how many people may use alcohol successfully to cure themselves of a potential neurosis.

Reduction in fear by prefrontal lobotomy. The operation for prefrontal lobotomy has been performed on some patients under a local anesthesia. These patients have reported a marked reduction in "tension" when the fibers were snipped (Freeman and Watts, 1942, pp. 106, 109–111). Afterwards their behavior was much less inhibited (Rylander, 1939; White, 1948, p. 476). It is known that prefrontal lobotomy helps to make pain more bearable (Falconer, 1948; Watts and Freeman, 1948). In the light of these facts we tentatively advance the hypothesis that prefrontal lobotomy produces a differential decrement in the pain-fear mechanism. If this is true, we would expect this reduction in the motivation to inhibit and repress to produce results somewhat analogous to those secured by the longer process of psychotherapy. As we shall see immediately, however, there would be important differences.

Comparison of three ways of reducing fear. According to our analysis there are three ways of reducing fear. One of these is by surgery; according to our hypothesis, prefrontal lesions produce a differential decrement in the fear-pain mechanism. Another is by drugs. Apparently certain drugs produce a greater decrement in fear than in other drives. The final way is by learning. This includes the related phenomena of discrimination, the extinction of fear, and the learning of habits specifically antagonistic to fear

The process of learning is likely to be slow, especially if strong fears must be extinguished. Furthermore, learning can occur only if the proper conditions can be established. The patient must be motivated to learn, must start performing some new responses in the presence of the correct cues, and must be rewarded for performing these responses. Finally, the special technique that we have been describing in the preceding chapters assumes that considerable portions of the patient's verbal responses are still intact. Under these conditions, techniques that depend entirely upon relearning are impossible or inefficient for certain patients. It should be remembered, however, that if the therapist were able to produce more drastic changes in the conditions of learning, he might be successful with cases that are now recalcitrant.

Though the process of learning has the disadvantage of being relatively slow, it has the advantage of being highly specific. Socially undesirable fears can be extinguished while socially desirable ones are reinforced. Under proper conditions, fine discriminations may be established in this way.

The advantage of surgery and drugs is that their action is relatively rapid and that they can be applied to certain patients whose symptoms and lack of motivation for psychotherapy make relearning difficult or impossible. On the other hand, we would not expect the drug or knife to be able to separate the socially desirable fears from the undesirable ones. These techniques should reduce all fears alike. This is, of course, what occurs. The person who takes alcohol to achieve the socially desirable effect of being less shy at a party may also achieve the undesirable effect of being indiscreet or driving recklessly on the way home. The same sort of thing seems to be true of lobotomy patients; they often do not show the socially desirable concern for the consequences of their acts, may be vulgar in public, insult policemen, and fail to show a proportionate concern for the future. (Brickner, 1936; Freeman and Watts, 1942, p. 140.)

With both alcohol and lobotomy, the fear mechanism apparently is only weakened but not completely eliminated. If the fears motivating socially desirable habits have been much more strongly established than those motivating the undesirable ones, the patient may receive certain benefits without too much loss. This is particularly true for the milder effects of a moderate amount of alcohol. Furthermore, since the fear mechanism is partially intact, some of the deficiencies can be made up by specific training. Apparently some people can learn to be careful, not to be indiscreet when mildly intoxicated, and to compensate by driving ten miles an hour slower for every cocktail. Similarly, after a number of painful experiences, some lobotomy patients show the relearning of certain socially desirable restraints. It seems probable that this relearning could be improved if special attention were given to establishing the optimum social conditions for it.

An obvious advantage of drugs over surgery is that the effects of the drug are reversible while those of the operation are not. Thus the drug can be used as a temporary aid to psychotherapy which, if successful, returns the patient to his normal nondrugged condition.

PART VII
SPECIAL ASPECTS OF THERAPY

CHAPTER XXIV

WAYS OF GETTING RID OF SYMPTOMS

In this part of the book various principles that have been discussed separately will be drawn together and organized around special aspects of therapeutic technique. Along with the novel applications, there will be a review of the basic principles brought together in new contexts.

The more clearly these fundamental principles are stated, the easier it will be to do effective therapy. But even in the remote future when all of the important principles have been clarified, their application to the wonderfully intricate variations of human personality is likely to involve a considerable element of personal skill. Therapists will differ in permissiveness, tact, compelling sense of authority, ability to explain, humor, conviction, hope, and love of people—in short, in everything that makes personal relations variable, colorful, warm, and beautiful. The problem of finding the most effective way to apply the principles will remain a challenge to the artistic skill of the therapist.

Interfering with the Symptom by Eliciting a Strong Incompatible Response

A learned symptom, like any other response, can be eliminated by a stronger response that is imcompatible with it.[1] A therapist with sufficient authority can sometimes elicit a response strong enough to do this by issuing a command or prohibition. The effect of such a command or prohibition can be strengthened greatly by hypnotism.

---

[1] One would not expect an incompatible response to be able to interfere with a symptom that was a direct physiological response to a state of high drive, e.g., the increase of stomach acidity produced by chronic fear. But if the drive was learned (i.e., response-produced), it should be possible for an incompatible response to eliminate it and hence, indirectly, the symptom.

Another way of eliciting a strong response incompatible with the symptom is by severe physical punishment.[2] Similarly, as has been pointed out, interpreting the function of a symptom or demonstrating its lack of organic basis elicits strong guilt that tends to cancel out the drive reduction and motivate the stopping of the symptom.

Finally the patient may find the therapeutic situation so anxiety-provoking that he is motivated to stop his symptoms so that he can leave therapy with a clear conscience. This process can occur unconsciously. The symptom reminds the patient of therapy and arouses increased fear that cancels out the drive reduction and motivates responses incompatible with the symptom. When the symptom stops the patient thinks: "I am cured and can leave therapy." This thought produces a reduction in anxiety that reinforces the responses involved in stopping the symptom. This mechanism may provide one of the ways in which the so-called "transference cure" can occur (Freud, 1924, Vol. I, p. 293; Alexander and French, 1946, p. 133). Once such a patient is completely out of therapy, we would expect the motivation to avoid therapy to fade out. Thus such a "cure" would be expected to be especially likely to be transient.

[2] According to our theory, there are two ways that punishment can function. First it may elicit a response incompatible with the symptom, and this response may be reinforced by the end of the punishment. For this method to be effective, the punishment must be given while the symptom is being performed, and it must be administered in such a way that it will elicit a response incompatible with that symptom. It must be terminated as soon as the incompatible response is elicited. The second way is by attaching fear to the cues produced by the symptom. The increase in this fear when the symptom is performed will tend to balance out the drive-reducing effects of the symptom and so remove its reinforcement. This fear will also motivate other responses and reinforce any responses that stop the symptom and remove the cues that it produces. Again the most effective method is to administer the punishment just as the symptom starts or while it is occurring. But an indirect and somewhat weaker effect can also be produced by associating the punishment with thoughts about the symptom or about distinctive cues that it produces. This technique will be effective only if similar thoughts are present when the symptom is performed and when the punishment is administered.

Increased drive from interfering with symptom. According to our hypothesis, a learned symptom must produce a certain amount of reduction in the state of high drive motivating it. Therefore, interfering with the symptom by any of the foregoing methods will be expected to throw the patient back into a state of high drive and conflict. This will tend to motivate the learning of new responses. These new responses may be either more adaptive ones or new, and possibly worse, symptoms.

According to our principles, the choice between these two types of new responses should depend upon the degree to which the adaptive goal responses are inhibited. If a more adaptive goal response is only weakly inhibited, the increase in drive will enable it to overcome the inhibition. Once this goal response occurs, it will be strengthened by reinforcement, and the fear motivating inhibition will be weakened somewhat by extinction. Thus this response will continue to occur.[3] On the other hand, if all of the adaptive goal responses are strongly inhibited, the persisting high drive will be able to motivate the learning only of maladaptive responses, or, in other words, symptoms.

The patient's close friends, relatives, and other members of society usually notice and condemn his symptoms. They urge him to give them up and suggest more adaptive responses. In effect this is similar to the procedure—increasing the motivation to approach the dangerous goal—that we have already dealt with in our discussion of conflict. We would expect most of the people who could respond to this kind of treatment to be cured without ever having to go to a therapist. We know that this sometimes happens; you will remember the case of the widower who gave up his neurotic heart symptoms and remarried after he had failed to get

[3] Sometimes the strongest inhibitions are not attached to the first occurrence of a goal response but to conditions that are likely to occur later. For example, a patient may have much less inhibition when he is caught off guard, so to speak, and sexual intercourse occurs with a new partner without premeditation, tender feelings, or obvious responsibilities. As the incident develops into a stable affair or threatens to lead to marriage and the public assumption of responsibilities, many new thoughts and other response-produced cues may appear, which in turn elicit fear motivating much stronger inhibition. In such cases the cure will be temporary or the patient will learn the inferior adjustment of seeking transient sexual encounters.

any of his daughters to sacrifice their own lives to take care of him. Because such cases usually do not reach the therapist, we have no idea of how frequent they may be.

We would expect the cases that do reach the therapist to be those who could not respond to the commands, prohibitions, and suggestions of their associates. In other words, we would expect them to be a specially selected group with such strong inhibitions and repressions that they cannot perform the more adaptive goal responses. The observations of therapists seem to confirm this expectation. They find, just as we would expect, that when the symptoms of their patients are merely suppressed or inhibited, the increased drive and misery are likely to motivate the learning of new symptoms. Furthermore, if they are private patients this increased misery is likely to motivate them to quit therapy.

We have pointed out that the patients that reach a therapist probably are a highly selected group that have especially strong inhibitions blocking their adaptive goal responses. Therefore merely interfering with their symptoms will not be likely to produce a favorable result. After the inhibitions blocking the more adaptive goal responses have been sufficiently reduced, however, we might expect different results. Then the increased drive produced by interfering with the symptoms might cause the goal response to become stronger than the weakened inhibition. In fact, this often seems to occur; after the fears motivating the inhibitions have been reduced, therapists often find it desirable to interfere with a symptom by an unfavorable interpretation. This is especially true if the immediate effects of the symptom, like an addiction or a perversion, are so drive-reducing that it is strongly reinforced and the motivation for new responses is kept low.

Example of the problem of masturbation. Masturbation presents a special problem to the therapist because it is a response that frequently occurs and produces a marked reduction in drive but is not the socially most desirable form of sexual adaptation. It is an inferior form of adaptation because it removes one of the strong rewards from marriage which seems to provide the best all-round basis for personal adjustment.

If the patient has too much fear to try any heterosexual responses, masturbation may be good as the first step toward the goal of normal sexual behavior. When the patient first tries masturbation, the orgasm produced in this way will reward the general attempt to try sexual behavior, help to define the goal, and give the patient a good chance to discover and extinguish some of his fears of sex. We will expect this extinction to generalize and tend to weaken the fear motivating the inhibition of heterosexual behavior. On the other hand if the therapist shows any signs of disapproval at this stage, he will strengthen the patient's fear, and this fear will tend to generalize to all forms of sexual behavior.

If the therapist allows masturbation to become established as more than a transitional habit, it will become so strongly reinforced that it may be hard to abandon. Furthermore it will tend to keep the sex drive so low that the heterosexual responses never can become stronger than their inhibitions. Finally, the patient may be having undesirable phantasies during masturbation. Associating the strong sexual reward of the orgasm with the cues involved in these phantasies may increase his appetite for childish, perverse, or extramarital sex outlets.

This theoretical analysis yields several practical suggestions. If possible, it is better for the patient to move directly toward a heterosexual marital adjustment. If the patient's inhibitions are too strong for this to be possible, it may be necessary for the therapist to be permissive toward masturbation at first. After masturbation is started, it may be desirable for the therapist to try to exert some control over the accompanying phantasies and direct them toward the heterosexual marital goal. Finally, after the patient's inhibitions have been weakened enough so that he will be able to try better responses, it may be necessary to discourage masturbation by pointing out the ways in which it is an inferior response.

Increased Repression and Inhibition

Our analysis of the approach-avoidance conflict showed that making the feared goal seem less dangerous will cause the subject to come nearer, and that when he comes nearer, both the tendencies to approach and to avoid will be stronger. Thus, paradoxically, it will increase the amount of fear and conflict elicited and produce a negative therapeutic effect

Conversely, an increase in the motivation to avoid can cause the subject to remain so far away from the feared goal that he is much less tempted and frightened. Although the example is clearest in a simple spatial situation, the same phenomenon will be expected in nonspatial situations. The first incipient responses will produce additional cues with learned connections to further responses in the sequence; and the cues produced by responses nearer the time of reinforcement elicit a still stronger tendency to continue. Similarly drive-producing responses seem to become stronger nearer the point of reinforcement. In this way a sequence of responses seems to pick up something analogous to momentum; it is much easier to stop the sequence before it gets started than after it is well under way. Therefore there is less conflict if the fear is strong enough to prevent any responses from getting started, or, in other words, if the patient gives up completely. This reduction in temptation, fear, and conflict will be expected to reduce somewhat the misery and motivation for symptoms. Therefore, increasing the strength of inhibition and repression by making the feared goal response seem much more dangerous can reduce some of the motivation for symptoms. This will be especially true if a large part of the drive is learned so that it can be prevented by inhibiting the responses producing it.

On the other hand, if a strong primary drive is involved, it will persist and be a chronic source of misery and motivation for symptoms. Therefore, whenever a socially acceptable goal response is available, the technique of reducing the conflict by increasing the inhibition would not be expected to be as effective as that of getting rid of the inhibition that is preventing the goal response from reducing the drive.

Where the conflict centers around a learned drive for a socially unacceptable goal response, such as homosexuality, but where there is a socially acceptable goal response available, these two techniques can sometimes be combined. After the inhibition for the socially acceptable response has been sufficiently reduced so that it can occur as a means of drive reduction, the temptation to perform the socially unacceptable response can be reduced by increasing the motivation to suppress or inhibit it Such inhibition or suppression is, of course, necessary wherever serious dangers or exceedingly strong social taboos are involved.

Effects of Supportive Therapy

A child usually feels braver when one of its parents is present to defend it or rescue it from any danger.[4] Similarly the moral support of the therapist as a prestigeful person may produce a considerable reduction in the strength of the patient's fear. Where the symptoms are the direct product of the fear, this will tend to weaken them. Furthermore, if the patient has strong needs for companionship, sympathetic attention, and encouragement, these can be gratified by the therapist. The net effect of this kind of a therapeutic relationship can be to reduce a considerable number of the learned drives motivating the symptoms and thus produce a remission in them. This is another mechanism that may be involved in the "transference cure."

The difficulty with this type of therapeutic relationship is that the patient is being rewarded for coming to the therapist for moral support, companionship, sympathetic attention, and encouragement. Since he is being rewarded for depending almost entirely on the therapist, that is what he will be expected to learn. Not learning independent habits of reducing his drives in real life, he is likely to relapse unless access to the therapist is continued indefinitely. This alternative can be afforded only by wealthy patients.

If the patient's difficulties are largely situational, or, in other words, the product of transient unfavorable conditions that are not likely to be repeated, supportive therapy may tide him over the situation. After the unfavorable conditions have been resolved, the patient may be able to resume his old form of adjustment without any essentially new learning. Similarly, supportive therapy may be necessary to tide a neurotic patient over a specific crisis, especially at the beginning of treatment, and gain for the therapist sufficient time to start using other slower techniques that will produce a more permanent, independent effect. In fact, by its

---

[4] The child has experienced pain in the absence of its parent and has been relieved or has avoided pain in the parent's presence until a discrimination has been learned; in Pavlovian terms, the parent and his approval have become a conditioned inhibitor of the fear response

very nature, almost any therapeutic situation is likely to give the patient a certain amount of moral support, but this can vary from playing a secondary role to being the major factor involved.

If the patient's fears are weak, the moral support of the therapist as a prestigeful person may reduce these fears enough so that the patient can overcome his inhibitions and perform in real life some of the goal responses that reduce his strong drives. In this case these responses will be reinforced and he will start learning new adaptive habits. In some cases the therapist may try to hasten this learning by using his own higher mental processes directly on the solution of the patient's specific daily problems. He may make specific plans and decisions, take the responsibility for these decisions, and lend the reassuring weight of his prestige to them.

One advantage of this procedure is that it may help the patient to make the correct responses that will reward him. But this procedure also has disadvantages. The therapist may not know what actually is best for the patient. Furthermore, the patient eventually will have to generalize from depending on the therapist to being independent. In order to complete his therapy he will have to learn to bear the conflict that the making of a difficult decision necessarily entails, to resolve that conflict by using his own higher mental processes, to make his own plans, and to try independently to carry them into action. If the therapist is forced to support the patient at first, he should be sure to facilitate the generalization to independent action by starting as soon as possible to shift gradually from an active to a more passive role.

Finally, the patient who has been strongly rewarded by the therapist or overawed by his prestige may be motivated to give up symptoms in order to please him. This reaction may also be involved in the "transference cure." It can be entirely unconscious. When the patient notices a symptom he can feel worse because he knows that this will displease the therapist; when he notices that the symptom is stopped, he can feel better, and this can reinforce the responses involved in stopping the symptom. Such cures are likely to be transient because the conflict which produces the high drives motivating the symptoms will remain and the motivation to suppress or inhibit the symptom will be reduced as soon as the patient stops seeing the therapist. The cure will be expected to be permanent only if, while the symptom is absent, the patient performs a response reducing some of the basic drives involved. Then he will be rewarded for performing this response and will thus learn a new and more adaptive habit that may persist in the absence of the therapist.

Removal of Inhibition and Repression

When the fear motivating repression is reduced, the patient is able to think of more adaptive ways to achieve his goals. When the fear motivating the inhibition of the goal responses is reduced, he is able to perform them and reduce his strong drives. Both the reduction in fear and the reduction in drive alleviate conflict and misery. Therefore, the subject is much less motivated to perform symptoms and is less reinforced for performing them. When this happens, the symptoms tend to drop out as the response of drinking water does when a person is no longer thirsty.

This process may be gradual, with the symptoms coming and going as the general state of conflict fluctuates. As has already been pointed out in our discussion of the negative therapeutic effect, a reduction in the fear motivating the inhibitions may even produce a temporary increase in conflict and symptoms. Once a superior, socially acceptable goal response is independently tried out in real life, however, we would expect the drive reduction to be a strong reinforcement. Hence this response should continue to be strengthened. Meanwhile the fears will continue to be extinguished. With both the drives in the conflict reduced, there will not be any strong motivation to learn new symptoms. Therefore the cure, once achieved, should be permanent as long as the conditions remain relatively the same.[5] When this kind of cure is contrasted with those previously discussed, it can be seen why the therapist usually should focus his attention on the underlying conflict rather than on the symptoms.

Examples from the Case of Mrs. A

When Mrs. A came to the therapist, her main concern was about her symptoms, especially her great fear that her heart would stop

[5] In some cases, however, important changes in the conditions are likely to occur. See footnote 3.

beating if she did not constantly concentrate on counting its beats. She was not thinking about her basic difficulty, the conflict that produced the high drives motivating the symptoms. The therapist did not focus his attention on these symptoms but concentrated on getting at the conflict.

By his permissive attitude he got her to talk more freely. When she told him how her foster brother had seduced her as a child, he maintained his calm, warm, accepting silence without giving her the punishment or disapproval that she seemed to expect. This produced a marked reduction in her fear. With this reduction in her fear, the symptoms abated. At the same time her sexual adjustment with her husband improved somewhat.

Since Mrs. A's tendency to get into situations where she was likely to be seduced or raped was exposing her to real danger, the therapist labeled this behavior for her as soon as he thought her fear was reduced to a point where she could accept his interpretation. Pointing out that she was seeking situations in which she could get sexual gratification without being responsible also helped to focus her attention on the basic conflict.

As Mrs. A began to think more fear-arousing thoughts and to do more fear-provoking things, to become a more sexually responsive woman and a more aggressive, less subdued person, some of her fears returned. For example, she became afraid of going out alone and acquired a fear of pregnancy. By labeling the clearly sexual elements in her wishes when clear-cut opportunities came up, and by failing to punish such sexual thoughts as she was able to express, the therapist helped her to become able to think about the real problem, namely, how to achieve good sexual relations with her husband. As she became able to put this into words, the generalized fears responsible for her irrational phobic symptoms, such as being afraid to go out on the street, were weakened. Securing more sexual satisfaction with her husband also tended to reduce the strength of the sex drive that motivated her to do foolish and frightening things on the street. The summation of both of these sources of fear reduction eliminated the phobia of going out alone on the street.

CHAPTER XXV

TECHNIQUES OF THERAPEUTIC INTERVENTION

Various techniques of therapeutic intervention have already been mentioned during the discussion of other topics. These will be brought together here in a convenient summary with the focus directly on the problem of how the therapist can influence the patient. It will be seen that the different techniques are not completely separate; there are intermediate blends, and they may be combined with infinite variety.

Suggesting, Urging, Commanding, and Forbidding

The techniques of suggesting, requesting, urging, commanding, and forbidding are commonly used methods of trying to influence another person's everyday social behavior. As has already been pointed out, because these techniques are so commonly used by the person's friends and associates, any difficulties that will respond to them are usually solved before he is driven to visit a therapist. We have shown that the patient with strong repressions and inhibitions is only thrown into more severe conflict when his motivation to approach the feared goals is increased directly by urging him to approach, or indirectly by forbidding his symptoms. These techniques usually do not reduce the avoidance, motivated by fear, which is the cause of the neurotic's conflict. Even where they are of some benefit, they often do not help to free the patient to use his own higher mental processes. Therefore, Freudian therapy and its various derivatives use these techniques much less frequently than they are encountered in normal social life.

There are a few special places where these techniques are used. The therapist commands free association; he urges the patient to say everything that comes into his mind and forbids holding anything back. Before the formal sessions begin, the therapist generally places a taboo on making any drastic decision of an irreversible nature during the course of the treatment. This tends to protect the patient from things that he might be driven to do when his conflicts are heightened by the negative therapeutic effect and to give him a chance to correct exaggerated first attempts at new problem solutions. It also takes the burden off the therapist; he does not have to disapprove specific major decisions but can always relax the taboo if he is convinced that this is in the best interests of the patient. In this connection Alexander and French (1946, pp. 37–41) emphasize that it is often a necessity of the cure that the patient make such decisions when he is ready for them and not wait for any routine date such as "end of therapy."

When the therapist judges that avoidance has been weakened enough so that approach to the goal is possible, he may request the temporary abstinence from a symptom that is too drive-reducing. For example, he may request a patient to try abstaining from a drug or to try going into a phobic situation.

Reward and Punishment, Disapproval and Approval

As has already been emphasized, the therapist does not control the important primary rewards and punishments in the patient's life; he usually does not even control the most important learned rewards and punishments. The exceptions to this are in the Armed Forces and in mental institutions, but even here the potential control usually is not used. Our moral codes and humanitarian customs set strict limits to the creation and use of strong drives to modify a patient's behavior. Thus hunger, pain, and fatigue may not be used in unconventional ways or degrees.

Approval and disapproval have strong learned reward and punishment value. They may be expressed either directly and openly, or indirectly and subtly. In ordinary social life they are commonly used methods of influencing another person's behavior.

Most neurotics have met with a preponderance of disapproval. The effects of disapproval are likely to generalize and heighten the fears responsible for repression and inhibition. Therefore, the therapist is careful about expressing disapproval. In cases where there is a real danger that the patient will do himself irreparable harm, the therapist must point this out and thus by implication disapprove the behavior.   If the therapist fails to predict real dangers, the patient will lose confidence in him.

The therapist uses approval to reward good effort on the part of the patient. He does not let approval lose its specific value by dispensing it randomly. He makes the patient work for approval but shows that he realizes how hard therapeutic work can be. Finally, he knows that the ultimate goal is for the patient to become able to win the approval of his own social group, outside the therapeutic situation.

Permissiveness: Failing to Criticize or Show Alarm as a Powerful Intervention

When the patient has said something that frightens him, the therapist's calm, accepting manner can be a striking contrast to the type of social response that has reinforced the patient's fears. Under the right circumstances, merely saying nothing can therefore be a powerful intervention that reduces fear and is a condition for its extinction. We believe that this is a necessary condition for "catharsis," and that, by contrast, no relief is secured by expressing a suppressed feeling of emotion if the other person shows signs of strong disapproval. It is permissive also, when the patient asks about topics that are usually shied away from or discussed with embarrassment, for a therapist to give him calmly and objectively the information he wants. It is important for the therapist to be a good model. Since he has a great deal of prestige, his calmness, courage, and reasonableness are imitated by the patient, who thus tends to become somewhat calmer, more courageous, and more reasonable. Because it reduces the fear motivating repression and inhibition, the therapist's permissiveness is an effective form of intervention.

Sympathetic Interest and Understanding

Warm, sympathetic interest and understanding are powerful rewards, particularly for those who are usually misunderstood and who have worn out the sympathy and interest of their friends. This is further heightened by the social prestige of the therapist. It rewards the patient for coming to therapy and continuing to try. Specific signs of interest may also reinforce specific types of behavior. Questions can serve as a sign of interest and reinforce talking about the general topic that elicited the question. Repeating or "reflecting back" (Rogers, 1942) what the patient has said is also a sign of interest and has the same effect. Since the therapist does not repeat everything that the patient says, the effect is bound to be differential. The patient will learn to talk about the topics that are reflected back instead of those that are ignored. In this connection the reader will remember Greenspoon's (1950) experiment on the reinforcing effect of saying "mmm-hmm."

Reassurance

Reassurance is a common way of reducing fear. By reducing fear, it can serve as a strong reward. The patient's friends usually have tried to reassure him, but this has not been entirely effective or else he would not have been forced to come to the therapist. The therapist is able to use this technique somewhat better than the friends because he is freer from anxiety himself and has more prestige. He will not have much better luck than the friends, however, with blanket reassurance. In order to succeed when they have failed, he must be better able to locate the important sources of fear and thus to give the right kind of reassurance exactly when and where it is most needed. Reassurance must be used to reduce fear so that new thoughts and acts can occur, and then to reward those new thoughts and actions. If it is used merely to make the patient feel better, it will only teach the patient to come for more reassurance.

Manifold Functions of Questions

As we have said previously, questions can serve as a sign of interest and hence can reward talking about the topics eliciting the question. On the other hand, as we have stated before, probing cross-questioning tends to evoke anxiety and thus cause the patient to stop sooner and allow more margin of safety the next time.

Suitable questions can help to focus attention, stimulate thought, cause the patient to discover incongruities, and see obscured relationships. The therapist often finds the Socratic method useful. For example, after the patient has reproached himself harshly, the therapist may ask: "Is your attitude toward this typical of other members of your crowd?" At another time he may ask: "Hasn't something like that happened before?"

An advantage of a skillful question over a direct assertion is that it forces the patient to respond by thinking and seeing relationships for himself. Thus he is less likely to learn to listen and more likely to learn to think. The ultimate goal, of course, is for the patient to ask the right questions for himself.

Functions of an Interpretation

Interpretations may have a number of different functions which are not necessarily mutually exclusive. An interpretation often implies permission or nonpunishment. The presumption is that what the therapist says he will permit the patient to say. When the therapist gives an interpretation (*e.g.*, "Perhaps you are angry with me.") in a calm tone of voice, he in effect says: "I already know and I am not shocked or angry at you for having those thoughts or feelings."

Another function of an interpretation is to label a drive, emotion, or type of behavior. It should be noted that a connection can be formed between the cues of the drive or emotion and the response of the label only when they are both present simultaneously. The beginning therapist often makes the mistake of thinking of an interpretation after the episode is over and telling the patient about it the next day. This is usually ineffective because the patient is not being stimulated by the drive or emotion at that time. In those rare cases where the therapist believes that the labeling is very important and that the appropriate situation may not occur again for a long time, our type of analysis suggests the theoretical possibility of asking the patient to remember and report as exactly as possible all the details of what he was saying at that time. If he is able to supply enough cues, he may elicit the proper emotions again so that they will be present to be labeled.

Without a label, the patient can respond only directly and unconsciously to the drive or emotion; with a label he can initiate an intervening series of cue-producing responses or, in other words, use his higher mental processes. Labeling a drive, a goal, or a means to an end may also help to define the problem and suggest a course of action.

On the other hand, interpretations may be used to block a course of action by attaching an anxiety-arousing label to it. Thus if the therapist interprets a certain pattern of behavior as "homosexual drinking" he attaches a label to it that tends to arouse anxiety and motivates the patient to avoid it. Similarly, by convincing the patient of the unacceptable, and hence previously unconscious, gains from a symptom the therapist pits the patient's conscience and guilt squarely against the symptom. In another case, one may ask the person who is continually psychoanalyzing one's behavior in social situations: "Am I getting all this valuable information free?" This calls attention to the person's hostile motivation and tends to stop him.

Finally, by predicting the patient's actions or the consequences of his action, an interpretation can aid foresight and put the patient on his guard. For example, Mrs. A told the therapist that if a man "tried to take advantage of her," she would probably faint. The therapist pointed out that fainting is exactly what would allow him to take advantage of her. Then the therapist went on to present her with other evidence for her unconscious wish to have someone take advantage of her. This type of interpretation supplied labels which helped to put her on her guard. As a result she stopped getting into dangerous situations.

CHAPTER XXVI

KEEPING THE PATIENT'S MOTIVATION TO CONTINUE STRONGER THAN THAT TO QUIT

The neurotic patient's basic conflicts are between thinking and repression and between goal responses and inhibitions. In addition to these, he also is in a conflict between seeking and avoiding therapy. This conflict is of special interest to the therapist. He must see that the balance is kept in favor of seeking therapy until the patient has completed his new learning. Many of the factors contributing to this conflict have already been mentioned in other contexts. In this chapter we shall draw them together and focus our attention on what the therapist should do. We shall begin by listing the main motivations that tend to drive the patient away from therapy and by discussing what the therapist can do to keep these at a minimum. Then we shall consider the motivations to seek therapy and what the therapist can do to keep them at a maximum.

Motivation to Avoid Therapy

Both pride and fear tend to keep patients from admitting that they need mental help by seeking a therapist. They are often ashamed to admit that they have mental problems that they cannot solve, and some fear that this admission is a sign they are going crazy. They do not want to expose their own helplessness and are afraid that, if they do expose themselves, the therapist will take some sort of unfair advantage of them. They are ashamed of what they have to say and are afraid that the therapist may gossip about them to others. The very hope for a cure elicits some of the fears that have prevented the patients from reaching their goals. Finally, they tend to fear therapy as something unknown and occult.

These kinds of fear and shame are usually most important before the patient has made his decision to come to therapy or during its early stages. The therapist reduces them by his warm, sympathetic attitude and his assured, professional manner. He implies that therapy is normal and, if necessary, points out that professionally he could not afford to reveal any of his patients' secrets. Fear and shame are further weakened by extinction as the therapist does nothing which scoffs at, takes advantage of, or reveals to others the patient's weaknesses.

As the process of therapy gets started, new motivations to avoid it are aroused. The free associations bring up cues eliciting learned drives such as fear, guilt, and wounded pride. According to our analysis, the repressions have reduced these drives so that uncovering the repressed responses must produce an increase in drive. Furthermore, the patient feels frightening impulses of love and hate directed toward the therapist. It is the very fact that the therapist does not punish that enables the most frightening responses to be generalized to him. This will be seen as a special case of the negative therapeutic effect produced by lowering the gradient of avoidance.

The fears and other strong drives that are elicited in the therapeutic situation tend to motivate the patient to avoid it; this avoidance is reinforced by the drive reduction (feeling of relief) when the patient leaves at the end of the session or remembers that it is a holiday so that he will not have to go to therapy. Moreover, as the patient tries to overcome his inhibition and strives for better goals in life, he provokes the fears that have been keeping him away from these goals. Any interference with his drive-reducing symptoms is another source of increased misery. Finally, the expense and inconvenience of therapy are additional factors motivating the patient to quit.

Dosing of Anxiety

Because it is inevitable that considerable motivation against therapy will be elicited, it is important that the therapist should not provoke any unnecessary drives to avoid it and should keep those that it is necessary for him to evoke below the strength of the patient's motivation to continue.

When the patient is a considerable distance from a feared goal, increasing the motivation to approach it produces a great increase in fear, while reducing the motivation to avoid produces much less of an increase. Thus the general strategy of minimizing the former and concentrating on the latter is one way of cutting down on the fear elicited in the patient.

Another way is to give the patient a graded series of tasks within his capacity. Letting the patient determine his own pace by the free-association technique (Freud, 1943, p. 96) and the relatively nondirective approach (Rogers, 1942) is a fairly automatic way of doing this. Whenever too much fear is elicited, the patient tends to take a slower pace. Unless he knows that the patient is able to stand a considerably greater amount of fear, the therapist allows him to slow down. This is hard for the novice because his own sense of insecurity as a therapist is aroused whenever the patient does not seem to be making progress. The experienced therapist is less disturbed by occasional doldrums; he gives the patient a chance to consolidate his gains and temporarily bask in the reward of minor successes before pressing on.

As long as the patient is making progress by himself, the therapist avoids disturbing him by making interpretations. This has a dual advantage. It does not increase the patient's anxiety by forcing him ahead too fast, and it allows the patient to make the correct responses for himself so that he will not have to generalize them from the situation of rehearsing what the therapist says to the different one of independent thinking. An example of the disadvantage of interpreting when the patient is making progress comes from the case of Mrs. A. While she was reasonably carrying out the instructions for free association, the therapist told her that she had shown, by her difficulty in talking, that she was too dependent and relied too much on others. "But you can be more independent now," he concluded. Since she was talking without difficulty at the time (although previously she had had trouble), the interpretation was not appropriate. To Mrs. A it sounded like a reproach. Rather than hastening her progress, it produced a temporary setback.

Often severely neurotic patients reach points at which they seem to fail to be able to make further progress by themselves. For example, they may have clearly shown an emotion several times without labeling it, or they may have approached near to a goal or a topic several times and then shied away from it without seeming to be aware of the fact that they were avoiding anything. That is the time for an interpretation. In keeping with the strategy of working on avoidance rather than approach, it is the fact that they are avoiding something that should be called to their attention first rather than what they are avoiding. From our analysis of conflict, it can also be seen that no attempt should be made to elicit responses by an interpretation unless the subject is fairly near to making those responses by himself. In other words, interpretations should not be too deep. The time to make an interpretation is when the behavior in question is occurring, when the patient is unlikely to see the point for himself, but when he is near enough to it so that undue fear will not be aroused.

When it is necessary to interpret unconscious "bad" motivation, the therapist should also point out the conscious "good" part of the conflict. In interpreting a motivation to avoid therapy that shows up in persistent coming late or shying away from the central topic, the therapist should make it clear that he does not challenge the patient's conscious determination to cooperate. For example, he should point out that the patient was driven to avoid but wanted to come and compromised by coming late. While he did partially avoid, he nevertheless came. This procedure tends to reward the conscious cooperation and other desirable impulses; it does not wound the patient's pride by making him feel that the therapist has exposed him as a swindler or a liar. Furthermore, when the therapist shows the patient that he does not have complete conscious control over his behavior, this revelation is certain to be frightening to him. At the same time that the therapist points out the patient's lack of complete control, the therapist should show him that he still does have some control.

If the therapist has any reason for suspecting that a given interpretation may arouse too much anxiety, he should make it tentative. Although he may have the facts at his disposal to make a case that will be completely convincing to the patient, he should deliberately not make an airtight case but should leave a face-saving way out for the patient to use if necessary.[1]

Finally, the therapist should watch his patients carefully for overt signs of fear such as perspiration, muscular tension, and agitation. He should also be on the alert for sudden flare-ups of symptoms, for signs of tendencies to quit therapy, and for any serious suicidal thoughts. As soon as a patient shows signs of greatly increased fear or starts making tentative moves to flee from therapy, the therapist should stop making fear-provoking interpretations, give general reassurance, and, if necessary, even try to reduce temporarily the patient's motivation to approach fear-provoking goals.

Increasing Motivation to Continue

Since the outcome of a conflict is determined by the relative strength of the opposing tendencies, the stronger the patient's motivation is to continue, the more he will be able to bear fear, guilt, shame, and other drives motivating him to quit. It is therefore the therapist's task to maintain the patient's motivation for therapy at a reasonably high level.

The patient's motivation for therapy comes from his misery, the inconvenience of his symptoms, his desire to achieve better goals in life, his fears that he may be going crazy or will "do something awful," and pressure from his friends and relatives. Different ones of these motives may be in the foreground with different patients. If the patient thinks that the therapist will cure him, these motivations elicit the response of seeking therapy.[2]

The patient is often confused and misled at first; he does not realize what his problems really are. For example, Mrs. A came to therapy with a general feeling of intense misery and the specific complaints that she was compelled to count her heartbeats for fear they would stop and was afraid that she was going crazy. She did not realize that her main problems were to adjust sexually to her

---

[1] We are indebted to Mr. Earl F. Zinn for emphasizing this point to us.

[2] It seems probable that this is a generalization from other situations in which the patient has been rewarded by getting help from people who had prestige as experts. Neither the theory nor the facts of this process have been worked out in detail.

husband and to express enough aggression to stand up for her rights against the domination of her mother-in-law.

One of the first tasks of the therapist is to help the patient to locate and start working on some significant aspect of his problem. Getting the problem properly defined can help to arouse verbally mediated, learned drives to work in therapy. It shows the patient what the disadvantages of his neurosis are. Sometimes the therapist may have to point these out in order to strengthen a complacent patient's drive for therapy. Furthermore the patient has more hope when he has something specific to work on. Concrete, tested plans are much more often rewarded than vague plans; hence hope is most often rewarded in connection with a definite program. This hope and the motivation to continue therapy are strongly reinforced as soon as the patient has experienced his first success in solving some aspect of his problem (Alexander and French, 1946, p. 40).

Along with defining the problem more clearly for the patient, the therapist must get rid of the false explanations and hopes that divert motivation from therapy. Most patients either consciously or unconsciously have unrealistic hopes for a miracle cure. Allowing a patient to hold such hopes is bad because they are almost certain to be frustrated. This will discourage the patient and tend to discredit the therapist. During the early hours of therapy the patient should be told that since he has been practicing his bad habits for many years he cannot expect to get rid of them overnight, but that when he does get rid of them he will have many years left to enjoy a better life.

Neurotic patients often try to attribute their difficulties to a physical injury in the remote past. Then there is nothing they can do about it. They do not have to bear the inconvenience of therapy and can relax with a free conscience. They may hope that they can be cured by a pill, diet, or sleep, or that the trouble will pass away with time.

Patients also frequently hope that they will get relief from a change in the environment such as moving to a new place, getting a new job, changing to a new girl friend or spouse. Occasionally a patient's trouble is purely situational; the therapist must be alert to this possibility. More often an environmental change will do no good, or the relief will be only temporary; the patient's same old conflicts will reappear in the new situation. The new and more remote situations will look good in prospect because the avoidance falls off more rapidly than approach with distance from a feared goal. If the patient's fears have become conditioned to the cues in his environment, he may even experience temporary relief when he changes to a new environment; the avoidance tendency will generalize to the new environment less strongly than approach. But as the patient tries to approach the goals that are the source of his conflict, he will encounter cues eliciting intense fear. These fears will become conditioned to the other cues in this new environment so that it will soon become as uncomfortable as the old one. Thus the relief will be only temporary.

The various false explanations and the unrealistic hopes based on them divert motivation from therapy. The therapist must test them to be sure that they are not reasonable. For example, he must send his patient to an internist or other specialist to rule out physical causation. After he is convinced beyond reasonable doubt, he must get rid of any persistent false explanations and hopes. He can point out their unreasonableness directly or by asking leading questions. He may ask, "Did that help before?" or he may ask, "How long have you waited for some change like this to occur?" He may say, "But you had a physical examination and nothing of that sort was found." Finally, he may simply deny the false explanation or hope with his authority as a therapist backed up by the findings of science.

The case of Mrs. A showed many examples of false explanations and hopes. She hoped at first that she could quickly describe her symptoms to the therapist and he would give her some medicine or advice that would immediately make her well. At the beginning of the second hour she said: "Aren't you going to suggest anything? I told you everything Friday." The therapist explained to her that cure was a slow process. Then she seized on the thought that time would cure her. The therapist had to point out that it was not the passing of time but what she learned from the treatment during the time that would make her well. Mrs. A hoped that if she just tried going out by herself she would be cured. The therapist pointed out: "You tried that, didn't you? You tried going out and found you were frightened. You'll have to find out why you are afraid, in order to get over your fear."

When Mrs. A expressed the belief that some physical ailment could be found to account for her neurosis, the therapist simply denied this possibility: "A specialist examined you and found nothing physically wrong; isn't that true? I think we can find the cause of your illness and then help you if you will continue to talk about whatever comes into your mind, as I asked you to do."

Mrs. A gave up smoking for a while. When the therapist asked why she did this she said, "My sister-in-law said that if I cut out smoking I might gain weight." The therapist answered, "But you know why you don't gain weight. It's because you don't feel like eating and can't keep anything on your stomach. We have to find out why you haven't any appetite and why you lose what you do eat—what it is that is bothering you."

Mrs. A did feel better while she was visiting her parents in N over the Labor Day week end. This was because her relation with her husband seemed less of a problem while she was away from home. But this gain would be only temporary. If she took her husband to N, she would have the same old conflicts, and if she left him behind, her sex drive would mount and precipitate new conflicts.

The desire to be freed from agonizing conflict is the main motivation for therapy. This is reinforced as the patient sees himself making progress toward the cure. Meanwhile there are other rewards in the therapeutic situation that reinforce the response of coming to it. The permissiveness of the therapeutic situation, the reduction in fear when the therapist fails to criticize or show alarm, has a rewarding effect. On the other hand, permissiveness that brings out too rapidly the temptation to do frightening things can help to drive the patient away from therapy.

Extending reassurance and hope is another factor increasing the motivation to continue. The very fact that the therapist accepts the patient for treatment implies that he believes that he can be cured. If the patient is very much disturbed, the therapist may go beyond this and say that he has seen others in similar or worse circumstances get well; he can point out that the patient is not uniquely bad. He may assure the patient that once he was a

small child with normal ability to feel and act, that something intervened to interfere with his normal abilities, and that this something
can gradually be removed. For instance the therapist said to Mrs.
A: "You were not always frightened about sex. It's because
your mother scared you so about sex that you learned to be
frightened of it. You had a normal capacity to react when you
were a very small child." The therapist thus held out to Mrs. A
the hope of having sexual pleasure without anxiety. Patients
who have thought of themselves as perennially inferior are often
encouraged by the assurance that they once were completely
normal.

Making the goals of normal behavior concrete for the patient is
a way of both defining the problem and extending hope. The
patient with sexual inhibitions should know that normal people
derive great pleasure and comfort out of tender personal feelings,
that they experience delight uncontaminated by anxiety during
foreplay and complete ecstasy from the orgasm. Patients in whom
all aggression has been stamped out should be made to see how
the normal person stands up for his own rights and defends himself.
This must be done judiciously, however, at a time when the increased motivation to approach will not arouse too much fear.

Finally, the patient is rewarded by receiving sympathetic attention from the therapist and knowing that a prestigeful person is
interested in helping him. The therapist can increase this effect
by showing on appropriate occasions that he remembers in considerable detail something that the patient has said a number of
sessions before. The therapist can strengthen the patient's motivation to come by showing that he takes the patient's struggle seriously and understands the fight that he is making against great
obstacles.

The Partial Cure

Often a critical point is reached after a patient has achieved
a partial cure. Outside the therapeutic situation the gradient of
avoidance is reduced enough so that the subject can achieve some
of his more superficial goals. There is a general reduction in
anxiety and misery and some of the most troublesome symptoms
have disappeared. Paradoxically, this gain reinforces the tendency

to come to therapy,[3] but it also reduces the motivation to come.

Furthermore the greater reduction in the gradient of avoidance within the therapeutic situation and the therapist's insistence that the patient say whatever comes into his mind are causing the patient to come nearer to some of his more strongly feared goals. The patient therefore feels more miserable in the therapeutic situation than he does outside it. This increases his motivation to leave therapy, while at the same time his motivation to continue is reduced by the rationalization that he is cured. Such periods put particular demands on the therapist. He must decide whether the patient really has achieved the best adjustment that he can and is reaching a point of diminishing returns or whether he should be strongly urged to continue. If the therapist decides that the patient should continue, he must point out the disadvantages of stopping at this time and the unsolved difficulties that remain, challenging the patient to continue to try to succeed on these problems.

Interpretation of Attempts to Escape Therapy

The therapist will often notice that the patient is doing something to escape from the work of therapy. He may be talking about other things to avoid a crucial topic, coming late, or taking unnecessary trips to avoid coming at all. When the therapist notices such escapes, he should first ask himself whether the patient's fears are being raised to such a height that he is forced to escape and, if so, what is increasing his fears to this point. If he decides the patient is being forced to bear too much, he should try to make things easier for him. The therapist may also want to interpret the escape. By labeling the response as an escape from therapy, he reduces the unconscious reinforcement for it and motivates the patient to stop it. For example, the therapist may show the patient that his conclusion that he is cured is not very realistic and is overdetermined by his motivation to escape the fears that are being aroused in the therapeutic situation.

---

[3] Because of the considerable temporal interval between the responses of coming and the gain, this reinforcement cannot be direct but must be mediated by cue-producing responses. The therapist should help to ensure the occurrence of such responses by getting the patient to rehearse the connection between the therapy and the gain.

CHAPTER XXVII

REQUIREMENTS OF THE THERAPIST AS A SPECIAL KIND OF TEACHER

We have already at many points referred to the work of the therapist. In this chapter we shall swiftly pull together our findings and add some new facts. This will help to give a picture of the therapist and his activity "all in one place."[1]

If we ask what the therapist is expected to *be*, we can answer only by reminding ourselves what he is expected to *do*. His skills must match his function. Within the therapeutic situation he must control and direct activity, keeping the patient at his work. He rehearses calmly what the patient says and observes what he does. He notes failures, inadequacies, and inaccuracies in the patient's accounts and in doing so makes some kind of construction as to what a true account of the patient's mental life should be. Naturally he does not make this construction all at once. He makes a preliminary attempt on the basis of his first information (Alexander and French, 1946, pp. 5, 107–131) and then a series of ever better approximations as the facts come in. When the patient cannot complete his account the therapist aids him to do so.

It may be worthwhile to name four attributes of the therapist as a teacher in the situation of psychotherapy. We suggest that he should be *mentally free, empathic, restrained,* and *positive.* These words refer only roughly to what we mean so we shall enlarge upon each.

Mental Freedom

The therapist must have much less anxiety than the patient or the general public about the "worst" things that bother patients He must be able to rehearse what the patient says without anxiety.

[1] We do not intend this discussion to be a complete practical guide to the conduct of therapy.

No degree of fear should compete with his tendencies to "complete the account." When the patient stops, the therapist should be able to carry on where the patient and others would be afraid. This lack of fear on his own part enables him to be permissive and therefore to set up one of the fundamental conditions which aid the patient.

This requirement may be easy to state, but it is very hard to meet. The topics patients have conflict about (and hence must learn to talk to the therapist about) are just those that are most anxiety-laden in our culture. The things that are "driving the patient crazy" are likely also to have some effect on everyone.

Very likely the socially disapproved aspects of sexuality will appear. Patients may talk endlessly about masturbatory phantasies and practices. Some patients will have had homosexual experiences. In the case of Mrs. A, after the eighteenth hour the main topic was sex. She discussed not only normal heterosexual feelings but also incestuous and perverse feelings. When the patient talks about these most private, most tabooed aspects of sex, the therapist cannot help being anxious if he has had the usual childhood training in our culture—unless he has done something to unlearn the anxiety that most people feel. Some patients will revel in anal thoughts and associations, and the therapist must be able to tolerate these. Others will impose on the therapist the burden of rehearsing and momentarily sharing strong hatreds. Mrs. A's hatred of her foster mother, for instance, was especially intense.

The patient therefore has a role very different from that of the "average" speaker in a social situation. This average speaker, who has made proper discriminations, can afford to keep many matters suppressed or even repressed. The patient, on the other hand, is in a different situation. He is sick because he is generalizing the punishments for forbidden acts to ones which are not forbidden. Tabooed impulses therefore must be talked about in order to help the patient make discriminations. He may have been punished for incestuous acts and phantasies in childhood. He must discriminate this childhood situation from that of his marriage. He may have had a cruel father or mother who evoked intense rage; he must discriminate these persons from those whom he meets in adulthood.

If the therapist is to help him make these discriminations, the therapist must be prepared to listen to the "worst" things. As Freud says (1924, Vol. II, pp. 328–329),

. . . the physician must put himself in a position to use all that is told him for the purposes of interpretation and recognition of what is hidden in the unconscious, without substituting a censorship of his own for the selection which the patient forgoes. . . . But if the physician is able to use his own unconscious in this way as an instrument in the analysis, he must himself fulfil one psychological condition in a high degree. He may tolerate no resistances in himself which withhold from his consciousness what is perceived by his unconscious. . . .

If the therapist is to listen and do his work he must be free of the fear ordinarily attending such discussions.

In listening without criticizing, the therapist is not saying that "anything goes." He is merely affirming that the past is past and cannot be changed. The conditions of the past must be identified and the habits they produced, be recognized. Only in this way can patients gain some faith that the conditions of the present are different and that the habits learned under past conditions are not appropriate to present conditions. Naturally if the therapist shows fear or avoidance when the patient fearfully communicates his thoughts, the therapist will strengthen rather than weaken repressive tendencies in the patient. The therapist will then be unable to learn what he needs to know to help the patient reconstruct his life.

Empathy

Except in the case of excessive fear, the therapist should have the conventional emotional responses attached to the sentences that he rehearses. If the patient refers to a pitiable situation, the therapist should, as he silently repeats the patient's words, feel a twinge of pity. When the patient reports a situation where rage is appropriate the therapist should feel the stirring of those rage responses. The account of a fearful situation should have its appropriate effect on the therapist.

When the therapist feels an emotional response along with common humankind but the patient apparently does not, the therapist is in possession of some important information, *i.e.,* that the patient does not have appropriate emotions attached to his sentences. The therapist should likewise feel in miniature the relaxation and relief which the patient feels when a correct verbal solution has been hit on. It may also be that various other kinds of empathy are important, such as a "sense of humor."

There are other essential aspects of empathy. When the patient's account is incomplete, its incompleteness must act as a stimulus to the therapist to which he responds with a learned drive to complete the account. If something is out of order or illogical, the learned drives to "connect" and to find the logical answer must be excited. It is the activation of these drives which produces the therapist's superior construction of what the patient's mental life ought to be. We have called all of this "empathic." Such an analysis brings the emotional as well as the intellectual dimension into the description of the therapist's work.

Restraint

The therapist must resist the strong tendency to conduct the therapeutic interview as a conversation. He must subordinate himself to his strategy of cure and say nothing that does not further this strategy. Whereas the patient vows "utterance," the therapist vows relative silence. It is our belief, incidentally, that almost all therapists talk too much or, rather, too loosely. They find it hard to subordinate themselves to the listening role. They interrupt the patient, prompt the patient, give him unnecessary reassurance, paraphrase his statements without essential clarification, and otherwise vocalize in a useless manner.

The therapist should restrain himself from giving any verbal cue which the patient can hit upon by himself and should allow good time for the patient to try. The therapist should remember who is paying and trying to learn something and who is being paid for his attentive silence. Of course the therapist must speak and speak pertinently at the right times, but this injunction hardly need be given. The errors are likely to be made on the other side.

Positive Outlook

The therapist must believe—and, better, believe on the basis of his own experience—that repression can be revoked and that neurotic conflicts can be eliminated. How else can he have the courage to drive and to help the patient along the blind way he must go? He must believe in the patient's capacity to learn. We agree with Rogers (1942, p. 28) that faith in the patient is a most important requirement in a therapist. But we would describe it as a belief in a capacity to learn rather than one in a capacity to grow because "growth" suggests physiological models which we do not believe are as appropriate or specific as the principles and conditions of learning. When we affirm the patient's capacity to learn we mean always "provided the right conditions are set up." Learning is not inevitable. Our view is better expressed by the belief that the patient will learn if he must. The therapist must be well forewarned of the forces which operate against learning and must set up the conditions carefully so that these forces can be defeated.

In this connection it is particularly important that the therapist urge and encourage the patient to make those overt responses in real life which are needed to reduce conflict. If his attitude is truly positive, the therapist will know that these responses must be made and will be willing to take the risks involved, along with the patient. The therapist will know, further, that as the patient is successful in making these conflict-reducing responses in the real world he will become more and more responsive to the stimuli of his real world and less and less to the therapeutic situation and the therapist. Obviously, the therapist must fully accept this separation and his chief motivation must be to have that separation occur.

If he is too fearful himself of trying the event in real life and holds his patient back, the therapist will of course cause his own therapeutic efforts to be abortive. He should watch particularly tendencies to "hang on to" the patient either through fear or self-interest. We are suspicious of those therapists whose patients never seem to "go away," who continue to circle around their therapists in some satellite role. We further consider it a great point of honor to Freud and his followers that despite the many wealthy people they have analyzed the number of major subventions to psychoanalytic causes has been so small. The therapist's attitude should be positive in a planful sense, indifferent to rewards other than his stipulated compensation, and remorseless in driving the patient into the real-world acts and relations by which alone he can be healed.

Tolerance of the Transference

As fear weakens, the needy patient begins to make ever more lively emotional responses toward the therapist. The therapist must be in a position to prove that these responses are "unreasonable," that is, not provoked by the stimuli of the interview. He can identify these transferred responses either by observing the patient's behavior or by noting his own responses to the patient. In the first case, the frightened patient will make responses indicating fear of the therapist. In the second case, the therapist first realizes that the patient is acting toward him by noting that he is reacting to the patient. The therapist finds that he can sense and identify within himself that incipient love which is called out by love or the hostility with which he has learned to meet aggression. He argues, as it were, "If I am defending myself, someone must be attacking me." The therapist should notice these emotional responses within himself while they are still weak. He can then suppress the building up of strong drive-producing trains of thought within himself and restrain overt counteraggression.

The cues of these nascent emotional responses should set off analytical chains of sentences within the therapist. What is the patient doing? What does he want of me? What does this behavior of the patient's indicate about him? Why is his reaction evoked at this time? How was the reaction learned? When these questions are answered, the transferred reaction must be fitted into the general picture as one of the facts that supports the therapist's construction and his consequent therapeutic plan. Tolerant behavior, then, amounts to a special skill in allowing and encouraging emotions to be expressed toward himself and not responding directly where it is not in the patient's interest. We have already noted that patients with fierce aggression may show real ingenuity in finding the weak spots in the therapist's armor.

At one point, Mrs. A was attempting to force the therapist to help her. She complained that free association was too hard. If only the therapist would suggest topics! She then brought up the example of a compliant therapist. "This boy who had a nervous breakdown in the Army said the Army psychiatrist suggested topics each day." Mrs. A continued, "If you'd just give me a hint!" When the therapist resisted this pressure and insisted that Mrs. A could follow the rule of free association, Mrs. A lashed out saying, "You are making me feel worse. I think you're just experimenting on me." Mrs. A, frustrated in her dependent demands, was attempting to hurt the therapist and provoke him into reaction by attributing a ruthless, conscienceless attitude to him. The therapist stuck to his task, and the accusation proved entirely transient.

There is another aspect to the emotional reactions aroused in the therapist. When these escape notice and labeling, they have been called "countertransference." Such unconscious reactions disturb the therapist's ability to perform his task because, obviously, he cannot help the patient to label what he cannot himself identify. As in the case of nascent reactions, if the therapist does finally note the countertransference, he will learn something about his patient and something about himself as well. The unskilled therapist may believe that he has accepted the patient's aggression as a necessary part of his behavior but may nevertheless retaliate at some unexpected moment. The appearance of such unexpected aggression is the cue which should start the therapist on self-examination. Any strong action of the therapist's which is "not according to therapeutic plan" is under suspicion of being unconsciously motivated.

Similarly, the unskilled therapist may be too sympathetic and fall in with the patient's unrealistic, defensive explanations. He may fail to perceive and point out incongruous or irrational elements in the patient's behavior. He may be afraid to name embarrassing drives because they are also unconsciously active within his own personality.

Every therapist will find evidence in himself of unconscious reactions toward his patient. His lack of repression is bound to be relative rather than absolute. He must therefore always be on the alert for behavior of his own which is not part of his rational plan. When such occurs he must indeed set out to "know himself" better.

Amateur therapists will inevitably display various faults of countertransference. They will be afraid of the patient and hence stiff and unbending. They will have maternal impulses to express and will therefore be too nice to the patient. They may want the patient to fall neatly into a category or react with a predicted response, and if he does not they may feel humiliated and punish him. Good supervisory work will, of course, aid apprentice therapists to identify and deal with these reactions.

Importance of Therapist's Training and Adjustment

Perhaps the most severe test of the therapist's restraint occurs when he has to take a patient who has some special claim or sociological leverage on him—as, for example, where a subordinate technician has to take the head of his own clinic in therapy. The therapist does indeed incur some risk in this case but less than that of the patient. The patient runs the risk that the therapist will not be able to do his duty, that necessary thoughts will not occur to him, that fear or tact will influence what is happening in the therapist's mind. The patient will be, by so much, deprived of that accurate "construction" which the therapist should be helping him to produce.

The battering effects of transferred emotions would be almost intolerable were it not for two facts. The first is that the therapist has an intelligent, technical perception of what is going on. He sees that the patient cannot have any other emotions than those he has. The therapist understands that he cannot label these emotions unless they are present. In the limited situation of therapy these emotions cannot prompt acts which have a really damaging effect on the therapist's life. He can afford to let them pass since he knows they are necessary, transitory, and of little real effect.

Secondly, the therapist is less likely to act under the influence of unconscious motives if he is living a strong, positive life himself. He who has vital sex habits outside the therapeutic situation is less likely to be accessible to sex temptation within it The therapist who is a professional success will have less need to hit back when his competence is unreasonably challenged. The therapist with genuine maternal feelings will recognize when the patient is in real need and when his demands are excessive; if the patient is dependently attempting to exploit the therapeutic situation, the strong therapist can play the role of the strong mother who recalls the child to its real-life duties.

Furthermore, it is not enough for the therapist to have self-knowledge, to be able to give himself a relatively complete verbal account of what he is doing. He should have, in addition, strong neurosis-resistant habits. He should *be* the kind of person his patient wants to *become*. We say that, other things equal and allowing for exceptions due to unusual circumstances, it is better that the therapist be married than single; that he have a stable *normal* rather than stable *perverse* sexual adjustment; that he show evidence of a good conscience in dealing with his personal affairs; that he be a professionally responsible and cooperative person rather than a lone wolf or a prima donna; that he have some viable sublimations rather than an incontinent preoccupation with professional work; and that he have a sense of humor. Although therapists will invariably fall short of the ideal in some respects, that ideal should be left to beckon them.

Psychotherapy for the therapist. The student therapist *may* be able to train himself by his own efforts at self-study, but this procedure is slow and its outcome uncertain. He should therefore submit himself to therapy and get the guarantee of a competent technician that repressions are reasonably revoked and conflicts resolved. Only thus can the therapist face his patient with a good conscience. The formalities of the matter are important from a legal but not from a moral standpoint. Morally the therapist is obliged to assure his patient that he has that mental freedom, empathy, restraint, and positive character which are his essential tools.

Rewards for therapy only. The therapist should be in such a position relative to his patient that he is rewarded for his therapeutic skills and for nothing else. The therapist should be sufficiently paid since economic rewards are the most suitable in our society. In some cases (and they are too few) the satisfaction of research drives may be a sufficient reward to maintain the therapist's integrity. When the going is slow and the course of events baffling, "sticking it out" becomes a real problem for the therapist. The patient needs to control rewards which will keep the therapist working throughout this period. Like every other good human relationship, the relationship of therapist and patient has to be an affair of reciprocal rewards. The patient should feel safer, also, if the therapist's rewards are sufficient, explicit, and conventional. Therapists who pretend to conduct the hard work of therapy "out of the goodness of their hearts" may actually be doing so out of the badness of unknown drives.

The therapist's knowledge of psychological principles. The therapist should have a practical knowledge of the psychological principles involved in neurosis and conflict. He should understand how repression and emotional conflicts are learned. Only in the light of such knowledge can the therapist "run the machine backward" as he must do in psychotherapy. Repression must be unlearned in order to gain the manifold advantages of verbal cues. Emotional conflict must be replaced by strong habits which reduce that conflict and stand as a barrier to its recurrence. We believe that the clearest exposition of the nature of neurosis and psychotherapy can be made in the behavioral concepts of reinforcement theory.

Strategy and tactics of therapy. Obviously the therapist must have much concrete experience in carrying on therapeutic work. He learns the rudiments through his own therapeutic experience. He should discuss the theory of psychotherapy in special seminars. (Preferably the theory should be based on the joint Freudian-behavioral approach discussed in this book.) He should serve an appropriate apprenticeship. Some of the errors of his many trials can be eliminated during the course of this apprenticeship.

We believe that it would be a great aid to apprentice therapists if they could watch the most experienced therapists working. In Freud's time it was not technically possible to make sound records of the therapeutic interview. Nowadays it is not only possible but easy (Redlich *et al.*, 1950). Model records of our best therapists at work should be available for study. Probably, also, the young therapist should record some of his own hours with patients, especially his earliest ones. With the aid of such recordings the supervisor can much more easily help the apprentice in establishing a correct and sensible technique. We assume that the supervisor can help his candidate better the more accurately he knows what this candidate is doing. We believe that the use of sound recordings will materially speed up the learning of the apprentice therapist. Correct indoctrination at an early stage might save the candidate from overlearning his first mistakes and having them only slowly culled out of his behavior in the blundering process of ordinary supervision by verbal report. Pioneer work in the field of recording has been done by E. F. Zinn and Prof. Carl Rogers.

The Therapist Must Know Social Conditions

The therapist's knowledge of the social conditions under which the patient lives and has lived is usually considered "intuitive," something given and not especially trained for. Such intuitive knowledge is roughly adequate in the middle and upper classes of the societies of Western Europe and their offshoots. The apparent reason why therapists are interchangeable among Western European societies is that the fundamental form of the family is the same throughout these societies. As a result, the fundamental circumstances of child training are similar and the neurosis-producing conditions of childhood are similar. Thus, one can pluck a therapist out of Berlin or Paris and find that he carries on his work usefully in London or New York. Since he deals with highly placed people in either city, his knowledge is rather readily transferable.

If psychotherapy is ever to be broadened from its present upper-group locus in society, therapists will have to acquire more specialized knowledge of social conditions. The usual circumstance at the present time is that a middle- or upper-class psychiatrist treats a middle- or upper-class patient. Some confusion may result in the case when the middle-class psychiatrist has an upper-class patient. Such a patient can always legitimately and realistically "snoot" the therapist, and the therapist will find rising within himself reactions which are not easily controlled and which cannot be explained by the psychodynamics of childhood. Psychotherapeutic results will be more predictable when the rudiments of knowledge of American social structure are taught in every American school where psychotherapists are trained.

When a middle-class therapist does occasionally treat a lower-class patient, he finds a culture somewhat different from his own (Davis and Havighurst, 1947, pp. 215–219). That same docility which is a favorable trait in a middle-class boy may be a character disorder in the lower-class boy. The masturbatory behavior reluctantly tolerated in the middle-class adolescent may be viewed as a perversion in the lower-class child (Kinsey *et al.*, 1948, pp. 375–377).

This matter was well exemplified in the behavior of a lower-class patient who had been a sailor. The patient was suffering from acute anxiety in connection with unconscious homosexual tendencies. In broaching this subject matter, he described various sexual temptations to which he had been exposed as a sailor. He said that in port cities enlisted men were often approached by youths who offered to perform fellatio on them. The patient deplored the fact that he could not accept the act as most of his companions did and forget about it. He could not comply and yet he could not get the matter off his mind. In the course of this discussion it became clear that the patient considered the stranger who performed fellatio "homosexual" but the man on whom it was performed normal. The performer was a "fairy." The compliant sailor, not. This patient's attitude was quite striking because in a middle-class definition of the situation both persons would be considered partners in a homosexual act and therefore homosexuals. If the therapist followed lower-class logic in this situation, his goal would have to be to make this sailor capable of passively enjoying fellatio. The patient's disturbance arose from the fact that he unconsciously wanted to be the performer; the anxiety attached to this inhibited wish generalized to the passive acceptance of the act.

Since many neurotic patients suffer social frustration in the course of an (unconscious) mobility campaign, it is often important for the therapist to understand the class structure and the needs and goals of socially mobile people. If the therapist does not understand this matter he will seriously misinterpret the conditions of the patient's life and may charge off to "unconscious forces" frustrations that are imposed by the actual conditions of the patient's life. Ruesch and Loeb (1946) have studied a group of patients in whom social class frustrations have seriously contributed to pathology.

What is "reality?" Social conditions plus physical dangers are often referred to by the vague and sometimes treacherous concept of "reality."   Behind the notion of "reality" is hidden the great variability incident to social and cultural conditions. It is much better for the therapist to have a clear statement of social stratification and the conditions which it imposes upon individual life than to trust to such a general notion (Warner and Associates, 1949; and Warner, Meeker, and Eells, 1949). Ideally we should like to avoid the twin errors made by some sociologists and psychologists, which for want of a better name may be called the sociological error and the psychological error. The sociologist may err by putting all of his emphasis on conditions and not noticing individual differences which indicate important constitutional factors and attitudes learned in early life. The psychologist, on his side, may err by putting too much emphasis on constitution and habit, thus underestimating the variability that may be produced by specific social conditions. As far as psychotherapists are concerned, we feel that a knowledge of social conditions is underdone rather than overdone. The favorite error of therapists is *not* that of sociologists!

Ability to Discriminate Functional from Physical

The ability to discriminate functional from physical causation is of great importance and yet, unfortunately, this problem becomes more, rather than less, difficult as time goes on. We intend to say only a few, essential things in connection with it. The medical therapist may choose, though many do not, to determine for himself whether somatic problems are involved in a psychoneurotic complaint. The nonmedical therapist should, in every case, insist upon a preliminary physical examination of his patient whether or not somatic problems are obviously involved.

When somatic symptoms arise in the course of psychological treatment, the medical therapist can diagnose them himself, but the nonmedical therapist should refer the patient to his "anchor physician," *i.e.,* the one who made the first examination. The nonmedical therapist may have to refer his patient to the physician more than once since he cannot judge somatic symptoms for himself. He should, in any case, err on the side of caution. As part of his caution, he should select a physician who will do his job as physician and nothing more; otherwise he will find an unskilled person meddling in the psychotherapeutic situation.

If therapy involves an admixture of medical and psychotherapeutic work—as sometimes it must when the patient needs sedation, shock, or other means to make him accessible to therapy—such treatment should be carried on by a medical therapist or under his immediate supervision. Psychoses should be treated by medical therapists since they routinely involve commitment and many accessory medical measures. The foregoing considerations are pertinent not only to treating but also to selecting patients.

We have emphasized the precautions important to psychologists who work as psychotherapists. In the same connection we stress that the ability to treat organic disease does not automatically carry with it a skill at psychotherapy. Nor does the possession of any degree such as Ph.D or M.D. routinely confer such skill. Only the knowledge of theory, the kind of character, and the supervised training discussed here can make a man a psychotherapist. Anyone who undertakes psychotherapy without such training is exposing his patient to real danger and committing a moral, if not yet a legal, fraud. We are not here concerned with the historical circumstances (including Freud's genius) under which psychotherapeutic techniques were invented, improved, exploited, or patented. We are concerned, at this time, with these questions: Upon what kind of scientific knowledge do psychotherapeutic procedures rest? What is the basic science of which psychotherapy is an application? How can this science be best advanced, and how can the arts based upon it be improved? As these questions are answered we will know better how psychotherapists should be trained and how they should be related to the patient and to society at large.

CHAPTER XXVIII

HOW THERAPY CAN GO WRONG

In this chapter we will highlight the points at which therapy can fail. The survey will be brief and will serve only as a crude check list. The material has been presented before but a résumé would seem to be useful.

From our standpoint, it is evident that the effort demanded from the therapist will vary greatly from case to case. Some patients will need only minor encouragement to make effective use of their higher mental skills. Others may require many months of laborious work to revoke repression and restore higher mental activity. Some patients may need only a nudge to take the vital step into drive-reducing action. Others will require a long period of slow testing in the therapeutic situation before inhibition of action is reduced. The goal is the same in every case, *i.e.*, an active mental life and effective behavior in the real world. The demands on the therapist, however, will vary according to the severity of repression and the strength of conflict.

Since there exist no scales to measure the degree of repression and strength of inhibition, it has also been difficult to evaluate the results of the therapist's activity. When the patient got the nudge that he needed, the activity could be scored as a success. But if he needed *two* years of intensive work and got only *one*, the outcome was necessarily scored as a failure.

There are even some difficulties about estimating when a conflict has been resolved and replaced by a strong drive-reducing habit. The family and friends of a patient who do the estimating may not know that the conflict exists. The new habit may appear in a private realm—say, in the relation between husband and wife—and therefore not be available for public judgment. It is likewise very difficult to credit a psychotherapist for disasters averted, though the arrest of a malignant course of events may be a great triumph.

There is urgent need for scales to measure severity of repression and strength of conflict. Likewise, there are needed measures for the strength of the habits which replace the neurotic conflict. Such measures would not only be of value in the treatment but would also enable us to identify the many cases in which brilliant work is done by the therapist.

Assuming, however, that we have in hand a patient with strong repressions and severe conflict, we will indicate some of the circumstances under which therapy may fail.

1. *If the patient is too proud to come to the therapist.* Mention of this may seem naïve, but many who do need help do not try therapy for this reason. If they do not try they cannot change. Such persons may feel that it is a humiliation to admit being in need of help, and their resentment of the therapist is immediately raised by this circumstance. Friends and family may stand helplessly by while such a proud person destroys himself.

2. *If the patient cannot meet the therapist's conditions of treatment.* Obviously, in this case again, the therapeutic relationship never occurs. We mention this case because, though the individual therapist does not fail, the craft or institution of psychotherapy does. Psychotherapy fails of its full social effect if all who need it cannot avail themselves of it. The patient may not be able to pay the therapist's fees—as is true of many lower-class and middle-class patients. They may not be able to come at the hours when the therapist can see them. Or they may not be able to pay long enough and stay long enough to do the necessary therapeutic work.

The result is that protracted psychotherapy is virtually unavailable to lower-class and lower-middle-class persons, even though it is often needed. For it must not be supposed, that lower-class people are so toughened or obtuse that they do not have neurotic disorders; they, too, have all been children. Although psychiatric and family case workers do excellent service for lower-income groups, often these workers do not have the specialized training or the time needed to do the best work in psychotherapy.

3. *If the patient is unable to learn.* Since psychotherapy is by its nature a learning situation, the patient who is for any reason unable to learn cannot profit by it. The stupid, defective, or brain-injured are thus at a disadvantage. The therapist cannot restore higher

mental processes if the necessary brain mechanisms do not exist.

If the patient is preoccupied by a psychosis or other intense internal stimulation (cancer, for instance) so that he cannot pay attention, he will likewise be unable to profit by psychotherapy. The patient must be able to rehearse and react to the therapist's sentences if therapy is to occur.

Where the socially desired habit is opposed by a strong competing habit, psychotherapy may be impossible. Thus, the perverse individual may find in some crevice of society the conditions which strongly reward his perversion. The existence of the perverse habit makes it difficult to learn the conventional one. We should also list in this connection the absence of a motive to learn a conventional habit. In general, neurotics have strong anxiety attached to the performance of unconventional acts. This anxiety persistently drives them to try to find drive-reducing acts which are conventional. In the case of the psychopath, anxiety impelling toward a conventional path of action is weak. Likewise, psychopaths have a defect in the ability to love and trust other persons. This defect they display in relation to the therapist who cannot get "a hold" on them. Training procedures for psychopathic persons could perhaps be invented, but they would be different from those described here.

4. *If the patient is not strongly motivated to "bear therapy."* Many patients who urgently need psychotherapy attempt the relationship but then stop. They find the work required of them too painful and their own motivation to continue is too weak to overcome this avoidance. It is important for the therapist at the earliest possible moment to show the patient that psychotherapy is the *only* way out of his neurotic conflict and thus get the full benefit of neurotic pain as a motive for the work. Persons without intense conflict are little likely to continue when the attempt at free association produces much pain.

5. *If conditions of therapy are not arranged in a proper, benign way.* The therapist may not know how to set up a permissive atmosphere. He may cross-question his patient and thus raise unbearable anxiety. He may fail to compel the patient to utterance and so never get him started on his proper work. Under such circumstances, naturally, the anxiety attached to verbal cues

cannot be extinguished and the patient will remain without the benefit of improved higher mental life.

6. *If the therapist cannot spot repression areas.* The therapist cannot repair what he cannot locate. His failure may be due to lack of correct theory, lack of specific, controlled practice, or presence of some repression in the therapist. Psychotherapy is a special skill which requires special training. It must be actually practiced under supervision. It is hard to learn from books. Psychotherapeutic skill does not come as a by-product of any academic degree whatsoever. It is an applied science based on a fundamental science whose nature is not yet entirely understood. We believe, however, that the laws of learning must be fundamentally involved.

7. *If the therapist does not understand transferred behavior.* In this case, the therapist cannot keep the patient "on the rails" and at his proper work. He loses essential knowledge as to the nature of inhibited drives. The therapist will find his patient motionless and the work blocked. He must be able to identify the transferred emotional response, convince the patient that it has not been "earned" in the course of therapy, and demonstrate that it does obstruct therapeutic advance. Motives to be reasonable and to be well are thus called out to compete with the tendency to luxuriate in obstructive behavior. Skill in identifying and exposing the negative transference is thus essential to getting the patient back at his work.

8. *If the patient does not try new responses outside the therapeutic situation.* The patient must generalize the new verbal units learned in the therapeutic situation. He must likewise generalize emotional responses, first practiced toward the therapist, to persons in his actual life. If the patient cannot thus generalize, he remains fixed in the impermanent and unreal therapeutic situation.

Similarly, the patient must try out entirely new responses, ones which have never been made in therapy. Unless he makes these actual, gross responses toward persons in the outside world, he cannot form new habits. This transaction is not necessarily automatic; although freedom to speak may often incite action, the therapist should also specifically encourage trying out such new responses. The cure should not remain at the "talking level" only. Such generalization and innovation of responses occur both during and after the end of the therapeutic sessions. It is highly important that the therapist witness the occurrence of some such responses *during* therapy.

9. *If real life does not reward new responses of patient.* The goal of the whole therapeutic situation is to resolve the neurotic conflict and to set in place of it a positive, drive-reducing habit. The conditions of real life must be favorable if new responses are to become strong habits. On the one hand, the real-life conditions must fail to reinforce the inhibitory arm of the conflict, *i.e.,* the patient must find in fact that self-expression is not dangerous. On the other hand, the responses produced by the inhibited drive of the conflict must be strongly rewarded.

Therapy often fails on this account, and former theories have not sufficiently emphasized the crucial character of these real-life circumstances. Many a therapist who has done his work correctly has blamed himself for failure when the fault was not his. If the patient's real life does not permit resolution of the neurotic conflict it cannot be resolved by the talking part of the cure.

10. *If reality circumstances do not remain favorable.* After therapy, habits retain the same changeability that they had before. Favorable circumstances must not only prevail at the time of the therapeutic sessions, but must be maintained; otherwise the misery of an unsatisfied drive, if not the conflict, will return. Such real-life conditions may improve or deteriorate after therapy. If the latter, therapeutic results may be lost. When this is the case, the therapist is powerless. There is no way of guaranteeing a permanent therapeutic result when the therapist cannot control the conditions which permit the reduction of strong drives.

Furthermore, life circumstances may evoke conflicts which were not present at the time of the original therapy. In such a case also the original therapeutic result will not suffice. It is not always possible at the time of therapy to provoke every conflict of which the patient is capable and which life circumstances may eventually evoke. If such a new conflict occurs, the patient should swiftly return to his therapist and complete the work.

New measures needed. As we move toward an exact science in this area, it will be necessary to invent systems for scaling or ranking a number of new variables (Kubie, 1950). We should have, and will eventually have, measures of some or all the following variables: *patient's ability to learn, degree of repression, strength of conflict, skill of therapist, strength of "positive" habit,* and *relative favorableness of reality circumstances.* As these new measures are devised we should be able to predict therapeutic outlook and result more exactly.

Needed Too: A Science of Child Rearing

The slowness, the labor, and the expense of psychotherapy are evident to all, especially to patients and therapists. Analysis of the forces involved does not make it seem likely that therapists will hit on swift, economical techniques for treating neurotic patients. The important inference from this fact is the following: neurosis must be prevented, not cured; its waste and loss must be avoided, not repaired late in life. Since we hold that neurotic behavior is learned, we also hold that it is taught—taught unwittingly by the confused practices of child rearing in our culture. As of today, there is no science of child rearing (Dollard, 1949). Fad after fad sweeps the field. The parents of today weep at the thought of the pseudo-science they practiced yesterday on their beloved children. Neurotic behavior in children is dismissed as a mere incident of growth. Research is conducted in the clinic—and the home, where all happens, is neglected. Advice given to parents is mainly "ad-libbed." It lacks the pattern and ordering which it might have were it derived from a powerful scientific theory. It lacks the power to prevent or to predict the disaster of a severe behavior disorder.

Further research in psychotherapy will teach ever new things about the higher mental life of human beings. But though such research is urgently needed and will contribute greatly to human welfare, it will never solve the problem of neurosis. That solution can come only by such a powerful and systematic knowledge of how children learn in our culture as to enable us to change those culture patterns which produce neurosis. We now know how to go about the needed research. New developments in learning theory offer a powerful systematic basis for development. The zeal and the resources to launch the research on child learning must be found.

PART VIII
TWO APPLICATIONS TO NORMAL LIVING

CHAPTER XXIX

SELF-STUDY

Higher mental processes are constantly in use by normal persons to solve emotional, social, scientific, mathematical, geographical, and other types of problems. We do not call this activity self-study but have described it as "the normal use of the mind in reasoning, forecasting, and planning." By self-study we mean a somewhat more deliberate activity. It usually begins with a recognized problem. A planned period of time is set aside. Some way of externalizing and conserving the flow of response is used. The goal is to discover repressed or partly repressed action tendencies and to label them. If this is achieved, the new labeling permits appropriate discrimination and generalization and novel efforts to resolve emotional conflict. The activity of self-study, as differentiated from ordinary reasoning, is based on the existence of formal psychotherapy and the theories of mental life which accompany it. Such self-study would not have been possible in the old days before Freud.

Though the normal person has been cynically called "one who has not been adequately studied," important differences between people in degree of repression and degree of emotional conflict are obvious. Thanks to a lesser degree of misery from conflict, normal people have less motivation for effortful self-study. Presumably they come out of childhood already equipped to resolve the conflicts which might produce such motivation. Though neurotic persons have been carefully studied, the work on normal people is much less thorough. We cannot be certain that they do not themselves, in the ordinary course of higher mental activity, uncover repressions and repair the effects of mild childhood damage.

In normals, as in others, the anxiety attached to verbal cues representing forbidden acts is always present to oppose self-study. Conventional people do not think of (and do not need to think of) unconventional things. Normal people have made the useful dis-

431

criminations. They do not, for instance, widely generalize anxiety from truly forbidden acts to others which are not forbidden, as neurotics tend to do. Normal people can afford to "let their minds alone." This matter might also be expressed by saying that in normal people the repressions and inhibitions of the individual coincide with the mores of the group, whereas in the neurotic, the individual repressions and inhibitions much exceed the strength and scope demanded by group mores.

Indeed, since normal persons are not forced to understand the nature of repression and conflict, they often do not credit neurotics with the misery they actually suffer. This attitude is bearable in lay people but entirely unworthy of scientists. There exist, nevertheless, strong movements within psychology and psychiatry which derogate the importance of neurotic phenomena, offer puerile theories to deal with such phenomena, and speak for coarse and hostile methods of treatment of the neurotic person. The normal person who values his conventional comfort above truth should avoid the study of these phenomena.

Need for Social Training in Self-study

We have said that normal persons have little motivation to prompt special efforts at self-study. The same thing is true of arithmetic. If motivation were not supplied from parents and school pressure, there would be little learning of mathematics. By analogy, it seems possible that children could be motivated and trained to use their mental skills to solve *emotional* problems. They get almost no training in this important skill at the present time. Examples of stupid or irrational behavior are dismissed, unnoticed, as a normal part of child nature. The displacement of emotional reactions should, nevertheless, be viewed as a failure to use higher mental processes. The child has been presented the problem and has failed to solve that problem in a rational way. The following example from real life is a case of such a failure.

A fourteen-year-old boy, George, had a Saturday date to go to the country with another boy. Both boys had looked forward to the day of freedom and had made detailed plans for their holiday. On the Saturday morning in question, George received a telephone call. The mother of his friend said that her son had a cold and could not go on the outing.

George was intensely disappointed. To his friend's mother he pretended to accept the circumstances. He suppressed his anger since he had learned it was no use fighting the inevitable.

Shortly thereafter George went to play in his back yard and there met his twelve-year-old sister. She teased him a little, as was her wont. He reacted strongly, striking her. She began screaming and he screamed back. An interactive quarrel flared up in which strong responses were called out in both children. The mother had to intervene. She found it hard to make sense of the affair because the original causes were obscured by angry claims and counterclaims. She ended by sending the boy to his room for the morning and drying the little girl's tears. The mother was not able to analyze the problem as a case of displaced aggression though she had the major facts, and she did not regard the incident as a failure in the use of higher mental processes on the boy's part.

Analyzed our way, the matter looks like this: To a slight cue of teasing produced by the sister, the frustrated boy reacted with disproportionately strong, aggressive responses. In the heat of the moment he passionately believed these responses to be warranted. He was unable to do anything except plunge into the quarrel. He had *displaced* to his sister the anger aroused by the nonappearance of his friend.

He had been prevented by fear of (respect for) his friend's mother from showing this anger during the telephone conversation. After this conversation he had continued to talk to himself about his lost goal and these reflections continued to excite angry responses. To the slight cue of the sister's teasing to which he would ordinarily react with counterteasing, he generalized the strong response of slapping.

This is the kind of behavior situation in which such a child could be taught important new units on the higher mental level. His mother, for instance, could have reminded him that he should have expected to be angry when he was barred from his goal. She should have told him that he could have expressed his disappointment and anger verbally to himself and to others. She could have forewarned him that when one is angry one is likely to try to "take it out on somebody else." She could have instructed him to *restrain* himself in such situation. She could have designated the aggressive action toward the sister as a "lower and poorer" kind of human adjustment—defining it as "bad" since someone gets punished who does not deserve it. She could have told the boy that the more he continued to think about the fun he could not have the angrier he would become.

At this point she could have taught the suppression unit. The best thing to do is to suppress the sentences and thoughts connected with the impossible plan, and by this act of suppression to stop creating hopeless motivation. The best way to suppress is to make other plans instead. Could some other boy, by chance, share the outing with him? Hadn't he been awaiting a chance to go to the rifle range and shoot? If he did his homework on Saturday, might he not look forward to going to the movies on Sunday afternoon? The latter activities were rendered impossible in this case by the outburst of anger which provoked punishment from his mother. By acting, literally, like a lower animal he was unable to canvass alternative solutions which might have greatly reduced both his frustration and his anger.

This may seem a laborious amount of training to inflict upon a child. We think, however, that this kind of training would not have to be invoked very long before the child would begin to get the hang of it. For all we know, it might be as easy to learn as the multiplication table. We have no doubt that however strange such training may seem at the present time it will sometime be part of the repertory of human culture.

The mind of the child could be trained to deal with such problems if the home and the school were able so to train it. Much that has later to be done by exhausting treatment of adults might be taught mass-wise at elementary levels. Both parent and elementary-school teacher must eventually learn to train children to use their minds in solving emotional problems. As adults, such children would then naturally have recourse to self-study when they were faced with bothersome problems.

Self-study for Neurotics without Therapy

Before they come to a therapist, neurotics regularly try to use their own higher mental processes to solve their problems. They talk about their symptoms endlessly, they canvass their cultural repertory for solutions, grasp at this and that vain approach. They dislike going to the therapist not only because of sacrifices of time and money but because they must ask for help and, to some extent, humiliate themselves by admitting they cannot solve their own problems.

The neurotic person who comes to therapy has plenty of motivation to prompt self-study, but when he attempts to solve his own problems he invariably fails. As he approaches repressed areas in his thinking, anxiety arises and tends to reinforce the stopping of thinking. He has no theories to go on. He has no habits or experience to direct him to what is repressed. His energies are not harnessed and focused on the important problems. Most important of all, he is alone and lacks the support which he needs to face his insupportable anxiety. Furthermore, he has no hope. He has had no positive rewards from self-study. On the contrary, he has a long record of failures in attempting to use his mind to reduce his misery. The unhappy fact is that self-study is most difficult, or impossible, just where it is most needed. The neurotic, therefore, must seek the support and direction that he needs from the skilled therapist. He is, so to say, one step away from self-study. He must accept the apprenticeship of the psychotherapeutic situation before he can take this step.

Self-study for the Neurotic after Therapy

In successful therapy there may be little or no need of self-study at the end of therapy. New drive-reducing habits have become strong and been overlearned. Verbal trial-and-error behavior, though necessary to excite early responses, may eventually drop out, since it is opposed by fatigue and not differentially reinforced. The person then may be viewed as quietly "happy," his adaptive habits clicking along with but little mental intervention.

Usually, however, the matter does not go quite so smoothly. After therapy there is a period of "working through." The patient is engaging in a kind of new practice, both mental and actual. He is generalizing his learning in the therapeutic situation to the cues of his actual world. He is innovating strong responses prepared for but not executed in the therapeutic situation. In this phase of things he may find self-study valuable. Occasionally he can make a real gain by taking time off to "figure things out," "pull things together," and make a plan. This kind of "working through" may go on in minor degrees for years. The sentences borrowed from the therapist may linger in the patient's mind, becoming attached to ever-new emotional and verbal stimuli. Patients often give evidence of this by suddenly thinking, "Oh, that's what he meant," a long time after the therapist's words were uttered.

New life dilemmas. New life dilemmas may create or bestir conflicts which have never been attacked in the therapeutic situation. Advancing age or death of a spouse may precipitate entirely new problems. It is desirable that the patient have some skill at the deliberate solution of emotional problems which we call self-study. In the ordinary case, this skill is a by-product of the original therapeutic training.

What are the cues for self-study? No person should, and no normal person will, undertake self-study unless genuinely motivated. It is entirely too effortful an activity to become an amusing habit. The most obvious cues which should prompt self-study are real-life conflicts which do not seem on their way to solution after ordinary mental working over. Marital conflicts of various kinds could excite such a canvass. Difficulties on the job, misunderstandings with friends, where one has the vague feeling of being at fault, may be cleared up by a period of self-study. If, however, the cues to such study are continuous and obsessive, the patient should accept this as a sign that therapy is radically incomplete and that he had better recur to his therapist for more specialized help. Self-study is an awkward, costly, and often futile way of solving a serious neurotic conflict.

Will the patient hit on it himself? If the formal period of therapy has produced strong rewards, the reinforcement of the habits which led to conflict resolution would be expected. Hence, we would expect that some of the habits practiced in the therapeutic situation with the therapist would generalize to problem cues alone and be tried out without the therapist. The patient has had a long period of practice in searching for new lines of verbal response and in bearing some anxiety while doing so. If he has been rewarded for this work, the tendency to continue the search and to bear some pain in the search should be strengthened. The more the patient has been left on his own and the more novel mental units he has himself created, the stronger should be the tendency to attack later problems by the same means. After therapy the patient knows that it can be done. He values more than formerly the search for the right labels and the combination of sentences into a useful plan. We believe, therefore, that a successful experience of psychotherapy should produce an individual who is prone to self-study and can make use of it when need arises.

What is tried out in self-study? To this we answer, "The identical activities which have been used during the course of formal therapy." The person stops to think instead of rushing into action. He attempts to see where blocks in association point and to decode dreams. He tries to trace vague anxieties to specific problem areas. He tests his reasoning for inconsistencies. He searches for missing units in his verbal series. In the privacy of his own mind, he will attempt to label irrational emotional responses which he is making to persons in his real life. He will try at least to be clear with himself when he is at fault. He wants to act reasonably and therefore he must identify his unreasonable behavior.

Undoubtedly, also, he consoles himself as the therapist would console him. He assures himself there is no punishment for merely thinking. He affirms that he is free "to think anything." If he hits upon a solution of a problem, he then goes into action exactly as he was expected to do by the therapist. If he has been unreasonable, he tries to make amends. If he has been stupidly afraid, he tries responding despite his fear. In short, the mental activity of self-study is designed to produce a more adaptive course of action in real life. It is not mere brooding or anxious self-preoccupation. Prolonged brooding is itself a symptom of mental malaise and not a positive use of the mind.

Can self-study be strengthened as a habit? It can indeed and by the very same means which have been referred to so often before. Consoling insights may occur immediately while the process is going on. This can and does happen. Self-students testify that they have often felt "the weight lift" while they were still working out their thoughts. It is easy to see how such a consolation can occur. Thoughts inhibitory of fear may pop up. Discriminations between present innocuous and past dangerous situations can be made. Similarly, new plans may be hit upon which seem likely of success and thereby bring an anticipatory reduction of tension.

If the plan is tried out and conflict is actually resolved, the effect of the terminal reward will work backward and strengthen all the acts incident to self-study. Those who have achieved it to some degree testify that such an ability to solve one's emotional problems produces a wonderful increment of self-confidence. The process is, however, lawful. If the terminal acts of the plan are not rewarded, the laborious activity of self-study is likely to be dropped.

Can training for self-study be given during therapy? We believe most certainly that it can. Activity analogous to self-study goes on between therapeutic hours. Continued conflict and misery keep on activating mental attempts to solve problems. Where such activity has no defensive function but is a genuine attempt to advance the work, it can be rewarded by the therapist's approval. If it is so rewarded, it is more likely to continue after therapy.

There is, however, a big difference between such interstitial self-study and the activity which occurs after the therapeutic interviews are over. During therapy the patient has the expectation of seeing the therapist again and can rely on the therapist to verify his findings and to help correct erroneous mental units. The patient will find it much more difficult when this support is lacking. He has to generalize his creative habits from the problem plus the therapist to the problem stimuli alone. He is less sure that he has the right answer and must risk overt action on his own, unaided judgment.

It is theoretically possible that special practice in self-study might be given during the latter part of a course of therapeutic interviews. The patient might be asked to practice solving particular problems and the therapist could act as a kind of control. The point would be to make the conditions of practice during therapy as similar as possible to those to be used after therapy. The therapist could reward the outside work of self-study by listening and confirming.

Technique of Self-study

The technique of self-study was first suggested by Freud in connection with his study of his own dreams (Freud, 1913, pp. 86–88). He suggested writing out dreams and the associations which appeared to them. The same rules prevail as in the condition of free association. The thoughts are written down as they come. The person compels himself to follow the rule relentlessly. He perseveres until tired.

Writing preserves responses which might otherwise be repressed. The ones occurring early in a sequence can be compared with ones occurring later. The document can be looked over from the standpoint of missing links and unreasonable emotions, hints of repressed forces. The self-student may destroy his production after it has served its immediate purpose. He may set aside time and try again another day so long as his problem is not solved.[1]

There is one disadvantage of self-study as compared with the activity of the therapist. When the patient gets around to canvassing and organizing his own associations he finds that many of the cues are "cold." They have lost the exact sense with which they were first written down. The therapist who intervenes from the outside can label and make linkages while the emotions and emotional cues are hot and strong.

A quotation from the book "Victory over Fear" (Dollard, 1942, pp. 55–56) will illustrate the concrete activity of self-study. The case is that of a "man who didn't want to go back home."

As a self-student he decided to turn his attention to the problem. All he was aware of at the outset was a kind of reluctance to return to visit his old parents. He had, of course, many excuses for not returning, but he knew in the privacy of his own mind that they were really excuses and not reasons. He was not really too busy to go home, etc.; he just didn't want to go home. He realized that he was fond of his parents and that they felt quite hurt because of his absence of several years. Starting from this problem, he wrote out his thoughts in approximately the following way:

1. Have been avoiding home for several years, why? Really ought to go—owe my parents a great deal.

[1] See "Victory over Fear" (Dollard, 1942) for suggestions concerning the technique of self-study.

2. Had a chance to go last year at the time of the convention but did not take it.

3. Perhaps I am ashamed of my parents—but I'm ashamed, too, to be ashamed of them.

4. Don't actually have a very good time at home. Last time I went they didn't listen to me. Tried to tell them about self, but they switched always to local gossip. Were proud of me in general but didn't care about my life as I live it now.

5. Made me feel small, like a child again. Ordered me around as if I were still a small boy. Bragged about me before my face, showed me off to the neighbors like a prize calf. Won't admit I've grown up.

6. They seem plain and dull now. Couldn't bring my friends home possibly. They wouldn't understand and family would be embarrassed.

7. Still it's fun to talk about old-time things for a little while.

When this student looked over what he had written he made himself a brief summary of the reasons why he didn't go home, somewhat as follows:

1. Parents humiliate me by treating me as a child.

2. I'm ashamed of them because they pushed me ahead while they have stayed behind.

The answer to the question that he had set himself was in reality a very simple one. He didn't go home because he was afraid to. He got punished when he went home, and he was avoiding the punishment situation.

He could see clearly that there was little possibility of changing the situation. His parents were too old and fixed in their ways to try to adapt themselves to him. In a sense, they were interested in what they could get out of his coming home and not in what he could get out of it. But he did have a certain grim affection for them, for those people who had fought his battle so well and launched him on a good career. Since he couldn't change the situation and couldn't change his reaction of fear and embarrassment, he went back to a good old solution of the problem. He decided to grin and bear it, to stand some punishment for his parents' sake, and found himself able at last to make his plans for the visit.

Vivid idea of strength of anxiety. If any normal person wishes to verify the fact that there are anxiety-protected areas in his own mental life he need only attempt self-study. He will find that mysterious forces arise to stop his work. He will find himself welcoming distractions and thinking of interesting plans for other things to do. Persons whom he would ordinarily shun are surprisingly welcome when they drop in. Hopeless thoughts easily come to mind. If the person persists, he will find himself facing the vague terror of anxiety. He will find indeed that the effect of past punishments will rise again when he contemplates the course of action that was punished. Such a normal person will then understand better the value of the reassuring presence of the therapist to the neurotic person and what resolution is required to carry on self-study outside the supportive context of the psychotherapeutic situation.

Self-study for Normals

Quite apart from the matter of revoking repression and resolving conflicts, self-study is independently valuable as "a chance to think." For most people, life goes by too fast. They find it hard to evaluate all the information that comes to them and assemble it into a useful plan of life. They find their security threatened in some oblique way; they forget the facts, but the event has registered and continues to bother them. A little reflection may enable them to recall the threat and estimate it at its proper value. Though "the mind" is highly honored and idealized in the abstract, it is surprising how little use most people make of it.

A second example from "Victory over Fear" (Dollard, 1942, pp. 43–44) will show the effect on behavior of a neglected observation and how self-study can aid adjustment by giving such an observation its true weight. The case is that of a novelist who was working on a story based on his own life, although the latter fact was not generally known.

He had a regular occupation and was writing the novel in addition to carrying on his daily work. His hope of being rewarded for carrying on the work of writing was very nearly balanced by his anticipation of failure and by the effort required to do the writing. It was, therefore, always touch and go as to whether he would get his weekly chapter done. He had set aside a Sunday for finishing up one chapter and sat down at his desk bright and early. When he sat down he had a sort of feeling that he would not be very productive that day, but he resolutely opposed this notion. It proved, however, to be all too true. He writhed and wrestled for most of the day, attempting to get his plot straightened out and his characters to behave as he felt they ought. Late in the afternoon he decided to stop work on the novel and to start work on why he was blocked. He began writing to himself about as follows:

1. Can't seem to finish this chapter—am I just lazy, losing my grip?
2. Have been blocked before. It went away—but hate to lose time today.
3. Book won't be any good anyway—I'm just wasting my time—guess I'll quit—no, finish.
4. That last chapter was good, anyway.
5. Perhaps I need someone to tell me it's all right, to go ahead—wish I had a contract for the book.
6. No use, for the moment, anyway.

So the author turned from his desk and gave it up as a bad job. He had tried to find out the source of his blocking by self-study and had failed. But he had a surprise coming. He went out to play with the children before dinner and, as it were, took the weight off his mind. As he was walking back to the house he had a revealing and releasing thought. Only the day before he had been talking to an important friend about his novel. The friend had not been encouraging, felt it would be difficult to get a publisher, thought it might be too obvious that the plot represented the author's own life. The writer had not taken any particular notice of these remarks at the time, although they were naturally unwelcome, and he and his friend had gone on to other topics of conversation. But the discouragement had registered even though the author was not aware of it. The fear of exposing himself was added to his other difficulties in writing. It provided just that little weight on the side of not writing the book which was needed to stop him. As soon as he realized that this was the discouraging element which had held him up, he was able to see that his friend's opinion was not necessarily decisive. After all, the friend had not read the book and did not know the detail of the project. Even if one friend didn't like the idea, another might. Perhaps the friend was envious, without being aware of it himself. Certainly the author was resentful and discouraged and he had been stifling both feelings.

These realistic and encouraging thoughts were enough to shift the balance once more in favor of creative work. The author felt released, as if from some witchcraft that had been perpetrated on him, and continued his writing. Without the preparation of the period of self-study he could hardly have realized the significance of the casual thought that struck him while he was walking with his children. It was the uncompleted part of the mental work which would not get itself done while he sat at his desk. Such minor triumphs of self-study deal only with everyday matters and the simplest of human situations. It would seem that a very large number of people could use the method to this extent.

Activity analogous to self-study can occur without the formalities of taking time off or of writing. An analyzed youth reports the following example: He had invited a girl whom he particularly liked but did not know very well to a formal dance. The girl had declined the invitation but said she would be glad to go to dinner before the dance. Trapped by her suggestion and his attraction to her he had agreed to take her to dinner. The boy found the dinner rough going. He was immediately attacked by a stomach-ache so severe that he thought he would be forced to leave the table. He was thus urgently motivated to understand his situation. One of the units learned in his analysis came flying to mind. He recalled that aggression against a woman frequently took gastric form in his case. Could it be that he was angry at the girl, and if so, why? He realized immediately that he *was* angry and had repressed his anger. He had felt exploited by her suggesting dinner when she could not go with him to the dance. He was just being used to fill in a chink of time before the dance. When these thoughts occurred, ones contradictory to them came up also. The girl did not seem like an exploitive type. Maybe she wanted to show that she really liked him. There would, after all, be another dance, so why not ask her then and there for another date. This he did, and she accepted with evident pleasure. The combination of this lack of cause for aggression and hope of the future brought relief; the stomach-ache disappeared.

It is interesting to note that the whole reaction occurred under the cover of a social situation and was invisible to his partner. She could have noted only a change from glumness to spontaneity. The incident shows, however, that units of self-study can be performed swiftly, without formal measures, when the subject has learned well some of the needed responses, and the solution involves chiefly a transfer of these units from past to present situations. Once the stomach-ache was labeled as aggression-produced, the rest of the solution appeared rapidly.

Even if nothing new is derived from self-study, that which is already known can be better integrated and applied if the person takes time off to think.   For normals, then, self-study becomes practice in assembling and evaluating knowledge and making mental forecasts.   Everyone should try it—not as a substitute for psycho-therapy but as an experience in active meditation.   None but a universal genius like Shakespeare or Freud will come upon new knowledge of the deeply repressed.   Everyone, however, can do a better job of solving his problems if he stops to think about them.

CHAPTER XXX

SUPPRESSING TROUBLESOME THOUGHTS TO GET FREEDOM FOR CREATIVE THINKING

Every creative worker knows the danger of distraction from his task. The buzzing telephone, the questioning letter, the visit from a friend may set up chains of thought in him which stop his work. After such an interruption he finds it difficult to get back on the track. Against such hazards the original worker can protect himself by not answering the telephone, not opening his mail, and, for a time at least, not seeing his friends.

Suppose, however, that the distracting stimulus comes from within the mind itself, that one vagrant thought leads to another and distracts the worker from his task. Can anything be done about this kind of interruption? The answer is in the affirmative. Although most people have not made any special study of the matter, they can control their thoughts to some degree. In this chapter we will examine the circumstances of such mental self-control. The mechanism is commonly called "suppression."

Persons who have been psychoanalyzed and have developed the invaluable habits of free association may learn with surprise that there are occasions when it is advantageous to do exactly the opposite of what they have learned. As a method of combating repression, the free-association technique is crucial, but this technique may be an actual impediment if an individual practices it when he has an urgent piece of work to be done. The time must come when he closes his mind to all stimuli irrelevant to his task, refuses to admit vagrant associations, and keeps his mind firmly on the problem to be solved. Suppression is thus a kind of opposite of free association.

Obviously each technique should be used where it is appropriate and avoided where it is not. Those who have strong habits of free association should also consider under what circumstances they should practice habits of suppression. Those who are skilled at suppression are often said to have the ability to "concentrate," that is, to perform a task in the midst of distracting stimuli or nerve-wracking emotional situations. In the previous chapter we have dealt with the cues which normally excite self-study. At this time we will deal with suppression, the motives which prompt it, the kind of response it is, the cues which should evoke it, and the manner in which it is rewarded.

We have already explained in Part III that emotional responses can be attached to verbal cues. These emotional responses can, in turn, produce strong drive stimuli. Thus, the thoughts we think can produce motivation which, in turn, prompts to further thoughts and action. If no action is possible, these response-produced drives elicited by our thoughts can make us miserable. We can seethe with anger at the thought of affronts or injustices that have been done to us. Wandering thoughts may produce strong sexual excitement. Forebodings about the future may give rise to intense fear. In each case we must bear the misery produced by such a drive or act in some way to end it. If no action is possible, the person is left helpless in a condition of strong motivation. If action is possible, committing oneself to it may take his attention from other and more vital tasks. It is therefore of considerable importance to be able to control the thoughts which produce emotional responses. To be accessible at all times to any and every thought and thought-produced motive may make it impossible for an individual to carry on a creative life.

Suppression Works for Learned, Not for Innate, Drives

Innate drives, such as pain, being produced directly by drive stimuli acting on nerve endings, cannot be suppressed. For instance, products of decay, acting on the nerves in a tooth will produce toothache, and it is not possible to "think oneself out of" the occurrence of this reaction. Naturally if a stimulus stronger than the tooth-pain stimulus occurs, the response to it may become dominant, and one may thus get one's attention off the tooth-pain response. The primary pain response, however, is still occurring and will be attended to once the stronger stimulus is removed.

The case is quite different with learned drives. If certain thoughts are eliciting strong emotional responses, such motivation can be entirely reduced by not thinking those thoughts. If the thoughts do not occur, they do not produce the emotional responses which produce the learned drives.

When a primary drive and a response-produced drive based upon it are occurring at the same time, the total motivation can be reduced if the stimuli evoking the learned drive can be avoided. Thus, a very hungry man can avoid "tantalizing himself" by not picturing delicious foods or giving himself descriptions of them. Similarly, it is possible, though perhaps rare, for a patient in a dentist's chair to bear only the pain of the drill and not the pain of anxiety at worse suffering to come. The dentist attempts to help the patient do this when he says, "Relax," "It won't be so bad," or "It's almost over now."

This discrimination is important to the person who would learn the techniques of suppression. He will find it of little avail where he is dealing with an innate drive, but he will find suppression highly useful and benign where he is dealing with a response-produced drive. The physiological reactions which produce innate drives are not under his control. The responses which produce learned drives (especially when they are mediated by verbal or imageal responses) are, to some extent and with practice, under his control.

The motivation to suppress. The drive to suppress arises from the urgent task or problem requiring mental activity for its solution. The writer must write, the scientist must create his theories, the painter must paint, and for the actor the show must go on. The book can wait no longer; the portrait must be finished; urgent problems must be solved no matter what else is done. There is no time to waste in brooding, basking, dawdling with remote problems, or worrying. The task requires a fixed, absorbed, preoccupying, exclusive attention. It is this imperious task which motivates suppression. The creative worker requires not only physical solitude but also the freedom from thoughts and motives which interrupt his necessary chains of thought. Under such circumstances he will find invaluable the ability to suppress. If he cannot suppress irrelevant responses and motives, he will live miserably in indecision and inaction, not accomplishing his necessary task and not going on to any other.

What Kind of Activity Is Suppression?

Apparently there is no direct mechanism for suppressing thoughts and producing a blank mind. Suppression does not operate like a hot iron taking the wrinkles out of a shirt. In order to suppress a train of thought a person must take his attention off the stimuli which are producing this train of thought and turn his attention to some other cues which produce an incompatible train of thought. The essential activity, therefore, is the freedom to manipulate attention responses. In a problem situation the individual is to some extent free to turn his attention away from some cues and toward others. As he turns his attention away from cues to which he does not wish to respond, the response to those cues is weakened and the emotions produced by this response are reduced. As attention is turned to new cues, these cues produce different responses, and these responses in turn produce new and different motivation—that to accomplish the task to which the person is addressing himself.

Some obvious attentive responses are the following: poising the head to determine the direction from which a sound is coming, fixing the eyes on the shoulders of a uniform to determine the rank of the wearer, opening the mouth to taste and sample food, beginning to read a book which one wishes to master, writing the first sentence of a poem, repeating to oneself the instructions which will get one to a certain destination, beginning to think about a particular problem so that one gets "tuned up" on it. As will be seen, all these responses are under some degree of voluntary control. When the drive to accomplish a specific task is strong and when such tentative responses are attached to the stimuli produced by this drive, the individual focuses on the problem concerned. As he does so, he eliminates from his mind other types of thoughts producing other motivations.

The delicate point in this transfer is that at which one stops thinking an old line of thought and begins thinking the preferred line of thought. The to-be-abandoned responses are still creating motivation which tends to keep the old thoughts going. The new line of thought to which one is beginning to attend is still producing weak stimuli which have only a weak motivating effect on this new line. The strong turning and fixing of attentive responses is probably what William James meant by a "heave of the will." The motivation of the unsolved problem is perhaps the strongest component in producing this heave. If the person can once get strongly involved in making the new line of verbal responses these will, in turn, produce stronger motivation to continue such responses. As this occurs, the individual is less and less reactive to the cues from which he is trying to turn his attention and more and more reactive to the cues of the problem situation.

When he is strongly involved in the new and necessary task he will find that he is reacting but little or not at all to the cues which were dominant a few minutes before. He will have to relax his attention to his task and stop making the task responses before the old cues can reassert themselves. Every creative worker knows with wonder and pleasure the experience of getting immersed in his necessary task and of abandoning obsessive, though futile, trains of thought. The crucial consideration here is that thoughts can be manipulated to exactly the extent to which attention responses can be directed and concentrated.

Cues Exciting Suppression

Suppression should be invoked when an urgent mental task is at hand and when other such tasks, though preoccupying, are either insoluble or can be postponed. The task may be insoluble on a temporary basis, as is the case in the frustration situation. A football game is postponed or an illness prevents attendance at a family festival. There may be delay in a necessary administrative action, expressed by the sentence, "Nothing can be done until the new dean is appointed." In the meantime, the frustrated person may suffer continuously by steadily imagining the hopeless goal, or he may, if he is able, turn his attention to something else and do something constructive while he is waiting. The football game, or another just like it, will be played, another family reunion will occur, and the dean will eventually be appointed. Such temporarily insoluble problems tend to produce misery for those who cannot turn away from the impossible goal and set themselves some other goal or problem.

Many other problems are, from the individual's standpoint, insoluble. The adult committed to one career line can hardly take up another. The citizen may foresee war for his country but be unable to affect the course of events. In the fact of death every human being faces his greatest insoluble problem. The individual may make the best of the career he has. He may plan and execute those measures which best guarantee safety in case of war and battle. As to death, he can take all due precautions, plan to avoid it as long as possible and to face it, as Shakespeare advised, when it comes and but once. With an insoluble problem the individual does what he can to make the best of his circumstances and then invokes suppression. He turns his attention away from the course of events that he cannot alter and toward the problems that he can solve.

When suppression is difficult. Suppression is sometimes difficult or even impossible. As already noted, it may be impossible to get one's attention away from a strong innate drive stimulus like a toothache. Even learned drives, such as fear, may be difficult to avoid. If the preoccupying stimuli are very strong, such as those evoking fear in battle, it may be impossible not to attend to them, and hence it may be impossible to begin attending to any other stimuli. For instance, although we are told that it is possible for veteran football players to play bridge during the evening before a big game it is probably hard to play dominoes in the interludes of ground combat.

Exciting stimuli are easier to avoid when they are outside the body. Internal stimuli are much more difficult to avoid, especially when they are unconscious. This is just the case with the neurotic whose anxiety is a response to unlabeled, internal cues. The response to such neurotic cues may, however, be suppressed if other, stronger responses occur. A neurotic person who has a strong artistic habit may make his artistic responses so strongly that he stops reacting with fear to internal cues. He thus finds a "zone of freedom" in his artistic activity.

One can also easily observe the effect of distracting stimuli and the responses they produce when one thinks of being involved in a sport like tennis. As is often observed, a good game of tennis "will drive your troubles right out of your mind." The tennis player must attend closely to the stimuli of the sport itself. He must make the strong responses of serving and running to get into position for a forehand shot. He must react to the cues produced by his opponent, such as the opponent's stroke and the angle of the ball returning over the net. With his attention thus fixated and with strong, physical responses occurring, a player is able to get his attention off the cues which produce worry or concern.

If, on the other hand, the player is "sick with anxiety," he may be too preoccupied to turn his attention to the stimuli of his favorite game. At such a time he will be unable to play because he is unable to react to the first weak thoughts of playing tennis. To the stimulus of the invitation to play he responds with refusal. The obvious lesson is that unless he can begin making the tennis responses strongly they cannot win over the response of worry. In this case, his friends may attempt to stimulate motivation to play and direction of response to the tennis cues by urging him to "snap out of it," "forget it for a while," etc. Sometimes this much help from others will enable him to play. Once he is playing, the strong responses of the game will crowd out all the ordinary worry responses.

Suppression Must Be Rewarded

If suppression is to become a strong and therefore useful habit it must be rewarded like any other habit. The exact habit to be learned is that of recognizing the urgent task, identifying the tasks which are insoluble or can be postponed, and concentrating attentive responses on the initial stimuli of the urgent problem. The suppression habit is rewarded in two ways, one immediate and the other delayed. The immediate rewards occur when attention is changed from the futile line of thought to that of the necessary task. As the futile responses drop out, the painful stimuli that they produce drop out and hence reward fixing attention on the useful effort. The person, so to say, stops worrying about what cannot be changed and starts acting on the problem that can be solved. The more remote reward occurs at the time of completion of the urgent task. The motivation which impelled this task disappears when the task is completed. Thus, completing the task is rewarded and all of the responses which made completing the task possible may be rein-forced by a complex chain of generalized learned rewards.

Learning theory suggests that this "spread" of the effects of the final reward to the first responses involved in suppression can be enhanced by rehearsing these first steps at the time one is experienc-ing the final reward. It can be helped by sentences like "I'm glad now that I stopped fretting about that disappointment and forced myself to start concentrating. I want to be sure to remember to do the same thing the next time I'm bothered by a hopeless prob-lem." Some persons appear to learn the suppression habit so strongly that they can switch rapidly, with little loss of effort, from one task to another. They can, as it were, turn their minds off and on.

Suppression vs. repression. Suppression has one very great ad-vantage over repression. In the case of repression, the verbal re-sponses are more or less permanently lost. They are crowded out by anxiety and are not recoverable except under the special con-ditions of psychotherapy already outlined. In the case of suppres-sion, however, the verbal responses are much more easily recovered. No anxiety opposes them. When the stimuli of the preoccupying task disappear, the stimuli of other tasks can recur and produce other trains of thought. The stimuli of daily life, shut out during the creative exercise, will excite appropriate verbal and mental re-sponses.

In the case of repression it might be said that the solution of a problem is put aside for all time. The verbal-mental means of solv-ing the problem are denied to the person who represses. In the case of suppression, on the contrary, the problems are put aside *for the time being* only. The verbal means of solving problems other than the immediate, pressing one are not completely lost but are only abandoned during the accomplishment of the pressing task. It seems, however, to be the way of human life that when one urgent task is accomplished, another more or less urgent one im-mediately suggests itself. The suppression technique provides most of the benefits of repression without the penalty of mental paralysis which is involved in recourse to repression. Furthermore, the at-tention responses themselves are under verbal control in the case of suppression; but the repression activity is automatic and cannot be verbally mediated.

Suppression is normal. Many normal persons learn and use suppressive techniques effectively. Since the rewarding effects of stimulus reduction are automatic, any person who happens to hit upon suppression and does reduce drives in the manner just described will emerge with a stronger suppressive habit. No special suggestion is needed in this case. It is probable, indeed, that life circumstances tend to give everyone some training in suppression techniques. Among these circumstances are terminal dates for school papers, deadlines for real-life tasks, plans of the individual which lay out work activity in a series of subgoals to be achieved, meetings of scientific societies which cannot be postponed, and so forth. Parents frequently create urgency by the instructions they set up such as, "You can't go out sledding until you finish your schoolwork." In this case, brooding about the pleasures of sledding delays enjoyment by obstructing the completion of the school task, and hence tends to be eliminated.

Some religions also give specific training in suppression. They teach their members to react to thoughts of sin, pain, disease, or death by turning to other thoughts. Members of such a religion should rank high on the scale of efficient use of the suppression mechanism, especially in regard to the matters they are taught to suppress. If many of the concerns that people ordinarily worry about in relation to sin, pain, disease, or death are actually futile, the members of such religions should experience a definite gain in well-being. If, on the other hand, the problems which are suppressed are ones where effective adaptive action can be taken by mental means, such religious persons should suffer a relative loss in well-being. To refuse to recognize the existence of a disease when there is a new and spectacular cure may make it impossible for the person to have access to this cure. Oftentimes it would seem adaptive to bear the anxiety of recognizing a disease in exchange for access to the measures for curing it.

Joint Use of Free Association and Suppression

Both free association and suppression have their uses in a constructive life. Each should be used when the stimuli for it are appropriate. Just as "rushing into action" must be inhibited in order to make self-study possible, so a free canvassing of alternatives must sometimes be inhibited in order to make action possible. Self-study should be used especially when a person is uncertain as to *what* to do. Suppression should be used when he knows what he should do but is afflicted by irrelevant thought sequences and the motivations they produce. Self-study is useful in making a canvass of alternative plans, in discovering what one really wants to do. Suppression is useful when plans have been made and ranked as to their urgency. Suppression then helps the individual to concentrate on the ranking plan.

If plans are vague and not clearly ranked, it is dangerous to suppress the brooding, canvassing, and labeling which we have described as "self-study." Rushing into action on any kind of ill-conceived plan should be inhibited. Suppression can also be dangerous if the individual suppresses the stimuli to tasks which must be solved. Thus, one does not turn away from the sight of his house on fire in order to continue a conversation with a friend; nor should one suppress thoughts about a dangerous cough for fear the doctor might diagnose it as tuberculosis. Suppression is dangerous if thus used, and the individual who uses it thus lives in a fool's paradise. The dangers of free and unlimited brooding are equally obvious. The brooding person may never get around to accomplishment of those critical tasks which are necessary to sustain his life.

Postponing to a specific time. As will be seen in the examples which follow, the work of suppression is greatly eased if a worker can be sure that the stimuli to the by-passed task will come up again. Everyone has some feeling that tasks which are abandoned now may not be accomplished at all, and he hesitates to stop thinking about a course of action which may be lost entirely if it is left uncompleted at the time.

Some system of "checking off" is a real help in this case. Ask your secretary to put the item in a tickler file; make a note instructing yourself to take up the problem again; ask someone to call you back. Thus the stimuli to the postponed task are not lost only to be rediscovered when it is too late. Motivation to "do it now" is greatly reduced when we are sure that stimuli to the deferred task will be aroused again later at an appropriate time.

When motivation to competing tasks is reduced, it is much easier to fix attention on the stimuli of the urgent task.

Some Examples of Suppressed Thoughts and Motivations

We present herewith some examples of suppression from a well-studied case. Obviously all references and names used are for cover purposes and are not those of real persons or institutions.

Mr. Smith had to prepare a budget which involved decisions on all manner of perplexing minor problems. He estimated that the task would take about a week of concentrated work. The budget had to be prepared in time to be submitted along with various other departmental budgets in his organization. He was forced, therefore, to sweep his life clean of other distracting issues in order to get at his budget problem.

First, Mr. Smith had to isolate himself temporarily from the telephone calls, visits, mail, and home stimuli which tended to intrude upon his working day and incite him to the performance of work other than his budget making. Once alone, however, he had the further task which we have called suppression, *i.e.*, he had to stop making those verbal-mental responses which aroused motivation and impelled him to undertake competing tasks.

The following is a list of chains of thought which Smith had to suppress:

1. There was a letter to a member of his family which should be written. He had been asked to support a common family project and had not been able to make up his mind whether or not to do so. He was worried that further delay might produce further misunderstanding. He decided, however, that this matter could wait for a week and that the letter would be at hand to remind him to take up the problem again.

2. Smith was engaged in the project of building a special research room. There had been much delay in this project, most of it justifiable and resulting from a careful casing of the problems involved in building. Still, he worried about what the Foundation that had made him the grant would think when so much time was passing with no action. Shouldn't he telephone the Dean and see whether or not one of the suggested plans couldn't be adopted? He decided that he could put this matter to one side. There was

no likelihood of his forgetting it once he dropped the budget matter.

3. Smith remembered that his wedding anniversary was coming up in a couple of weeks and that a present for his wife would be appropriate—at least send flowers! He asked his secretary to make a note which would help him get this matter off his mind. Thoughts of his wife, however, were not yet ended. He remembered that he had promised to take her watch to the repair shop and that he had it at that moment in his pocket. Shouldn't he take some action on this immediately? He decided that the watch matter would wait.

Thoughts of his wife, once started, kept on intruding. He thought of what a complete woman she was, how real and warm, and what a wonderful job she was doing. The budget stimuli, however, intruded, and he decided that he could safely turn to them, leaving his appreciation of his wife to take some later form.

4. Smith had been asked to do a small text piece for an important magazine. A goodly fee was in prospect. Could the piece wait for a week? Smith decided that it could and that if necessary he would risk not getting the fee. The budget was more important.

5. The daily mail brought its suggestions which required decisions. One colleague wanted him to prepare a chapter in a book. Smith doubted that this would be possible but was not yet dead sure. Another colleague invited him to give a seminar which he knew he should not take time to give, but there were the slight anxious feelings as to whether he might miss something, offend somebody, and the like. He put both letters aside, knowing they would be there to answer when his budget task was done.

6. Smith had some undergraduate advisees. One of them was reported from the Dean's office as being on "general warning." Wasn't it Smith's duty to see this student immediately and do what he could to help? It was, of course, his duty but he felt that probably one week more or less would not make too much difference. The Dean's letter would not escape notice later.

7. Smith had an important lecture coming up for a large undergraduate class. He was as yet unprepared and felt he should be mentally preparing himself, brooding over the materials, finding examples, integrating new data. He would have only a day at the end of his week to prepare this lecture. He turned away from these thoughts and allotted to the lecture the "Number Two" priority.

It would be the first thing taken up when the budget was done.

8. There was the letter from Don lying on his desk unanswered for many months. He enjoyed his handwritten correspondence with Don. Though their letters were episodic, too much time had passed. Definitely the letter should have been answered. But Don, Smith decided, would wait as he had always done.

9. Smith had recently presented a research project to a Foundation. This had been submitted to a committee of three unknown persons. Smith assumed that somebody must think they were scientists. In any case, they had advised the Foundation to reject Smith's project. He thought, with some anger, that he would try to find out who they were. They would henceforth be in his "bad books." On second thought, of course, he felt this resolve to be silly. The unknown advisers had undoubtedly done what they thought was right. Anyway, a Foundation is such a thing that it is, as the spiritual says of the Lord, "too high to get over and too low to get under."

10. The Smiths also needed a new car. Their present one was ten years old and was causing constant trouble. The one grievous blemish on the Smith family life was Mrs. Smith's constant concern over the rackety old car. Inquiry of automobile dealers, however, had shown a perplexing state of affairs. There was the problem of body style, of color, and model. It would take a few days' good time to settle all these issues in which each member of Smith's family had a vote. There was an expert in town who knew the pros and cons as to various cars quite well. Smith resolved to call him and find out the best car and order it blind. He realized that actually he would never be able to do this, but the possibility served to put the problem off and enable him to turn back to his budget.

The foregoing trains of thought produced different kinds and degrees of motivation in Smith's mind. The acquired drives of anxiety, anger, and love can be clearly identified. Any one of these motives could have led to action which would have competed with the essential task and sopped up the time and energy required by it. If any of these thoughts had been allowed to mount and run free they would have choked off the thoughts necessary to the performance of the urgent task.

We believe that such examples give a clear idea of the nature of thought-produced motivation. They also show that suppressing the thoughts which produce motivation will cause such motivation to disappear. Once involved in his budget task, Smith got the benefit of the dropping out of these other motivating thoughts. As he began to make the responses needed to solve the budget problem, it became more commanding and preoccupying. The increase in stimulation produced by thinking about his budget problems further motivated the train of thoughts needed to solve these problems.

The use of suppression has been exemplified here by the situation of a commanding task and a baffling series of distracting problems. Suppression can be equally useful in the converse case, that is, when the person is faced by a major problem, about which nothing can be done, while a series of small but important tasks of daily life pile up. In this case the person is likely to prepare for the remote important eventuality and neglect the real and soluble problems of the moment. The remote issue may arouse fearful brooding or joyous anticipation, but either will preoccupy the mind to the exclusion of concern with immediate duties. The same techniques of suppressing mental reaction to the remote event and plunging into the smaller problems at hand are found useful here. As in the case of the urgent task, suppression helps to avoid waste of mental time and to get important work done.

Use of Suppression in Psychotherapy

In psychotherapy, as elsewhere, suppression should be used when the patient knows what to do but lacks the ability to get into action. Suppression is particularly necessary in the phase of "trying out in the real world" the new plans that have been made in the period of free association. Eventually the patient must abandon brooding and reflection, form a dominant plan, make a decision to act, and put the plan at hazard. Only thus, as we have shown, can he achieve real reduction of the drives which have been producing misery.

In the usual course of psychotherapy, training in suppression is not given. This failure involves the risk that the patient will generalize to the situation where action is imperative the same habits of reflection which are so adaptive in overcoming repression. Such reflective habits are plainly maladaptive in the situation requiring action. The therapist should aid his client to discriminate between the habits necessary to revoke repression and those appropriate to real-world action. In the first case the patient properly "lets everything come into his mind"; in the second, he shuts out all thoughts that do not aid in carrying out the plan arrived at. Such resolute steps to action are not automatic. Many patients need to learn them. In such cases the therapist should require action in the same steady and benign way that he has earlier required reflection and "not rushing into action." Since he must teach free association first, in order to overcome repression, he must be particularly alert to the danger that the patient will continue to practice thinking when the time for deeds is at hand.

SUMMARY

The stimuli which excite suppression are those of an urgent problem. The essential responses are those of shifting attention and actually beginning the first responses necessary to the accomplishment of the urgent task. The cues to suppression are those of hopeless or postponable problems. Suppression is rewarded by reducing the stimulation involved in canvassing irrelevant problems and of finishing the urgent task, thus eliminating the motivation to it. Suppression has a great advantage over repression in that it is temporary. Once the urgent task is over, suppression can be abandoned and the cues to other tasks arise and produce new trains of thought. Free association and suppression can be used as complementary measures. Free association helps the individual to discover what he wants to do, what comes first. Suppression aids him to knock out irrelevant trains of association and motivations so that the task of greatest importance can be accomplished. It is dangerous to suppress at the point where motivation has to be discovered, alternative solutions canvassed, and a first-ranking plan selected. Free association likewise is dangerous when the urgent task is at hand. The therapist must be alert to the danger that his patient will continue to practice free association when it is the time for action in the real world. He should first teach habits of free association to overcome repression, then later insist upon suppression and that real-world action which alone can reduce misery.

BIBLIOGRAPHY

ADATTO, C. P., 1949. Observations on criminal patients during narcoanalysis. *Arch. Neurol. Psychiat.*, 62:82–92.

ADRIAN, E. D., 1928. "The Basis of Sensation." Norton, New York.

ALEXANDER, F., and FRENCH, T. M., 1946. "Psychoanalytic Therapy." Ronald, New York.

ALEXANDER, F., and FRENCH, T. M., 1948. "Studies in Psychosomatic Medicine." Ronald, New York.

ALLPORT, G. W., 1937. "Personality." Holt, New York.

ALLPORT, G. W., 1946. Effect: a secondary principle of learning. *Psychol. Rev.*, 53:335–347.

ANDREWS, T. G. (ed.), 1948. "Methods of Psychology." Wiley, New York.

ARNOLD, M. B., 1946. On the mechanism of suggestion and hypnosis. *J. abnorm. soc. Psychol.*, 41:107–128.

ATKINSON, J. W., and McCLELLAND, D. C., 1948. The effect of different intensities of the hunger drive on thematic apperception. *J. exp. Psychol.*, 38:643–658.

BARD, P., 1934. On emotional expression after decortication with some remarks on certain theoretical views. *Psychol. Rev.*, 41:309–329, 429–449.

BEACH, F. A., 1942. Effects of testosterone propionate on copulatory behavior of sexually inexperienced male rats. *J. comp. Psychol.*, 33:227–247.

BEACH, F. A., 1947. A review of physiological and psychological studies of sexual behavior in mammals. *Physiol. Rev.*, 27:240–307.

BEKHTEREV, V. M., 1932. "General Principles of Human Reflexology." International, New York.

BERITOV, I. S., 1924. On the fundamental nervous processes in the cortex of the cerebral hemispheres. *Brain,* 47:109–148; 358–376.

BIRGE, JANE SILL, 1941. "Verbal Responses in Transfer," Ph.D. dissertation. Yale University, New Haven.

BLECKWENN, W. J., 1930. Narcosis as therapy in neuropsychiatric conditions. *J. Amer. Med. Ass.*, 15:1168.

"Blue Laws of Connecticut. Capital Laws. Code of 1650," 1861. Section 14. Duane Rulison, Philadelphia.

BRENMAN, M., and GILL, M. M., 1947. "Hypnotherapy: A Survey of the Literature." International Universities Press, New York.

BRICKNER, R. M., 1936. "The Intellectual Functions of the Frontal Lobes; a Study Based upon Observation of a Man after Partial Bilateral Frontal Lobectomy." Macmillan, New York.

BROWN, J. S., 1942. The generalization of approach responses as a function of stimulus intensity and strength of motivation. *J. comp. Psychol.*, 33:209–226.

BROWN, J. S., 1948. Gradients of approach and avoidance responses and their relation to level of motivation. *J. comp. physiol. Psychol.*, 41:450–465.

BUSH, VANNEVAR, 1945. "Science, the Endless Frontier; A Report to the President by Vannevar Bush, Director of Scientific Research and Development." Government Printing Office, Washington, D.C.

CANNON, W. B., 1929. "Bodily Changes in Pain, Hunger, Fear, and Rage." Appleton-Century-Crofts, New York.

CARLSON, A. J., 1916. "The Control of Hunger in Health and Disease." University of Chicago Press, Chicago.

COFER, C. N., and FOLEY, J. P., JR., 1942. Mediated generalization and the interpretation of verbal behavior: I. Prolegomena. *Psychol. Rev.*, 49:513–540.

COFER, C. N., JANIS, M. G., and ROWELL, M. M., 1943. Mediated generalization and the interpretation of verbal behavior: III. Experimental study of antonym gradients. *J. exp. Psychol.*, 32:266–269.

COLLIAS, N. E., 1944. Aggressive behavior among vertebrate animals. *Physiol. Zool.*, 17 (No. 1).

CONANT, JAMES, 1947. "On Understanding Science: An Historical Approach." Yale University Press, New Haven.

CONGER, J. J., 1949. "An analysis of the Effect of Alcohol upon Conflict Behavior in the Albino Rat," Ph.D. dissertation. Yale University, New Haven.

COWLES, J. T., 1937. Food tokens as incentives for learning by chimpanzees. *Comp. Psychol. Monogr.*, 14 (No. 5).

DARWIN, FRANCIS, 1898. "Life and Letters of Charles Darwin," Vol. I. Appleton, New York.

DAVIS, ALLISON, 1948. "Social Class Influences upon Learning, The Inglis Lecture, 1948." Harvard University Press, Cambridge, Mass.

DAVIS, ALLISON, and DOLLARD, JOHN, 1940. "Children of Bondage." American Council on Education, Washington, D.C.

DAVIS, ALLISON, and HAVIGHURST, ROBERT, 1947. "Father of the Man." Houghton Mifflin, Boston.

DEWEY, JOHN, 1910. "How We Think." Heath, Boston.

DOLLARD, JOHN, 1942. "Victory over Fear." Reynal and Hitchcock, Inc., New York.

DOLLARD, JOHN, 1943. "Fear in Battle." Yale University Press, New Haven.

DOLLARD, JOHN, March 9, 1945. Exploration on morale factors among combat air crewmen—memorandum to research branch, information and education division. *Psychol. Service Center J.* In press, 1950.

DOLLARD, JOHN, 1935. "Criteria for the Life History." Yale University Press, New Haven. Reprinted by Peter Smith, New York, 1949.

DOLLARD, JOHN, 1949. Do we have a science of child rearing? In "The Family in a Democratic Society," Anniversary Papers of the Community Service Society of New York, pp. 41–55. Columbia University Press, New York.

DOLLARD, JOHN, DOOB, L. W., MILLER, N. E., and SEARS, R. R., 1939. "Frustration and Aggression." Yale University Press, New Haven.

DUNBAR, HELEN, 1943. "Psychosomatic Diagnosis." Hoeber, New York.

FALCONER, M. A., 1948. Relief of intractible pain of organic origin by frontal lobotomy. *Res. Publ. Ass. nerv. ment. Dis.*, 27:706–714.

FENICHEL, O., 1945. "The Psychoanalytic Theory of Neuroses." Norton, New York.

FISHER, VARDIS, 1932. "In Tragic Life." Caxton Printers, Ltd., Caldwell, Idaho.

FOLEY, J. P., JR., and COFER, C. N., 1943. Mediated generalization and the interpretation of verbal behavior: II. Experimental study of certain homophone and synonym gradients. *J. exp. Psychol.*, 32:168–175.

FORD, C. S., 1937. A sample comparative analysis of material culture. In G. P. Murdock (ed.), "Studies in the Science of Society," pp. 225–246. Yale University Press, New Haven.

FORD, C. S., 1939. Society, culture, and the human organism. *J. gen. Psychol.*, 20:135–179.

FORD, C. S., 1949. The arbitrary values of mankind. *Amer. Merc.*, 68 (No. 306): 746–751.

FRANKLIN, J. C., SCHIELE, B. C., BROZEK, J., and KEYS, A., 1948. Observations on human behavior in experimental semistarvation and rehabilitation. *J. clin. Psychol.*, 4:28–45.

FREED, H., 1946. Narcosynthesis for the civilian neurosis. *Psychiat. Quart.*, 20:39–55.

FREEMAN, W., and WATTS, J. W., 1942. "Psychosurgery." C. C. Thomas Company, Baltimore.

FRENCH, T. M., 1933. Interrelations between psychoanalysis and the experimental work of Pavlov. *Amer. J. Psychiat.*, 89:1165–1203.

FREUD, SIGMUND, 1913. "The Interpretation of Dreams." Macmillan, New York.

FREUD, SIGMUND, 1924. "Collected Papers," Vols. I–II (2d ed.). The International Psycho-Analytical Library, Hogarth, and The Institute of Psycho-Analysis, London.

FREUD, SIGMUND, 1925. "Collected Papers," Vols. III–IV (2d ed.). The International Psycho-Analytical Library, Hogarth, and The Institute of Psycho-Analysis, London.

FREUD, SIGMUND, 1930. "Three Contributions to the Theory of Sex" (4th ed.). Nervous and Mental Disease Publishing Company, Washington, D.C.

FREUD, SIGMUND, 1933. "A New Series of Introductory Lectures on Psycho-Analysis." Norton, New York.

FREUD, SIGMUND, 1936. "The Problem of Anxiety." Norton, New York.

FREUD, SIGMUND, 1943. "A General Introduction to Psychoanalysis" (3d ed.). Garden City Publishing Company, Inc., Garden City, New York.

FRY, CLEMENTS C., 1942. "Mental Health in College." Commonwealth Fund, New York.

FULTON, JOHN, 1949. "Physiology of the Nervous System" (3d ed. rev.). Oxford, New York.

GESSELL, ARNOLD, 1940. "The First Five Years of Life." Harper, New York.

GLUECK, B. C., JR., 1946. Pharmacological therapies in psychiatric practice. In B. Glueck (ed.), "Current Therapies of Personality Disorders." Grune and Stratton, New York.

GREENSPOON, JOEL, 1950. "The Effect of Verbal and Mechanical Stimuli on Verbal Behavior." Personal Communication.

GREGG, ALAN, 1949. The future of nursing. *Yale J. Biol. Med.*, 21:279–285.

GRINKER, R. R., and SPIEGEL, J. P., 1945a. "Men Under Stress." Blakiston, New York.

GRINKER, R. R., and SPIEGEL, J. P., 1945b. "War Neurosis." Blakiston, New York.

GUTHRIE, E. R., 1935. "The Psychology of Learning." Harper, New York.

GUTHRIE, E. R., 1938. "The Psychology of Human Conflict." Harper, New York.

GUTHRIE, E. R., 1939. The effect of outcome on learning. *Psychol. Rev.*, 46:480–484.

GWINN, G. T., 1949. The effects of punishment on acts motivated by fear. *J. exp. Psychol.*, 39:260–269.

HALL, C. S., 1941. Temperament: a survey of animal studies. *Psychol. Bull.*, 38:909–943.

HALVERSON, H. M., 1938. Infant sucking and tensional behavior. *J. gen. Psychol.*, 53:365–430.

HARTSHORNE, HUGH, and MAY, MARK, 1928. "Studies in Deceit." Macmillan, New York.

HASTINGS, D. W., WRIGHT, D. G., and GLUECK, B. C., 1944. "Psychiatric Experiences of the 8th Air Force." Josiah Macy Jr. Foundation, New York.

HENRY, G. W., 1948. "Sex Variants" (1-vol. ed.). Hoeber, New York.

HILGARD, E. R., 1948. "Theories of Learning." Appleton-Century-Crofts, New York.

HILGARD, E. R., and MARQUIS, D. G., 1940. "Conditioning and Learning." Appleton-Century-Crofts, New York.

HIROA, T. R., 1932. Ethnology of Ranihiki and Rakahanga. B. P. Bishop Museum Bulletin, 99.

HOLMBERG, A. R., 1950. Nomads of the Long Bow: the Siriono of Eastern Bolivia. *The Smithsonian Institute of Social Anthropology*, Publication No. 10, Washington, D.C.

HORSLEY, J. S., 1943. "Narco-Analysis." Oxford, London.

HORTON, DONALD, 1943. The functions of alcohol in primitive societies: a cross-cultural study. *Quart. J. Stud. Alcohol,* 4:199–320.

HULL, C. L., 1929. A functional interpretation of the conditioned reflex. *Psychol. Rev.,* 36:498–511.

HULL, C. L., 1930. Knowledge and purpose as habit mechanisms. *Psychol. Rev.,* 37:511–525.

HULL, C. L., 1931. Goal attraction and directing ideas conceived as habit phenomena. *Psychol. Rev.,* 38:487–506.

HULL, C. L., 1932. The goal gradient hypothesis and maze learning. *Psychol. Rev.,* 39:25–43.

HULL, C. L., 1933. "Hypnosis and Suggestibility: An Experimental Approach." Appleton-Century-Crofts, New York.

HULL, C. L., 1934a. Learning: II. The factor of the conditioned reflex. In C. Murchison (ed.), "Handbook of General Experimental Psychology," pp. 382–455. Clark University Press, Worcester, Mass.

HULL, C. L., 1934b. The rat's speed-of-locomotion gradient in the approach to food. *J. comp. Psychol.,* 17:393–422.

HULL, C. L., 1935. The mechanism of the assembly of behavior segments in novel combinations suitable for problem solution. *Psychol. Rev.,* 42:214–245.

HULL, C. L., 1943. "Principles of Behavior." Appleton-Century-Crofts, New York.

JACKSON, E. B., OLMSTED, R. W., FOORD, ALAN, THOMS, HERBERT, and HYDER, KATE, 1948. A hospital rooming-in unit for four newborn infants and their mothers; descriptive account of background, development, and procedures with a few preliminary observations. *Pediatrics,* 1:28–43.

JENKINS, J. J., and HANRATTY, J. A., 1949. Drive intensity discrimination in the albino rat. *J. comp. physiol. Psychol.,* 42:228–232.

JENNESS, ARTHUR, 1944. Hypnotism. In J. McV. Hunt (ed.), "Personality and the Behavior Disorders," Vol. I, pp. 466–502. Ronald, New York.

JONES, M. C., 1924. Elimination of children's fears. *J. exp. Psychol.,* 7:382–390.

KELLOGG, W. N., 1939. "Positive" and "negative" conditioning, without contraction of the essential muscles during the period of training. *Psychol. Bull.,* 36:575.

KINSEY, A. C., POMEROY, W. B., and MARTIN, C. E., 1948. "Sexual Behavior in the Human Male." Saunders, Philadelphia.

KLEIN, MELANIE, 1948. "Contributions to Psycho-analysis 1921–1945." Hogarth and the Institute of Psycho-Analysis, London.

KUBIE, LAWRENCE S., M.D., 1950. "Practical and Theoretical Aspects of Psycho-analysis." International Universities Press, Inc., New York.

LAWRENCE, DOUGLAS, 1950a. Acquired distinctiveness of cues: I. Transfer between discriminations on the basis of familiarity with the stimulus. *J. exp. Psychol.* (in press).

LAWRENCE, DOUGLAS, 1950b. Acquired distinctiveness of cues: II. Selective association in a constant stimulus situation. *J. exp. Psychol.* (in press).

LEVY, D. M., 1934. Experiments on the sucking reflex and social behavior of dogs. *Amer. J. Orthopsychiat.*, 4:203–224.

LINDEMANN, ERICH, 1931. Psychopathological effect of sodium amytal. *Proc. Soc. exp. Biol.*, 28:864.

MacCORQUODALE, K., and MEEHL, P. E., 1948. A further study of latent learning in the T-maze. *J. comp. physiol. Psychol.*, 41:372–396.

MAHL, G. F., 1949. The effect of chronic fear on the gastric secretion of HCl in dogs. *Psychosom. Med.*, 11:30–44.

MAHL, G. F., 1950. Anxiety, HCl secretion and peptic ulcer etiology. *Psychosom. Med.*, 12:140–169.

MAIER, N. R. F., 1949. "Frustration: The Study of Behavior without a Goal." McGraw-Hill, New York.

MASSERMAN, J. H., 1943. "Behavior and Neurosis." University of Chicago Press, Chicago.

MASSERMAN, J. H., 1946. "Principles of Dynamic Psychiatry." Saunders, Philadelphia.

MASSERMAN, J. H., and YUM, K. S., 1946. An analysis of the influence of alcohol on experimental neurosis in cats. *Psychosom. Med.*, 8:36–52.

MAY, MARK, 1948. Experimentally acquired drives. *J. exp. Psychol.*, 38:66–77.

McCLELLAND, D. C., and ATKINSON, J. W., 1948. The projective expression of needs: I. The effect of different intensities of the hunger drive on perception. *J. Psychol.*, 25:205–223.

McCULLOCH, T. L., 1939. The role of clasping activity in adaptive behavior of the infant chimpanzee: III. The mechanism of reinforcement. *J. Psychol.*, 7:305–316.

McGEOCH, J. A., 1942. "The Psychology of Human Learning." Longmans, New York.

MEAD, MARGARET, 1928. "Coming of Age in Samoa." Morrow, New York.

MEAD, MARGARET, 1949. "Male and Female." Morrow, New York.

MEEHL, P. E., 1950. On the circularity of the law of effect. *Psychol. Bull.*, 47:52–75.

MENNINGER, W. C., 1948. "Psychiatry in a Troubled World." Macmillan, New York.

MILLER, N. E., 1935. "The Influence of Past Experience upon the Transfer of Subsequent Training," Ph.D. dissertation. Yale University, New Haven.

MILLER, N. E., 1941. An experimental investigation of acquired drives. *Psychol. Bull.*, 38:534–535.

MILLER, N. E., 1944. Experimental studies of conflict. In J. McV. Hunt (ed.), "Personality and the Behavior Disorders," Vol. I, pp. 431–465. Ronald, New York.

MILLER, N. E., 1948a. Studies of fear as an acquirable drive: I. Fear as motivation and fear-reduction as reinforcement in the learning of new responses. *J. exp. Psychol.*, 38:89–101.

MILLER, N. E., 1948b. Theory and experiment relating psychoanalytic displacement to stimulus response generalization. *J. abnorm. soc. Psychol.*, 43:155–178.

MILLER, N. E., 1950. Learnable drives and rewards. In S. Stevens (ed.), "Handbook of Experimental Psychology." Wiley, New York (in press).

MILLER, N. E., and BAILEY, C. J., 1950. Effect of sodium amytal on behavior of cats in an approach-avoidance conflict (in preparation).

MILLER, N. E., and DOLLARD, JOHN, 1941. "Social Learning and Imitation." Yale University Press, New Haven.

MILLER, N. E., and KRAELING, DORIS, 1950. Displacement: evidence for more generalization of approach than avoidance in an approach-avoidance conflict generalized to a new stimulus situation (unpublished manuscript).

MORGAN, C. T., 1943. "Physiological Psychology." McGraw-Hill, New York.

MOWRER, O. H., 1939. A stimulus-response analysis of anxiety and its role as a reinforcing agent. *Psychol. Rev.*, 46:553–566.

MOWRER, O. H., 1947. On the dual nature of learning—a reinterpretation of "conditioning" and "problem solving." *Harv. educ. Rev.*, 17:102–148.

MOWRER, O. H., and ULLMAN, A. D., 1945. Time as a determinant in integrative learning. *Psychol. Rev.*, 52:61–90.

MURDOCK, G. P., 1934. "Our Primitive Contemporaries." Macmillan, New York.

MURDOCK, G. P., 1949. "Social Structure." Macmillan, New York.

MYERS, J., 1949. The Reinforcement Value of the Sight of Food for Rats that Are Not Hungry. M.A. thesis. University of Iowa.

NUTTIN, J., 1947. Respective effectiveness of success and task-tension in learning. *Brit. J. Psychol.*, 38:49–55.

OGBURN, W. F., 1922. "Social Change." Viking, New York.

PARSONS, TALCOTT, 1942. Propaganda and social control. *Psychiatry*, 5:551–572.

PARSONS, TALCOTT, 1942. Age and sex in the social structure of the United States. *Amer. sociol. Rev.*, 7:604–616.

PAVLOV, I. P., 1927. "Conditioned Reflexes," trans. by G. V. Anrep. Oxford, London.

PERKY, C. W., 1910. An experimental study of imagination. *Amer. J. Psychol.*, 21:422–452.

REDLICH, FREDERICK C., DOLLARD, JOHN, and NEWMAN, RICHARD, 1950. High fidelity recording of psychotherapeutic interviews. *Amer. J. Psychiat.*, 107:42–48.

RICHTER, CURT, Dec. 2–3, 1949. Anatomic, physiologic, and behavior reactions during stress in domestic vs. wild animals. Proceedings of the Association for Research in Nervous and Mental Disease, New York.

ROGERS, CARL, 1942. "Counseling and Psychotherapy." Houghton Mifflin, Boston.

RUESCH, JURGEN, LOEB, M. B., *et al.*, 1946. "Chronic Disease and Psychological

Invalidism: A Psychosomatic Study." American Society for Research in Psychosomatic Problems, New York.

RYAN, T. A., 1948. Recollecting, Imagining and Thinking. In E. G. Boring, H. S. Langfeld, and H. P. Weld (eds.), "Foundations of Psychology," pp. 185–214. Wiley, New York.

RYLANDER, G., 1939. Personality changes after operation on the frontal lobes. A clinical study of 32 cases. *Acta psychiat.*, Kbh., and *Neurol.*, Suppl. XV, London.

SARGENT, W., 1942. Physical treatment of acute war neuroses. *Brit. med. J.*, 2:574.

SAUL, L. J., 1944. Physiological effects of emotional tension. In J. McV. Hunt (ed.), "Personality and the Behavior Disorders," pp. 269–305. Ronald, New York.

SCOTT, J. P., 1945. Social behavior, organization and leadership in a small flock of domestic sheep. *Comp. Psychol. Monogr.*, 18 (No. 4).

SCOTT, J. P., 1948. Dominance and the frustration-aggression hypothesis. *Physiol. Zool.*, 21:31–39.

SEARS, R. R., 1936. Functional abnormalities of memory with special reference to amnesia. *Psychol. Bull.*, 33:229–274.

SEARS, R. R., 1944. Experimental Analysis of Psychoanalytic Phenomena. In J. McV. Hunt (ed.), "Personality and the Behavior Disorders," pp. 306–332. Ronald, New York.

SEARS, R. R., DAVIS, H. C., *et al.*, 1948. Effects of cup, bottle, and breast feeding on oral activities of newborn infants. *Pediatrics*, 2:549–557.

SEARS, R. R., and WISE, G. M., 1949. Relation of cup-feeding in infancy to thumbsucking and the oral drive. *Amer. J. Orthopsychiat.*, 20:123–138.

SHAFFER, L. F., 1947. The problem of psychotherapy. *American Psychologist*, 2:459–467.

SHEFFIELD, F. D., WULFF, J. J., and BACKER, ROBERT, 1950. "Reward Value of Sexual Stimulation without Ejaculation" (in preparation).

SHEFFIELD, V. F., 1949. Extinction as a function of partial reinforcement and distribution of practice. *J. exp. Psychol.*, 39:511–526.

SHOBEN, E. J., JR., 1949. Psychotherapy as a problem in learning theory. *Psychol. Bull.*, 46:366–392.

SKINNER, B. F., 1938. "The Behavior of Organisms." Appleton-Century-Crofts, New York.

SPENCE, K. W., 1947. The role of secondary reinforcement in delayed reward learning. *Psychol. Rev.*, 54:1–8.

SPENCE, K. W., 1950. Theoretical interpretations of learning. In S. S. Stevens (ed.), "Handbook of Experimental Psychology." Wiley, New York (in press).

SPOCK, BENJAMIN, 1946. "Baby and Child Care." Pocket Books, New York.

STRATTON, G. M., 1897. Vision without inversion of the retinal image. *Psychol. Rev.*, 4:341–360; 463–481.

SUMNER, W. G., and KELLER, A. B., 1927. "The Science of Society." Yale University Press, New Haven.

THORNDIKE, E. L., 1932. "The Fundamentals of Learning." Teachers College, New York.

THORNDIKE, E. L., and ROCK, R. T., JR., 1934. Learning without awareness of what is being learned or intent to learn it. *J. exp. Psychol.*, 17:1–19

TOLMAN, E. C., 1949. There is more than one kind of learning. *Psychol Rev.*, 56:144–155.

VON FELSINGER, JOHN, 1948. "The Effect of Ovarian Hormones on Learning," Ph.D. dissertation. Yale University, New Haven.

WARNER, W. L., and LUNT, P. S., 1941. "Yankee City Series, Vol. I: The Social Life of a Modern Community." Yale University Press, New Haven.

WARNER, W. L., and ASSOCIATES, 1949. "Democracy in Jonesville." Harper, New York.

WARNER, W. L., MEEKER, MARCHIA, and EELLS, KENNETH, 1949. "Social Class in America: A Manual for the Measurement of Social Status." Science Research Associates, Chicago.

WATSON, J. B., 1925. "Behaviorism." Peoples' Institute, New York.

WATSON, J. B., and RAYNER, R., 1920. Conditioned emotional reactions. *J. exp. Psychol.*, 3:1–14.

WATTS, J. W., and FREEMAN, W., 1948. Frontal lobotomy in the treatment of unbearable pain. *Res. Publ. Ass. nerv. ment. Dis.*, 27:715–722.

WEISS, EDWARD, and ENGLISH, O. S., 1949. "Psychosomatic Medicine" (2d ed.). Saunders, Philadelphia.

WERTHEIMER, MAX, 1945. "Productive Thinking." Harper, New York.

WHITE, R. W., 1948. "The Abnormal Personality." Ronald, New York.

WHITING, J. W. M., 1941. "Becoming a Kwoma." Yale University Press, New Haven.

WHITING, J. W. M., and SEARS, R. R., Nov. 28, 1949. "Projection and Displacement in Doll Play." Laboratory of Human Development, Cambridge, Mass. (mimeographed prospectus).

WICKERT, F. (ed.), 1947. "Psychological Research on Problems of Redistribution," Army Air Forces Aviation Psychology Program. Research Reports No. 14. Government Printing Office, Washington, D.C.

WILCOXON, H. C., 1951. "Abnormal Fixations and Learning," Ph.D. dissertation. Yale University, New Haven.

WOLFE, J. B., 1936. Effectiveness of token rewards for chimpanzees. *Comp. Psychol. Monogr.*, 12 (No. 60).

WOODROW, H., and LOWELL, FRANCES, 1916. Children's Association Frequency Tables. *Psychol. Monogr.*, 22 (No. 97), 110 pp.

WOODWORTH, R. S., 1938. "Experimental Psychology." Holt, New York.

WOODWORTH, R. S., and WELLS, F. L., 1911. Association tests. *Psychol. Monogr.*, 13 (No. 57), 85 pp.

YOUNG, P. C., 1941. Experimental hypnotism: a review. *Psychol. Bull.*, 38:92–104.

NAME INDEX

A

Adatto, C. P., 369
Adrian, E. D., 46
Alexander, F., 193, 233, 276, 303, 313, 337, 338, 350, 384, 394, 404, 409
Allport, G. W., 50, 62, 91
Andrews, T. G., 314
Arnold, M. B., 461
Atkinson, J. W., 179, 180

B

Backer, R., 41, 142
Bailey, C. J., 370, 376
Bard, P., 82
Beach, F. A., 53, 85, 162
Bekhterev, V. M., 52
Beritov, I. S., 175
Birge, J. S., 101, 218
Bleckwenn, W. J., 369
Brenman, M., 196
Brickner, R. M., 380
Brown, J. S., 53, 71, 162, 173, 354, 355
Brozek, J., 211
Bush, V., 7

C

Cannon, W. B., 82
Carlson, A. J., 211
Charcot, J. M., 169
Cofer, C. N., 101
Collias, N. E., 84
Conant, J., 7
Conger, J. J., 185
Cowles, J. T., 78–80

D

Darwin, F., 208
Davis, A., 45, 62, 94, 108, 154, 420
Davis, H. C., 86
Dewey, J., 45

D (cont.)

Dollard, J., 25, 28, 34, 35, 37, 40, 42, 45, 48, 62, 69, 76, 84, 87, 92, 97, 101, 117, 118, 128, 129, 148, 156, 158, 246, 428, 439, 441
Doob, L. W., 463
Dunbar, H., 193

E

Eells, K., 421
Einstein, A., 6
Eitingon, M., 246
English, O. S., 193

F

Falconer, M. A., 378
Fenichel, O., 163, 171, 196, 233
Fisher, V., 14
Foley, J. P., 101
Ford, C. S., 38, 62, 94
Franklin, J. C., 211
Freed, H., 369, 376
Freeman, W., 378, 380
French, T. M., 9, 193, 233, 276, 303, 313, 337, 338, 350, 384, 394, 404, 409
Freud, S., ix, 3, 5, 6, 9, 71, 123, 127, 129, 136, 140, 141, 144, 169, 171, 183, 190, 196, 198, 217, 220, 241, 252, 253, 256, 260, 261, 277, 279, 288, 299, 305, 331, 332, 335, 338, 363, 384, 401, 411, 413, 422, 431, 439, 444
Fry, C., 306
Fulton, J., 178

G

Gesell, A., 130, 135
Gill, M. M., 196
Glueck, B. C., 369
Greenspoon, J., 43, 44, 92, 288, 396
Gregg, A., 281
Grinker, R. R., 77, 165–167, 195, 196, 201-203, 342–344, 369, 371, 372, 374, 375

471

SUBJECT INDEX

A

Abnormal behavior, 5–6
Abreaction, 372
Act, 26
  (*See also* Response)
Acting out, 248–249
Adaptation, 46*n*.
Adaptiveness, 165–166, 187–190, 322–325
Adjustment, 4, 187
  in selection of patient, 236–237
Adjustment levels, 123–124
Adulthood, 131, 314
Age-grading, 90–91, 236, 305
  and regression, 171
Aggression, 77, 183, 225, 272, 323, 373, 443
  displaced, 151
  and frustration, 84, 148–154, 432–434
  learning of, 82–84, 148–154
  toward therapist, 269
  in young children, 83*n*.
  (*See also* Anger)
Alcohol, 185–187, 332, 369–370, 377–380
  self-therapy, 377–378
Ambition, 88
Ambivalence, 272, 366
Amnesia for traumatic situation, 73, 371
Amnesias, 201–202, 225
Anger, of children, 148–149
  and fear, 272
  as learned drive, 82
  projection of, 181
  reduction in, as reinforcement, 84
  reinforcement of, 83
  unlearned reactions, 194
  (*See also* Aggression)
Animal experimentation, rationale of, 63
Anticipation, 133
Anticipatory goal response, 111
Anticipatory response, 202
  in communication, 60–61

Anticipatory response, definition of, 57
  discrimination of, 59–60
  involuntary, 58
Anxiety, 133, 135, 138, 142, 440–441, 450–451
  castration, 145–147
  chronic, 68–69, 193–194
  dosing of, 231, 243, 247, 292, 350–351
  evoked by sentences, 241, 249–250
  faced by patient, 230–231, 241
  relation of, to fear, 190–191
  sexual, 141–148, 257, 317
  (*See also* Fear)
Apathy, 132–133
Appetites as learned drives, 85–86
Apprehensiveness, 132–133
Approach, 268
  gradient of, 352–355
  increasing drive to, 357
Approach-approach competition, 365–366
Approach-avoidance conflict, 191, 355–363
Approval, 92
Assumptions, 26*n*., 30*n*., 40*n*., 42*n*., 44, 69, 70*n*., 81, 99*n*., 100, 172–173, 315, 352–354
Attention, 35, 103, 117, 245, 309, 374, 407, 447–449
Authority, reactions to, 147–148, 244, 262, 268
Automatic defense reactions, 275
Automatic habits, 98
Avoidance, 268
  gradient of, 352–355, 370–371

B

Barbiturates, 369–377, 379–380
Bed phobia, 142, 159–160
"Belle indifférence," 170, 196
Birth control, 235
Blank mind, 255–256, 271
Blocking, 255

SUBJECT INDEX

Perception, 34n., 87, 178–181
cue-producing, 178
influence of drive on, 179
Permissiveness, 230, 240–259, 286, 306, 395
Personality, 3–6, 10, 25, 94, 136, 149, 152, 155–156
inhibited, 152
role of learned drives and reinforcements in, 62–63
sex-typing of, 143
(See also Individual differences)
Perversion, 85, 143, 147–148, 234, 425
Phobia, 157–163
arousal of, by temptation, 159–160
extinction of, 162–163
origin of, 161
Planning, 110–115, 219, 278, 300–301, 324-325
essential steps in, 115
Pleasure principle, 9
Postponing, 454
Prediction, 7
Prejudice, 217
Preoccupation, 224
Present vs. past, 331–332
Prestige, 92, 244, 262, 268
Pride, 90, 93, 424
Principles, psychological, 3, 9, 10
Private assumptions, 242
Privation in therapy, 288
Problem defining, 113–114
Problems, emotional, 97–124
physical, 97
Prognosis, 233–239, 341
Projection, 119, 174–175, 181–184
Psychoanalysis, 3, 284, 445
misinterpretation of, 11
(See also Freud; Therapy)
Psychological error, 421
Psychological principles, 3, 9, 10
Psychopath, 236, 425
Psychosis, 141, 237, 425
Psychosomatic symptoms, 193–194, 383n., 443
Psychotherapy, 3–6, 147, 286, 305, 317, 342–344
availability of, 419, 424
conflicts as focus of, 391

Psychotherapy, creation of normality by, 5, 406–407
false hope of easy cure by, 267
and laws of learning, 89
as learning situation, 7–8, 233, 379–380, 413
limiting factors of, 122
as opportunity for observation, 3–6, 98
role of, not intellectual exchange, 275
role of suppression in, 458-459
time consumed in, reasons for, 257–258
(See also Therapy)
Punishment, 51, 134, 139, 159–160, 188–189, 248, 384
delay in, 187–188, 333
fear of, 189, 207n.
functions of, 75–76, 384n.
mediated, 207
in repression, 204
role of fear in, 75–76
role of thinking in, 75–76

Q

Questioning by therapist, 242, 396–397
Quibbling, 271, 278

R

Rationalization, 119, 177–178, 263
Reaction formation, 184–185
Real-life situation, 10, 231, 279–280, 291
Reality, 119, 180, 250
Reasoning, 110–115, 219, 281–282, 324–325
absence of, in infants, 130–131
copied sentences in, 116–117
eliciting correct response by, 38
essential steps in, 115
example of, 111–113
social training in, 116–124
(See also Higher mental processes; Planning)
Reassurance, 244, 251–252, 321, 396
Reconstruction, 317–318
Recording of therapeutic interviews, 259, 419
Recreation as escape, 200
Reflecting back, 289, 396